Gender Issues in Learning and Working with Information Technology:
Social Constructs and Cultural Contexts

Shirley Booth
University of the Witwatersrand, South Africa
University of Gothenburg, Sweden

Sara Goodman
Lund University, Sweden

Gill Kirkup
Open University, UK

 INFORMATION SCIENCE REFERENCE

Hershey • New York

Director of Editorial Content:	Kristin Klinger
Director of Book Publications:	Julia Mosemann
Acquisitions Editor:	Lindsay Johnson
Development Editor:	Elizabeth Ardner
Typesetter:	Greg Snader
Quality control:	Jamie Snavely
Cover Design:	Lisa Tosheff
Printed at:	Yurchak Printing Inc.

Published in the United States of America by
  Information Science Reference (an imprint of IGI Global)
  701 E. Chocolate Avenue
  Hershey PA 17033
  Tel: 717-533-8845
  Fax: 717-533-8661
  E-mail: cust@igi-global.com
  Web site: http://www.igi-global.com/reference

Library of Congress Cataloging-in-Publication Data

Gender issues in learning and working with information technology : social
constructs and cultural contexts / Shirley Booth, Sara Goodman and Gill
Kirkup, editors.
     p. cm.
  Includes bibliographical references and index.
   Summary: "This book deals with diffe four features of the burgeoning knowledge society: gender, equity, learning, and information technology with the focus on gender - not in the taken-for-granted biological sense of sex but in the socially constituted sense of it"--Provided by publisher.
   ISBN 978-1-61520-813-5 (hbk.) -- ISBN 978-1-61520-814-2 (ebook) 1. Women in technology. 2. Technology and women. 3. Technology--Sociological aspects. 4. Information technology--Sociological aspects. I. Booth, Shirley, 1945- II. Goodman, Sara. III. Kirkup, Gill. T36.G44 2010
   305.43'6--dc22
                                                    2009044849

British Cataloguing in Publication Data
A Cataloguing in Publication record for this book is available from the British Library.

All work contributed to this book is new, previously-unpublished material. The views expressed in this book are those of the authors, but not necessarily of the publisher.

Editorial Advisory Board

Table of Contents

Section 1
Being and Becoming IT Professionals

Chapter 1

Women, Men and Programming: Knowledge, Metaphors and Masculinity
Inger Boivie, Guide Konsult AB, Sweden

Chapter 2

New Gender Relations in the Transforming IT-Industry of Malaysia
Ulf Mellström, Luleå University of Technology, Sweden

Chapter 3

Women in computer science in Afghanistan
Eva Maria Hoffmann, Technische Universität, Germany

Section 2
Working with and Preparing to Work with IT

Chapter 4

For Me it Doesn't Matter Where I put my Information: Enactments of Agency,
Mutual Learning, and Gender in IT Design
Johanna Sefyrin, Mid Sweden University, Sweden

Section 3
Representation in Media

Section 4
Adult Education

Detailed Table of Contents

Section 1
Being and Becoming IT Professionals

This section contains research on the higher educational experiences of women who are studying to be information technology professionals. The case studies are from Sweden, Malaysia and Afghanistan.

Chapter 1
    Inger Boivie, Guide Konsult AB, Sweden

This chapter examines whether and how computer science practices contribute to a strict separation between "experts" and "users" in a way that serves to exclude women from "real" computing. The author focuses on epistemological issues of what constitutes computing as both knowledge and practice and what type of knowledge is valued in the profession.

Chapter 2
    Ulf Mellström, Luleå University of Technology, Sweden

Mellström investigates how and why computer science courses in Malaysia are dominated by women, in contrast to the situation in most other countries discussed in this book. The research is grounded in social anthropology, feminist studies of technology and highlights the Anglo-centric bias of gender and technology studies.

This chapter analyses a survey of Afghani women computer science students and discusses the opportunities that they feel a computer science education will give them in helping rebuild their society, as well as the challenges they face both culturally and economically. The author discusses the importance of setting up networks for these young women to provide a safe physical and virtual space.

Section 2
Working with and Preparing to Work with IT

This section contains three pieces of research with women who are IT users and IT professionals. Two of the chapters are qualitative in-depth research of the processes and interactions carried out by people using IT in the workplace. The third is a survey of IT professionals who reflect on the route by which they became professionals.

This chapter is an ethnographic study of the design process in an IT business analysis project. The author uses a particular theoretical approach to analyse her research data: "agential realism", a new "feminist materialism", using metaphors from the world of theoretical physics in which humans and technology are viewed as mutually engaged in producing the material world.

This chapter explores the IT-intensive life of two groups of women who work in Swedish local authority administration, gathered through interactive workshops with the women and analyzed to give voice to their everyday lives. 'Agential realism' is also used to understand the experience of working in new IT-intensive administrative work, where claims for the efficiency of IT processes are a prime justification.

Chapter 6

Marie Griffiths, University of Salford, UK
Helen Richardson, University of Salford, UK

The authors carried out a survey of women in the ICT sector in the UK examining their paths into their profession. They discovered that most women computer professionals in their sample came from single-sex schools where they studied mathematics and science.

Section 3
Representation in Media

This section focuses on the representation of women and of technology in three different media: newspapers, computer animations, and television 'soap operas'. It illustrates the ways in which traditional gender stereotyping continues, alongside notions of gender complementarity. It is also shows that in some circumstances young adults prefer to work with less stereotypically gendered virtual characters.

Chapter 7

Agneta Gulz, Lund University, Sweden
Magnus Haake, Lund University, Sweden

The authors designed and implemented four virtual characters with different degrees of femininity, masculinity and androgyny and used them with high school students. The students showed a preference for the more androgynous female and male presenters, in comparison with the more stereotypical feminine and masculine virtual characters. The implications for this in designing online information systems are discussed.

Chapter 8

Martha Blomqvist, Uppsala University, Sweden

This chapter gives a gender-sensitive analysis of the discourses about IT and gender issues in Swedish newspapers in the years 1994 to 2004. Blomqvist carried out a textual analysis of the content of these newspapers and found little evidence of any discourses which could further the debate on the participation of women in IT in a new or productive way.

Chapter 9

Els Rommes, Radboud University, The Netherlands

Rommes uses Dutch TV 'soap operas' to explore heteronormativity, i.e. the normalised expectation that men and women are attracted to each other because of their presumed gender difference and gender complementarity. In the examples of popular media that she studies, not only do men and women have stereotypical gender roles with respect to technologies, but they also play these as complementary to each other and as constructing gendered relationships

Section 4
Adult Education

This section looks at the experience of women in three different adult education situations: doing adult education computer courses, engaging in distance education, and preparing to enter traditional campus-based higher education. These chapters show that, although women are the majority sex in adult and higher education in the countries in question, there are still issues of lack of empowerment for adult women learners.

Chapter 10

Shirley Booth, University of the Witwatersrand, South Africa & University of Gothenburg, Sweden
Eva Wigforss, Lund University, Sweden

This chapter contains in-depth case studies of two women who take part in an adult education course to induct them into the academic practices of the university. The authors show that the differences in the ways the women experience their relationship to higher education can be ascribed to the relations to people and practices they encounter in their everyday experienced places of home and work.

Chapter 11

Annika Bergviken-Rensfeldt, University of Gothenburg, Sweden
Sandra Riomar, University of Gothenburg, Sweden

This chapter questions the assumption that distance education is open, flexible and liberating through an examination of the gendered use of technology, and of the home as the location for learning. Distance education, the authors argue, creates spaces that risk disempowering women in comparison with traditional higher education which takes people out of their domestic environment.

Chapter 12

Minna Salminen-Karlsson, Uppsala University, Sweden

Salminen-Karlsson carried out a survey of computing courses in adult education centres in Sweden. This chapter describes her findings that, while men reported greater computer competence, even in younger age groups, there was no gender difference in regard to interest or attitudes towards computing between men and women. Despite this women, were more critical and more dissatisfied with their courses than men.

Section 5
Digital Learning

This final section looks at information technology used by learners, teachers and scholars, and asks whether gendered practices are being reproduced through these new technologies. The three chapters look at different technologies: in particular online forums for students, and blogs and wikis for scholars. They all argue for the importance of adopting a critical perspective in one's own practices of teaching and scholarship in particular incorporating feminist perspectives.

Chapter 13

Kirkup uses feminist theories of gendered knowledge production to question whether some of the new forms of Web 2.0 knowledge production are more gendered than traditional print technologies. She sees blogs in particular as being more aligned to what have been described as a women's way of writing, and argues for critical engagement with Web 2.0 technologies by women scholars and students in particular.

Hughes uses the metaphor of bees in the hive, to explore gendered 'performance' in collaborative online groups. She took as a case study the students she taught and she analyzed their behavior in online forums. She concludes that a shift from face-to-face to online does not necessarily promote shifts in gender performances, and that students and teachers need to find new ways of performing gender online if they are to maximize the potential of collaborative work.

The chapter critically analyses current developments from gendered theoretical perspectives and calls for consideration of the feminist work on embodiment, knowledge, power and ethics to be built into e-learning policies as well as into the practical applications in the classroom and used by teachers.

Foreword

It gives me great pleasure to write the foreword to this book, Gender Issues in Learning and Working with Information Technology: Social Constructs and Cultural Contexts. One of the first projects I initiated as CEO of the Knowledge Foundation[1] in Sweden was the research programme on Learning and IT, LearnIT, and one of the remits of that programme was to contribute to the work of the Foundation in terms of its research orientations and research output – to benefit the knowledge society which was taking shape in Sweden. Of the many research projects, masters and doctoral theses, books and conferences that came from the programme, which ended in 2008, one that might have spread its wings furthest is the research network on Gender, Learning and IT (GLIT) which Shirley Booth and Sara Goodman ran from 2001 until 2008. This network provided the core of the chapters which make up this book. However, it also made contact with other networks and researchers in the field to expand the final set of chapters with contributions about research from the UK, mainland Europe, Afghanistan and Malaysia.

The origins of GLIT were in the perceived shortcomings of the Foundation itself, when it came to policy and principles for adjudicating applications for research and development funding. Indeed, one of its later activities was a symposium at the headquarters of the Foundation in 2007 when some of the work that had been financed was presented to the whole staff to act as catalyst for the development of our own structures. Most of the work of the Foundation involves financing projects, research and development and dissemination, that are intended to contribute to the building of a viable infrastructure for Swedish development in terms of information technologies, and we have come to see that such issues as gender and equity awareness are essential aspects of a strong ethical and sustainable policy for our work.

The chapters presented here, from work carried out across the world, suggest that there are many common assumptions about such social issues, but it takes research and theorizing in the social sciences, closely allied to the technical sciences, to inform us at a deeper level than assumption. I recommend that policy makers globally should engage in reading such books as this one in order to embrace the values that can lie at the foundation of a just society even in the technologically rich future. The chapters of the book embrace one of the principles of the original LearnIT research programme: that research and development need to be aimed at three levels of society – to the individual, to groups or classes of individuals and to society as a whole. Thus the chapters take on issues from individual women making their way to higher education with the help of IT, to forming networks for women taking on a new role of computer scientist in the restrictive culture of Afghanistan, and to proposing a manifesto for e-learning that would embrace all higher education and place it on a footing of a feminist ethic.

I wish the book well, and the networks that have come together to write it all success in the future.

Madeleine Cæsar
Former CEO of the Knowledge Foundation, Sweden

Madeleine Cæsar was the Chief Executive of the Swedish Knowledge Foundation (The KK Foundation) 1999-2009. She was Head of Operations at the Foundation during 1995-1998 and was responsible for education and research programmes. The Knowledge Foundation was established in 1994 by the Swedish Parliament and promotes a broad use of IT in society, and supports research at Sweden's university colleges and new universities. Cæsar is on the board of the Government owned company Rise Holding AB, which owns shares in Swedish industrial research institutes as well as also on the board of the Interactive Institute, Blekinge Institute of Technology and KTH Royal Institute of Technology's Holding Company. Madeleine Cæsar has served during 1970-1995 at the Ministry of Industry and has been Head of Division Industrial Research and Development. 1992-1995 she was Director and Head of Division responsible for budget coordination and planning of the Ministry of Industry.

ENDNOTE

[1]   KK-stiftelsen, Stiftelsen för kunskaps- och kompetensutveckling.

Preface

The fifteen chapters that make up this book all deal to different degrees with four features of the burgeoning knowledge society: Gender, Equity, Learning, and Information Technology. The main interest, which all the chapters take as a theme, is that of Gender – not in the taken-for-granted biological sense of sex but in the socially constituted sense of the major category of human being in the world. Equity is a broader term than gender, but here it is restricted to the ethical equity that can be neglected or overlooked in relation to gender and societal development where male role models and male power players have predominated. Learning is the number one prerequisite for the emergence of an equitable knowledge society, learning to use and shape the new tools that support the society and ensure that its development includes greater social justice rather than mere change alone. And finally, Information Technology, IT (or ICT, Information and Communication Technology as it is almost synonymously called) is the overridingly important innovation in our knowledge society, both driving it and being driven by it, being taken for granted in homes and workplaces at the same time as new implementations and applications are being introduced daily.

The book is situated in the social studies of information technology: how IT skills are learned and how these skills are gendered. It draws on the disciplines of sociology, education, cultural and media studies, and gender studies. The authors use a variety of research methods and theoretical perspectives. The case studies in the book approach gender and IT in different contexts: education settings, work settings and everyday life. The book comes from a European perspective but with a global dimension. Certainly there is a growing awareness in the research field that it is no longer adequate to have only American and European studies. The field of IT is global, and international practices need to be included in the field of knowledge. The social and symbolic operation of gender is different in different cultures and consequently has a different impact on women's relationship with IT. A unique feature of this book is that gender relations and IT are examined in a multidimensional way.

Gender, Equity, Learning and Information Technology can be seen as intersecting to form a theoretical and abstract field of knowledge emanating from very concrete lived experiences. That field is being researched from a number of different points of view, with different starting points and different theoretical assumptions, addressing issues from different areas of the field. The reader will find significant differences in the issues being tackled, the methods being applied, the theories being espoused and the contexts in which the research takes place, but taken together they will offer a rich insight into both the issues themselves and the field of research which they represent.

The chapters have their origins in the work of members of two research networks – GLIT (Gender, Learning and IT) from Sweden and ATHENA (The Advanced Thematic Network of Women's Studies in Europe) which is a European network – both of which we wish to introduce now. While the GLIT network has contributed chapters that are mostly Swedish in context, or at least in authorship, the Athena network has contributed papers from around the world, thus adding an important international dimension to the book.

In 2000 a research programme on Learning and IT (LearnIT[1]) was initiated in Sweden under the auspices of the Knowledge Foundation of Sweden (KK-stiftelsen[2]) and one of the editors (Booth) took up a research fellowship there. It turned out that the Foundation had virtually no principles on gender or equity in their research and development funding, or even in their own organisation, and an investigation was initiated by LearnIT into the ways in which their enormous investments in bringing IT into schools – one of their main remits – had treated gender and equity issues. The result was startling (Booth & Booth, 2000)[3] – of 660 projects they had financed, a search on gender-related terms in both Swedish and English gave only 91 hits; of those only 45 took up issues that could be related to gender and equity in the IT-society specifically, and less than half of these focused directly on gender or equity or both. Funding was quite soon granted by KK-Stiftelsen, through LearnIT, to form a network of Swedish researchers who could contribute to the debate that was obviously needed. The network, led and administered by Booth and Goodman, in time obtained funds from the same sources to finance six peer-refereed research projects, five of which are reported here, and to continue with symposia and conferences which have also contributed chapters to the book.

The ATHENA network is an EU funded programme which brings together 80 funded institutes who do work in gender and women's studies. It has operated since 1999, and has produced a wealth of publications, research projects and curriculum developments. One aspect of Athena has been to explore best practices for using digital technologies and e-learning for gender studies programmes. Goodman and Kirkup had worked together in this network previously, producing a volume of papers on IT use in Women's Studies (Goodman et al., 2003)[4]. The three editors decided that there was enough interesting material coming from both networks to produce a published collection that would make a significant contribution to the field.

In this introduction we will introduce the chapters of this book so that you, the reader, can find more easily those that interest you as well as giving you an overview of the whole. We will present the chapters in five themes, Being and becoming IT professionals, Working with and preparing to work with IT, Representation in media, Adult education, and Digital learning. Finally we will look briefly at the methodological and theoretical underpinnings of the different contributions.

The first theme, Being and becoming IT professionals, begins with an in-depth qualitative study on *Women, men and programming – knowledge, metaphors and masculinity* by Inger Boivie. In her research with computer programmers and future programmers, Boivie, herself a computer and programming professional in Sweden, formerly of Uppsala University, explores the world of computing as a discipline in universities, and examines the issue of whether and how computer science has practices which contribute to a strict separation between "experts" and "users" which further exacerbates the exclusion of women from "real" computing. To illuminate this question Boivie focuses on aspects of the gendering of computer science and IT, related to epistemological issues of what constitutes computing as both knowledge and practice and what type of knowledge is valued in the profession.

In the paper on *New gender relations in the transforming IT-industry of Malaysia* Ulf Mellström from Luleå University of Technology in Sweden also takes as his subject the gendering of computer sciences in a professional and educational context in Malaysia. He investigates how and why computer science courses in Malaysia are dominated by women, in contrast to the situation in most other countries discussed in this book. In his work he strives for "more culturally situated analyses of the gendering of technology or the technology of gendering with the Malaysian case exemplifying the core of the argument." He grounds his research in social anthropology, feminist studies of technology and a critique of both the 'black-boxing' of gender in gender and technology studies and the Anglo-centric bias of gender and technology studies. Mellström argues for the importance of intersectional analysis so that one understands the cultural specificity of the context.

The third chapter in this theme also extends it geographically, turning attention to computer science education in Afghanistan, where a larger number of young women are studying undergraduate computer science courses than the rest of the world might expect. Eva Maria Hoffman from the Technische Universitaet in Berlin, Germany, writes of *Women in computer science in Afghanistan*. She has surveyed Afghani women students and discusses the opportunities that they feel a computer science education will give them in helping rebuild their society, as well as the challenges faced by them in studying in a country where there are both cultural and economic challenges for women students. She discussed the importance of setting up networks for these young women, computer science professionals and students to provide both a physical and virtual a space where they can get to know one another and exchange ideas and information.

The second theme in this collection concerns Working with and preparing to work with IT, and it opens with an ethnographic study of the design process in an IT business analysis development from Johanna Sefyrin, from Mid-Sweden University. Her title starts with a quote from an interview and finishes with the key theoretical ideas underpinning work: *"For me it doesn't matter where I put my information" – Enactments of agency, mutual learning, and gender in IT design*. This chapter offers a detailed analysis of a moment in a particular design process where the material and social relations are inextricably intertwined with the issues of agency, mutual learning and gender. The theoretical approach she uses is from Karin Barad – a theory which is variously described as "agential realism" or a new "feminist materialism" and draws on metaphors from the world of theoretical physics in which humans and technology are viewed as mutually engaged in producing the material world.

The second chapter in this second theme also uses Barad's theoretical framework, now applied to understanding the reality of working in new IT-intense administrative work, where women are the main groups of employees submitted to ever-sharpening claims for efficiency and effectiveness in the rationalization process of local authority administration. In *Attaching people and technology: between e and government*, Christine Mörtberg from Oslo University and Umeå University and Pirjo Elovaara from Blekinge Institute of Technology paint a picture of the IT-intensive life two groups of women are leading at work in Swedish local authority administration, gathered through interactive workshops with the women and analyzed to give voice to their everyday lives.

The third and last chapter in this section looks at the issues associated with recruiting women into ICT-related careers. Marie Griffiths and Helen Richardson, both from the University of Salford in the UK call their chapter *Against all odds, from all-girls schools to all-boys work-places: Women's unsuspecting trajectory into the UK ICT sector*. On the basis of a survey of women in the ICT sector with respect to their paths into their work, they find that, even after many years of special initiatives in UK schools and a significant reduction in the numbers of single sex girls schools most women computer professionals in their sample came from single-sex schools where they studied mathematics and science. This suggests that in the UK at least aspects of gendered school education as still being played out in the careers of women

Having looked into the reality of the gendered nature of working and preparing to work in various sectors of ICT, the third theme *Representation in the Media* looks into what is considered to be an important factor in producing a gendered world: how the sexes are represented in ever-day media The first chapter in this section looks at the different ways in which potential computer students experience being told about studying computer engineering by a range of virtual characters in a computer environment designed to attract new students to the field. Agneta Gulz and Magnus Haake from Lund University in Sweden designed and implemented four virtual characters with different degrees of femininity, masculinity and androgyny and exposed final year high school students to them in recruitment software. In the broadest terms, they found that school students showed preference for the more androgynous female and male presenters, in comparison with the more stereotypical feminine and masculine virtual characters. The implications for this in designing online information systems is discussed in the chapter.

Absent women: Research on gender relations in IT education mediated by Swedish newspapers is the next chapter where Martha Blomquist from Uppsala University in Sweden presents a gender-sensitive analysis of the discourse with which IT and gender issues – predominantly the lack of women in the field – were discussed in Swedish newspapers in the years 1994 to 2004. She carries out a textual analysis of the content of these newspapers and identifies that there is both a masculine discourse – in which an assumption is made of technology as a male preserve – and a feminised discourse – that women have qualities that are needed in the IT field – but she found little evidence of a more nuanced differentiated discourse which could lead the debate on more fruitful paths.

The third paper in this section on media points again to the masculine nature of the IT related discourse, this time in the popular media, in the form of Dutch soaps that are very popular with teenagers. Els Rommes from Radboud University, Netherlands, in *Heteronormativity revisited: Adolescents' educational choices, sexuality and soaps*, explores the notions that heteronormativity, the normalised expectation that men and women are attracted to each other because of their presumed gender difference and gender complementarity, can offer an explanation for the persisting association between masculinity and technological and computer competence. In particular, she explores two aspects of heteronormative gender relations, namely sexual attractiveness and the heteronormative division of labour. In the examples of popular media that she studies, not only do men and women have stereotypical gender roles with respect to technologies, but they also play these as complementary to each other and as constructing gendered relationships.

The fourth theme and section in the book is on the theme of Adult education, both using IT as a medium of communication and having IT as the subject of education. Shirley Booth from the University of the Witwatersrand in South Africa and Eva Wigforss from Lund University in Sweden have studied two women who take part in a university-based distance course to induct them into the academic practices of the university, in preparation for a possible entry to higher education. In *Approaching higher education: A life-world story of home-places, work-places and learn-places*, they show that there are differences in the ways the women experience the relationship to higher education which can be ascribed to the relations to people and practices they encounter in their everyday experienced places of home and work, and that is seen to impact on the ways they enter higher education.

Following that, Annika Bergviken-Rensfeldt and Sandra Riomar from the University of Gothenburg address Swedish policy on distance education using a gender and space analysis to ask how spaces of distance education are gendered and what power asymmetries are produced. In *Gendered distance education spaces: "Keeping women in place?"* they question the assumed open, flexible and liberating nature of distance education by considering the spaces that are created in terms of their off-campus nature, the gendered use of technology and location of the home as the place for learning. These, they conclude, create spaces that risk keeping women in their place, by disempowering them in comparison with the norms of higher education which take people out of their domestic environment.

This fourth section closes with a chapter that looks at adult education for competence in using computers and information technology. Minna Salminen-Karlsson from Upsala University in Sweden carried out a survey of computing courses in adult education centres in Sweden. She discusses the results of this in her chapter *Computer courses in adult education in a gender perspective* and raises practical questions about gender differences in computer competence and women's feelings of technical inadequacy. She asks how educators can take advantage of women's interest in computers while aligning this with their expectations about their future life chances. She found, on the basis of a survey of a broad spectrum of adult learning centres, that while men reported greater computer competence, even in a younger age group, there was no gender difference in regard to interest or attitudes towards computing. Despite this women, were more critical and more dissatisfied with their courses than men.

The final section comprises three chapters on the theme of Digital learning. The first chapter in the section asks about the gendering of two of the most commonly used features of what has come to be called Web 2.0: the range of online applications that encourage social networking, and group content creation. Gill Kirkup of the Open University in the UK– who has been involved with the Athena network since its inception and with the GLIT network since being one of the first invited speakers at its symposia and invited keynote speaker at the final conference – considers the role of blogs and wikis in creating gendered knowledge in *Gendered knowledge production in universities in a Web 2.0 world*. She begins by discussing the historical achievements that women have made in first gaining entry to learning at universities and more recently becoming scholars who are fully engaged as knowledge producers in universities alongside men. However drawing on feminist theories of the gendering knowledge production she asks whether some of the new forms of Web 2.0 knowledge production are more gendered than traditional print technologies. She argues that blogs appear to be are more aligned to what have been described as a women's way of writing, while wikis could allow invisible power hierarchies to create gendered knowledge. She argues for critical engagement with Web 2.0 technologies by women scholars and students in particular.

In the second chapter in this theme, Gwyneth Hughes, of London Institute of Education, in the UK, looks at the uses the metaphor of bees in the hive, to explore gendered 'performance' in collaborative online groups. She took as a case study the students she taught and analyzed their behavior in online forums. She describes different behaviours she observed as: frustrated queens, workers and excluded drones and argued that these different kinds of gender behaviours did not lead to harmonious and productive collaboration. She concludes that a shift from face-to-face to online does not necessarily promote shifts in gender performances and that students and teachers need to find new ways of performing gender online if they are to maximize the potential of collaborative work.

And finally, as befits such an internationally grounded book with gender, learning and IT in focus, there is a chapter from a group of European feminist researchers and teachers of gender studies who call for, justify and describe a move *Towards a Feminist manifesto for e-learning* against a background of the current developments in the field which are strongly driven by economic and technical concerns. The manifesto critically analyses current developments from gendered theoretical perspectives and calls for consideration of the feminist work on embodiment, knowledge, power and ethics to be built into e-learning policies as well as practical applications in the classroom and use by teachers. They offer this paper as the first step towards a more detailed radical manifesto, which would take up some of those issues discussed by other authors in their chapters: intersectionality, culture and context being some of the key ones.

The fifteen chapters of the book come from a number of different, largely social science, research perspectives and exemplify a number of different methodological approaches to the field. These differ in the extent to which they embody gender and feminist theory even though all take up issues that put gender in focus. Three of the chapters use a distinctive theoretical perspective that originates in the work of Karen Barad, a theoretical physicist turned feminist researcher, and uses the inter-actions of physics phenomena as metaphors for the inter-actions of people and the material features of their environments in the creation of a material world that we understand. This material is likely to be the least familiar to most readers, but it demonstrates some of the new directions in feminist theories of creation of gender in bodies and social systems. There are references in several chapters to more familiar feminist theory in particular the pioneering work published, first by Carol Gilligan and then by Belenky and colleagues, on what they call women's ways of knowing. This literature remains controversial in the fields of psychology and education in which it first emerged, but it underpins a great deal of work which still continues trying to understand the nature of gendered differences in how people relate to the world and each other. Further, two significant theoretical underpinnings in a number of the articles are, first, the concept of intersectionality which emphasizes the complex intersections of social categories including gender, ethnicity, class, sexuality, religion and disability, and, second, the feminist pedagogical theories which have taken inspiration from critical and Freirian pedagogy. Then there are the approaches to research that do not emanate from gender research or feminism, such as the quantitative work of surveys and the phenomenological analysis of the every-day life-world, which can also turn attention to gendering and learning. These draw on a variety of theoretical frameworks to explain their findings.

Depending on the ideological perspective, learning is dealt with in different ways, too, sometimes more and other times less explicitly. A broadly socio-constructivist thinking underpins much of the work reported in the book, learning being characterized as socially constructed when people work together with their knowledge and their tools. The ideas of learning being associated with acquiring and adopting new practices of work and thought are to be seen in several chapters. Learning as coming to see new aspects of the world and the salient phenomena in the every-day life-world underpins the phenomenological and phenomenographic work reported.

In lots of ways the chapters in this book give a flavour of the kind of research that is now being carried out in the interdisciplinary field of gender, education and work, in particular where that education or work entails the use of technologies or has technologies as its content. There is still a great deal of work to be done. We have seen dramatic changes across the world in the last century with respect to the participation of women and girls in work and education, but where that intersects with technologies, it remains gendered in ways that other areas of education and work no longer appear to be. There continues to be a need for further research and intervention.

Editors
Shirley Booth
University of the Witwatersrand, South Africa
University of Gothenburg, Sweden

Sara Goodman
Lund University, Sweden

Gill Kirkup
Open University, UK

ENDNOTES

[1] www.learnit.org.gu.se/english/
[2] KK-stiftelsen, Kunskap och Kompetens, www.kks.se
[3] Booth, A. C. & Booth, S. A. (2000). Genus och jämställdhet i IT-samhället: En inledande genomgång av KK-stiftelsens satsningar. (Gender and equity in the IT-society. A review of the projects funded by the Knowledge Foundation of Sweden.) Retrieved 15th October 2009 from http://www.learnit.org.gu.se/digitalAssets/759/759137_booth_o_booth_2000.pdf
[4] Goodman, S., Kirkup, G. and Michielsens, M. (Eds.), (2003) *ICTs in teaching and Learning Women's Studies- Perspectives and Practices in Europe,* Athena, Universiteit Utrecht, Centre for Gender Studies, Lund University

Acknowledgment

Producing this book has been quite a long process and there are many people to acknowledge and thank for their contributions, apart, of course, for the authors of the chapters.

The first step towards a book was the start of the network that later became GLIT – Gender, Learning and IT – and for that network we must thank the research programme LearnIT and its leaders, who gave a small sum of seed money. Thank you, Professors Ulf P Lundgren and Roger Säljö, respectively chair and scientific leader for the LearnIT programme, for acknowledging the need for a gender perspective in the area of Learning and IT. Then the network grew, and received generous funding through LearnIT, from its host and funder, the Swedish Knowledge Foundation, for continued network activities and associated research projects, the second important step. Thanks must go to Madeleine Caesar, who was at that time Chief Executive Officer of the Knowledge Foundation. Lund University gave a home to the network within its centre for research on learning in the activities and enterprises of higher education, Learning Lund, and we thank those who made possible the meetings in the sunny conference room there with its outlook over the Bishop's House in Lund.

The network, now comprising a number of research projects, worked together for three years, meeting regularly to discuss the ongoing research, most of which is represented in this book. The culminating event was a conference held in Helsingborg, Sweden, where network members presented their work, and invited international researchers complemented our work with theirs. This marked a third step towards the book, for there a book was outlined with a new international presence, which was later strengthened through close contact with the European Athena network and its conferences. Thank you, all who attended the respective conferences and contributed to the discussions there.

The fourth step was engaging with IGI Global and the assigned editor Beth Ardner. Thank you, Beth, for your ever ready and helpful advice, offered professionally, concisely and cheerfully. And thank you for the opportunity to extend our boundaries to a wider international audience of gender and IT researchers.

Finally, the fifth step was to collect, collate, review, edit, administer, and archive the material we received, with the invaluable help of our panel of expert reviewers. Having come this long, we think that an acknowledgement to one another as editors would not be out of place, for good collaboration.

Section 1
Being and Becoming
IT Professionals

Chapter 1
Women, Men and Programming:
Knowledge, Metaphors and Masculinity

Inger Boivie
Guide Konsult AB, Sweden

ABSTRACT

This chapter explores aspects of the gendering of computer science and IT, related to epistemological issues of what computing is and what type of knowledge counts. The chapter is based upon an interview study of how students and professionals in the field of computer science, perceive programming in a broad sense. Much of the earlier research on the under-representation of women in IT education and the IT industry has tended to focus on factors and aspects where women and men differ in their relation to IT and computers. Inspired by feminist research, it is suggested that developing an understanding of the problem of gender and IT requires a more complex analysis than a dualistic focus on differences between men and women. This chapter analyzes interviews with a range of Swedish male and female students and professionals from the field, in relation to gender with respect to metaphors of programming, inclusion and exclusion, the notion of beautiful code, understandings of masculinity and programming, and the idea of dedication.

INTRODUCTION

Some 25 years ago, I took a mandatory course in programming as part of my engineering program. At the time, I found programming very dreary, and something that only nerds could enjoy. I had little sympathy for my (primarily male) classmates who seemed obsessed with programming problems and told stories about waking up in the middle of the night with the long sought for solution to a particular problem and writing it down on whatever empty surface that was at hand. Some twenty years later, I was back at university, doing a PhD in Human-Computer Interaction, and decided to do a course in java programming, constructing user interfaces. To my great surprise, I was completely and utterly enraptured. I found programming great fun, creative, and virtually addictive. In fact, I so much enjoyed

DOI: 10.4018/978-1-61520-813-5.ch001

programming that I seriously regretted my 20 year old decision never to program, and never to enter a career in programming.

Being a woman, I am certainly not alone in making that decision. Women are under-represented in nearly every sector of education and professional life in which work with IT (information technology) is the main focus, i.e. designing, developing, operating and maintaining systems or products based on IT.

There is a large body of research on the under-representation of women in IT education and the IT industry internationally (see, for instance: Trauth et al., 2004; Selby et al., 1998; Camp, 1997). Much of this research focuses on factors and aspects in which women and men differ in their relation to IT and computers; that women have less experience with computers and programming from young age, for instance, and that women have less confidence in technical areas. Whereas some research seems to relate the problem to biology, discussing inherent differences in men and women (the essentialist approach), most of the research is grounded in a social constructionist perspective focusing on the social construction of male and female identities in relation to IT and computing (Trauth et al., 2004).

The number of women in IT-related educations and programmes in Sweden is currently low and even falling. The same trend has been reported in the US, the UK and a number of other Western countries. Extensive efforts have been made to reverse this decline in women's participation in the IT sector, not least in the area of recruiting and retaining women in higher IT education. In a two-plus-two year program at the Carnegie-Mellon University, the authors identified a number of key factors for the success in getting women students to their computer science program (Fisher & Margolis, 2002). Despite the success reported at Carnegie-Mellon, few other universities seem to have been able to reproduce their results. In Sweden, Chalmers University of Technology introduced a reformed Computer Science and Engineering program (D++[1]) in order to increase the number of women. Despite an initial success, the initiative has been a failure as regards recruiting and retaining women students (Wistedt, 2001).

Feminist research suggests that the problem of gender and IT is far more complex than a mere matter of under-representation that focuses on differences between men and women. Corneliussen (2003) uses the concept of subject positions to discuss how gender is constructed in relation to computers, shaping the way real men and women orient themselves in relation to these gendered subject positions. Björkman (2005) suggests that the problem is an epistemological one, i.e. a problem of what knowledge counts and whose knowledge counts in computer science and IT. Cukier et al. (2002) discuss the narrow definition of IT that dominates the discourse, and advocate a broader definition of IT including not only the technical bits but also the applications. Clegg (2001) discusses the relation between gender, education and computing and argues that gendered practices have pervaded the area of computing throughout its history and that these practices have maintained an "outsider" position for women and girls.

In this paper, based upon my recent study of how Swedish students and IT professionals perceive computer science and programming, I discuss some aspects of the gendering of computer science and IT.

Social Construction of Sex/Gender

Sex or gender is one of the most basic and persistent categorisations that people make in understanding ourselves and our surroundings (West and Zimmerman, 1987). It is a categorisation that is never silent, which means that there is virtually no human activity that is "gender neutral". There is never a situation in which an individual is not a girl/woman or a boy/man. The development and use of IT are emphatically not gender neutral.

West and Zimmerman (ibid) describe gender as an accomplishment, a complex of "micro-activities" that we perform in the virtual or real presence of others who are equally involved in the production of gender. The authors suggest three concepts for analysing the gendering mechanisms in society: sex, sex category and gender. Sex is a determination based on socially acceptable biological, observable, criteria, and we are *placed* in a sex category in accordance with these criteria. Gender, on the other hand, are the activities we perform and the conduct we display in order to place ourselves in a sex category. These three concepts are independent. For example, it is possible to claim membership in a sex category without having the outward characteristics of the corresponding sex. Zimmerman and West describe doing gender as an "ongoing process embedded in everyday interaction" (p 130). Doing gender is about adapting one's gender-marking or gender-displaying activities to every particular situation at every time, i.e. a skilful, ongoing reading of a situation and aligning one's response and activities to it in such a way that one's membership in a particular sex category cannot be questioned. At the same time, the sex categories of the members is one of the circumstances that attends virtually all our interactions. Thus, sex/gender is produced in a situation and at the same time shapes it (West & Zimmerman, ibid).

Doing gender is therefore about creating differences between male and female in social interaction, differences that are social constructions, having little to do with biology or essential differences between men and women. Despite arguments to the contrary, the sex categories of the actors in a situation or social setting are always part of that situation or setting. Women may be accorded respect for their professional or academic performance within a male domain, such as computer science, but they are always *also* evaluated against norms for appropriate behaviour of women which has little to do with their skills as computer scientists (see for instance Peterson (2005) for an account of how gender is done in the context of IT consultancy work.)

The Study

My understanding of computing or computer science is also a social construction[2]. In this paper, I explore how students and IT professionals perceive computer science, in particular programming – i.e. the production of the code which computers are "run on". I, and my informants, use the term programming in a broad sense, including not only the actual writing of code but also the work that leads up to and incorporates the coding. This work is difficult to delineate, since it is highly individual and situated, but it includes activities such as designing different parts of the system (e.g. client and server), structuring different parts of the code (e.g. classes and methods in object oriented programming), testing and debugging code, etc. Some of the informants made a distinction between programming and systems development.

Informant: *Programming, that is to write code. The way I see it, you're a programmer, you get a spec [specification] in your hand, like program these classes. Someone else has... everything is already done... like defined, it's just to start implementing. That is programming.*

Interviewer: *But that includes also to... not only writing the code line by line but also to use ready-made components and to put them together and these tools that are a bit more...*

Informant: *Well... the concepts [programming and systems development] are a bit fuzzy. I usually say developer. And then there is more of problem solving and stuff... perhaps... the spec is more generalised... it includes a bit broader... you get to analyse and design and then program and test and..." (Male IT professional)*

The students I talked to were not always aware of the distinction between these two concepts, not having been in contact with systems development in practice. They nevertheless do the activities described in the quote in their programming work. I have therefore primarily used the term programming in my discussions with my informants, applying a broader interpretation of it.

I have chosen to explore how the informants perceive and construct the concepts of programming and computer science without making gender an explicit part of my discussions with them. In accordance with the standpoint outlined above, that gender is displayed in virtually all activities and social settings in which we are members, it is not necessary to discuss gender explicitly in order to identify gender-marking activities or understandings.

This paper is written from an "insider" point of view. I have an engineering background, albeit not in computer science, and I have more than 15 years of practical experience of IT development. I have worked as an IT consultant focusing on usability issues and user involvement in IT systems development projects. This means that to some extent, I share common ground (Clark, 1996) with the informants, e.g. educational background and practical experiences. I have also basic knowledge about the internal logic and workings of a computer. Being a member of the social setting I explore, I am immersed in the discourse of computer science and systems development, creating an insider vantage point from which I have a sensitivity towards and appreciation for the informants' points of view. However, I also recognize that my in-depth familiarity with systems development makes it difficult for me to maintain the distance required to critically reflect on and problematise my informants' accounts of the concepts of programming and computing. I have therefore chosen to problematise the relations between these concepts and the process of doing gender.

Computer science is a diverse area including, for instance, hardware-related issues, software-related issues and programming, and data com-munication. The focus of my study has been programming, since it is the primary means with which we interact with and control computers. It also reflects the internal logic of a computer. In this study, I have therefore focused on how computer science students and IT professionals (systems developers) understand, think about and talk about the concept of programming.

The Interviews

In total, I have interviewed 13 people.

- nine computer science students (six men and three women) from two universities (engineering faculties) in Sweden, ranging from first-year students to final-year students and one student from another engineering program. This informant had taken programming courses and did quite a lot of programming as part of a master's thesis.
- two IT professionals – currently active in the IT industry – one man and one woman
- one male PhD student at my own department
- one woman who had an educational background in computer science, but did not work within the area – not out of a lack of interest, but because the she was not able to find an IT-related job when she had finished her degree, times being tough in the IT industry at the time. This interview was only summarised since the recording failed.

I knew some of the informants from before, and contacted them directly. I got in touch with the student informants by putting up notes about the study at the two universities represented in the study.

In the interviews, I used a semi-structured, rather informal approach, based on an interview guide including questions about:

- what do you associate with the concepts of computer science, information technology and programming?
- what does a programmer do?
- what does it take to be a really good programmer?
- what are your own strengths and weaknesses as a programmer?
- what makes programming fun?
- what do you find difficult/frustrating in programming?

In order to elicit answers that went deeper than the general, unreflected ones, I tried to make the informants relate to real people and settings from their everyday lives as students or systems developers. I also used follow-up questions extensively, which turned the interviews into informal discussions and in-depth reflections about programming and computing.

The interviews were taped and transcribed, partly verbatim, partly with less detail, summing up what was being said. The level of detail in the transcription was adapted to the topic of discussion, and in what ways it related to the research questions.

I analysed each interview by arranging the data in accordance with themes or codes based on my interpretation of what the informants said. The codes were partly determined by the themes and questions used in the interviews, and partly they emerged during the process of transcribing and analysing the interviews. Then I categorised the interview data across the individual informants.

In the analysis, I identified several themes relating to the perception of programming, computer science and IT. Below, I discuss three of the more salient themes. These are some of the metaphors used to talk about and think about programming, abstract and concrete knowledge in programming, and finally the notion of dedication and concentration associated with programming and with good programmers. I have related these three themes to gender-marking processes using quotes from the interviews to illustrate the themes. I have translated these quotes from Swedish, retaining the spoken and everyday characteristics of the language to the best of my ability. I have also "sanitized" the quotes in order to make them more readable.

Metaphors: Inclusion and Exclusion in Programming

Eriksson (2003) describes metaphors as a bridging process between different fields of meaning. The use of metaphors implies a process of interpretation and understanding of a phenomenon rather than the mere transfer of meaning, unchanged, from one area or object to another. The metaphor creates associations between the fields, which move beyond the initial meaning of the referenced object or area.

The informants talked about programming using various metaphors. In this paper I focus on two of these metaphors. They are programming as mathematical/logical problem solving, and programming as construction work.

Programming as Mathematical Problem Solving

Traditionally, programming has been described and seen as mathematical/logical problem solving (see for instance, Turkle & Papert, 1990; Cukier, 2003). References to this type of problem solving were frequent in the interviews. The informants talk about programming as problem solving, in particular the type of problem solving taught and applied in engineering and mathematics.

Interviewer: *What do you associate with the concept of programming – what does the concept mean to you?*

Informant: *The first thing I would say is problem solving ... I really do associate directly to that ... then ... what else is programming ... creativity too, to create things. (Male student)*

However, explaining what problem solving actually means was more difficult for the informants. The notion of problem solving is deeply inscribed in engineering disciplines in general, including computer science/programming. It is taken for granted and therefore difficult to elaborate on. Gedenryd (1998) argues that engineering-oriented problem solving is about defining delineable problems that can be described and solved by means of mathematical models or by applying a number of pre-defined, discrete, rational steps. The problem must be transformed into a set of parameters that can be defined in advance, since this approach does not allow for "unknowns" or uncertainties. It can only solve "tame" or "benign" problems where an exhaustive problem formulation can be stated in advance and where there is a stopping rule, clearly stating when the problem is solved (Rittel & Webber, 1973). This way of understanding phenomena in the world as well-defined problems, described by sets of characteristics or parameters is sometimes referred to as "boxology"[3]. The way the informants talked about programming, and how they approach and solve a programming problem shows that the "boxology" way of thinking is an integral part of programming and computing. Some informants talked about the need for structure, i.e. the need to understand the problem as a structure describing well defined units and their inter-relations. They also described lack of structure as a problem and even anxiety provoking, for instance, if the programming problem does not lend itself to being sub-divided into separate units and well-defined relations.

The problems the students work within their programming courses range from very simple ones in the beginning, such as making the computer display a sentence on the screen, or do simple calculations and display the results and then moving on to problems that deal with data structures, data storage and sorting algorithms. Over time, the problems become more complicated and gain more of an "everyday" nature.

Interviewer: *What is a problem in your world?*

Informant: *... A problem could be 'do I need two bags to pack these things that I've bought at the supermarket or do I need one? Is one enough?' That is a typical computer science problem that you could [...] When you went shopping and put things in your trolley, if they were scanned, their volume and stuff, then the trolley would be able to calculate for you, calculate that, well, this number of bags. So problems are nothing strange really, they are really small things, and what it is all about is transforming all these strange things in computer science to little everyday problems, like packing a bag. (Male student)*

The problems given to the students are typically well defined. One of the informants described an assignment, where the problem was not defined exhaustively from the beginning, Instead, the teacher changed the nature of the problem along the way. The informant found this very annoying.

Informant: *... And then, when I did it that way it was 'no thank you', they didn't want it that way. So, OK, I have rewritten [the code for the assignment]. And then, the second time, then it was 'no', they wanted each part on its own, not all together. [...]*

Interviewer: *So, it's partly... what it says in the instructions doesn't fit with how you then...*

Informant: *Yes... that was primarily why I got so angry." (Female student)*

To my informants engineering-oriented/logical problem solving is taken for granted as a natural part of computer science/programming. Several of them (both men and women) talked about problem solving as a motivating factor. They said that they enjoy solving problems, for instance, puzzle problems, and talked about the feelings of reward, joy and even pride when they manage to solve a particularly tricky problem.

Informant ... *It's this... if you like solving puzzle problems... the bottom line is that you should like to solve things... quite a few people who like programming... I think that they describe the feeling that when you have really solved it, and it works, it's some kind of relief, it's the confirmation that you could do it. It could be a mathematical problem, or it could be that you have managed to program whatever you were supposed to program, or it could be solving a sudoku, and get it sorted out. Puzzles. (Male IT professional)*

The relations between gender and mathematics/engineering played out in the interviews have been extensively discussed in the literature. For example, in their study on Swedish engineers, Berner & Mellström (1997) describe a historic process in which women have been first excluded and then segregated and subordinated within the engineering educations and professions.

Programming as Craft: As Construction Work

In addition to the mathematical, logical aspects of programming, the informants also talk about programming using concrete, physical terms related to construction work. The informants also refer to the concrete, almost embodied, knowledge about the tools they use to create the programs.

Interviewer: *The knowledge that the child needs is in certain ways.... It's pretty physical stuff.... The analogies you bring up are all pretty physical... while programming is extremely abstract and intellectual...*

Informant: *But you still have to understand what side of the hammer you have to use to hit the nail with. You still have to understand that it's the sharp end that goes down. It's not enough to do it at random. Even if you could learn by doing that... there is some kind of understanding there as well. But, of course, programming is more intellectual... but it's the same thing really, a bit... One of the lecturers here... (authors' note: name of lecturer) perhaps. He talked about throwing a basket ball... most people who do that don't know how to do it, they use a lot of the muscles in their arms, they don't know how to do it, so they swing and twist and it doesn't go straight at all. Then, the more you practice, the fewer muscles you start to use, you understand what it is that counts. And, above all, it becomes automatic, muscle memory. And when you sit there programming and you're not that used to it, then every little step is difficult. And then, after a while, you quickly scribble down large parts of the code purely automatically since you know that this and this and this have to be there. So it just gets there, you don't have to think about why. (Male student)*

Often, the informants refer to this concrete, embodied aspect, in terms of "building". References to craft, carpentry and construction work were abundant in the interviews. Nearly all the informants talked about programming as "building".

Interviewer: *This thing with building, what do you think about when you say building? What is it you build?*

Informant: *It is to build the software, to build it up. First you build it like a structure in your mind – this is the way it should be, this is the way it should work – and you keep thinking about it. And then... well to build it in the code, to make it work. (Female IT professional)*

Many made explicit analogies to constructing and building a house, using hammers and nails and pieces of wood to create things. They talked about tools – and compared the tools used in programming to the tools a carpenter or construction worker would use, for instance, a hammer or a spanner.

Interviewer*: You talk about building... that recurs in many interviews. What is it in programming that has to do with building?*

Informant*:... The question is where that word comes from... perhaps it's that you almost... it's about compiling and linking things together and that is easily seen as something you have to build... you have a number of boards that you put together... in programming, you have small elements that you put together. That's what you do. That's where the thing with building comes from, I believe... build programs... because often you may have ready-made components that you use as well. There are little parts that you build together in your program as well... like you re-use somebody else's half-finished house and continue building on that. (Male student)*

One interesting parallel is that of building with Lego.

Informant*: I think programming is like building with Lego. You take the ready-made pieces you've got... where they fit in... and if you don't have the ready-made pieces, then you'll have to manufacture them." (Male PhD student)*

Metaphors from building/construction are formally and informally used in programming, for instance, a "build" is a compilation of all the code that makes up a particular version of a system/application or a part of it. Programming is often referred to as "building" a program or a system. In western societies, the metaphors of "building" and "construction" have a male connotation and this aspect of masculinity in the metaphors is not something that is easily changed.

The Creative Aspects of Programming

The construction metaphor extends to include the creative aspects of programming. The informants talked about creativity and how they feel that they create something. They talk about creating something that is tangible and usable, something that works, not necessarily because they want to use the programs they create. Instead they talked about how creating something gives rise to feelings of reward and contentment, making programming fun and enjoyable.

Interviewer*: Is it about creating things?*

Informant*: Of course! Everything you do, you create. At least I think that the joy of creating something is what makes programming fun, in the same way it was fun to build with Lego. It wasn't because you wanted to play with the Lego, it was because you built something. As a side effect, you may use the program you have created, but that's not the thing. Perhaps, you get really happy with your program and you think that that's exactly the way I wanted it. Great, now I've got it. But, it's not the same thing as when you're programming – that's two completely different things. When you're programming, if you think that's fun, then it's the joy of creating something, And I have no answer to what that is. (Male PhD student)*

The informants talk about creativity primarily in a constructive sense of the word, not so much in an artistic sense of creativity. It is a productive, object-oriented creativity, aimed at constructing or creating *things* where the thing in itself is the outcome of the process, not its use or its effect on other people. However, one important factor to some of the informants was the reactions they got from other people from making their programs available to others. In their opinion, it is not only about the thing in itself – it is also about how other people relate to it. One of the informants described graphic programmers and the demo scene and compared their attitudes to his own:

Informant: *(...) There are endless numbers of game programmers and graphic programmers, and I think that it is very much about the internal reward there: 'sh*t, that turned out really nice, I'm really happy with that'. People can look at it and go 'that was really cool', but you can't get the same response as when someone sends you a mail 'Well, this was really good, but I would like to have this feature as well, could you fix that?'. Or that you get continuous response 'I use this everyday and I think it's really great, but could you please fix this feature as well?'. Something like that is really good to get. When other people tell you that it is good, then you also think it's good – that's the fun part of it. (Male student)*

By making the program available to others, this informant places it in some kind of public sphere to test the reactions he gets from other people, like placing a piece of art in a museum or in a public space to have other people look at it and react to it.

Metaphors: Mechanisms for Inclusion and Exclusion

I find the metaphoric use of building and construction in programming interesting, since it is an explicitly masculine metaphor. Building and construction work is an almost exclusively male domain in Sweden. The few women who work in the building/construction industry typically work in "white collar" positions, e.g. architects, construction engineers, etc. The building/con-

struction industry is a typical "hard" domain/technology. Hard technologies are large-scale and associated with power (e.g. industries, space shuttles, weapons) whereas soft technologies are small-scale or organic (e.g. kitchen appliances, life sciences) (Faulkner, 2000b).

In North European and North American cultures, the mathematical/logical problem solving metaphor is also masculine. Mendick (2005) describes how mathematics is cast as masculine by means of a number of inter-related binary opposites, where those concepts that align with being good at maths, also align with masculinity and a higher value than the opposing, feminine, concepts in each pair.

Hence, the metaphors used casting programming as building and mathematical problem solving simultaneously typecast it as masculine i.e. relate it to traits and characteristics that are traditionally associated with the male sex category and doing the male gender.

The use of metaphors highlight certain aspects of a phenomenon, but obscures others, thus reducing the complexity and ambiguity of the phenomenon being described (Öhman Persson, 2004). In this process of highlighting/obscuring aspects, metaphors act as ideologies in that they create specific interpretations of a phenomenon. Metaphors provide a way of creating a common ground and understanding, including actors who share this understanding. At the same time they exclude other actors, i.e. those who are not part of the metaphor, who cannot relate to the understanding expressed in the metaphor.

Metaphors and metaphoric use in language are often gendered. For example, Eriksson (2003) describes how metaphors (animals, sports, war, other masculine occupations) are used to describe surgeons in ways that simultaneously gender the profession, casting it as masculine. However, metaphors create associations to masculinity or femininity on a symbolic level. They do not describe how real men and women relate to the concept or area. For example, the use of masculine metaphors to describe surgery does not disqualify real women surgeons, but typecasts it as a male arena and the stereotypical surgeon as a man. Similarly, typecasting programming as a male arena and the stereotypical programmer as a man does not imply that real women are automatically excluded. Nor that all men are included. Individual men and women relate to the metaphors in various ways depending on their background, interests and preferences.

Professionals vs. Non-Professionals: Being in or Out

The informants also talked about programming and computing in terms that tell stories about being in or out. Although no one talked explicitly about women being out, these stories indicate a gendering mechanism.

I asked them about the differences between computer science and information technology (IT). Many of the informants made distinctive differences between the two concepts, placing themselves very clearly in the area of computer science. The following excerpts illustrate how the informants talked about IT versus computer science.

Interviewer: *Is there a difference to the concept of IT?*

Informant: *Yes, personally I think that IT feels like a concept that is used for people who don't really understand what it's all about – it's like a buzzword only, that is bandied about just to make people think that 'Oh, this is new and cool, new and modern'. The IT concept is just a buzzword. (Male student)*

and

Informant: *When I started [the computer science program], most people thought then, in '98, that IT was one of those ridiculous, stupid words that business guys had made up ... but it's taken over since then.*

Interviewer: *In what ways was it stupid?*

Informant: *That probably came from the fact that it was "Aftonbladet" (author's note: a major evening paper in Sweden) and papers like that that wrote about IT ... like that was the cool thing ... since it was. While everyone who worked with it seemed to talk about computer science ... at least the ones you met. That is to say that that word [IT] was used outside the actual sphere where it should be used. So it was pushed on from the outside rather than emerging within. That's how I perceived it, at least at the time ... when I was a poor student. (Male PhD student)*

There are differing voices in the interviews, describing computer science as a sub-area of IT where IT is attributed a higher status than computer science, rather than as two fundamentally different things. However, the perception of computer science as the real thing and IT as a nonsensical concept is more prominent in the interviews. This perception tells two stories of exclusion. IT is for people outside the area who do not know anything about computers and computing. It is used by "business guys" and journalists without the discretion and knowledge to use the proper word (computer science) appropriately. It is moreover used by amateurs and dilettantes within the area as illustrated in the below excerpt:

Interviewer: *What did they write [about IT] that was so stupid?*

Informant: Oh... I don't remember exactly what they wrote about it... but it was the big thing, IT, at the time, it was. Everything with IT was so cool... and everyone was supposed to be doing IT. If you'd managed to create your own web page, then you were doing IT, you were in the IT industry. I suppose that was why it was stupid, that everyone could be in the IT industry in some way, if it only meant that you'd managed to build an incredibly ugly homepage with purple colours on green background, then you were suddenly an IT engineer or IT professional. (Male PhD student)

There are two distinctions being made here – IT is used by those who do not know anything, not being a part of the area at all, and by those who participate in the area on "false" premises, faking it as IT professionals.

Having worked within the IT industry, as an *IT* consultant for more than 10 years, I was quite surprised by the emphasis the informants displayed in making distinctions between computer science and IT. Setting up and marking boundaries to those who do not know, or are amateurs, is typical for the professionalisation of an area (Birkett and Evans, 2005). Looking up the ACM[4] digital library, there are a great number of papers, workshops and panels calling for an increased professionalism within software engineering and the IT area, for instance by means of licensing software engineers (developers), uniform definitions of the curricula of computer science education programmes and calls for a code of ethics. There are no explicit references to gender-marking mechanisms in the discussions about who is "in or out" in my interviews. However, Valian (1998) argues that professionalisation as such implies the exclusion of women in that most high status or high paying professions are male-dominated. Women, being women, fit less well to our notions about professions and professionalism since these are rooted in notions about masculinity. In western society, men are seen as "… capable of independent,

autonomous action (agentic, in short), assertive, instrumental, and task-oriented. Men act..." whereas women "… nurture others and express their feelings." (ibid, p 13). The IT industry is no exception to this. Nielsen et al. (2003) describe, for instance, how women have to adapt to the IT industry as a masculine domain, and Hoplight Tapia (2003) describes how women IT professionals have to contend with an implicit hostility towards women.

Abstract and Concrete Knowledge in Programming

The metaphors used to describe programming also describe two different types of knowledge; abstract, formal knowledge versus concrete, situated knowledge.

Traditionally, computing and programming have been closely related to mathematics and analytical/logical problem solving based on the formal, propositional way of knowing and abstract knowledge. However, computer science and IT, being engineering areas, also relate to a more direct, physical interaction and knowing about the material at hand. Wendy Faulkner (2000a) explores issues of dichotomies in a study of a software development project in an American telecommunications company, and she suggests that some software developers not only work with their code in abstract, formal ways, but also relate to it through "rituals of tinkering". Based on work carried out at Massachusetts Institute of Technology, and using a number of their previous studies on researchers, computer science students and children, Sherry Turkle and Seymour Papert (1990) identified and discussed different ways of doing computing/programming by examining how novice programmers learn to program. They describe, for instance, the planner's way of structuring and dividing the program into abstract sub-procedures as compared to the bricoleur's way of working with objects as parts of an evolving whole. These two approaches represent different types of knowledge – the formal and abstract versus the concrete and direct.

Similar ways of thinking about and doing computing and programming are played out in the interviews in my study. For example, some informants made a clear distinction between designing the program and writing the code, even saying that they would like to hand the actual coding over to somebody else (the planner approach). Others talked about designing and writing the code as inseparable (more similar to the bricoleur approach). They described writing the code as part of designing the program, since new questions and problems come up throughout the whole process.

Informant*: ... You have a picture in front of you, and you have the problem all set up, like, what you are programming, and you have it in a bigger context. It takes a little while... every time you sit down it takes a little while to build this up, like, you have to think about what you have done, and where you were. That may be a reason also, why you tend to sit for a long while. So, when you program, you have to... like you have to finish, you cannot stop in the middle of it, because then you get lost. And sometimes, when you get a really good idea, you have to hold on to it, and write it down and get it down in code. (Female student)*

The excerpt tells a story about close interaction with the material at hand, about getting a hold on your problem and immersing yourself in it. This requires concrete, if not physical, at least virtual contact and interaction with the code. It requires knowledge and know-how that are situated and concrete. The problem and its solution is not something you can make completely extraneous to yourself on a piece of paper.

Turkle and Papert (ibid) describe these two approaches as contradictory, and a matter of personal style and preference. However, in my interviews, the same informant would describe different ways of relating to and thinking about programming, indicating that it is not just a matter of personal style and preference, but that programming involves many different aspects and skills. In particular, they talk about beautiful code, which at the same time represents the abstract, logical and formal aspects of programming, and the more concrete, situated, embodied know how of the programmer.

Beautiful Code

Beautiful code is pure, simple and optimal. It is not messy, not littered with superfluous bits and pieces or "quick and dirty" solutions. There is no "copy-and-paste" code, i.e. code that has been copied from another program or another part of the same program and then modified here and there.

Informant*: Well, it should be clean, there shouldn't be a lot of error handling, no obscure jumps to different places and things like that. It... one of the most common characteristics of beautiful code is that it is a short, concise, efficient solution to a problem. It should... it should be easy to see everything that happens without the code becoming unwieldy and long. I've seen some example of people who have written... to search a graph, and have done it in four lines. Then you think 'well if I'd do it, it would take me half a page to do that'. But someone's managed to squeeze it into four lines by thinking really hard. (Male student)*

and

Interviewer*: Yes, I understand.... Clean code, what does that mean?*

Informant: *... Imagine that you were to leave here... (...)*

Informant: *Just next to here, I think, there is a door to the stairway. If I want to go to the stairway, I could walk through that door, and then come back in through the other door. But I could also walk out through this door, walk to the main entrance, down to the street, and then walk all the way round and come back in through the backdoor and be in the same place. That's the difference. (Male IT professional)*

Somebody compared it to the beauty you find in mathematical formulae:

Informant: *(...) The first time you come across the Fourier transform, it's like... it's the same thing in a way. The F transform is really.. is really just... a few lines long. But when you understand what the F transform does, then you realise that it is really beautiful. It does.... It solves extremely many problems in a beautiful way. And it's the same with code in a way. You come across... you have a problem... and you think it's a bit messy, this is hard work, it's going to take very long time to solve. I have to write a hundred special cases to take care of everything. And then you see someone who's solved it in fifteen lines. And you understand every single line and you can see exactly how the code interacts." (Male student)*

The concept of purity is quite interesting – pure code is not messy, it is beautiful in its simple and clear-cut logic. There are no disturbing or disruptive parts, no distracting information or pieces. There are no emotions, no social debris cluttering the picture. There are no humans. When humans (users) enter the picture, it becomes more difficult to write beautiful code, since humans are prone to making mistakes. They are unpredictable, their actions are situated rather than abstract and rational in the classic sense of the word.

Informant: *Well... it has to be clean... clean... free of everything that is not needed. It has to be very... If you have error handling or special cases, then it's no longer beautiful. That's why it gets... then you're back in the ordinary messiness... the messiness of ordinary code where you have... many programs consist of nothing but error handling. You try to catch every stupid thing a user could possibly do to the program. (Male student)*

The beauty of the simple and the pure reflect the privileged position of abstract knowledge in western society. Such knowledge where the situation, the social and the emotional are peeled away (Faulkner, 2000a) and only the pure abstract logic remains. Excelling in the art of writing this kind of code requires that you are "IQ smart". The informants talk about the importance of being traditionally "IQ smart", good at maths and logic, in order to be a good programmer, as in being able to do the really difficult stuff. You also need to be able to "see structures", i.e. abstract away from the context, the concrete situation.

Interviewer: *So smart, that is to be smart in a mathematical way?*

Informant: *Yes, old traditional IQ smart so to speak... (Female student)*

and

Informant: *(...). He gets along... he has a very good ability for systems, to see systems, and to penetrate problems. He has a lot of practice in that, and he has it from the start. His mother is very logical and stuff like that. So he has... she grilled him whenever he didn't have logical arguments... (Female student)*

It also requires a natural talent, a genius to see the brilliant solutions.

Interviewer*: Let's go back to the really good programmer. What you bring up is the ability to be dedicated...*

Informant*: Or rather, to see the solution straight away... perhaps. I think there is... there are the geniuses who in some way manage to... and there are those who practice a lot.*

Interviewer*: Ok, so the geniuses are those who see the solution right away?*

Informant*: Yes... or perhaps they see a different solution than the one you'd think of spontaneously. I don't know how common that is, there may also be people who get these genius solutions without being able to explain how. (Male IT professional)*

Here, programming and engineering become gendered through their associations with science which emphasises objectivity, emotional detachment and rationality, all of which are historically associated with masculinity (Fox Keller, 1985). Such characteristics that are peeled away in the simple, pure and logic belong on the feminine side of the masculine/feminine dualism in gender making. This, of course, is not to say that real men and women do not display characteristics, abilities and traits across these lines, which Faulkner points out in her ethnographic study of software developers (ibid).

The Art of Writing Beautiful Code

Beautiful code may be about abstract knowledge and pure, simple, clean logic, but writing beautiful code is about emotions and dedication. It may even become an end in itself, a driving force as described in the following excerpt.

Interviewer*: One of the people I interviewed talked about beautiful, elegant code and some kind of ideas and notions about it being code that is smart, that does things in an incredibly elegant and smooth and efficient way. Little code that does much. Is that anything that you have...*

Informant*: No, it's a bit like... I can see a difference from NN. He can sit and read and become enthusiastic. Because they had those... at his old workplace, where they tried to do something in as few lines of code as possible. And to do as tight loops as possible, and the time critical core, and then you have to create that really tight loop because then there's time... That's something that he is really fascinated by. (Female IT professional)*

Indeed, some informants claimed that being an excellent programmer, requires that you are virtually addicted to programming.

Informant*: I think you have to dedicate yourself to coding to an incredible extent, in order to be an efficient programmer. You have to code a lot, everyday surely, which I believe very few who consider themselves programmers actually do. Above all, I think you have to program in your spare time, you have to like programming so bloody much that you do it whenever you get the chance.*

Interviewer*: Does that mean that you have to be completely dedicated in order to be a really good programmer?*

Informant*: Yes I believe so. (Male IT professional)*

However, not everyone shared this viewpoint.

Interviewer*: Well... but you don't think it necessary to have it as a hobby, to completely dedicate yourself to it, in order to become a really good programmer?*

Informant*: That it is necessary to program in your free time in order to be a good programmer?*

Interviewer*: Yes.*

Informant*: No.*

Interviewer*: You don't think so?*

Informant*: Oh, well... of course they're good, but...*

Interviewer*: You can get there anyway?*

Informant*: Yes. They'll surely be a lot faster than me, and have much more efficient solutions than I'll ever be able to produce... possibly (...). But personally... I don't think you should do in your spare time what you do for a living. Or... sure, they're good at programming.*

Interviewer*: But it's not necessary so to speak. You can become a good programmer even if you're not prepared to spend all your...*

Informant*: Well, I really want to become a good programmer. I'm OK. And I want to be good. But I'm not going to spend my spare time just to become good. (Female IT student)*

But, dedication is not enough. Being an excellent programmer, i.e. one who is able to write that kind of code, is also about concrete and situated knowledge of programming. Experience and practice are important aspects, and being open-minded about how to solve a particular problem. And also some kind of tenacity, i.e. an ability to persevere and not give up when you have found a solution that works.

Informant*: Partly the problem, the programming language, how you want to solve it, the ability to see other ways of solving the problem, to be able to find the right tool for the task. That is one thing, to me at least, that distinguishes a good programmer from a poor programmer. A poor programmer knows C and does everything in C. A poor programmer who writes something in java, does java like C. While a good programmer is not limited by the choice of language or choice of technology, or stuff like that, but knows how to adjust and to still produce a good solution. (Male student)*

Interviewer*: So it takes a certain amount of persistence, not to turn a blind eye to the problem?*

Informant*: Yes, absolutely. It's really easy to... you often see that with the students... in their assignments. Those who are not that good they've managed to get it to work once, and then they don't touch anything. They hand it in straight away, virtually before it breaks on its own accord. While those who are really good, they have run tests on it properly, and tested different imaginable scenarios, where different things happen in different ways. To see if there are any problems like 'if this and this, then that will happen'. Those solutions will be much more robust, since they anticipate these things. (Male PhD student)*

These excerpts complement the picture of programming requiring abstract knowledge and a logical, rational ability and the notion of the genius, (s)he who can write beautiful, elegant programs seemingly effortless. They tell a story about the necessity of having concrete and situated knowledge as well as strong emotions and dedication.

DEDICATION: TO PROGRAMMING OR TO PEOPLE

As discussed above, programming seems to require the time, the tenacity and the devotion to pursue it not only as an occupation but also as a main interest in life. This was one aspect of programming, where gender explicitly came into the picture in the interviews. Women do not display the same kind of dedication.

Interviewer*: But, these women that you've met, who're really good. In what ways are they really good?*

Informant*: You can see that it's this particular way of thinking, and the really quick solutions, they're really quick at solutions. But then you also hear.... It's been people who've been in the same class as me here at XXX, or with whom I've done... worked a bit together with, and so you've heard from other people that she's really bright, she can do it... is really good at programming, can use it so to speak. But on the contrary... the difference between the guys and the girls is that I've never met a woman that I know has it as an interest in her spare time and an interest at school... or specialisation at school. The women I've met who program, they only do it at school because they have to, or... well... they probably like it but they often have other things... They don't have it as their main interest in their spare time, they didn't start as small kids and programmed*

some little box, like... (Female student)

Where does this interest and space for pursuing programming as a hobby come from, or rather where do the obstacles come from that stop women from focusing their time and efforts on programming as a singular pastime? The woman IT professional discussed the differences between herself and her husband (also a professional IT worker) in that he takes the time to learn new things thoroughly, out of sheer interest, in his spare time. She described how he had spent four weeks learning a new operating system (Linux) in the evenings.

Informant*: He has enormous... this is new, this is fun, I want to learn this. And so... he just penetrates that. That's what he's working with now. That's how he got his current job.*

Interviewer*: Does he spend the evenings and nights programming, just for fun?*

Informant*: He reads a lot. But at that time, he built a Linux machine and downloaded Linux programs so that he got a whole Linux system and then he executed stuff on it, and did things... And he tests... Well, if he has to do something small, like if the kids need a multiplication table for practising, then he'd test to do it in JavaScript and would practise doing that. While I sit down and write it on paper. He's a completely different type of human in that regard.*

This situation is naturally overlaid with the division of responsibilities for the family and the home – but indicates that he has the time, the interest and the opportunity to focus on programming tasks (regardless of whether or not they are a primary object in the situation) and to block out others, for instance, in this case the children who do not need a JavaScript-based multiplication table as such, but something that will help them practise their maths. Whereas she would orient herself towards her children (people), writing down something simple on a piece of paper to meet their immediate needs providing care and support.

Many of the informants describe being absorbed by a problem, getting some kind of "tunnel view" that blocks everything else out. The following excerpt gives a compelling account of how the informant literally disappeared into a world of her own, forgetting everything but the programming problem she was struggling with. In my question I refer to my own experience of programming as being completely absorbing.

Interviewer: ... Do you find it difficult to let go of the problem? Because, that's how I felt, I just wanted to try this out, and this, and this.

Informant: Yes, I can tell you about one thing. It was in my first year... I had a class, three classes, or two classes that day, and then I had a meeting later. The first class was ten to twelve. And that first hour, I came up with something... I thought that I should change that line in my code. So we were sitting in X and I thought that I will come out during break, before I forget it. [...]. So, during the eleven o'clock break, I came here (authors note; the computer class room), and sat down and changed that line, and it didn't really get right, so I kept on with it, and the next time I looked at the time, it was six.

Interviewer: Six! My god, it just disappeared?

Informant: Yes, it just disappeared.

Interviewer: Seven hours later...

Informant: Seven hours later, and I hadn't felt anything...

Interviewer: You weren't even hungry?

Informant: No, I wasn't even hungry. I hadn't even thought of anything... I just... sh*t, six o' clock. I'd missed my class, I'd missed my meeting. (Female student)

Other informants describe similar experiences of being absorbed, not being able to let go of a problem and the strong feelings of reward when they finally solve the problem. But there is another side of the same coin, the frustration of being stuck, not being able to solve a problem, also known as "coder's block".

Informant: ...Other things that are dreary and hard is when you get stuck... you can get what is popularly known as 'coders' block'. You have a problem and you just cannot find the solution to it. It is... I've been in situations where I've been sitting for three-four days with something that I've had to write, and just haven't been able to find a way to solve the problem... and literally banged my head on the desk in the attempts to come up with something. You just don't get anywhere. (Male student)

The stories about being absorbed and the stories about coder's block both indicate that programming requires concentration and a very strong focus on the task at hand. One of the informants discussed the importance of being able to focus.

Informant: Being able to focus very hard on one and the same thing, preferably for a long time.. and that you... well, you have to be able to focus because if you are interrupted than you easily... well that you lose everything. (Female student)

Hence, this need for and ability to focus on the task at hand, to exclude everything around you and to become completely absorbed with your programming problem is very important. The train of thought that helps you solve the problem is easily disrupted, negatively affecting the quality of your work and your efficiency as a programmer. However, focusing on a task and excluding everything extraneous to it also implies excluding other people, where task-orientation is typically associated with masculinity and conflicts with people-orientation which traditionally is considered a feminine trait (Valian, 1998).

This need for complete dedication described above, and the need for focus, concentration and task-orientation may be contrasted with the concept of "availability for doing caring work" (Widerberg, 1992). In many situations, not least in the workplace, women are expected to take care of relationships and to provide for a good and friendly atmosphere as well as provide social support, sympathy and understanding (Widerberg, ibid). Carstensen (2004) describes such expectations within the university, expectations in which women PhD students are seen as providers of care, support and sympathy.

Being available for doing caring work requires continuous people orientation which conflicts with task orientation, and the "tunnel view" in programming described by my informants. Hence, these expectations placed on women, by men and women alike, may make it more difficult for women to focus on the programming task, and to enter that state of "blocking out" the surroundings. The people-orientation expected from women may also make it more difficult to display the kind of dedication that some of the informants described as necessary for becoming a brilliant programmer.

If dedication and single-minded concentration are what it takes to become a really good programmer, women are disqualified from the start. As one of the female students pointed out.

Informant: *I think... that's a thing that I've talked with my friends about... why did so many women start my year and the year before that... And I think that perhaps many of the women do not have the computer interest from the start... not so incredibly interested in computers as many of the guys who come here. Instead they see it as a smart career move, 'Now, I want to get a good education and this seems to be a good one'. And when the [IT] business went down, they moved on to other education programs, and that's why there are so few now. And that's probably why many of the women remain now. Since many of the guys they move on to jobs instead, they work within computer science, since they have quite a bit of knowledge and experience from before [before university] and do not need to finish. But many of the women don't have that and so they feel that they have to finish [the education] in order to get a job within the area.*

DISCUSSION

The starting point of this paper, and the research, was West and Zimmerman's concept of "doing gender". West and Zimmerman emphasise the interactional aspects of gender, how we constantly do gender by performing "socially guided perceptual, interactional, and micropolitical activities" (West & Zimmerman, 1987, p 126) in social situations. Gender is something we do constantly in every walk of life. It is an ongoing, interactive process and a categorisation that is never silent. In every social situation, we do gender – we place ourselves in relation to the situation and in relation to gender within that situation. Doing gender means behaving, acting and interacting in such ways as to prove oneself a legitimate member of either sex category. There are no gender-neutral situations or arenas. Being a woman in a male domain, for instance, being employed in men's work means that you have to continually prove that you are a woman, despite your professional role, actions and interactions. You have to remain the 'other' in relation to men, in order to keep your feminine identity.

Information technology, computer science and programming are indeed not gender-neutral arenas. Had they been, we would not have had the under-representation of women we face today. In this paper I have discussed the building metaphor and the mathematical problem solving metaphor used to describe programming. These metaphors represent different ways of thinking about, talking about and feeling about programming. They also represent different ways of "doing programming" and constructing programming as an activity or area. Both metaphors are associated to traits and characteristics that are traditionally considered masculine in western culture, in particular in Northern Europe and North America. Hence, by talking about programming as building or solving problems, we also talk about it as a male arena, typecasting the stereotypical participant as a male.

The use of the building metaphor and its associations to hard technology and masculinity is no coincidence. One could argue that any metaphor describing the process of creating something whole out of pieces would be equally valid to describe this aspect of programming, for instance, doing patchwork[5]. However, such a metaphor connotes soft technology and women's work in the domestic sphere and would change the perception of programming. Faulkner (2000b) argues that technology in itself cannot be understood without reference to gender in that it is populated by men and based on a gender-segregated labour division which equates technical expertise with masculinity. Moreover, cultural images of technology and technical artefacts, knowledge and practices are all associated with masculinity.

Furthermore, the focus on rationality and abstract, formal aspects places the area within the tradition of masculine knowledge and skills. Notions about the importance of pursuing programming as one's main interest in life and a

single-minded dedication to it may also act as gendering mechanisms in that women are expected to be people-oriented and providers of caring work.

The masculine gendering of computing/programming makes it more difficult for women to take part and feel at home. As in other professional areas, women have to prove themselves as legitimate members of the profession, *and* as women. It may seem that women in computing/programming are restricted to two choices; maintaining their femininity by defining themselves as women and 'other' than men and thus defining themselves out of the area, or re-defining themselves as 'one of the boys', which they can never be anyway, since they obviously cannot define themselves into the male sex category.

However, the emerging picture in my interviews was more complex. Despite the gendering of programming, the women I talked to did not differ much from the men in the way they related to programming. They expressed excitement about solving tricky programming problems, and joy of creating or constructing programs, putting together pieces to make a whole. With a few exceptions, they did not talk about feeling as outsiders, but seemed to have made programming "their own". One of the women talked about being a nerd. She identified herself with and seemed to feel at home in a group of students who took pride in being nerdy, even competing in "nerdiness".

Informant: ... the nerd culture... because I think that there (author's note: in the nerd culture) one appreciates somehow intelligence rather than other things, and that's something I like. So I suppose I'm quite nerdy. I like all of that ... culture... that those who are smart are considered superior to those who have big silicon boobs. [...] I'm quite happy with being nerdy. (Female student)

As discussed above, metaphors act on a symbolic level. The associations we make, we make on an abstract, generalised level. As individual men and women in a particular context, we do not necessarily act in accordance or comply with the ideologies created by the metaphors. Rationality, mathematical and abstract analytical/logical problem solving may be associated with traditional male characteristics, but this does not mean that individual women do not possess these abilities and take pride and feel joy in applying them. Building and construction work may be male arenas, but this does not stop women from being excited about creating and constructing programs that work as intended.

Informant: Well... it's fun to sit and program, then the solution comes. "This was fun, I'm proud of myself... well, when I've finished the assignment. (Female student)

and

Interviewer: What was fun with programming – what was it in programming that made you move into the area when you were at XXX (author's note: a department at the university the informant attended)?

Informant: It was this thing with building things, and... well to build logical structures and see connections... and I was probably quite good at it. And then I really enjoyed debugging. To see what happened when you single stepped a program. How it works and all that. (Female IT professional)

RE-DEFINING COMPUTING AND PROGRAMMING?

Our understanding of IT, computing and programming is a social construction based on the discourse – how we think about and talk about the area, the metaphors and language we use. We shape what computing and programming are

through the way we talk about them, and we may re-shape them by changing the way we talk about them, by changing the discourse. Björkman (2005) suggests broadening the epistemological base of computer science and Cukier et al. (2002) argue that the area of IT should be re-defined to include the applications in addition to the technical bits. This would certainly help in opening up these areas to other influences and groups of people with other life stories than the rather limited experiences of middle class white men.

However, I do not feel altogether comfortable with this line of reasoning as a way of addressing the problem. There are aspects, I believe, that are obscured in this argument.

Firstly, computer science and IT cannot be re-defined outside the capacity or possibilities inherent in the technology. Clegg (2001) argues that in order to understand the relations between gender and computing, it is necessary to understand the technology not just as social relations, but also as a set of real material capacities. Technology cannot be reduced to either just science and the machine nor to social relations only – "Science and technology are mutable social practices but they operate on the stuff of a stratified real world" (p 310). Our understanding of computers and computer science is a social construction, but it emerges from and revolves around the material constraints and capacities embodied in the machine. The social construction of the area relate to and are part of a sense-making process of these capacities and constraints. Thus, in order to understand information technology, computer science, or computing, one cannot disregard the capacity of the technology itself. Modern computing is based on discrete mathematics, algebra and logic, forming part of the epistemological base of computing and programming. Working with programming requires at least basic knowledge and abilities in these areas.

Secondly, I believe that arguing for the re-definition of computing/programming on account of its being cast as a masculine domain may reinforce traditional constructions of gender. I believe it is important not to conflate the aspects of masculinity contained in the metaphors used to describe programming with aspects that are not desirable, i.e. abilities and characteristics that women do not or ought not possess. By doing that, we risk excluding women on the basis that they cannot be anything but averse to programming, reinforcing the traditional stereotype of women as emotional, people-oriented and always available to provide care, social support and sympathy.

I suggest we need to look at the problem from another viewpoint. The above reasoning is based on the notion that there is only one way of being a woman – namely that of not being a man, i.e. remaining within the constraints of the dualistic definitions of masculine/feminine gender. This may explain why so many women do not feel at home in computing/programming, but it does not explain why most of the women I interviewed embraced programming with such joy and warmth. As described above, they gave expression to a genuine interest and were truly enthusiastic about programming, which aligns with my own experience of programming as completely engrossing.

I think that the research on women and programming needs to problematise the notion that women are outsiders and even victims in a male-dominated world of computing. The process of describing them as such, reinforces the definition of them as 'other' than men, and reinforces the normative masculine gendering of the area. We need to start asking questions about why some women enter and stay in computing and programming, enjoying it, perhaps not being completely comfortable but nevertheless feeling sufficiently at home to stay there. We need to acknowledge that women want to take part of computing and programming, not because they necessarily feel that they can contribute with typically 'female' experiences and skills such as communicative skills, but because they simply enjoy it (Corneliussen, 2003).

I do not argue with the importance of analysing and criticizing the dualistic definitions of women versus men and problematising the ways in which traditional female attributes, characteristics and skills are devalued. However, there is a paradox here. By describing women as different from men, we may reinforce the conception of women as the 'other', implicitly expecting women to embrace and act out traditional values of femininity.

Some Personal Reflections

I started on a personal note and I will also end with some personal reflections. Broadening the epistemological base and the definition of IT would not allow me to redefine myself as a woman in relation to computing. I would perhaps be more welcome within IT and computer science were they to encompass broader perspectives, viewpoints and groups of people. But, it would not redefine me as technically able on par with the men. I would still be defined as a woman, i.e. 'other' as compared to men. I would still be expected to be different, and to bring different experiences, values and viewpoints. I would be expected to bring people-orientation, emotions and care-taking into the picture. But I, and perhaps many other women, do not particularly want to do that. I do not want to be the 'bearer' of femininity, being some kind of moral compass, bringing other, better values into the area of computer science and IT.

Knowing that gender is something we do continuously, I realise that I can never escape being the 'other', in IT or programming. So the hope of participating in that particular community out of sheer interest in computing and programming on some kind of gender-neutral basis is impossible, but I would still like to ask the same question as Corneliussen (2003) does:

[W]hy can't women's pleasure in working directly with the technology be used to recruit women? It is as if the stories about women's pleasure in this field don't stick, they are drowned in the hegemonic

discourse which claims that 'women don't care for computers'." (p 10).

We need to bring forth these stories of women enjoying programming for the sake of getting a kick out of it.

ACKNOWLEDGMENT

Thanks are due to the KK-Foundation (The Knowledge Foundation of Sweden), its research programme LearnIT, and GLIT, its network for research on Gender, Learning and IT, for financial support for the research on which this chapter is based.

REFERENCES

Berner, B., & Mellström, U. (1997). Looking for Mister Engineer. Understanding Masculinity and Technology at two Fin-de-Siecles. In Berner, B. (Ed.), *Gendered Practices. Feminist Studies of Technology and Society*. Stockholm: Almqvist & Wiksell.

Birkett, W. P., & Evans, E. (2005). Theorising professionalisation: a model for organising and understanding histories of the professionalising activities of occupational associations of accountants. *Accounting History, 10*(1), 99–127. .doi:10.1177/103237320501000105

Björkman, C. (2005). *Feminist Technoscience Strategies in Computer Science*. Doctoral Dissertation, Blekinge Institute of Technology, Sweden.

Camp, T. (1997). The incredible shrinking pipeline. *Communications of the ACM, 40*(10), 103–110. .doi:10.1145/262793.262813

Carstensen, G. (2004). *Sexuella trakasserier finns nog i en annan värld: Konstruktioner av ett (o)giltigt problem*. (Sexual harassment probably happens in another world: Constructions of an (in)valid problem in academia). Doctoral Dissertation, Uppsala University, Sweden. (In Swedish).

Clark, H. H. (1996). Using language. Cambridge, UK: Cambridge University Press. doi:10.1017/CBO9780511620539

Clegg, S. (2001). Theorising the Machine: gender, education and computing. *Gender and Education, 13*(3), 307–324. .doi:10.1080/09540250120063580

Corneliussen, H. (2003, November 14-16). *Negotiating gendered positions in the discourse of computing*. Presented at Information Technology, Transnational Democracy and Gender. Luleå.

Cukier, W. (2003, April 10-12). Constructing the IT Skills Shortage in Canada: The Implications of Institutional Discourse and Practices for the Participation of Women. In *Proceedings of the 2003 SIGMIS conference on Computer personnel research*. Philadelphia.

Cukier, W., Shortt, D., & Devine, I. (2002). Gender and Information Technology: Implications of Definitions. *SIGCSE Bulletin, 34*(4), 142–148. .doi:10.1145/820127.820188

Eriksson, K. (2003). *Manligt läkarskap, kvinnliga läkare och normala kvinnor: Köns- och läkarskapande symbolik, metaforik och praktik*. (Physicianship, Female Physicians and Normal Women: The Symbolical, Metaphorical and Practical Doing(s) of Gender and Physicians). Doctoral Dissertation, Uppsala Universitet, Sweden. (In Swedish).

Faulkner, W. (2000a). Dualisms, Hierarchies and Gender in Engineering. *Social Studies of Science, 30*(5), 759–792. .doi:10.1177/030631200030005005

Faulkner, W. (2000b). The Power and the Pleasure? A Research Agenda for "Making Gender Stick" to Engineers. *Science, Technology & Human Values, 25*(1), 87–119. .doi:10.1177/016224390002500104

Fisher, A., & Margolis, J. (2002). Unlocking the Clubhouse: The Carnegie Mellon Experience. *SIGCSE Bulletin, 34*(2), 79–83. .doi:10.1145/543812.543836

Fox, K. E. (1985). *Reflections on Gender and Science*. New Haven, CT: Yale University Press.

Gedenryd, H. (1998). *How Designers Work – making sense of authentic cognitive activities*. Doctoral Dissertation, Lund University, Sweden.

Hoplight Tapia, A. (2003, April 10-12). Hostile_work_environment.com. *Proceedings of the 2003 SIGMIS conference on Computer personnel research*. Philadelphia.

Mendick, H. (2005). A beautiful myth? The gendering of being/doing 'good at maths'. *Gender and Education, 17*(2), 203–219. .doi:10.1080/0954025042000301465

Nielsen, S. H., von Hellens, L. A., Beekhuyzen, J., & Trauth, E. M. (2003, April 10-12). Women Talking About IT Work: Duality or Dualism? *Proceedings of the 2003 SIGMIS conference on Computer personnel research*. Philadelphia(68-74).

Öhman, P. J. (2004). *The Obvious and the Essential: Interpreting Software Development & Organizational Change*. Doctoral Dissertation. Uppsala University, Sweden.

Peterson, H. (2005). *Gender, Power and Post-Bureaucracy: Work Ideals in IT Consulting*. Doctoral Dissertation, Uppsala University, Sweden.

Rittel, H. W. J., & Webber, M. M. (1973). Dilemmas in a General Theory of Planning. *Policy Sciences, 4*, 155–169. .doi:10.1007/BF01405730

Selby, L., Ryba, K., & Young, A. (1998). Women in computing: what does the data show? *SIGCSE Bulletin, 30*(4), 62a–67a. .doi:10.1145/306286.306318

Senger, P. (1998). *Anti-Boxology: Agent Design in Cultural Context. CMU-CS-98-151*. Pittsburgh, PA: Carnegie Mellon University.

Trauth, E. M., Quesenberry, J. L., & Morgan, A. J. (2004, April 22-24). *Understanding the Under Representation of Women in IT: Toward a Theory of Individual Differences*. Presented at SIGMIS'04, Tucson, AZ.

Turkle, S., & Papert, S. (1990). Epistemological Pluralism: Styles and Voices within the Computer Culture. *Signs, 16*(1), 128–157. .doi:10.1086/494648

Valian, V. (1998). *Why So Slow? The Advancement of Women*. Cambridge, MA: The MIT Press.

West, C., & Zimmerman, D. H. (1987). Doing Gender. *Gender & Society, 1*(2), 125–151. .doi: 10.1177/0891243287001002002

Widerberg, K. (1992). Om kjønnets logikk. (About the logic of gender). In Brantsaeter, M. C., & Widerberg, K. (Eds.), *Sex i arbeid(et)*. Norway: Tiden Norsk Førlag. (In Norwegian)

Wistedt, I. (2001). *Five Gender-Inclusive Projects Revisited. A Follow-up Study of the Swedish Government's Initiative to Recruit More Women to Higher Education in Mathematics, Science, and Technology. National Agency for Higher Education*. Stockholm: Högskoleverket.

KEY TERMS AND DEFINITIONS

Social Construction of Gender: This the idea that gender is created through social processes and that it is not related essential qualities.

Doing Gender: This term developed by West and Zimmerman (1987). They argue that gender is something that people, do, perform and accomplish in everyday interactions. Doing gender means carrying out activities that create differences between women and men. These created differences come to be viewed as "essential".

Beautiful Code: This is a term from Computer Sciences that is used to attempt to capture qualities of programming. Beautiful code is considered pure and logical.

Masculinity: Within feminist research masculinity refers to social characteristics, positions, behaviors and identities attributed to men. Masculinities are contextual and change historically and between societies and groups.

Metaphors: Metaphors can be viewed as a bridging process between different fields of meaning. The use of metaphors implies a process of interpretation and understanding of a phenomena rather than the mere transfer of meaning, unchanged, from one area or object to another (Eriksson, 2003).

ENDNOTES

[1] D++ is the name of the reformed CS program at Chalmers University of Technology. It is based on the name of the original program (D for Data), the first plus indicates that it will be better for women and the second plus indicates that it will be better for everyone! It is a play upon the name of the C++ programming language, and typical Chalmers University humour.

[2] Obviously, our understanding of computer science, or any phenomena, is not one single social construct, but an infinite network of different but inter-related, individually, socially and culturally situated understandings and interpretations. But for the sake of simplicity, I use the term social construction in singular.

[3] "Boxology" applies to approaches that describe a phenomenon in the world as consisting of tidy boxes with limited interaction, presumably summing up those characteristics of the phenomenon that are of interest. See for instance Senger (1998).

[4] Association for Computing Machinery "ACM delivers resources that advance computing as a science and a profession." From the ACM web site, www.acm.org.

[5] The concept of "patch" is actually used in programming, but has a slight negative connotation. A patch is a piece of code that is used to fix a bug or a security vulnerability.

Chapter 2
New Gender Relations in the Transforming IT-Industry of Malaysia

Ulf Mellström
Luleå University of Technology, Sweden

ABSTRACT

This chapter investigates how and why computer science in Malaysia is dominated by women. Drawing on recent critical interventions in gender and technology studies the paper aims at opening up for more culturally situated analyses of the gendering of technology or the technology of gendering with the Malaysian case exemplifying the core of the argument. The paper argues along four different strands of critical thought: (1) A critique of the 'black-boxing' of gender in gender and technology studies; (2) A critique of the Anglo-centric bias of gender and technology studies advocating more of context sensitivity and focus on the cultural embeddedness of gender and technology relations; (3) In line with that, also paying more attention to spatial practices and body politics in regard to race, class, and gender in gender and technology relations; (4) A critique of 'western' positional notions of gender configurations and opening up for more fluid constructions of gender identity including the many crossovers between relational and positional definitions of femininity and masculinity.

INTRODUCTION

This article addresses an old concern about the inclusion of women in science and engineering. Women's participation in science and engineering varies a good deal around the globe, but there still seems to exist, as Lagesen (2005, p. 19) states, a lingering notion of an all-encompassing masculine culture of science and engineering transcending time and space. By using empirical data from Malaysia in the context of computer science this paper generally aims at opening up for more culturally situated analyses of the gendering of technology that serve to undermine any notion of a global masculine culture of science and engineering that transcends cultural and national differences. Inspired by recent critical interventions and new analytical openings in gender and technology studies, (cf. Landström

DOI: 10.4018/978-1-61520-813-5.ch002

2007, Lagesen 2005, 2007a, 2007b, Rommes 2007, Bray 2007) this paper points to the Anglo-centric Western bias of gender and technology studies and argues for cross-cultural work and, intersectional understandings including race, class, age, and sexuality. With the Malaysian case exemplifying the core of the argument, I argue more specifically that as a consequence of a broader intersectional framework gender and technology studies need to investigate configurations of masculinity and femininity in a cross-cultural perspective more thoroughly. The focus in this article will stay on the relational dependence of male and female categorisations in gender relations, underlining that gender and technology relations are always deeply embedded in cultural contexts shaping the use, design and production of technologies and its co-production of gender and technology. In this it draws on earlier closely related work (Lagesen 2005, 2007b) but it also differs in focus in so far that my aim is to explicitly draw in aspects of Malaysian culture, society, and history in relation to my empirical data to illustrate the cultural embeddedness of gender and technology relations. However, the Malaysian situation within computer science is in this paper primarily used as an example to highlight how an intersectional analysis take form rather than a full-fledged critical analysis of the multifaceted and divergent power dimensions of the Malaysian society.

The article has three substantive parts. I will first present the so called "woman problem" (Lagesen 2005) in gender and technology studies and contemporary critical thought in feminist technology studies, invoking the theoretical tenets that possibly succeed this critique and how this feeds into the Malaysian situation. Secondly, I will present my case in terms of material, method, and the cultural specificities of computer science in Malaysia. Thirdly, a discussion of the empirical case follows in which I argue that the gender relations of computer in Malaysia must to be understood in relation to five strands of intersecting explanations (1) Quotas, ethnicity, and gender;

(2) A situated body politics; (3) Techno-optimism and techno-nationalism; (4) Under achieving men; and (5) A critical mass of women and a shortage of computer professionals.

The "Woman Problem" in Gender and Technology Studies

The so called "woman problem" within gender and technology studies, meaning the exclusion of women in science and engineering, has been thoroughly investigated. In spite of the fact that women are becoming the majority of the student population in most academic settings around the world, the relative absence of women from science and engineering is puzzling (Quinn 2003, Lagesen 2005). This is not in the least so as regards information technology (hereafter IT). Although far from being a universal pattern similar explanations describe the "woman problem". Women's non-use is seen as deviant and men regarded as the norm (Kramer and Lehman 1990). Learning environments are non-friendly to women (Siann 1997, Henwood 2000). Computer science technology grew out of the military complex and it's aura of combat and war has never attracted women (Mörtberg 1987, Edwards 1990) and so forth. In reviewing the literature Lagesen concludes that the "woman problem" in computer science mainly has been understood as an issue of exclusion and little is known about the women who actually decide to study computer science (Sørensen 2002, Lagesen 2005, 2007a). The history of gender and computer science as well as IT in general seems to follow a well-known theme in western history of technology. Throughout this history, men have centred themselves in central positions and technology has been associated with masculine values and at the core of masculinity in a number of ways whether it concerns machinery or digital technologies (cf. Cockburn 1983, 1985, Hacker 1989, 1990, Mellström 1995, 2002, 2003, 2004, Oldenziel 1999, Salminen-Karlsson 1999, Faulkner 2000, 2001, Lie 2003, Wajcman 1991, 2000, 2004).

In the western world, it seems that little has changed and there are for instance even fewer women in computer science today than compared to the late 1980s and the beginning of the 1990s (Salminen-Karlsson 1999). Still, when looking outside the western world, in different developing countries including Malaysia, there are a growing number of studies that diversify the picture (Wajcman and Le 2007, Ng and Mitter 2005, Saloma-Akpedonu 2005, Kelkar et al. 2005). Women's position in the IT industry and in new rapidly transforming digital economies in countries such as the Philippines, Brazil, Malaysia and Vietnam gives hope for an emancipatory concern for a more gender-balanced division of labour. In an investigation in the Philippines Saloma-Akpedonu (2005, p. 100, see also Wajcman and Le 2007, p. 6) reports that women constitute thirty percent of the Philippine Computer Society and that women's position in the IT industry has not resulted in a devaluation of status. In their study the gender relations of software work in Vietnam Wajcman and Le (2007, p. 23) concludes, "Compared to women's employment in previous eras, IT work is a significant improvement. Women in the IT sector have higher levels of education and earn more than women working in agriculture or the service sector. The IT industry does provide a vehicle for women to gain both higher education and economic power in Vietnam." Contributing to such a relative optimism concerning gender and technology relations and women's position in the IT industry in developing countries, is undoubtedly also the Malaysian situation where women in software work and education equals men, not least so at computer science departments. However, before moving to the case of this article I will touch upon some emergent epistemological dilemmas in gender and technology studies, articulated by a number of researchers that currently are re-reading the intellectual agenda of the field.

Analytical Openings in Gender and Technology Studies

Recently, critical interventions in the field of gender and technology studies, (cf. Landström 2007, Rommes 2007, see also Faulkner 2001) has for example drawn attention to how heteronormative assumptions form empirical research in feminist technology studies. Landström (2007) has in her critical re-reading of what she labels feminist constructivist technology studies, addressed the divide between theoretical discourses collapsing gender binaries and empirical research that relapse into old deterministic gender binaries. In a similar vein Els Rommes (2007) shows how the heterosexual imaginary is constantly at work reproducing gender dichotomies and hierarchies associated with computers and how through heteronormativity, technologically competent women become masculinised on various dimensions (Ibid, p. 13). Closely associated and overlapping with Landström's and Rommes queer interpretations is also the work of Vivian Lagesen (2005, 2007a, 2007b) and Francesca Bray (2007), addressing the 'black-boxing' of gender in gender and technology relations, where gender often is represented as stable while technology is open to interpretative flexibility. Although Lagesen and Bray does not problematise the "semiotics of heteronormativity" (Landström 2007, p. 14), they nevertheless points to the common analytical asymmetry in the process of co-production in gender and technology studies. (see also Landström 2007, Gill and Grint 1995). Another critique that has been addressed at various stages in social studies of science and technology and in the branch of feminist science and technology studies (MacKenzie and Wajcman 1999, Wajcman and Le 2007, Bray 2007), but now seems to reappear stronger than before, is the lack of studies of gender and technology relations in non-western societies. In short, this new wave of critical thought in feminist technology studies originating from sexuality studies, material-semiotic, and postcolonial approaches is seminal and point to the need of addressing a wider range of analytical themes that capture the inherent complexities and ambiguities of gender and technology relations such as the intersections of gender, race, bodies and sexuality.

However, for the purpose of this article, the critique centred on the lack of studies of non-western gender and technology relations is what feeds into my analysis. This is, as Francesca Bray (2007, p. 17) points to, a dimension that has been underestimated in the production of gender and technology relations, also implying the cultural embeddedness of such relations. She argues that "in focusing so closely on the gender-technology nexus itself FTS (Feminist Technology Studies, authors note) sometimes neglects deeper-lying ideological dimensions within which any regime of truth concerning gender and technology must ultimately be understood" (Ibid, p. 19). Thus, furthering gender varieties in gender and technology studies also opens up for cross-cultural interventions, comparisons, and intersectional understandings. The huge spectrum and variation of gender subjectivities in relation to artefacts and technology is still a field open to analyses that can bring new perspectives to the field. This also implicitly means addressing the lack, past and present, in gender and technology studies of non-western contexts and bringing in a wider range of cultural contexts to this field, varying gender relations embedded in a diverse range of settings investigating how technology is gendered or how gender subjectivity forms technology. Studies of gender and technology relations, and of technological change in general, consequently require attention to how gender as well as class and race often are instigating factors of changed social and cultural balance in nationalist projects such as the Malaysian one (see also Harding 2006).

In reviewing existing literature in gender and technology studies, I found one conclusion seemingly inevitable and that is the lack of studies that go beyond gender and technology as analytical parameters and include intersectional understandings

of the gendering of technology. In other words, if gender and technology are in theory mutually co-produced, (Faulkner 2000, 2001, Lagesen 2005), so are ethnicity and technology, age and technology, sexuality and technology, and class and technology (see also MacKenzie and Wajcman 1999, pp. 25-26). Still, generally within STS these latter dimensions of cross-cultural comparisons and intersectional understandings are, with a only few notable exceptions (cf. Traweek, 1988, Traweek and Reid 2000, Dyer 1997, Verran 1998, 1999, Adams 2002), and in particular this is the case regarding gender and technology studies. My purpose in this article is to invoke cross-cultural comparisons and intersectional readings in general, and when it comes to Malaysia in particular, to exemplifying this with the gender symbolisation, codification, and spatial practice of computer science in Malaysia. I believe cross-cultural comparative studies are of vital importance in taking studies of gender and technology further.

Consequently, my gender analysis is grounded in an intersectional understanding (cf. Peletz 1996, Collins 1998, Crenshaw 1991, Young 1997, Yuval-Davis 1997), where issues of inclusion and exclusion, power and powerlessness are to be understood by an integrative analysis of gender, race, age, class and nation. As the Malaysian feminists Cecilia Ng and Carol Yong (1995, p. 178) argue, "...while new technology skills are being polarized by gender, it also evident that women are entering computer professions in both the developed and developing countries, leading to a class polarization within the female labour force itself." It is therefore also important to look at the wider picture in which technology; labour relations and education are embedded. From their Malaysian horizon they also argue (Ibid.) "Since society is based on hierarchy, and technology is a medium of power, one needs to understand how power is negotiated." In a postcolonial and multiethnic society as Malaysia this also becomes most pertinent since class and ethnic differentials often are as important as gender differentials.

THE MALAYSIAN CASE

What make the Malaysian case of particular interest for gender and technology studies are the gender ratios observed in computer science and in the information technology related sector of Malaysian industry. For instance, for the 2001/2002 academic year at the School of Computer Science at Universiti Sains Malaysia (USM), the ratio of female students was 65 percent. At the Faculty of Computer Science and Information Technology at the University of Malaya 66 percent of students were women (Lagesen 2005). Already back in 1990/1991 female students comprised 51 percent of the total intake in computer related courses in tertiary institutions (Ng and Yong 1995). In 2003 over 50 percent of master students and PhDs at USM were female and seven out of ten professors at the department were women (the year 2003). There are likewise a high percentage of women in the professional ICT-sector. Although Malaysian labour force statistics are not broken down according to specific educational attainment, women comprise 44 percent of professionals and 38,9 percent of technicians and associate professionals. ICT and computer science professionals are normally categorised in of these statistical strata.[1]

This is noteworthy and very encouraging in terms of gender equality and something that can be regarded as a possible catalyst of change in a developing country where a substantial part of the population is currently reworking their social and ethnic identities (cf. Goh 2002, Gomes 1994, Kahn and Loh 1992). However, this grand narrative of a specific Malaysian modernity must also according to Kahn and Loh (1992), be understood in terms of a fragmented society where an emerging substantial middle class is a conspicuous feature in the current development. This new emerging middle class is in many ways portrayed as the symbol and hope of coming beyond a society that traditionally is marked by sharp ethnic divides between the three major ethnic groups, Malays,

Chinese, and Indians. Various political measures and programmes under the New Economic Policy (NEP) in 1971 and the New Development Policy (NDP) in 1991, have been aimed at strengthening the national economy and unite the country's ethnic groups in which the Malays make up 58% of the total population, Chinese 27%, and Indians 7%. Still, there is a number of current socio-economic divides between the ethnic groups of Malaysia. This national balancing act is played with the stakes of race and interracial harmony and is something that continues to pervade contemporary Malaysian society. In this balancing act, Chinese and Indian people has been marginalised, as non-Muslims, when the Malaysian state has been promoting a "national culture" based on indigenous Malay culture with a distinctly Islamic "governmentalism" as a central feature (Nonini 1998). "Malayness" is usually identified in terms of language, religion and royalty (*bahasa, agama, raja*) and exclude anything "Chinese" or "Indian". This balancing act is codified in the ethnic division and official politics between *bumiputeras* (meaning son's of the soil), which are the indigenous Malays and a number of other indigenous groups and *non-bumiputeras*, which are the Chinese and the Indians.

Simultaneously, the emerging middle class works as a powerful symbol and contravening force in the shaky ethnic and racial balance of contemporary Malaysian society which is to be united by relative prosperity, and technical development. The supraethnic nationalist rhetorics and politics of the country has almost an obsession with modernity by way of technological development. In this rhetoric, technology in general and information technology in particular holds notably positive connotations and is seen as the major source of individual and national empowerment. As a post-colonial society, Malaysia has nationalist politics which are most conspicuously manifested in *Vision 2020* (Mahatmir 1991). The politics of *Vision 2020* include the goal of Malaysia becoming a fully developed country, a

K-society (knowledge society)is and Malaysians being directed towards a 'common destiny' by means of technology and modernity. In such efforts of building and creating a subjective sense of commitment a 'common destiny' is crucial for the construction of nationhood rather than emphasizing a common past (Yuval-Davis 1997). To build the country through technological visions of modernity and development is thus an effective way for the Malaysian State to generate a national collective and a sense of belonging. Recurrent public campaigns such as the *Malaysia boleh* (Malaysia can, is able) crusade in the late 1990's and the beginning of 2000's persistently declare that a Pan-Malaysian identity (*Bangsa Melayu*, see Ariffin 1993) is built through technology and development. This Pan-Malaysian identity is very much defined as a national body and is seen as something primarily economic and technological and as such set in the future (Williamson 2002, p. 419) This fusion of a new middle-class are sometimes described as the 'haves' in contrast to the 'haves-not' in the current development where economic growth is aimed at reshaping the society into an imagined nation beyond ethnic tension by way of technical and financial nationalism (Ibid.). Access to a knowledge society and information technology seems to be the dividing line in this process between the 'haves' and 'haves-not' (Ng and Yong 1995).

In regard to gender studies and in the vein of Malaysian feminism and more broadly in the research field of Gender, Technology and Development Studies, the relationship between gender (here almost exclusively defined as women) and technology in Malaysia has been investigated from different perspectives (cf. Ong 1987, (ed.) Ng and Munro-Kua 1994, Ng and Yong 1995, Levidow 1996, Ng and Mohamad 1997, Ng and Thambiah 1997, Ng 1999, Ng and Mitter 2005, Lagesen 2005). As indicated earlier, rapid industrialisation, appropriating information technologies, globalisation are, in the Malaysian context, among other things, leading to class cleavages within the

female labour force (Ng and Yong 1995:178). For instance, within the electronic components industry (semiconductors, disk drives, etc.) low-skilled technology employment is predominantly female and will probably remain so. But at the same time, leading female professionals within ICT-related businesses are occupying executive positions to an impressively high degree (Ibid.). The number of women who partake in this imagined as well real formation of a new middle class leading the Malaysian nation into the future and aligning themselves with modernity, is also impressively high. Paradoxically, part of the explanation why women have come to dominate computer science in Malaysia is due to the intensive ethnification of the Malaysian society and its consequences for higher education, which will be explored in the following sections of the paper.

Consequently, an important conclusion that can be drawn from the work of feminists and others in a Malaysian context is that theories of gender identity need to consider that ethnic and class gaps are often as important as gender differentials. This means that we cannot focus on gender per se, but must also investigate the complex interrelationship of gender, class, age and ethnicity in a multi-ethnic society such as Malaysia. With a point of departure in an intersectional understanding of the highly complex multiethnic and stratified society of Malaysia, I intend to explore how cultural dynamics influence and shape the construction of computer science as a woman friendly technological field.

Material and Method

Material for this article was collected through policy documents, newspaper articles, labour employment statistics, popular writings, but also drawing on a long-term period of gender research in the country since 1997 (Mellström 2002, 2003, 2004). Moreover, in 2005, and with the help of lecturers and professors at the Computer Science Department at Universiti Sains Malaysia in Penang, I conducted a questionnaire with one hundred-fifty students in a computer science class, ten interviews with students in the same class as well as complementing that data with periods of participant observation in lecture halls and at campus. I also had numerous informal conversations with lecturers, post-docs, and professors at the department. Out of the 150 students 111 were females (73%) and 39 males (27%). 68 were Malay females (45%), 38 Chinese females (25%), 5 Indian females (3%), 20 Malay males (13%), 17 Chinese males (11%), and 2 Indian males (less than 1%). The students in class were taking a course in computer ethics, which might have caused that a higher number of women were taking the course but according to lecturers at the department the gender ratios were similar in most courses given at the department. In other words, it was an overwhelming majority of women.

The questionnaire focused on gender, ethnicity, family structure, educational choice, and career plans. The ten interviews followed up on the themes laid out in the questionnaire and in the interviews I could deepen my knowledge by discussing the themes in a more reciprocal manner. I also sat in, in computer science classes and talked to students in between lectures, at lunches, and at various social gatherings. I used English as the main medium of interviewing but occasionally also Hokkien, which is the dominating Chinese dialect of the island of Penang on the northwest coast of Malaysia.[2] The multifaceted data collected combined with previous experience of working in Malaysia is thus the empirical grounding upon which the themes that will follow in regard to gender and computer science draw. This web of overlapping themes is proposed here as an explanation of why computer science is dominated by women in Malaysia. In the tone of intersectional analyses, this paper draws on a certain methodological eclecticism working with both historical and discursive understandings of Malaysian society as well as individual and ethnographic evidence. Combining such diverse

levels of interpretation and data are here used as steps towards forming an intersectional analysis of a truly complex web of historical circumstances, contemporary politics and mundane realities.

Quotas, Ethnicity and Gender

As noted earlier the Malaysian nation is continuously balancing issues of interracial harmony and disruption as one of the fundamental socio-cultural dimensions of this society. It is literally inscribed into the history, the present and the future of this relatively newly founded nation, not least in the division between *bumiputera's* and *non-bumiputera's*. The colonial division once implemented by the British sharply separated Chinese, Indians, and Malays, and this policy was reinforced in the first period of self-government after independence 1957. This reinforcement of ethnic politics eventually resulted in the racial riots and bloodshed of May 13, 1969, when nearly two hundred people were killed. The memory of this traumatic event is still to be overcome and has a strong symbolic significance in today's politics and constantly balances against the Pan-Malaysian creation of *Bangsa Melayu*. Yet, after over thirty years of economic progress and reform (NEP, NDP), aimed at eliminating the identification of race with economic function, the inter-ethnic economic imbalance still prevail but are slowly being balanced according to some analysts. The still existing ethnic boundaries, are however, most manifest through the *bumiputera* policy where Chinese and Indians are disfavoured on the grounds of race "negative", while the *bumipetera's* (sons of the soil) rights to special privileges are inscribed in the Malaysian constitution. The special position and privileges of Malays and the Malay-related groups are inscribed in Articles 152 and 153 of the Constitution. The privileges range from quota protections in the field of education, scholarship, employment, training, trade, business permits and so on. When it comes State legislated favours, *bumiputera's* have clear advantages in relation to the other two major ethnic groups, Chinese and Indians. This is by the *non-bumiputeras* sometimes referred to as *kulitification* (*kulit* is Malay for skin, race) in contrast to qualification. These privileges were implemented under various programmes under the New Economic Policy (NEP) in 1971 and the New Development Policy (NDP) in 1991. The special privileges of the Malays stated in the Malaysian Constitution under article 153, is a most sensitive issue. To exemplify, in December 2000, a number of Chinese organisations asked for equal rights to all Malaysians, the so called Suqiu claims, which upset a lot of *bumiputera's* and especially the ruling UMNO (United Malay National Organisation) youth party. They as well as other UMNO leaders claimed that the Chinese were trying to create racial unrest in the country by demanding the abolishment of special privileges of Malays and natives of East Malaysia (Sabah and Sarawak). UMNO vice-president Tan Sri Muhyiddin Yassin said that if the Government accepted the Suqiu demands "national integrity will suffer and Malaysia will not be able to maintain unity, economic growth and racial harmony enjoyed since independence." (The Star, 001216) The special privileges of Malays concerns a number of different societal areas but when it comes to higher education it means that the *bumiputera's* will be granted special scholarships, free tuition and special opportunities to study overseas, among other things. Until 2005, when students were entering any of the state universities they were divided according to if they belong to the *bumiputera's* or *non-bumiputera's*. This quota-system guaranteed that at least 50% of the students were *bumiputeras*. It differed between different subjects pending on popularity. Since a much higher number of Chinese and Indian students generally apply for universities, in practice it meant that the *non-bumiputeras* have had much higher qualifications to get accepted into the state universities. According to the principles of race, each race thus had to compete within their quota of the system. Since 2005 the system has been

slightly changed with a preparatory college year (matriculation) organised according to race-based principles. It is currently heated domestic debates around whether the *bumiputera* matriculation schools where only Malay students attend, do live up to the same standards as *non-bumiputera* colleges. Critics argue that this is not the case.

However, the race-based quota system for university admission is of special interest here. The special *bumiputera* privileges have opened up an arena for Malay girls to study a classic masculine subject as computer science, at least from a western point of view. They are favoured on the grounds of race "positive" and possibly granted more student places than they would have been without the quota-system. As Lagesen also notes (2005, p. 50), the proportion of Malay women in computer science courses and at the faculty level of University of Malaya (UM) was strongly influenced by the quota-system. It is harder for *non-bumiputera* men and women to be admitted into the state universities in Malaysia. As other researchers also have shown (Lagesen 2005, Luke 2002, Ng 1999, Ng and Thambiah 1997), Chinese and Indian women and men feel disfavoured by the race-based politics. This was also articulated, off-record, by the Chinese and Indian students although never openly spoken about in class or neither mentioned by senior academic staff. Viji, an Indian male student pronounced that he was considering doing his Master's in computer science in Chennai, India, because as he said: *We non-bumis are not getting a fair chance in this system.* In informal conversations with other non-*bumi* students similar concerns were recurrently raised. On an aggregate level there is also apparent indications that the system disfavour non-*bumis* since, of the approximately 60 000 Malaysian students that study overseas each year (Lee 1999), a vast majority are non-*bumiputera's*.[3]

In this perspective race becomes a more pertinent and pervading social categorisation than gender and possibly and somewhat paradoxically operates more effectively to include women than many other inclusion strategies seen so far. However, in this case there are Malay women being positively affected by these inclusion measures while Indian and Chinese women are not.

Situated Body Politics

The articulation of gender, race, and class in Malaysia has long been informed by state policies, nationalist discourses and not least religious cosmology bearing on metaphoric understandings as well as concrete spatial practices of the different ethnic groups, and the differences within the ethnic assemblages (Peletz 1996, Nonini 1998). Nonini (1997, 1998, 1999) points to how Malaysian public spaces are distinctively divided by race, class and gender. The work of Henri Lefebvre (1991) shows how public spaces can be understood in regard to three forms of spatiality: spatial practices; representational space; representations of space. In trying to understand how women dominate computer science I concur that understanding the politics of space and bodies are crucial. Spatial practices are according to Nonini (1998, p. 441) the embodied habitus and routines people engage in as they move through and appropiate space as users, while representational space is space affectively marked in perceptions and memories, and representations of space are visual signs such as maps. The concepts of spatial practice and representations of space are of foremost interest in the following analysis. In the multiple modes of spatiality developed and practised, race, class, and gender mark out complex webs of spatial practices and representations of space. Race, gender, and class are deep reaching and fundamental social categories and in Malaysian society they continuously operate in public as well as in domestic spaces. The dynamics of a situated body politics then has to be understood in various intersections of these social categories. As race to a large extent can be understood as a hierarchy of bodies, something that also has become inextricably mixed with the hierarchy

of masculinities (Connell 2000), and femininities, bodies are configured and governed to such local gender discourses. The female domination of computer science in Malaysia is a case that illustrates this point.

The spatial association and practice of computers in relation to masculine and feminine bodies were a recurrent theme in the interviews and the survey (see also Lagesen 2005, 2007b). A comment made by one student, Zaharah: *IT for me is sitting in an office and do some business.* Many men think that the IT-section is not real like engineering and media" illustrates a viewpoint expressed by almost all the interviewees, namely that computer technology is spatially associated with in-door spaces and that in-door spaces are suitable spaces for women. This means that the gendered associations of computer science that are so prevalent in western studies of computer science is more or less absent. Lagesen (2007b) also points to the close spatial association between women and in-door technologies such as computers. In other words, the spatial segregation of what counts as female and male spaces seems to precede the gender codification of the technology. None of the computer science students whom I interviewed, indicated an association of computer technology with any specific masculine characteristics. Rather, they were genuinely surprised that this was the case in Western Europe. As Lagesen (Ibid., pp. 14-15) also notes, it is instead networking that is characterised as a masculine field because it is more physical and involves outdoor exposure not suitable to women according to her interviewees. Again, a spatial gender segregation of which bodies belong to which representational space, seems to precede the use and production of the technology and enactment of gender and technology through different spatial practices.

However, a division only by gender would be a misrepresentation of the complexity of the hierarchy of bodies if one examines which women are supposed to be situated in the woman-friendly indoor spaces symbolically connected to computing.

Thus, computer science was generally perceived as a suitable occupation for women irrespective of other social categories while civil engineering were defined as a masculine field because of its outdoor working environment and exposure to critical situations such as confronting foreign labourers at construction sites and the like (see also Lagesen 2007b).[45] Still it seems that even here there is a certain degree of interpretative flexibility in regard to what counts as 'genuine' women in relation to gender, race, and spatial practices. For instance, at a dam-project on the northern part of the island, an interviewed Malay male engineer told me that women engineers are not fit for civil engineering (Mellström 2003, p. 49). That is, they are not fit for outdoor engineering in the hot sun. At that very moment I could not help wondering about the mainland China chief engineer of the large project, who was a woman and had evidently spent uncountable hours in the hot sun managing the project. Just as if the Malay engineer had read my mind, he was saying: *Well, I mean the female engineers in Malaysia. Engineers from China, they are different.* This is one of many examples in my material that show how gender intersect with race as a social category that operates through different spatial practices, and help men to create spaces of their own or keep women circumscribed by a situated body politics with a plethora of rules regulating what certain women can't do and possibly some what they can do.

Still, in the bigger picture it is no doubt so that computer science as an occupational activity and the IT-sector as an industrial realm in Malaysia have opened up new emancipatory possibilities, spatial practices, and representational spaces for women, although it may not be the Cyberfeminist Utopia (compare Lagesen 2007b) that possibly could have been hoped for. So, even though the liberating effect of computing being associated with femininity is regulated within a nationalist, and local gender discourse, there is still hope for a relative optimism in the observations that computer science and IT-work are a major im-

provement of women's situation in the Malaysian labour market, navigating in between influences of 'western modernity' and an emerging Islamic modernity.

Techno-Optimism and Emancipation

According to a number of Malaysianists, gender politics in Malaysia has almost always been superseded by race (cf. Ariffin 1999, Mohamad 2002) often making it a non-problematized issue in relation to the totalizing ethnic politics pervading Malaysian society. The women's movement in Malaysia has been organised either within women's groups entrenched in ethnic party politics often supporting ruling ethnic elites or by feminist organisations organised in NGO's and at universities. Maznah Mohamad (2002, p. 217) sees this in terms of a women's movement at the centre versus a women's movement at the periphery but also concludes that even if there is "an ongoing contest between these two streams there were also been moments when they colluded for common gains". Although there has never been a multicultural feminist movement in Malaysia certain causes have united women from different ethnic groups. This was evident in the labour movement and the anti-colonial struggle of early independence days in the 1960's, and later in struggles against domestic violence and opening up the labour market for women.

The latter is here of special interest in regard to how Malay women entered IT-work and the related electronics industry. Before the influx of large-scale export-led industrialisation in the 1970's and 1980's, few Malay women were part of the non-agricultural labour-force, and Chinese women formed the majority of women industrial workers (ibid, p. 223). When Malaysia opened their economy to the global market in the 1970's, export-oriented industries were favoured such as textiles, garments, and electronics, hundred thousands of Malay women were pouring into new job opportunities not least for their perceived dexterity and docility (cf. Ong 1987, Lie & Lund 1994, Levidow 1996).[6] The mass recruitment of a female rural Malay labour force was both changing the ethnic composition of women industrial workers in the electronics industry sector, and it also opened up a new labour market for Malay women making the electronics industry symbolically associated with femininity as well as opening up a representational space for women. This space is implicitly and explicitly referred to in the interviews with the students who have had mothers or female relatives working in the electronics industry. As Penang (where USM is located) was a Free Trade Zone (FTZ) already back in 1970's, much of the early electronics industry in Malaysia were established here, and as many as 34 students (50%) of the Malay female students have had a female relative working in the electronics industry in Penang.[7] The answers given in the survey and the interviews, indicate that there are even more of the respondents that associate electronics in general and IT-work in particular as being a suitable labour market for women. Farah, a twenty-two year old Malay female student from the neighbouring state of Kedah says: *Two of my aunts were working for AMD, two of my cousins for Sony. They all do assembly work. Many women in my kampung (village) are going to Penang for work in the factories.*

What this suggests is that the conscious efforts to recruit low-paid women into this industrial sector early on also have had bearing on the symbolic effects and gender codification of IT-work. As such this sector came to represent a new industrial segment without the old gendered and racialised associations of the manufacturing industry connected to pre-independence days. In combination with a general undersupply of 'womanpower' in the electronics industry and a general shortage of computer professionals in the IT-sector, there has thus been what one might term a reversed symbolic gender appropriation of the how computing, electronics, and IT-work are perceived, in comparison to 'western' conceptions of this industrial segment.

However, as been pointed out earlier, the electronics industry and IT-work has also fragmented the female labour force dramatically. On the one hand there is the low-skilled technology employment with the image of the "nimble-fingered" docile female worker and on the other there is the female professional IT-worker. It is thus a highly charged and ambivalent space but nevertheless a space symbolically occupied by a high degree of women in a critically important industrial sector in the developing Malaysian nation. As such it have had impact on wider gender relations in the Malaysian society as well as challenging notions of an all-encompassing global culture of masculine values and symbolism connected to computing.

Under Achieving Men

The fact that women dominate computer science and many other academic fields also goes hand in hand with a long-standing concern and worry that Malay women outperform Malay men in Malaysian academia as well as many parts of the society. This concern aimed directly to boys and men, and in particular Malay men. For example this concern has been publicly expressed by the former prime minister and Malaysia's dominant political figure for two decades Dr. Mahatmir Mohammad has argued that young Malay boys are not ambitious enough and that Malay girls are more serious. In an interview in the English language newspaper New Straits Times December 29, 2000, Mahatmir says:

In the universities today, over 60% of the students, especially among the Malays, are women and they are studying serious subjects – engineering, science, management, etc, whereas the boys are studying simple subjects which they think they can pass, such as Bahasa Malaysia, Islamic Studies, and Social Sciences (sic!). And when they come into the government, where are we going to place them? They don't have the capacity to deal with administration, while the women in the universities are studying serious subjects to become the lawyers, the doctors, the engineers, and the scientists. They have shown that they can deliver, for example, a woman who had been sent to space saying that she is highly qualified. So, do I send an unqualified man because he is a man? No, I think it is not the choice that I would choose."

What Mahatmir expresses is also mirrored in recurrent media debates and articulated at different levels of the Malaysian educational system, not least at the state universities. In this sense, gender debates are part of the Malaysian public discourse as well as local concerns. In regard to computer science, the female professor and head of the computer science department at USM stresses that she would like to see more young Malay male students enrolled at her department but as she says: *They don't seem motivated enough and we also have problems with young men dropping out of class.* She also mentions that the department has launched recruitment campaigns at local matriculation colleges and continues: *...but we mostly seem to reach the young girls.* The topic was recurrently up for discussion at the department voiced differently depending on person and possibly position. Upon my question, a young female lecturer at the department puts it more crudely when she says: *Boys are raised that way. Always used to roam around and not taking responsibility. I guess they think they will be head of families anyway so why bother?*

The arguments in this public debate revolve around the idea that Malay men need to change their mind-sets and wake up to a new world where their lives are to be lived in a K-society of modernity and technological development. Moreover, in the creation of a pan-Malaysian identity Malay men lag behind. They are viewed as being still stuck in their *kampung* mentalities and needing to mature and take on more responsibility. In the meeting with a new form of *Bangsa Melayu* character Malay men are often portrayed in effeminate terms, not seen as men enough to cope with a modernity ruled by a globalised market economy, glossy consumerism and financial nationalism.

The emerging new middle-class needs Malay men that conform to a State politics that both emphasise *agama, raja and bahasa* on the one hand, and on the other, modernity through technological and financial nationalism, i.e. Islamic modernity which is the Malaysian State doctrine. Thus, a combination of a heavily male-dominated bureaucratised Islam and a nationalism formulated in terms of a modernity ultimately based on a global business masculinity (see Connell 2000). However, such a combination and definition of masculinity is in itself considered as a 'foreign' or 'western' conception of manhood for many Malay men, although huge variations are evidently part of the picture. This is an image in which: "The 'State' is metaphorised in men and the village in women, and the former seems more visible than the latter, and hence more powerful and dominant." (Karim 1995, p. 26). As such it does not necessarily comply with a bilateral view of gender where social relationships in many ways diffuse distinctions of hierarchy and difference in relationships of rank, class and gender. The bilateralism of gender relations typical for South-East Asia and Malay cultures in particular, emphasising lack of formality and avoidance of open conflicts, tend to be overlooked by 'Eurocentric' analyses of power relations. As Errington (1990, p. 5) would have it: "We also tend to identify 'power' with activity, forcefulness, getting things done, instrumentality, and effectiveness brought about calculation of means to achieve goals." The prevalent view in many parts of island South-East Asia, however, is that "to exert force, to make explicit commands, or to engage in direct activity – in other words, to exert 'power' in a Western sense – reveals a lack of spiritual power and effective potency, and consequently diminishes prestige." (Karim 1995, p. 17). Apparently, this is a notion of power and manhood rooted in the sphere of production, the public arena, assumingly a heteronormative masculinity based on a successful participation in the market-place competition (Mellström 1995, p. 170). Kimmel (1994, p. 122ff.) discusses this as the market-place manhood, a kind of masculinity that sets standards for other men and women and against which other men and women are measured. This is a career-oriented form of masculinity where a new emerging middle class are supposed to be agents of change and embody larger spatial-temporal patterns of modernity and a globalised industry.

Traditional rural Malay men accustomed to the confines of custom (*adat*) and a culture of kinship-relationality is here pinpointed as a problem. They are village (*kampung*) people rejecting change and men associated with a *kampung* lifestyle metaphorised as women in this lingua of State and market forces. This 'foreign' and globalised notion of a competitive market-place manhood based on an industrialised masculinity thus resonates badly with classical Malay notions of (heteronormative) masculinity and men's identities and senses of self being formed and based in kin and village relations. These relational forms rather than positional (Peletz 1996, p. 322ff.), defined masculinity not by men's roles or positions on the labour market, or in the politics, nor in the economy, or in terms of citizenship, nationality, or religion, but in terms of relations. This means, forms of masculinities being enacted through a number of different locally grounded social categories in daily life such as brother, father, son, uncle, friends and husband. This is also to say that certain male relational roles such as father or husband may well dominate the category of maleness or male rather than position on a so called public arena, although such a 'westernised' concept may not apply here. It is a different form of heteronormativity at stake. Masculinity is thus being performed or enacted in the interrelation between these categories and in regard to equivalent female roles. This is not say that masculinity stands on any equal footing to femininity, but to suggest that this classical Malay (heteronormative) masculinity as a social category is composed by a number of relational roles in contrast to notions of masculinity based in the sphere of production. To conclude, such a

relational notion of masculinity not primarily connected to a gender enactment achieved in a public arena also leaves space for women's participation in the positional sphere of a newly industrialising nation such as Malaysia. This is seen in the way that many of the young women in the survey and the interviews resonates around their anticipated careers and future life space in regard to family and in more general terms also in relation to masculinity, class and race. The politics of space and as shown earlier a situated body politics is here of outmost importance to understand the fact that women can make headway into, in the western world, a traditional masculine outpost such as computer technology.

The Co-Production of Computing and Gender in the Malaysian Context

In this last part of the article I will look more closely into this co-production computing and women's work by following threads evident in the interviews and the survey, and which also links closely to previous research (cf. Ng & Yong 1995, Ng & Mohamad 1997, Ng and Thambiah 1997, Margolis & Fischer 2002, Lagesen 2005, 2007a, 2007b). In the upper echelon of women's IT-work, and where we most probably will find many of the interviewed students of the computer classes at USM in the future, it is evidently so that numbers and role models matter. As many as 51% of the female students answered that they thought that IT- work in various positions such as systems analysts, programmer, lecturer at the university and web designer were possible future work tasks because they had seen other women doing this kind of work. The students mentioned female lecturer's at USM as inspirational sources (see also Lagesen 2005, 2007b) as well as alumnis, that, on a regular basis, lectured at the department. Azlina, in her third year: *This former USM student came the other week, and she was really successful, and everything she said was so inspiring.* There are in other words reasons to believe that a gender-balanced composition of computer science in combination with a number of women acting as role models in their sheer capacity of lecturing, and working in IT-businesses outside academia, are of great importance in regard to the representational space of computer science as a subject. As Lagesen (2007b, p. 87) also notes, this combination opens up for a more flexible gender coding of computing and computer science in particular. Whether or not this also brought about a significant change in the social environment was outside the scope of questions of this study but there are all reasons to believe that this is the case or rather so that it has never been a problem since men never dominated computer science in Malaysia. A question concerning the topic as such is often met with surprise and counter-replies such as the second-year student Maimunah's response: *Why do you ask that? Is that a problem?* What followed from such responses was that I had to explain that it is a problem in western countries and that was the reason why I was interested in the Malaysian case. The theory of a critical mass of women in order to secure a gender-balanced recruitment and that is frequently discussed in the context of inclusion of women in science and engineering in general and computer science in particular, (cf. Margolis & Fischer 2002, Lagesen 2007b) has never been posed as a problem in the Malaysian context, neither at an academic arena nor as it seems as a discourse of everyday life in computer science departments. Through its character of a non-issue in this context, the frequent occupation with the question from western researchers like myself comes out as a bit odd in the local context and something that is being imposed upon the research subjects. It is rather race and class interspersed with certain mainstreamed gendered questions that are on the agenda in terms of exclusion vis-à-vis inclusion in the realm of higher education and professional middle-class careers. Gender is not necessarily articulated as an issue in the professional sphere as long as it is confined to the proper symbolic as well as material spaces as been discussed previously. In

other words, in certain positional spaces gender is much more of a non-issue in relation to race and class. However, the combination of relational and positional roles rather comes in focus, i.e. that is how the 'public and private' interrelate or how the women in computer science and IT-work manage the juxtaposition between them. A great deal of the female students answers in the survey and interviews revolve around how to manage a life with family and career.

Atikah, a Malay female student: *It is very important that I can take care of my family first but also to make a career.* Most of the female students, irrespective of race, anticipated a full responsibility for their future families, meaning that they had the major responsibility of raising children and household work.[8] Male students did not at all anticipate this dilemma to same extent although five men mentioned it. One conclusion that can be drawn from the respondent's answers is that the domestic division of labour was by no means something that was questioned. Rather, it was the female students who anticipated ways to find viable solutions for managing a professional career in combination with family responsibilities. Zaharah would phrase it like this: *I will pursue a career until I reach 35, maybe 40, and then I will stay home with my children and husband.* Whether or not the interviewed female students will withdraw from the labour market in later family formation phases of life and stop pursuing a professional career is of course hard to anticipate but many of the students say that they have chosen to study computer science because it can possibly be combined with family responsibilities. Here it is apparently imagined to be easier within academia as Atikah also points out: "I would not mind to become a lecturer because it seems to be flexible with family and everything" (see also Lagesen 2005). Family obligations are seen to be compatible with an academic career according to many of the interviewees.

Employment statistics indicate[9] that there is a "leaky-pipe line" effect in the ICT-sector as a whole but segregated due to the class and ethnic cleavages. Many urban professional career women pursue a full-time career up till around the age of 55 (average female retirement age in Malaysia) in industry and academia without seemingly losing status and career opportunities, while many low-income factory women tend to move out earlier because of family obligations, pregnancies and childcare. Thus, a tentative conclusion would suggest that a fragmented female labour force in combination with a highly stratified multiracial society also is mirrored in the opportunity structure for women in science, engineering, and technology, where race, class and age are as crucial factors in determining career chances, as gender is. A general "leaky pipe-line" effect concerning women in science, engineering and technology is consequently hard to trace but can surely be observed in particular industrial sectors where many women move out form the labour market after the age of thirty-five to forty as well as never enter pending on race and class.

A great deal of ambivalence could also be seen in the replies, most likely mirroring the different pressures that confront many young women in contemporary Malaysia.. There are social demands such as performing within a complementary and relational gender paradigm working in parallel with a positional labour market where many young women are performing exceedingly well in an occupational space that for many years has encouraged them to do so and has been open to them pending on factors such as a race-based quota-politics, a shortage of computer professionals, a flexible gender codification of computing, and not least a gender order still very much based in relational characteristics and the 'politics' of family relations.

Included in the latter are also the state and the nation being metaphorised as an extended family (see Hylland-Eriksen 1998, Yuval Davis 1997). In a newly developing post-colonial nation as Malaysia, with a distinctive Malay nationalist state politics building on *agama, raja,* and *bahasa,* citizens are expected to share a familial sense of commitment

to these values. This is something that evidently varies a lot among the different ethnic groups, due to past and present politics of inclusion and exclusion in the imagined community (Anderson 1991) of the Malaysian nation, but the very idea also hosts gender relations of importance to how computer science and IT-work is loaded with techno-optimism in regard to a paternal gender order manifested through a metaphoric language of family and kinship relations. It seems that many answers of the students can be interpreted in this naturalized and 'primordial' image of the nation (Yuval-Davis 1997, p. 15), where the educational and occupational choice is connected to and dependent upon familial relations. Two quotes may illustrate this: *My parents want me to be someone that can give something in order to help my country* (Zanir, 2nd year student), *I must help to develop our country to be more technologically advanced* (Azikah). The will to help and build the nation is strikingly recurrent in the answers of Malay female students and this is something they can do by going into an field filled future promises for themselves, their families, and their nation. They are very explicit about the responsibility they feel for their families and their country. In contrast, this is not the case among the Chinese and Indian students, irrespective of gender but it also shows in the answers of the male Malay students but not to the same extent. The sense of communality is understandably much less pronounced among the *non-bumiputeras,* as the very term suggests. Approximately half of the *non-bumiputera* students say that they opt for a transnational job market with countries such as U.K, U.S.A, Australia, New Zealand, and Japan as the most popular ones mentioned. Considering the often vast transnational diasporic networks generally available among the Chinese and Indian populations in Malaysia (Mellström 2003), this does not seem to be an utopian claim but rather within the mobility realm of their ethnic assemblages.

In sum, a number of factors are salient in the co-production of gender and computing in the

Malaysian context. My conclusion is that this points to the variability and flexibility of gender and technology relations in time and space, and that a fruitful analysis and understanding of gender and technology relations requires and depends upon a thorough and informed local gender analysis to see where, why and how technology is being symbolised and codified, and which also feeds into the conclusive remarks.

CONCLUSION

In this article I have, by using an eclectic set of data in regard to women and computer science in Malaysia, stressed the importance of investigating gender and technology relations within their cultural embeddedness. With the aim of opening up gender and technology studies to cross-cultural comparisons and intersectional analyses I have taken an age-old question and concern with the inclusion of women into science and engineering to a case where women dominate, what is in western countries, a masculine field such as computer science. Inspired by recent critical interventions in the field of feminist technology studies, I argue that gender and technology studies need to pay more attention to culturally situated analyses where the analytic unit of gender and technology also needs to bring local gender discourses into the picture. What is charged with powered masculinity in one context such as computing is in many western countries, is non-charged in another due to local gender discourses situating the contested gender terrain in another space and location. It is then crucial to investigate the relational aspects of gender relations, including the position of women and men, in addition to other relevant social categories intersecting and shaping gender relations. In particular, I believe it is of crucial value to situate men, power, and technology if one is to understand where and why women are located where they are. I have also addressed the analytical asymmetry in the process of co-production in gender and technology studies by discussing a case where certain spatial practices dictating gender-appropriate spaces precedes the use of an artefact and technology such as computers, and thereby also showing that any idea of a common notion of an all-encompassing masculine culture of science and engineering transcending time and space is dubious. Following from this is also a critique of an Anglo-centric western bias of gender and technology studies that to narrowly focuses on these two parameters which to often lead to context insensitive analyses of the cultural situatedness of gender and technology relations.

ACKNOWLEDGMENT

Thanks to the *KK-Foundation* (*The Knowledge Foundation of Sweden*), its research programme *LearnIT*, and *GLIT*, its *network for research on Gender, Learning and IT*, for financial support for the research on which this chapter is based.

REFERENCES

Adams, V. (2002). Randomized Controlled Crime: Postcolonial Sciences in Alternative Medicine Research. *Social Studies of Science, 32*(5-6), 659–690. doi:10.1177/030631270203200503

Anderson, B. (1991). *Imagined communities: reflections on the origin and spread of nationalism*. London: Verso.

Ariffin, O. (1993). *Bangsa Melayu: Malay Concepts of Democracy and Community 1945-1950*. Oxford, UK: Oxford University Press.

Ariffin, R. (1999). Feminism in Malaysia: A Historical and Present Perspective of Women's Struggles in Malaysia. *Women's Studies International Forum, 22*(4), 417–423. doi:10.1016/S0277-5395(99)00039-4

Bray, F. (2007). Gender and Technology. *Annual Review of Anthropology, 36*, 1–21. doi:10.1146/annurev.anthro.36.081406.094328

Cockburn, C. (1983). *Male Dominance and Technological Change*. London: Pluto Press.

Cockburn, C. (1985). *Machinery of dominance: Women, men and technical know-how*. London: Pluto Press.

Collins, P. H. (1998). It's All in the Family: Intersections of Gender, Race and Nation. *Hypatia, 13*(3), 62–82. doi:10.2979/HYP.1998.13.3.62

Connell, R. W. (2000). *The Men and the Boys*. Berkeley, CA: University of California Press.

Crenshaw, K. W. (1991). Mapping the Margins: Intersectionality, identity politics, and violence against women of colour. *Stanford Law Review, 43*(6), 1241–1299. doi:10.2307/1229039

Dyer, R. (1997). *White: Essays on race and culture*. London: Routledge.

Edwards, P. N. (1990). The Army and the Microworld: Computers and the Politics of Gender Identity. SIGNS. *Journal of Women in Culture and Society, 16*(1), 102–107. doi:10.1086/494647

Errington, S. (1990). Recasting Sex, Gender, and Power: A Theoretical and Regional Overview. In Atkinson, J., & Errington, S. (Eds.), *Power and Difference: Gender in Island Southeast Asia* (pp. 1–158). Stanford, CA: Stanford University Press.

Faulkner, W. (2000). Dualisms, hierarchies and gender in engineering. *Social Studies of Science, 30*(5), 759–792. doi:10.1177/030631200030005005

Faulkner, W. (2001). The technology question in feminism: A view from feminist technology studies. *Women's Studies International Forum, 24*(1), 79–95. doi:10.1016/S0277-5395(00)00166-7

Gill, R., & Grint, K. (1995). *The Gender and Technology Relation: Contemporary Theory and Research*. London: Taylor and Francis.

Goh, B. L. (2002). *Modern Dreams: An Enquiry into Power, Cultural Production and the Cityscape in Contemporary Urban Penang, Malaysia*. New York: Cornell University Press.

Gomes, A. (1994). *Modernity and Identity: Asian Illustrations*. Bundoora, Victoria: La Trobe University Press.

Hacker, S. (1989). *Pleasure, Power and Technology*. Boston: Unwin Hyman.

Hacker, S. (1990). *Doing it the hard way: Investigations of gender and technology*. Boston: Unwin Hyman.

Harding, S. (2006). *Science and social inequality: feminist and postcolonial issues*. Urbana, IL: University of Illinois Press.

Henwood, F. (2000). Engineering Difference: Discourses on Gender, Sexuality and Work in a College of Technology. *Gender and Education, 10*(1), 35–49. doi:10.1080/09540259821087

Hylland-Eriksen, T. (1998). *Common denominators: ethnicity, nation-building and compromise in Mauritius*. Oxford, UK: Berg Publishers.

Kahn, J., & Loh, F. (1992). *Fragmented Vision. Culture and Politics in Contemporary Malaysia*. Sydney, Australia: Allen & Unwin.

Karim, W. J. (1995). *'Male' and 'Female' in Developing Southeast Asia*. Oxford, UK: Berg Publishers.

Kelkar, G., Shrestha, G., & Veena, N. (2005). Women's Agency and the IT industry in India. In Ng, C., & Mitter, S. (Eds.), *Gender and the Digital Economy: Perspective from the Developing World* (pp. 110–131). London: Routledge.

Kimmel, M. (1994). Masculinity as Homophobia: Fear, Shame, and Silence in the Construction of Gender Identity. In Masculinities, T. (Ed.), *H. Brod & M* (pp. 119–141). London: Sage.

Kramer, P. E., & Lehman, S. (1990). Mismeasuring women: A critique of research on computer ability and avoidance. SIGNS: Journal of women in culture and society, 16(1), 158-171.

Lagesen, V. A. (2005). *Extreme Make-Over? The Making of Gender and Computer Science. PhD-Dissertation, STS-Report 71.* Trondheim, Norway: NTNU.

Lagesen, V. A. (2007a). The Strength of Numbers: Strategies to Include Women into Computer Science. *Social Studies of Science, 37*(1), 67–92. doi:10.1177/0306312706063788

Lagesen, V. A. (2007b). A Cyberfeminist Utopia? Perceptions of Gender and Computer Science among Malaysian Women Computer Science Students and Faculty. *Science, Technology & Human Values, 33*, 5–27. doi:10.1177/0162243907306192

Landström, C. (2007). Queering feminist technology studies. *Feminist Theory, 8*(1), 7–26. doi:10.1177/1464700107074193

Lee, M. N. N. (1999). The Impact of the Economic Crisis on Higher Education in Malaysia. *Industry and Higher Education, 15*, 26–27.

Lefebvre, H. (1991). *The production of space.* Oxford, UK: Basil Blackwell.

Levidow, L. (1996). In Ghorayshi, P., & Bélanger, C. (Eds.), *Women, Work, and Gender Relations in Developing Countries* (pp. 43–56). Santa Barbara, CA: Greenwood.

Lie, M. (2003). *He, She and IT revisited. New Perspectives on gender in the Information Society.* Oslo, Norway: Gyldendal Akademisk.

Lie, M., & Lund, R. (1994). *Renegotiating Local Values: Working Women and Foreign Industry in Malaysia.* Richmond, UK: Curzon Press.

Luke, C. (2002). Globalisation and Women in Southeast Asian Higher Education Management. *Teachers College Record, 104*(3), 625–662. doi:10.1111/1467-9620.00174

MacKenzie, D., & Wacjman, J. (1999). Introductory essay: the social shaping of technology. In MacKenzie, D., & Wacjman, J. (Eds.), *The social shaping of technology.* Philadelphia: Open University Press.

Mahatmir, M. (1991). *Malaysia: The Way Forward.* Kuala Lumpur: Centre for Economic Research and Services, Malaysian Business Council.

Margolis, J., & Fischer, A. (2002). *Unlocking the Clubhouse: Women in Computing.* Cambridge, MA: MIT Press.

Mellström, U. (1995). *Engineering Lives, Technology, Time and Space in a Male-Centred World.* Linköping, Sweden: Linköping Studies in Art and Science.

Mellström, U. (2002). Patriarchal machines and masculine embodiment. *Science, Technology & Human Values, 27*(4), 460–478. doi:10.1177/016224302236177

Mellström, U. (2003). *Masculinity, Power and Technology: A Malaysian Ethnography.* Aldershot, UK: Ashgate.

Mellström, U. (2004, April). Machines and masculine subjectivity, technology as an integral part of men's life experiences. Men and Masculinities, Special Issue: Masculinities and Technology, (Eds) Faulkner, W. & Lohan, M., 6(4), 368-383.

Mohamad, M. (2002). At the Centre and the Periphery: The Contribution of Women's Movements to Democratization. In F. Loh Kok Wah and Khoo Boo Teik (Eds.), Democracy in Malaysia: Discourses and Practices, Richmond, UK: Curzon Press.

Mörtberg, C. (1987). *Varför har programmer-aryrket blivit manligt? (Why have programming become a male occupation?). Research report, 1987:42*. Luleå, Sweden: Luleå University of Technology.

Ng, C. (1999). *Positioning women in Malaysia. Houndsmill, Basingstoke*. Hampshire, UK: Macmillan Distribution Ltd.

Ng, C., & Mitter, S. (2005). Valuing Women's Voices: Call Centers Workers in Malaysia and India. In Ng, C., & Mitter, S. (Eds.), *Gender and the Digital Economy: Perspective from the Developing World*. London: Routledge.

Ng, C., & Mohamad, M. (1997). The Management of Technology and Women in Two Electronic Firms in Malaysia. *Gender, Technology and Development*, *1*(2), 177–203. doi:10.1177/097185249700100201

Ng, C., & Munro-Kua, A. (Eds.). (1994). *Keying into the Future. The Impact of Computerization on Office Workers*. Kuala Lumpur, Malaysia: Vinlin Press.

Ng, C., & Thambiah, S. (1997 March 5-6). Women and Work in the Information Era: Levelling the Playing Field? Paper presented at the Regional Conference on Women and Work: Challenges in Industrializing Nations, Putrajaya, Sepang.

Ng, C., & Yong, C. (1995). Information technology, gender and employment. A case study of the telecommunications industry in Malaysia. In Mitter, S., & Rowbotham, S. (Eds.), *Women Encounter Technology: Changing Patterns of Employment in the Third World*. London: Routledge.

Nonini, D. M. (1997). Shifting Identities, Positioned Imagineries: Transnational Traversal and Reversals by Malaysian Chinese. In Ong, A., & Nonini, D. M. (Eds.), *Ungrounded Empires: The Cultural Politics of Modern Chinese Transnationalism*. New York: Routledge.

Nonini, D. M. (1998). 'Chinese Society', Coffeshop Talk, Possessing Gods: The Politics of Public Space among Diasporic Chinese in Malaysia. positions: east asia cultures critique, 6(2), 339-369.

Nonini, D. M. (1999). The dialectics of 'disputatiousness' and 'rece-eating money': class confrontation and gendered imagineries among Chinese men in West Malaysia. *American Ethnologist*, *26*(1), 47–68. doi:10.1525/ae.1999.26.1.47

Oldenziel, R. (1999). *Making technology masculine: Men, women, and modern machines in America, 1870-1945*. Amsterdam: Amsterdam University Press.

Ong, A. (1987). *Spirits of Resistance and Capitalist Discipline. Factory women in Malaysia*. Albany, NY: State University of New York Press.

Peletz, M. G. (1996). *Reason and Passion: Representations of Gender in a Malay Society*. Berkeley, CA: University of California Press.

Quinn, J. (2003). *Powerful Subjects. Are women really taking over the university? Stoke on Trent*. UK: Trentham Books.

Rommes, E. (2007 August 23-25). Heteronormativity Revisited; Teenagers and their Occupational Choices for IT. Paper presented at the Symposium on Gender, Learning and IT, Helsingborg Sweden.

Salminen-Karlsson, M. (1999). Bringing women into computer engineering. Curriculum reform processes at two institutes of technology. Linköping, Sweden: Linköping Studies in education and psychology, no 60.

Saloma-Akpdeonu, C. (2005). *Female Spaces in the Philippines' ICT Industry'. Gender and the Digital Economy: Perspective from the Developing World*. New Delhi: Sage Publications.

Siann, G. (1997). We Can, We Just Don't Want To. In Lander, R., & Adam, A. (Eds.), *Women and Computing*. Devon, UK: Intellect.

Sørensen, K. H. (2002). Love, Duty and the S-curve: An Overview of Some Current Literature on Gender and ICT. In Sørensen, K. H., & Stewart, J. (Eds.), *Digital Divides and Inclusion Measures. A Review of Literature and Statistical Trends on Gender and ICTs. STS Report 59*. Trondheim, Norway: NTNU, Centre for Technology and Society.

Traweek, S. (1988). *Beamtimes and Lifetimes: The World of High Energy Physicists*. Cambridge, MA: Harvard University Press.

Traweek, S., & Reid, R. (2000). *Cultural Studies of Science, Technology, and Medicine*. New York: Routledge.

Verran, H. (1998). Re-imagining Land Ownership in Australia. *Postcolonial Studies*, *1*, 237–254. doi:10.1080/13688799890165

Verran, H. (1999). Staying True to Laughter in Nigerian Classrooms. In Law, J., & Hassard, J. (Eds.), *Actor Network Theory and After*. London: Routledge.

Wajcman, J. (1991). *Feminism confronts technology*. London: Polity Press.

Wajcman, J. (2000). Reflections on gender and technology studies: in what state is the art? *Social Studies of Science*, *30*(3), 447–464. doi:10.1177/030631200030003005

Wajcman, J. (2004). *Technofeminism*. London: Polity Press.

Wajcman, J., & Anh Pham Lobb, L. (2007). The Gender Relations of Software Work in Vietnam. *Gender, Technology and Development*, *11*(1), 1–25. doi:10.1177/097185240601100101

Willamson, T. (2002). Incorporating a Malaysian Nation. *Cultural Anthropology*, *17*(3), 401–430. doi:10.1525/can.2002.17.3.401

Young, I. M. (1997). *Intersecting voices: dilemmas of gender, political philosophy, and policy*. Princeton, NJ: Princeton University Press.

Yuval-Davis, N. (1997). *Gender and Nation*. London: Sage Publications.

KEY TERMS AND DEFINITIONS

Computer Science: Study of computers, their design (see computer architecture), and their uses for computation, data processing, and systems control, including design and development of computer hardware and software, and programming.

Intersectional Analysis: An analysis that bring together different social categories and power dimensions and weigh them against each other.

Gender: Refers to a social, cultural, and historical product varying across time and space, including and implying diversity in terms of culture, religion, age, sexuality, race, ethnicity and nationality.

Body Politics: How different forms of bodies are regulated and expected to be located in certain spaces such as in-door (women) and out-door (men) spaces.

Race: To denote a division of humankind possessing traits that are transmissible by descent and sufficient to characterize it as a distinct human type.

ENDNOTES

[1] (Source: Labour Force Survey Report, First Quarter 2007 MALAYSIA, Series No. 10 No.2/2007, August 2007. Department of Statistics)

[2] A dialect I master to a certain degree because of earlier anthropological fieldwork in Penang (cf. Mellström 2003).

3   http://aei.dest.gov.au/AEI/Publication-sAndResearch/MarketDataSnapshots/ MDS_No05_Mal_pdf.pdf

4   This is not least fed through the xenophobic characterisations of foreign guest workers in Malaysian media, "aliens" as they sometimes are referred to (The Malaysian Daily, The Star 14/1 2000)

5   From 1970 to 1980 female worker in the manufacturing sector increased from around 70.0000 to around 300.000 (Mohamad 2002, footnote 5)

6   Many of the students are locally recruited meaning that they come from the close by northern states of Malaysia such as Penang, Perlis, Kedah or Perak. A relative can here also mean a person in the extended family, and generally Malay families are large.

7   73 % of the female students.

8   In the Malaysian labour force participation rates by sex and age group we can see that in the age group 25-34 males comprise 97.2 percent and women 61.6 percent, age group 35-44 98.3-52.1 percent and in the age group 45-54, 94.7-44.5 percent. This is however fluctuating very much depending on industrial sector, occupation, and educational diplomas. In the upper and high-income branch of the ICT-sector, it seems to be a less pronounced difference according to interviewed lecturers and professors at USM. However, there is no available data to confirm this.

APPENDIX

Table 1.

Ciri-ciri	Jumlah	Lelaki	Perempuan	
Characteristics	Total	Male	Female	
Penduduk (juta) Population (million)	26.6	13.5	13.1	
Penduduk umur bekerja ('000) Working Age Group	16, 834.0	8,563.1	8,270.9	
Tenaga buruh ('000) Labour Force	10,628.9	6,843.5	3,785.4	
Penduduk bekerja ('000) Employed Persons	10,275.4	6,618.6	3,656.8	
Bilangan penganggur ('000) Number of Unemployed	353.6	224.9	128.7	
Luar tenaga buruh ('000) Outside labour force	6,205.1	1,719.6	4,485.5	
Kadar penyertaan tenaga buruh (%) Labour force participation rates	63.1	79.9	45.8	
Kadar pengangguran (%) Unemployment rates	3.3	3.3	3.4	
Pekerjaan Occupation	10,275.4	6,618.6	3,656.8	
Penggubal undang-undang pegawai kanan dan pengurus Legislators, senior officials and managers	829.6	635.7	193.8	
Professional Professionals	565.9	314.9	251.0	
Juruteknik dan profesional bersekutu Technicians and associate professionals	1,307.5	797.7	509.8	
Pekerja perkeranian Clerical Workers	968.3	289.7	678.6	
Pekerja perkhidmatan, pekerja kedai dan jurujual Service workers and shop and market sales workers	1,597.1	888.5	708.6	
Pekerja mahir pertanian dan perikanan Skilled agriculutural and fishery workers	1,335.9	993.4	342.5	
Pekerja pertukangan dan yang berkaitan Craft and related trade workers	1,154.8	1002.0	152.7	

Operator loji dan mesin serta pemasang Plant and machine operators and assemblers	1,408.0	1,004.4	403.6	
Pekerjaan asas Elementary Occupations	1,108.4	692.3	416.1	

Chapter 3
Women in Computer Science in Afghanistan

Eva Maria Hoffmann
Technische Universitaet, Germany

ABSTRACT

In Afghanistan, the development of information technology (IT) as an industry and an educational field is still quite young, but this provides the country with an opportunity – especially for women - to participate actively in the process of rebuilding, and to strengthen their role in Afghan society. This chapter gives an overview of the situation at Afghan universities and the women who are studying Computer Science there. Afghan female computer science students are young, open minded and very motivated. Nevertheless they are often limited by social boundaries within Afghan society. The situations and circumstances of these female students are largely unknown; hence a survey has been done to discover more about these women's world. Female students from Kabul and from Herat University have been interviewed and the data from these interviews is presented here as a foundation for designing measures aimed at integrating Afghan women into the world of IT in the near future.

INTRODUCTION

For 20 years, Afghanistan was isolated from the world. The reign of the Taliban had a strong impact on the nation's history. The many years of war and the reign of the Taliban have left an unstable nation, politically as well as economically and socially. By now, as civil reconstruction processes have begun, progress is clearly visible in all sectors. In every area there are projects conducted and supported by the international community.

Just a few years ago there was little use of modern technology in the country. Recently information technology (IT) has spread, but only a few modern and complex systems exist. Heterogeneous IT structures that have grown in industrialized countries over the past years can in parts be useful and adapted to the situation in Afghanistan. For example, the Open Source movement has the potential to gain a greater share of the market in Afghanistan than in

DOI: 10.4018/978-1-61520-813-5.ch003

western economies, since Afghan users and their technology still have the potential to be shaped due to a lack of prior experience or commitment to prior technical structures (Ghosh, 2004).

This, however, will require a sustainable strategy. To quote the Afghan Ministry of Communication: *"[...] Afghanistan will use Communications and ICTs to improve Government and social services expeditiously and foster the rebuilding process, increase employment, create a vibrant private sector, reduce poverty and support underprivileged groups."* (Ministry of Communication, 2003)

Currently, the IT sector and the use of computer technology are generally dominated by men. Many obstacles prevent women from using these technologies. For example, using computers and computer technology demands prerequisite literacy, and less than a third of the total population can read and write. Of that literate population only 12% are women. Therefore, less than 2 million women have the necessary entrance requirements for IT training or other forms of education. A second obstacle in Afghanistan is English language skills: most of the IT applications are only available in English. (CIA, 2009)

The living conditions of most Afghanis prevent free access to digital technologies. Infrastructural basics like stable power supply or reliable Internet access are not available nationwide, especially not in rural areas. Since only a small percentage of households own their own computer, most people go to Internet cafés and public computer centers. Here again, women face difficulties due to their restricted freedom of movement. They cannot access these centers as easily as men, as they are mostly not allowed to leave their homes on their own, and in addition, they are not always allowed to be in the same room with unrelated men or strangers.

Despite these obstacles, many Afghan women are curious and very interested in IT and its applications, and this is reflected in the high numbers of female students studying courses related to computer science and information technology.

Based on my work as a lecturer at Herat University, this paper presents a picture of the most recent developments in the area of Computer Science (CS) in higher education in Afghanistan. The current status of the subject at Afghan universities will be described and a group of female students has been researched to get a deeper understanding in their lives as students. On the basis of interviews and questionnaires the aspirations, problems and motivations of the female students have been captured. It is intended that the results of the research can be later used for the development of measures to empower Afghan women in the area of IT.

Current Developments at Afghan Universities

One of the most important elements of the reconstruction process in Afghanistan is education. Education statistics are a measure of the progress of the nation. The future of the nation will lie in the hands of the next generations of the academic offspring.

The vision of the Afghan Ministry of Education is described in the concept of national education: *"Our vision is to facilitate the development of vibrant human capital by providing equal access to quality education for all and enable our people to participate and contribute productively to the development, economic growth and stability of our country."* (Ministry of Education, 2006) Hence, a modern, effective and reliable educational system is to be established. The most important goal of the development of the whole education system is the assured supply of a free basic education, an increase in the quality of education, a steady-going development of education in both urban and rural areas of the country as well as increasing the education of teachers.

Afghan society appreciates this: many Afghans are eager to study, they know how important education is for them and their future. But only a small fraction of Afghan youth has the necessary skills

Figure 1. Enrollment by Grade 2007

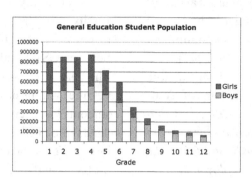

or has access to education to gain these skills. Currently, about 5.4 million pupils are enrolled in elementary and secondary school, about 35% of whom are girls. In elementary schools, girls form more than a third of all pupils enrolled. In secondary schools the overall the number of enrolled pupils generally decreases, but this is especially true for female pupils. Many pupils do not have the opportunity to finish their school career beyond primary school, and only about 5% of the age group is enrolled in the upper secondary school (grades 10 - 12) (cf. figure 1) (data obtained from Ministry of Education, 2007). Even so, not all school graduates will be provided with a place to study at a university, as the universities lack the capacities to satisfy demand throughout the country. In 2009, 79,175 school graduates applied for enrollment at university. Only 19,982 students however were admitted.

There are 19 universities and some institutions of higher education in Afghanistan. During the years of war, most of the institutions of higher education and the infrastructure have been destroyed. In 2002, there was no electrical power or water supply on the university campuses.

Additionally, there is a severe lack of teachers. This is a result of the emigration of the intellectual elite during the war, little attention to tertiary education in the past, low quality and lack of standardization in the education system and the administrative load carried by professors. Under-qualification, significant lack of motiva-

tion and low salaries are typical characteristics of the education system in Afghanistan. This results in poorly educated students and a deficient curriculum. Furthermore, there is a lack of technical literature in the Afghan native languages, few libraries and a little good organization.

Regarding the status of women in particular, the following deficits and shortcomings can be seen:

- At Afghan universities, the only decision-making body for all matters concerning women is the head of the administration.
- At all universities and faculties, all questions and subjects specifically concerning women are still discussed without their participation.
- At all universities, there are still no structures specifically oriented to act on behalf of, and for women's issues; thus women have no possibility to define their position.

This emphasizes the need for adopting mentoring as a concept and for structures which allow discussion of the questions specifically concerning women.

All in all, there are more than 42,000 students registered at universities in Afghanistan in 2009. Kabul University, the biggest university of the country, has 9,000 students. During the reign of the Taliban women were excluded from schools, many girls and women are currently trying to

Figure 2. Students at Afghan Universities

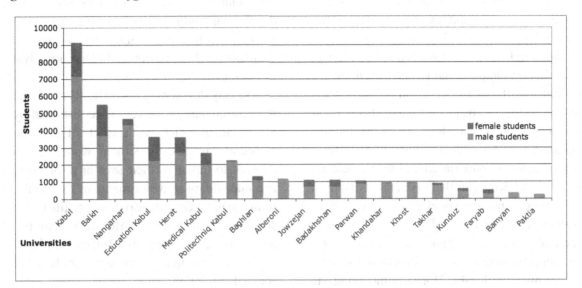

get their high school diploma. Despite these circumstances, the percentage of students enrolled at Afghan universities who are female is up to 45%, varying from region to region. Especially in smaller states and rural environments the numbers tend to be quite low, as society is still very conservative. The highest percentages of female students are at Kabul University, Herat University and Balkh University. Additionally, a great number is enrolled at Kabul Education University and Kabul Medical University.

Most female students enroll to study courses like literature, education, and law. Only a few choose to study medicine, computer science or economics. Nevertheless, when compared to the female-to-male ratios at universities in industrialized countries, the percentage of Afghan women is still high. To apply to an Afghan university, the applicant has to take an entrance exam (Concours Examination), which takes place in Kabul. He or she can apply for their desired course of study. Most of the applicants, female and male, apply for medicine, engineering, and law, but are not accepted due to the small admission numbers.

The enormous demand for IT experts from private companies and NGOs, makes study-

ing computer science (CS) attractive for many students. Until a few years ago, many students did not know anything about computer science, or related areas. From 2006 onwards however, this course of study has gained some prestige. Particularly among women, CS is the favourite subject among the technical areas.

WOMEN IN COMPUTER SCIENCE

Women in Computer Science in Developing Countries

Observing the percentage of female students in computer science enrolled in Dubai (50%), in Malaysia (60%) or in Africa (30%), women seem to be over-represented compared to the percentage of female students enrolled in IT study courses in industrialized countries. There is a multitude of reasons for this which relate to the specific circumstances in individual countries. (Nitsche, 2006) (Othman & Latih, 2006). In developing countries, access to universities and education is primarily dependent on social origin. Most female students have a background in the upper class of a society, are members of the educated elite and hence do not represent the female population overall. Upper class children have grown up having equal rights, men and women have access to education on almost equal terms. Still there are qualitative differences: Sons from wealthy families often study abroad to get the best education possible, whereas daughters stay in the country and are much less often sent abroad. Therefore, in developing countries in general, the percentage of female students enrolled in university is high. Plus, there is no fear about enrolling in a field of study dominated by male students. Often the standard as well as the rank of a course of study is lower at the national universities than overseas, which lowers the threshold for enrollment, and has an impact on the salaries of graduates afterwards (Schinzel, 2004). For Afghanistan the situation is different, as there exist few opportunities to study abroad.

The percentage of people in the population with access to a computer or the Internet is quite low in developing countries, especially in Africa and Central Asia and parts of South America, where around only 1% (ITU, 2007) of inhabitants own a PC. Only in urban regions and bigger cities, where the educated elite lives, is an IT infrastructure is present, and the rural population does not have access to IT in any way. Hence the percentage of the population with the privilege of being able to use IT is comparably small. (Hafkin & Taggert, 2001)

Hafkin & Taggert (2001) argue that women have significantly more domestic pressure and are burdened with many time-consuming family duties. So primarily it is the lack of time that impedes girls and women from using and getting familiar with IT. At first, women have to acquire new skills with the technology, which poses an additional workload, before they can begin to use the technology to reduce their workload.

Hafkin and Taggert (2001) also observe that all costs related to the purchase of a computer and other IT equipment including an Internet connec-

tion cannot be borne by most of the population in developing countries. Hence access to a computer is usually only possible at one's workplace, and even there an Internet connection is normally not available.

In many developing countries women's freedom of movement is even more restricted by a conservative society with strict religious and/ or social customs. Sometimes women are not allowed to travel on their own or to be present in a male dominated environment. Especially in rural areas where infrastructure is still lacking, considerable distances have to be overcome to get access to a computer and/or Internet, and this is not possible for many women due to these strict societal regulations.

Some social systems prohibit contact between men and women outside family bounds, which also impedes access to IT for women. In all Internet cafés, computer rooms, universities, IT training centers contact with men cannot be avoided. One possible solution is to define days or times where only women have access to these rooms and hence access to the Internet, computers or educational courses. Unfortunately this solution often cannot be realized, as men will complain about *"an inequitable treatment"*. Sometimes unfounded accusations may arise. Buder (2003) argues that men keep women away from these opportunities because they fear losing control over women in their society.

Getting access to computers within the family is often even more complicated for girls and women. As they are on the lowest level within the family hierarchy, their spouses, fathers and brothers block them.

There is of course that danger that when more women are working in one sector of employment is more likely that this sector becomes feminized and this can have disadvantages. For example: the more women work in IT, the less value this work might be seen to have. This could lead to salary decreases, deterioration of working conditions, and a disrespect for the area of expertise. One study about gender, IT and developing countries made by the Academy for Educational Development (a sub-organization of USAID) advises against the feminization of IT professions as follows: ' *As computer-based skills become more commonplace, and as the need for more workers to use them in a greater variety of ways grows, more women will be again recruited. But this will be at a lower wage because these will be no longer be considered specialist skills, merely something that women can do.* ' (Hafkin & Taggart, 2001, p.35)

Despite all these disadvantages, women should enter these fields of employment because they will get a salary for their work that will raise their status within the society. In most countries, regions and areas with a high literacy rate there is a positive impact for women

Women in Computer Science in Afghanistan

At present, there are three CS departments and two CS faculties at Afghan Universities. The first CS department was founded at the University of Kabul in 1995. At first there was no equipment at all, and only four professors carried out all the education. By 2009, the curriculum was modernized, and 4 PC pools (150 PCs in total) were built, and a specialized library was opened. The department was upgraded recently to a faculty of Computer Science and is now employing 15 lecturers, among them five women.

These universities offer bachelor level courses in computer sciences. In 2003, the Technische Universitaet (TU) Berlin supported the foundation of the IT Center at Kabul University (ITCK). At first, courses in computer applications like word processing were offered at the ITCK, for all members of the university: lecturers and students. Today computer administrators for the different faculties are trained, as the needs and demands of the university have changed. The ITCK has become the center of the IT infrastructure for the whole university. Together with the trained faculty administrators, the whole campus will soon be interconnected, and the education network will be further expanded.

In Herat a CS faculty was founded in 2007. Currently the TU Berlin is responsible for the further development of the faculty, and it both supports academic structures and conducts most of the lectures. This includes the education of qualified lecturers for the faculty. Currently six out of 14 lecturers are female and participate in a TU Berlin masters program for future CS lecturers. Based on the model of Kabul University, an IT Center will be established at Herat University (ITCH) as well.

The proportion of women on CS courses in both universities is relatively high: at the University of Herat 73 out of 285 students (26%) are female and at the University of Kabul there are 64 female students out of 210 (30%) in total. There are also courses in computer science at Kabul Polytechnic University, Kabul Education University and Nangahar University. In these institutions there is no exact data on female students, as no statistical data has been collected, and at the time of writing the courses have just started.

Establishing academic structures at the University of Herat is supported by the TU Berlin. A curriculum for computer science was developed at TU Berlin, designed to respond to local Afghan demands. The goal is to implement this curriculum at all Afghan universities. Besides the curriculum, lecturers from TU Berlin supported the computer science course on location in Herat with academic expertise. Some of the students faced difficulties in understanding the lecturers, due to a lack of English language skills. Additionally the new teaching methods were unfamiliar to many students. A tutorial model was drafted to support learning. This group of tutors and the staff for the computer science library, self-organized by students, and the network administrators, who are maintaining the PC labs at the faculty, were all selected with equal representation of female and male staff. The achievements and effort of female students are acknowledged and in addition these female tutors, administrators and librarians serve as role models for all fellow students. Both motivation and self-confidence has grown among female students and for all newly enrolled female students access to the course is now facilitated thanks to female advisors.

The image of computer science as an occupation has a generally positive connotation. All female students consistently emphasize that their study is motivated by the contribution they want to make to their country. When women discover their ability and technical talent they consider computer science as an important field for themselves as well as providing an opportunity to support the development of their nation by using their capabilities. (Hafkin & Taggart, 2001)

SURVEYING CS EDUCATION IN AFGHANISTAN

Experience in other developing countries suggests that the emerging IT developments in Afghanistan can provide an opportunity to include women in this stage of the country's development. For example, the founder of the Tanzania Media Women's Association (TAMWA) said: *"We must recognize that information technology is here to stay [...] What we have to decide if we either play the game and turn it to our advantages or lose out completely"* (Hafkin & Taggert, 2001, p.14)

In her assessment all the risks in participating at the information or knowledge society are minor compared to the potential disadvantages resulting from a refusal to join the IT society. Developments in IT are of great importance for development and form some of the most influential factors, a situation which will continue to be the case during the next decades (Hafkin & Taggert, 2001).

The current circumstances of women in Afghanistan were surveyed, to deduce measures aimed at integrating Afghan women into the world of IT. A questionnaire as well as interview topics were developed to gather a closer insight into the Afghan way of life. Much data has been collected by others about IT and developing countries, and based on this and observations in Afghanistan both a questionnaire and a standardized interview were designed.

Results of a Questionnaire for Afghanistan Students

Based on surveys of CS in other countries an interview and a questionnaire was designed to get a closer knowledge of the women studying CS in Afghanistan. The results gathered from this research will be presented here but no comparison can be made directly with data from other developing countries.

In 2006, a first survey was conducted to analyze the situation of women at the universities in Kabul and Herat. Female students from both the University of Herat and Kabul were surveyed. Out of all 156 female students, who are studying in Kabul, 20 were surveyed with the help of the questionnaire. In Herat, 10 female students were interviewed, as well as in Kabul. A second survey was conducted in 2009; a group of 73 female students at Herat University was questioned, on the basis of the same questionnaire as in 2006. In addition, standardized interviews were conducted with 15 female students (see Table 1).

All interview subjects were chosen from the students participating at the questionnaire. The interviews aimed to concretize the results found within the questionnaires, and to ask further questions. In the questionnaire all female students were given the opportunity to speak anonymously. The personal interviews were chosen to better capture the thoughts and the situations of the students, and to ask specific follow-up questions. These interviews were conducted with students who were fluent in English and who were willing to say more about their personal situation. The situations and circumstances of female students are largely unknown, as Afghan society does not allow the

Table 1. Number of surveyed students

	Kabul (2006)	Herat (2006)	Herat (2009)
Questionnaire	20	-	73
Interview	10	10	15

publicizing of private living conditions. Hence the interviews are one opportunity to discover the women's world.

All the female students in the sample were currently enrolled on bachelor level courses in computer sciences. This bachelor's study program requires eight semesters of study to graduation. At the time of the survey in 2009 the number of female students in the first semester was 25 out of 122 students in total (20%), in the third semester 26 out of 70 (37%), in the fifth semester 15 out of 54 (27%) and in the seventh semester 7 out of 39 (18%).

The results from the questionnaires and interviews have been analyzed and grouped into three main areas:

- **The family situation:** Questions about the family situation that asked about the existence of role models for academic education within the family and the value gender equality has in the family. In addition participants were asked about the existence of a computer in the household as well as the general use of computer.
- **School education:** Questions about school education were asked to gather information about their previous knowledge and interests of the female CS students
- **The course of study:** Questions about the reasons for choosing CS, and any difficulties arising during their studies, fields of interest in the area of CS and assumptions about job opportunities.

The Family Context

The parents of the female students surveyed belong to diverse occupational groups, so that a categorization was not possible. But it is remarkable that 58 participants (79.5%) have mothers in employment. Almost all of the students surveyed were unmarried; only one was married and one engaged. The age of the students varied between 18 and 25 years, with an average age of 20 years.

Compared to the survey done in 2006, the average age of female students had declined from 23 to 19.75 in 2009. This can be explained with the fact that young female students of 2009 are no longer so strongly affected from having being banned from school, which girls were during the reign of the Taliban, as the female students questioned in 2006 indicated. 61 students (83.6%) were financing their studies exclusively through support of their parents or family, nine students (12%) through their own work and the rest (three students) were getting funded through scholarships. The majority of the students worked, in their profession, primarily as network administrators.

A computer was present in 70% (51) of the households of the students, not all of which had access to the Internet. The following reasons for a missing Internet connection were stated as: *"It needs money", "telephone line is necessary"* and *"we can't support it"*.

Half of the participants from these 51 households had installed an operating system at least once on their own and 12% declared that they had installed a computer network on their own at least once. All of them tried to solve problems by themselves. If this did not work then most of them asked their brothers for help. Some tried to

Figure 3. Help by computer problems

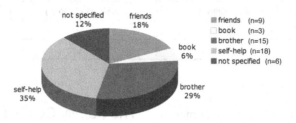

get help from friends, or they used books, tutorial programs or the system 'help' facility of the computer or they simply continued to try to solve the problem by themselves. (cf. fig. 3).

61 of the women students (83.6%) chose not to reply to the question of whether they would quit their studies in the event of a pregnancy. The rest stated that they would continue their studies and can imagine getting support from their husbands. It might seem surprising that this answer was given by unmarried students. Experience however shows that female students in later semesters will be engaged or married.

Schooling

51 of the students in the 2009 survey (70%) finished their school education in Afghanistan and 22 students (30%) in Iran. In comparison to the survey conducted in Kabul in 2006, the same results became apparent, with only one slight difference: female students who did not finish their school education in Afghanistan did finish it in Pakistan. This however is due to geographical reasons, as Kabul is closer to Pakistan, and Herat is closer to Iran.

In response to the question about their favorite school subjects, the students named mathematics without exception, followed by English language and further subjects in the area of science like physics, chemistry and biology.

The command of English of those participants who finished their school education abroad is superior to their classmates. Also, some of those

students who were educated abroad got basic computer literacy skills there. Most of them considered the state of the PC lab rooms and hardware equipment in their Afghan university as not good enough.

There were no PC labs at the schools they had attended, with the consequence that there was no education in computer technology on a regular basis. Those students who went to school in Afghanistan had no access to computers whatsoever. More than 80% of the female students directly enrolled in their CS course after graduation from school.

Studying CS at University

To the question: why they were studying CS, 58 students stated 'personal interest', the rest that they studied because of the good job opportunities CS would provide. The personal interests of the female students are mainly about the acquisition of new technologies, improving the economic situation of their parents and to actively strengthen the role of women within Afghan society. Software engineering, followed by operating and communication systems, technical computer science and database systems can be clearly identified as the main focuses within the CS course which are of interest to the female students. Some of the women also stated that they liked theoretical computer science, and computer science and society. Pure theoretical courses hardly existed in the curriculum; the courses were all application-oriented or at least had a practical background. (cf. fig. 4)

Figure 4. CS study course

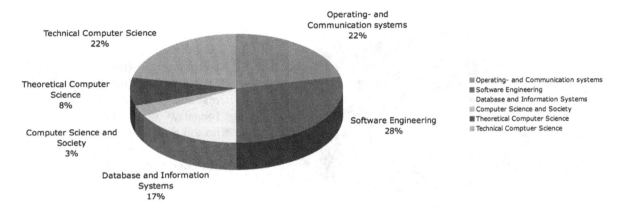

Most of the difficulties students reported resulted from weak English skills (51 students, 70%). At the University of Herat all lectures and courses are held in English. Some of the female students also had difficulties establishing the relationship between their subjects and topics, some had problems with mathematics and/or programming. Eleven students (15%) reported problems with the exams.

Half of the female students found that their expectations of the course had been fulfilled. 28 students (38%) however did not. In addition, 15 of the female students (20.5%) stated that they did not gain any computer skills during the course of their study. Twelve of these students (80%) who stated this were from fifth and seventh semester. The reasons for the high proportion of 80% of responses are still unknown, and efforts are currently underway to identify difficulties of this kind earlier in order to counteract the situation.

According to the survey, most female students (22 students) aim to make teaching their profession. The second biggest group (19%) considers research, and 17% want to work in the industry, despite the fact that there is no IT industry or research in Afghanistan. A small percentage aim to do web-design and about 8% are undecided about career goals. Until now, there is no typical occupational image for computer scientists in Afghanistan. (cf. fig. 5)

Examples from the Interviews

Additionally to the topics of family situation, education and social life, the following questions were asked:

- "Why do you study computer science?"
- "Why is Afghanistan in need of IT?"
- "What do you wish for your future?"
- "What kind of problems did you face during your course of study?"

To get an impression of the students' attitudes here are some of their answers:

I found Computer Science a noble and great profession; when I can improve my lessons, I really love it, also when I learn it practically and I hope I can continue my lessons very well.

In the progressive countries like Afghanistan it's a must to learn computer science. For me it's the most important field of study because everything is about to become digitalized and computerized. After becoming a student of Computer Science I got interested in programming, networking and web designing.

Figure 5. Future job possibilities

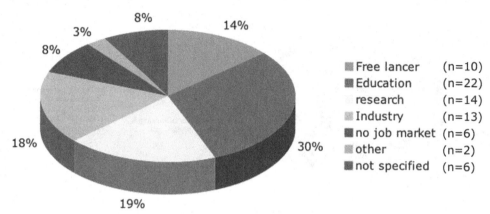

I like Computer Science too much; it's new in Afghanistan and the young generation, where I belong to want to promote step by step with technology.

There are different reasons why I studied Computer Science. First there are personal reasons, it matches my interest, I want to help my country and I want to make my family proud. The social reasons are that the study matches the modern world demands and it is possible to get a good position in the society.

According to this, the female students rate studying computer science very positively. For women, studying is a privilege.

All the female students seem to agree with the idea that IT is very important for their nation. Most female students consider studying to be a way to support the nation, and doing this is important to them. Exemplarily, a student's quote can be stated: *"We want to take part at the international information exchange and we want to be equal with other countries."*

Asked about whether Afghanistan is in need of IT, another student said: *"Internet is in Afghanistan maybe even more important than in other*

countries, both for the communication within our country as well as with foreign countries. Even now there are no streets between some cities. Here the Internet can bridge the missing interconnection. All of our cities next to the border are only connected to the neighboring countries. Access to information and knowledge in the world however is important, if we want to develop our country. "

In addition, the students surveyed were asked about what they wished for their own future and the future of their faculty in the university. The answers are proof of their immense motivation for action and their great pride in their studies and their institutions. *"I hope that our faculty can attract students. I wish we have experienced teachers and we have our lessons in a good methodical arrangement. I wish that we are able to follow the lessons series, I wish, that we are able to study lessons and work at society practically. I want that we can be the persons for the future of our country."*

"I hope that I can witness the day, that our faculty in Herat is becoming a place like Technical University of Berlin. Organized, academic, with advanced technologies and equipment and with best teachers. I don't only want to witness that day, rather I want to be one of the constructors of my faculty, so we can achieve this one day."

"I wish that someday I can also act as a computer science teacher in my faculty, I want to transfer the knowledge what I learned from my lecturers, because I really can imagine how my country needs this technology." "I wish that all women have the same rights as men in our country and women can work in their profession. I like the area of IT a lot, even I can't work in the future. But I can do something for myself." Asked about the problems they face in their studies, many students pointed out that they could achieve more but lacked time. One of the female students described the learning environment at her home. Late at night she finishes her household duties and only then is she able to study, for example to do her homework assignments. The only space she can use is in the kitchen where there is always somebody working. She does not have a quiet room for herself. Plus, after a long and hard day she isn't able to concentrate anymore.

Homework assignments or preparing for lectures are activities where students suffer from a great lack of time. Despite these problems, most female students show a pronounced eagerness to learn and study: *"Some subject were new for me, like database, and some were hard like Java but learning them was not impossible. I can say that I learned in every subject something new."*

Another student said: *"About programming in the language Java, I had a little problem and I think that it was not just difficult for me, of course it was difficult for all of my classmates too."*

In most of the households (70%) of students in the survey there was a computer, which needed to be shared among the family members. Three of the students complained about having to wait until their brothers had vacated the computer. These three have also never installed an operating system, as the brothers did not allow any changes to the system.

Reflections from Experience

An analysis of the questionnaire and interviews seems to reflect the viewpoint of women who are quite self-confident, goal-oriented and hopeful. However, in my experience as a lecturer in CS in Afghanistan this does not reflect reality. Most female students feel privileged, hence are highly satisfied with their course. Only a few freely admit to encountering some problems. Having trouble with anything is often regarded as someone's personal weakness therefore most female students try to conceal it. Particularly in Afghanistan, problems or personal matters are not discussed outside the family.

A significant difference can be observed between the female students in Kabul and Herat. Most of the students in Herat are from more conservative families and environments. Hence, they did and still do separate themselves quite strictly from their male fellow students. For example, they will seat themselves in the first rows of the lecture hall, whereas men sit in the back. Female students often behave passively and shyly. Sometimes they refuse to speak in front of the class or submit exercises.

As a teacher my first impression was that these women were not interested in their chosen course. Only after learning more about them and their life I realized my misunderstanding. The public image of women in Afghan society does not include studying. Women are expected to be quiet, not talk in public and not to draw attention to themselves. Hence female students do not ask questions during class or exercises but try to acquire the learning material together after class. Upon asking whether they had understood in class all would nod without exception. *"Problem-oriented thinking is mostly unknown for all students. Team assignments, or even participatory lessons, have never been applied in the past. Mostly, students would just memorize. Questioning or even arguing was not accounted for, all learning matter was only recited and reproduced without criticizing. (Mahr & Peroz, 2006)"*

A lot of patience is necessary to acquaint the students with new teaching and learning methods. At first new methods frustrate and unsettle the students and some of them fight the new ways. Their frustration shows in complaints about the form of instruction in class, about the level of difficulty in class, and the amount of homework assignments. Those students simply copy the assignments from classmates, do not attend the exercises or attend but do not participate in the problem solving process, let alone ask questions.

One female student described her problems with finding a suitable learning environment at home. Due to household work female students often lack the time to learn and study. Additionally, they lack a proper place where they can learn and study without getting interrupted. Hence it is of great importance to offer a secured room for women at the university. Trust has to be built, so women will confide their problems to each other and try to find a solution together and/or with their lecturers.

If asked about their occupational perspectives all female students will give the same answer: in theory, these are great. In reality, most of them see their future in the field of education. Integrating women in the professional world and a working environment is difficult and was impossible in past times. Currently, the Afghan economy is recovering from the years of conflict and war.

Afghanistan is still a very poor country and totally dependent on foreign support, on their agricultural products and trade with neighboring countries. On the other hand, the reconstruction processes in Afghanistan is considerably dependent on skilled workers. As a consequence there is a huge lack of professionals in every sector. Hence it could be expected that all university graduates will be easily integrated in the job market.

In the city of Kabul women can be seen in the working environment, they perform various occupations. Kabul however is an exception. In all other cities throughout Afghanistan women are less present in public. In rural areas they are only present in the domestic environment. Kabul offers a wide and multifaceted job market since all ministries and governmental institution are located in the city. Most NGOs and private companies as well have chosen Kabul for their head offices. The latter are desirable employers, since they pay salaries well above average. In other cities there are only a few NGOs or private companies and fewer in rural areas. The international community and financial support are based and focused on Kabul and some of the bigger cities.

Only a few of the companies will actually hire female graduates for different reasons. One of their prevailing prejudices is of women having less practical experience than men or not being able to perform physical tasks like laying out cables and networks. It is still assumed that men need less vacation, are more focused on their work and are more capable to deal with pressure.

Women are not granted the freedom of movement and flexible time scheduling making it impossible for most of them to work in commercial organisations. Hence most women are employed in governmental organizations and institutions. Familial pressure is quite high for Afghan women due to their duties with children and household. Most women are married and have children. In bigger cities there is a transportation system for the female employees: from Saturday to Wednesday at 3 pm and on Thursdays at 12 noon they are picked up with buses. In contrast to men, women are dependent on this kind of transportation system.

Due to these inflexible structures and the partially ill founded apprehension that women will not be able to balance professional work and family, many private companies will avoid conflicts by not employing women in the first place. Women still have to take on dual capacities whenever wanting to pursue a profession. Despite their jobs they still are expected to do all the housework.

The job descriptions for female graduates in computer science significantly differ from those of their male counterparts in most cases. Women are employed merely as assistants, aides, web designers or secretarial helps. In casual talk most of them do not even complain about the fact that almost all companies do not hire them permanently but assign them to assistant or temporary jobs. Moreover, most women make excuses for these companies by claiming family and childcare to be the highest priority in their lives. And this attitude is clearly not reflected by the self-confident answers given in the survey. Over many years now women have been excluded from the professional world in Afghanistan. Until now, women hesitate to apply for jobs in a working environment dominated by men.

In conclusion it can be stated that women are still not as successful in pursuing their professional careers as men. The main cause is the generally poorer position of women in Afghan society overall rather than any particular issue with CS.

Outlook for the Future

A totalitarian system has ruled Afghanistan until very recently. Women and girls have been pushed out of the society and could not and cannot contribute something to the development of their country.

An awareness of the potential role of women in Afghan society is completely missing. The unequal access to knowledge and economic possibilities for women has been culturally legitimized. Not only have women to overcome external constraints like the acceptance by men of the right of self-determination for women, they have internal constraints like their own understanding of their potential role. If women can work successfully in their professions, not only they will profit from this, but also their families and Afghan society as a whole. However without external support from other countries it is unlikely that Afghan women will get equal opportunities in education or in professions.

The empowerment and the integration of women in higher education in Afghanistan are especially important, because the future elite will be edu-

cated here. Neglect of women's disadvantages in higher education will reinforce problems in the whole society. The successful integration of women into Afghan society needs a certain basis. Equal basic rights for both women and men have already been legislated, but this has yet to be acted upon. At the university level, this implies for example the integration of women in decision-making processes, and the nomination of women's representatives. Women should be incorporated sustainably and with an integrated approach at all Afghan universities. This integration task can often be solved locally, but it has to be accounted for by a centralized policy. The Ministry of Higher Education and the universities are the decision makers and have to support these changes. Women are highly motivated, but are unable to develop their capabilities and their potential due to their culturally restricted and secondary role. The desire to participate in the reconstruction of their country is obviously present and expressed by all female students in my research. Now steps have to been taken to ensure that the students can fulfill their aspirations.

There are women, who are fighting for their ambitions and developing their ideas at the universities in Herat and Kabul. Only if these young women get enough support and assistance will they be able to apply their experience and their knowledge in a useful way. These young female students, graduates and lecturers in the area of CS will be the role models and multiplicators for many other women. They should be helped to retain interest in technical courses like CS. and to discover the many possibilities that IT offers as a career They should be allowed to play an active role in Afghan society as they wish to do, and so be an active member in the process of reconstructing their country.

REFERENCES

Buder, C. (2003). Frauen und Informations- und Kommunikationstechnologien im globalen Süden. In Frauen und IKT im globalen Süden – Research Report (pp. 37–50). Wien: Frauensolidarität.

CIA-The World Factbook. *Afghanistan*. Retrieved April, 2009, from https://www.cia.gov/library/publications/the-world-factbook/geos/af.html

Ghosh, R. A. (2004). *The opportunities of Free/Libre/Open-Source-Software for developing countries*. Retrieved December, 2006, from: http://www.iprsonline.org/unctadictsd/bellagio/docs/Gosh_Bellagio4.pdf

Hafkin, N., & Taggart, N. (2001). Gender, Information Technology, and Developing Countries: An Analytic Study. New York: Academy for Educational Development (AED)

International Telecommunication Union. (2007). *ITU ICT Eye*. Retrieved July 2008 from ITU. Website: http://www.itu.int/ITU-D/icteye/

Mahr, B., & Peroz, N. (Eds.). (2006). Establishing Academic Structures in Computer Science at Herat University. Frankfurt, Germany: IKO Verlag.

Ministry of Communication. (2003). *Information and Communication Technologies (ICT) Policy*. Retrieved July, 2008, from Ministry of Communication/Afghanistan. Web site: http://www.mcit.gov.af/Documents/PoliciesandLaws/Afghanistan%20ICT%20Policy-english.pdf

Ministry of Education/Afghanistan. (2006). *National Education Strategic Plan for Afghanistan 1385-1389*, Retrieved July, 2008, from Ministry of Education/Afghanistan. Web site: http://moe.gov.af/National%20Education%20Strategic%20Plan.pdf

Ministry of Education/Afghanistan. (2007). *School Survey 1386 Report*, Retrieved January, 2009, from Ministry of Education/Afghanistan. Web site: http://www.moe.gov.af/EMIS/School%20Survey%201386%20Report%20v2.3_2.zip

Nitsche, S. (2006, July). Null Bock auf Technik – warum sich in Deutschland nicht mehr sondern weniger Frauen für ein Ingenieurstudium entscheiden. *TU Intern - University Press*, p. 12.

Othman, M., & Latih, R. (2006). Women in Computer Science: No Shortage Here! Communications of the ACM, 49(3), 111–114. doi:10.1145/1118178.1118185doi:10.1145/1118178.1118185

Schinzel, B. (2004). *Kulturunterschiede beim Frauenanteil im Informatik-Studium*. Retrieved July, 2008, from, University of Freiburg, Department of Modelling and Social Impacts. Web site: http://mod.iig.uni-freiburg.de/cms/fileadmin/publikationen/online-publikationen/Frauenanteil.Informatik.International.pdf

KEY TERMS AND DEFINITIONS

Literacy: The skills of reading and writing.

Faculty: In Afghanistan (as in many countries) the university is divided in faculties, each faculty has its dean, administration, and lecturers. They are subdivided in departments, for example: Faculty of Computer Science.

Department: A faculty is divided in departments, these departments deal with a specialized field of knowledge, for example: Department of Software Engineering.

Concour Exam: In Afghanistan this is the application for admission to a university. School graduates have to pass the concour exam. It takes place once a year. Questions from all subject areas are asked. Students can chose entry for a specific university and field of study, and it is possible to choose several options. The Ministry of Higher Education distributes the students, based on the points achieved in the exam in their field of study.

Kabul: Capital city of the Islamic Republic of Afghanistan.

Herat: Second largest city in western Afghanistan, near to the border of Iran.

Section 2
Working with and Preparing to Work with IT

Chapter 4

"For Me it Doesn't Matter where I put my Information":
Enactments of Agency, Mutual Learning, and Gender in IT Design

Johanna Sefyrin
Mid Sweden University, Sweden

ABSTRACT

In information technology (IT) design it is essential to develop rich and nuanced understandings of messy design realities. In this chapter Karen Barad's agential realism is used as an analytical approach in order to obtain such a multifaceted understanding of a local IT design project. The purpose of the paper is to explore entanglements of agency, mutual learning, and gender in a business process analysis. The main argument here is that these issues were inextricably intertwined with each other and with the sociomaterial relations of which they were part. All empirical material used in the chapter was collected with the help of ethnographic methods. Finally the chapter concludes with a discussion about agential realism as an analytical approach.

INTRODUCTION

In information technology (IT) design it is important to obtain rich and situated understandings of relevant design contexts, and this requires proper analytical methodologies. Analytical methods which result in simplified understandings can lead to a range of various problems. If the analytical methods are too simplified we might (in an IT design context) end up with categories such as 'users' and 'designers', without understanding that behind these categories there are a number of different professional identities and working relations (Suchman, 2002). If this happens we might also be unable to see that those who at first seemed to be users might, related to an IT systems design project, also be considered designers. A part of any methodology for understanding situations in all their complexities might be to develop an awareness of gender. Otherwise there is a risk of using gender blind methods in IT design. Such gender blind design methods might lead to the exclusion of certain groups of female users, even though the intention was to include everybody (Oudshoorn et al, 2004). Researchers in Participa-

DOI: 10.4018/978-1-61520-813-5.ch004

tory Design have underscored the importance of user participation in IT design. They mean that if the (work) practices which an IT system is supposed to improve are not understood in all their intricacies, chances are good that the users will not be able to use the IT system in a way that can help them conducting their assignments (see e.g. Bjerknes & Bratteteig, 1995, Bødker et al, 2004). What our analytical tools make visible as relevant is a question of ethics, moral and politics, since our understanding of reality regulates what can be designed, and thus the kind of world that can be created (see Löwgren & Stolterman, 2004, Beck, 2002). We need analytical tools which are sensible enough to make visible these and other kinds of problems that may appear in technoscientific practices such as IT design. How is it possible to see and understand technoscientific practices as complex processes, consisting and dependent of a range of interrelated issues, instead of understanding them in a simplified and isolated manner? There is always a risk that analytical tools sort out issues that might at first seem irrelevant, but later turn out to be highly relevant. Consequently it becomes central to consider what is included and what is excluded as relevant in IT design situations – and who gets to decide this. In order to reach deeper understandings it is essential to learn to see and understand in richer ways, to include rather than to exclude what is taken into account as relevant. How and what we see also shapes what becomes possible to do. Donna Haraway (1991b, p. 190) writes: "Feminist objectivity is about limited location and situated knowledge, not about transcendence and splitting of subject and object. In this way we might become answerable for what we learn how to see". Several research traditions have attempted to develop methods for how to see and understand the world as something dynamic, multiple and situated. Some of these attempts come from feminist technoscience[1]. Within the tradition of feminist technoscience Haraway's figuration of diffraction (see Haraway 2000, 2004, 1997) is one such attempt, and Karen Barad's agential

realism (1998, 1999, 2003, 2007) is another. In this paper Barad's agential realism will be used in order to explore some of the complexities of one specific technoscientific practice; the design of an IT system. The purpose of the paper is to explore entanglements of agency, mutual learning, and gender in a business process analysis. The argument in the paper is that these were deeply and inextricably entangled in each other and with the sociomaterial relations of which they were part, and that changes in one of these resulted in changes in the others.

The paper is structured in the following way: after the introduction there is a section which is concerned with the case study of an IT design project, the project group that was researched, and the IT design method used. The third section concerns the theoretical framework, and consists of a discussion of mutual learning and of feminist technoscience and agential realism. Then follows a fourth section concerning the research methodology, which provides details of how agential realism was used in the analysis. The fifth section presents the analysis of the empirical material, and the final section provides a concluding discussion of the results, and of the use of agential realism for this type of analysis.

THE IT SYSTEMS DESIGN PROJECT

The empirical material in the paper is based on an ethnographic study of an IT systems design project in a government agency in Sweden, here referred to as The Insurance Agency (TIA). At the time of the observations (2005-2006) TIA had approximately 320 employees, and its core business was the administration of a part of the Swedish public social insurance system. The project started in September 2005; it was extensive and spanned several years, and was considered to be critical for TIA. The (initial) name of the project was 'Project IT support for administrative officers'.

There were two different objectives associated with the project. One objective was to provide IT support for the administrative officers for their case administrating tasks. The IT support was expected to ease the work of the administrative officers and also to minimize simple, monotonous and repeated tasks. The administrative officers formed the largest professional group within the organization; 200 out of the total of 320 employees. Of these administrative officers 80 percent were women. Another objective of the project was to automate as much as possible of the case administration. These two objectives were partly conflicting, and contributed to making the project somewhat complicated. In the beginning there was only talk about the IT support for the administrative officers, but after a while it became clear that the automation objective was the most prioritized.

The Business Process Analysis Method and the Project Team

The project was conducted according to an internally designed business development method, of which the business process analysis constituted one part. The business process analysis method included three steps: a) describe the current system, b) formulate a better system for tomorrow (five years ahead), and c) formulate a better system for the future (20 years ahead). These steps were supposed to be conducted sequentially, but in practice they overlapped in some respects. The analysis appeared to focus on the first and second steps of the model. As part of the business process analysis the business analysts (see below) developed and used paper prototypes of graphical user interfaces (GUIs) in order to discuss what the administrative officers wanted from the IT-support of tomorrow.

The project was conducted in-house, and consisted of a project team made up of a project manager (Ingrid[2]), a client (John), and a project steering committee. A map of the project organisation is presented in Fig. 1. The role of the cli-

ent was to determine how to allocate the project resources and what the result of the project would be[3]. The project steering committee was supposed to function in an advisory capacity for the client. The project team consisted of a large number of people, who worked part-time or full-time in the project. Among these was a project core team consisting of five members who were working full-time with the business process analysis. Hence during the business process analysis there was a larger project team consisting of less involved people, and a smaller project core team working full time. The project core team will henceforth be referred to as business analysts. The business analysts were:

- Sonja, administrative officer.
- Maria, administrative officer.
- Ulf, "business client". He was supposed to act as a link between the business part of the organization and the IT part.
- Jacob, an expert in graphical user interfaces (GUIs).
- Hans, an expert in the business process analysis method, was leading the day-to-day work of the business analysts.

Roles and responsibilities in the project were assigned to the participants according to a division between 'IT'[4] and 'business'. 'Business' seemed refer to all organisational activities apart from the IT department. The IT department of an organization can be understood as an important part of the overall business, so there are no clear boundaries between the two. However in TIA 'business' and 'IT' were referred to as different units. According to this division, within the project context, the business department was supposed to formulate the requirements and the IT department was supposed to present the solutions. Following this logic, individual participants in the project were seen as representatives for either business or IT. Hence, the business analysts were seen as the formulators of the business requirements and

Figure 1. Model of the project organisation.

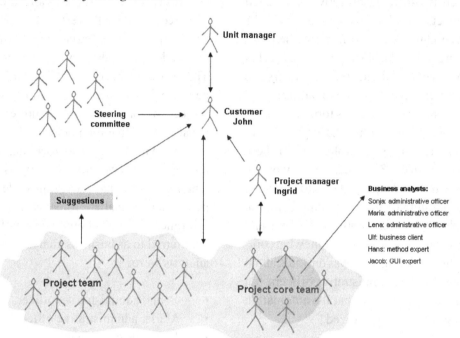

as representatives of business, although not the same part of the business. Ulf, one of the business analysts, was employed as a "business client"; a position which was intended to act as a link between business and IT. However, this position seemed to be rather vaguely defined, and it was unclear exactly how Ulf was supposed to link business and IT within the project. The boundaries between IT and business appeared to be an important part of the organisational culture, and had material implications in the form of organisational structures and divisions of labour in the organisation as a whole and in the project.

THEORETICAL FRAMEWORK

In this paper a range of various voices and perspectives will be heard and thus contribute to the paper. Some of these come from Participatory Design (PD), but the most important contributing

voices come from feminist technoscience. The use of the term 'mutual learning' is inspired by the Scandinavian tradition of PD, a large research tradition concerning IT design, which is particularly influential in the Scandinavian countries. According to the ideas of mutual learning users will be unable to imagine a new IT system if they lack knowledge about the possibilities given by technology, and developers will be unable to design an IT system which meets the requirements and needs of the future users if they do not know the work practices associated with it. Mutual learning in IT design is about allowing the users to learn about the possibilities offered by information technologies (ITs), and about allowing the designers to learn more about the situation of the users, their (work) practices and routines (Kyng, 1991, Bratteteig, 1997, Bratteteig, 2004, Bødker et al, 2004). The idea of mutual learning is central in PD, in which the focus is on designing IT systems for a particular group of users (often in an organisational setting). Therefore PD requires knowledge about these users' work situations. A basic concern for PD researchers is the involvement of future users of IT systems in the design process of the systems. PD is presently a widespread field of research with several different branches, but originally the idea of PD was to improve work place democracy, and to democratize design processes (Bjerknes & Bratteteig, 1995, Bødker et al, 2004). Other important ideas are that knowledge of the future use situation will improve the system, and that the systems will become more easily accepted by the end users if they are involved in the design process (Bjerknes & Bratteteig, 1995). A common problem in IT systems design projects is that the (power) relations between users and developers often are asymmetrical (Suchman, 2001, Boivie, 2005).

Feminist Technoscience and Agential Realism

Agential realism can be considered part of the larger tradition of feminist technoscience[5]. Feminist technoscience is the use of feminist research as a resource "in the creation of alternative understandings of technoscience" (Mörtberg, 2003, p. 57). Feminist technoscience goes beyond the relations of women and men and focuses instead on broader epistemological and ontological issues (Barad, 1999, Elovaara, 2004), that is, issues of knowledge production and of how (human and non-human) bodies materialise. Donna Haraway is the most important theoretician in the area of feminist technoscience. In an interview Haraway (2000, p. 156-158) explains how she understands feminist technoscience:

"Understanding technoscience is a way of understanding how natures and cultures have become one word. So the analysis of technoscience, the understanding of what kind of world we are living in, is what we call technoscience studies. Feminist technoscience studies ... involves technoscientific liberty, technoscientific democracy, understanding that democracy is about the empowering of people

who are involved in putting worlds together and taking them apart, that technoscience processes are dealing with some worlds rather than others, that democracy requires people to be substantively involved and know themselves to be involved and are empowered to be accountable and collectively responsible to each other. And feminist technoscience keeps looping through the permanent and painful contradictions of gender".

From a feminist technoscience perspective it is important to ask whose knowledge is dominant and whose knowledge is marginalised in technoscientific practices, and what the consequences of this are. Karen Barad writes: "We are responsible for the world within which we live not because it is an arbitrary construction of our choosing, but because it is sedimented out of particular practices that we have a role in shaping" (1999, p. 102). The citation underscores how we are responsible for what is created as a result of particular technoscientific practices such as design practices, and research practices for seeing and understanding (i.e. research methods), since these practices can be reconfigured. Barad writes about accountability to "marks on bodies" (2007, p. 340), and this includes both human and nonhuman bodies. Consequently feminist technoscience is the use of feminist research to critically analyse and reformulate technoscience, to point to alternatives and to how things could be different, and in this work, to keep a particular eye on gender.

An important issue in feminist technoscience is to reach situated and differentiated understandings of the world, and to deconstruct simplifying dichotomies such as the 'material' or 'natural', and the 'cultural' or 'discursive'. Barad's agential realism (Barad, 1998, 1999, 2003, 2007) is one such approach which specifically aims at deconstructing the boundaries between the material/natural and the cultural/discursive. Barad (2003, p. 808) "calls into question the givenness of the differential categories of "human" and "nonhuman," examining the practices through which these differential boundaries are stabilized and destabilized". In an agential realist account, humans and nonhumans have no prior existence as separate entities; instead they are seen as constituting each other, or as the results of their encounters with each other (Suchman, 2007). The focus in agential realism is on the (ontological) becoming of subjects and objects. Thus it becomes important to explore the genealogical becoming of the human and the non-human. In order to do this, agential realism makes use of concepts such as *apparatuses*, *material-discursive practices*, *intra-actions*, and *cuts*. These concepts are not self-evident but require further explaining.

Apparatuses are physical and cultural arrangements and practices such as gendered divisions of labour, existing IT systems, and IT design methods. Examples of apparatuses when studying carbon atoms through a scanning tunnelling microscope are, apart from the scanning tunnelling microscope: "the high value accorded to visualization… techniques… such as the geologist's practice of cleaving certain crystals like graphite with scotch tape… gendered and raced divisions of labor… the privileging of realist discourses… that is, getting the microscope to "work" involves a range of practices including judgments identifying certain aspects of images as artifacts and others as constituting "data," and under what conditions, and so forth" (Barad, 1999, p. 2). Apparatuses are specific material-discursive practices. The concept of material-discursive practices is similar to Haraway's concept material-semiotic[6]. Related to the example above, the apparatuses listed are specific material-discursive practices which in various ways made possible and produced the image of the carbon atoms in the microscope.

Intra-actions take place in material-discursive practices. "Whereas the construct of interaction suggests two entities, given in advance, that come together and engage in some kind of exchange, intra-action underscores the sense in which subjects and objects emerge through their encounters with each other" (Suchman, 2007, p. 267). The term intra-actions indicate that entities

are produced in their encounters with each other, and are inseparable from the material-discursive conditions which produce them. In Suchman's words (2007, p. 268) there is an "intimate co-constitution of configured materialities with configuring agencies". Through the intra-action in specific material-discursive practices entities such as humans and nonhumans come into existence as separate from each other. For instance how to define a human body is not a given. Haraway writes: "Why should our bodies end at the skin, or include at best other beings encapsulated by skin?" (Haraway, 1991a, p. 178). Thus apparatuses are boundary making practices.

In an agential realist account, humans and nonhumans emerge as a result of the intra-actions in material-discursive practices, as the results of differently performed *cuts*. "The line between subject and object is not fixed, but once a cut is made (i.e., a particular practice is being enacted), the identification is not arbitrary but in fact materially specified and determinate for a given practice" (Barad, 2007, p. 155). At a certain point in time, through the enactment of a particular practice, boundaries are performed, and thus objects and subjects are sedimented out. Practices which perform cuts can be an observation or a research analysis. In between cuts, the world is unknown and concepts are fluid and undefined. At the time of a cut the world is frozen and defined.

Agency is central in feminist thought and usually refers to the freedom and power to act and influence one's life (see e.g. McNay, 2003, Parkins, 2000, Fraser, 1992). In an agential realist framework agency is rather about intervening in the world's becoming. In fact, as we are part of the world, we always intervene in one way or the other; it is rather a question of how we intervene and with what consequences. Thus to analyze agency from an agential realist point of view is to ask about how responsibility and accountability are performed. Barad highlights how at every moment there are particular possibilities to act. These possibilities imply the responsibility to intervene in processes of becoming and to challenge and reconfigure what is included and what is excluded (2003).

RESEARCH METHODOLOGY

The empirical material was gathered through the use of ethnographic methods (Aull Davies, 1999), since I wanted to focus on practices. I conducted participant observations of the project from the start of the project in September 2005 until March 2006, mostly through being present at work meetings of the business analysts. My observations took place during the phase of business process analysis. I also talked to the project manager, the delegated client and the method expert in order to understand the organization and the administration of the insurance, as well as to understand what was happening within the project. I took field-notes, photographs, transcribed the notes to electronic documents, and recorded discussions and meetings. I was also able to collect a great deal of project documentation. The time I spent at TIA usually involved two to three days a week, for a total of approximately six months. After this initial period, I was still following the project, but from more of a distance, through participating in occasional meetings and talking to the project manager. The empirical material consists of project documentation, field notes, photographs, recorded discussions and interviews, and transcribed discussions. For the analysis of the empirical material, the ideas of agential realism have been used.

Research Practices are also Apparatuses

In agential realist terms cuts, which result in the emergence of entities such as agency or participation, are enacted in the intra-actions of specific material-discursive practices. These material-discursive practices can be a number of different

physical and discursive circumstances and conditions, such as organisational settings, methodological practices and divisions of labour which regulate for instance whom gets to talk about what. When a research analysis is conducted, research practices also form an important part of the practices which intra-act to produce certain results. Formulating a purpose for the paper is one part of several such research practices. Other research practices associated with this analysis were those that allowed me to participate in a "real" IT design project as a researcher, the theoretical framework that I used, the research methods used, and my choice of discussion extract. Thus agency, mutual learning and gender as specific entities were produced by a number of intra-acting material-discursive practices, among other research practices, which thus performed a cut in agential realist terms. So without this specific empirical material and these specific research practices, another result would have been produced. The idea that the researcher and the research practices are integral in the production of a certain analysis and its result, is not new, but can be found in several research approaches. Hence in a similar way, Henriksen (2002), a researcher in the field of multi-sited ethnography, argues that the researcher is active in constituting the field site and the object of study, through research practices such as selecting, seeing, connecting and analysing. Another researcher in this tradition, Bossen (2008), describes the process of (qualitative) research as a dance between theory, method and encounters with the world of 'creative mess'.

As part of the research practices referred to above, I chose one discussion transcript for this paper. This discussion transcript was chosen because it shows how in the discussion some material-discursive practices were cited as relevant, and seemed to contribute to the production of specific entities such as various groups, boundaries and positions in the project. Language is a discursive practice in which boundaries are enacted, and in which subjects and objects are constituted. However, recall the above discussion about how the discursive and the material are intertwined. Thus discourse, in this account, is not what is said, but "that which constrains and enables what can be said" (Barad, 2007, p. 146). In this paper a genealogical analysis of the becoming of the business analysts' agency, of mutual learning, and of gender will be carried out In order to analyse the genealogy of the human (or the nonhuman), an exploration of the apparatuses that contributed to the materialization are required. Hence one part of the analysis is the identification of relevant apparatuses. The work of Judith Butler helped me see how (some) material-discursive practices were cited in the discussions I listened to and thus invoked as relevant (Butler, 1993, 2006). One example of this was when a business analyst referred to the method; thus the method was cited as a relevant apparatus.

ENACTMENTS OF AGENCY

According to the business process analysis method, the business analysts were supposed to work on their own to analyse the business process and formulate requirements from a business perspective. After that, a systems requirements formulation process was supposed to take place. In this process the IT representatives were supposed to depart from the business requirements, analyse them from an IT perspective, and examine whether or not they were technologically feasible. This meant that the IT representatives would be able to modify or reject some of the business analysts' requirements[7]. These steps – business process analysis, systems requirements formulation – were supposed to take place sequentially so that the business analysts would not cooperate much (or at all) with the IT representatives. However, after having worked for some months the business analysts began to consider how realistic their requirements were. They seemed to fear that if they were to formulate requirements without knowing anything about the technical

conditions, there was a risk that their requirements might not be used as they intended. Instead they wanted to make realistic requirements that would be carried through. They were prepared to change their requirements in order to make them more technologically feasible. They could only learn about how to formulate technologically feasible requirements from the IT representatives. So they asked for more cooperation with the IT representatives. Their requests were heard, and in order to increase the mutual learning between business analysts and IT representatives several workshops with those two groups were arranged. The division of labour described here very much sets the boundaries for the business analysis work.

The transcript presented below is from the third workshop with the business analysts and the IT representatives. At this workshop all of the business analysts (see above) except for Sonja were present. Additionally Ingrid and John (the client) were present, plus Lydia and Niklas who represented other parts of the business department. Representatives from the IT department were Peter and Sven, systems managers, Lars, an IT architect, and Anne, who worked with documentation from an administrative perspective. Additionally there was Karl, a systems architect, Helga, who was appointed manager of the systems requirements formulation process, and Roger, one of the systems architects. Finally I and my MP3 player were there too. The group were discussing technical solutions to requirements made by the business analysts, and what was technically feasible or not[8].

John: like even if we still use these excel spins on sick insurance and insurance benefit then we still can't create a window that registers them into benefits

Lars: precisely

Ingrid: yes

Peter: and store them

John: and store them in

Ingrid: yes

John: instead of storing them in CICS [one of the existing systems] like we do today

Roger: then we do get a more secure administration

John: cause it, it, I think kind of, kind of, one has to look on one level, like those who are architects, like those who work with that, if you want it like that it's not a problem for us to have a window and, and register it directly at, is it

Ingrid: no sure

John: even if, even if the other benefits [inaudible]

Ingrid: yes, for a start, to refine this

Roger: // [inaudible, speaks at the same time as Ingrid] the problem is, like the problems that are caused by doing like this and shove it here and [inaudible]

Ingrid: // mm

John: yes it's like, I think it's such a big requirement from your side so in some way we have to (.) we don't have, we don't think

Maria: no for us it doesn't matter

John: it kind of doesn't matter

Maria: for me it doesn't matter

Ingrid: // no

Maria: where I put my information

Ingrid: // no (.) no

Maria: I don't have any requirements regarding that but

Ingrid: // right

Maria: that's like

Peter: no, it's a coordination, it's like, it's debt [another organizational department] and, that has

John: so it seems as though everyone rather agrees on that

Lars: mm

The transcript makes visible how this discussion was not an isolated phenomenon but part of and produced by a complex context consisting of, for instance, organisational structures, project organisation and project method. These and other issues were invoked, or cited, as relevant in the discussion. Thus an existing system was cited as being a relevant apparatus ("these excel spins on sick insurance and insurance benefit", "CICS"). A new system was cited as relevant too ("and stores them in … instead of storing them in CICS like we do today"). In John's and Maria's talk about "us" (the business analysts), "your side" (the IT representatives), and "we" (the business analysts), the division of labour used in the project was cited, and this had to do with the business process analysis method. Through these citational practices boundaries were performed and groups came into being. Thus the business analysts and their relation to a system were constituted ("no for us it doesn't matter"). When Maria said: "for me it doesn't matter … where I put my information … I don't have any requirements regarding that but", she constituted herself as an administrative officer, and as different from a business analyst. Then as an administrative officer she talked about her tasks in the project. In other words she cited the division of labour. In this her position as a specific type of administrative officer came into being. This position was to be interested only in the user aspects of the system; not to care about technical aspects such as where she put her information. This kind of administrative officer was not (and was not allowed to be) interested in how things worked behind the screen, or in the deeper functionality of the system. This reading of Maria's statements makes sense also since in several previous situations Maria said similar things, constituting herself as an administrative officer and a user of the system that was being developed.

When looking at the model presented in Fig. 1 it is easy to get an impression that the project organisation was rather clear-cut and existed isolated from other organisational influences. However, this was far from the case; instead the project took place in, and was inseparable from, a rather complex organisational context. The project was dependent on a number of variables such as the resources allocated to the project, the project structure, and ideas about a new and improved system for the administrative officers, the project method, and the associated division of labour. There were several departments in TIA that were in one way or the other involved and/or interested in the project, and there were also several parallel projects running, and some of these partly intermingled with the project described here. These other divisions and projects in TIA occasionally had representatives participating in meetings for this project. Also, there were informal discussions between members of different projects and organisational divisions. Decision making in TIA followed both formal and informal structures – as in most organisations. Furthermore the project was initiated as a response to the Swedish eGovernment initiative, and from this ideas were translated to fit the organisational context of TIA. The business process analysis was also affected by the existing system with its current work practices, and information technologies, the division of labour in TIA (in which 80% of the administrative officers were women), and the organisational culture in TIA with the taken for granted boundaries between the IT department and the business. Related to the project and thus the business process analysis there were a number of stakeholders such as other projects and departments, internal and external customers (organisations and citizens), the IT department, and the administrative officers. Additionally there were a lot of ideas – produced by different stakeholders and involved agencies – about a new system, both in terms of IT support for the administrative officers and about a system for automated administration. Several of these issues that affected the project were interrelated and co-dependent, such as the organisational culture of TIA, the project method, the project organisation and the organisational structure of TIA. All these issues constituted conditions or prerequisites that were integral to and produced the project; without these specific conditions the project would been something else. This underscores how it is impossible to separate the entities that are produced from the material conditions produce these entities. These prerequisites can be seen as apparatuses, or in other words specific material-discursive practices that constituted the business process analysis, the discussion above, and what was constituted in the discussion. In the discussion several entities were constituted, such as various groups (IT representatives, business analysts, administrative officers), and positions (business analysts, administrative officers).

Furthermore, the result of the analysis conducted in this paper is dependent not only on the material-discursive practices discussed above, but also on the research practices. These include the theories and methods that were used, the purpose that was formulated, and the issues that were the focus of the analysis; agency, gender and mutual learning. The focus on these issues too can be seen as specific material-discursive practices that – together with the empirical material – produce the result of the analysis. This is nothing new or controversial; with other theories, methods and/or with another purpose and something else as the analytical focus, the result of this analysis would have been something else. The researcher and the research practices are deeply embedded in the research analysis, and are thus inseparable from the produced results. In Fig. 2 an illustration of the material-discursive practices that in some way affected the business process analysis and the research analysis is presented.

Figure 2. Illustration of what went into the business process analysis and into the research analysis.

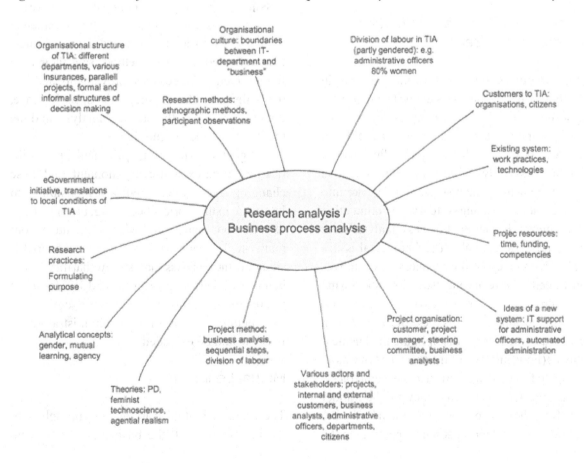

What Came Into Being in the Material-Discursive Practices?

In the following section the becoming of agency, mutual learning and gender will be explored. In an agential realist account, borders and properties of human and nonhuman bodies are performed in material-discursive practices and as a result of their intra-actions. Thus related to the project, the meaning of 'agency', 'mutual learning' and 'gender' came into being in the intra-actions in the material-discursive practices such as the business process analysis, the discussions at project meetings, and the research practices. This does not mean that any universal or general meaning of these concepts was constituted, but that *a particular kind of* agency, mutual learning and gender came into being in these material-discursive practices, depending on the specific material-discursive practices that were included.

Agency – Possibilities to Intervene in Processes of Becoming

In the above discussions agency came into being in talk about what the business analysts did or were supposed to do as business analysts. An example from the first discussion is when Hans said: "in the BA work we don't have any such limitations" (BA: business analysis). Hans cited the method in which the business analysts should not take into consideration an existing system when formulating requirements. In fact the business analysts were not supposed to care about technological issues at all. The agency of the business analysts was constituted in the recurrent discussions about what they were supposed to work with – or not work with. In Foucauldian terms these discussions can be seen as practices for disciplining the business analysts (Foucault, 1975). In other words it was an attempt to force them to return to the 'right track', when there was a risk that they might wander away from the course allocated to them by the BA method. This method in some respects gave the

business analysts certain possibilities to exert their agency, but limited them in other respects. In this method the ideas of the business analysts might be deemed technically unrealistic by other actors in the project such as the IT representatives. Thus their requirements risked not being used at all; and their suggestions could easily be disregarded by other actors in the project. It seemed as though the relations between the business analysts and the IT representatives were asymmetrical in the way that they had unequal possibilities to influence the project (Suchman, 2002, Boivie, 2005).

The business analysts realised that they were part of asymmetrical relations and decided to do something about it. They suggested a closer cooperation with the IT representatives, with the intention of formulating more realistic and technically informed business requirements. Thus even though the method did not initially provide much leeway for this type of mutual learning, the business analysts were given the agency to change the method in this respect. In this way they broadened their agency to include methodological issues; they reflected over the method, saw their own limited agency, suggested improvements, and saw the realisation of their suggestions. In this case, both the agency of the business analysts and the method were reconfigured.

In agential realist terms "[p]articular possibilities for acting exist at every moment, and these changing possibilities entail a responsibility to intervene in the world's becoming, to contest and rework what matters and what is excluded from mattering" (Barad, 2003: 827). Translated to this situation, the business analysts saw that they risked being excluded from mattering, and decided to act to prevent a situation in which their suggestions for a better IT support for the administrative officers would be excluded.

Mutual Learning

The issue of mutual learning was brought into the project through the business analysts who wanted to meet with the IT representatives and learn from them in order to avoid the formulation of business requirements that would not be technically feasible. The business development method was sequential, and did not provide any leeway for these types of meetings. When the business analysts wanted more mutual learning than was available from this method, the method was reconfigured, and workshops between business analysts and IT representatives were initiated as a response to the demand for more mutual learning. My reading of the demand for mutual learning is that the business analysts wanted to move beyond their roles in the project, and that they wanted to extend their agency. In agential realist terms the method together with mutual learning and the agency of the business analysts were not only reiterated, but were in fact reconfigured, or in other words changed. The issue of mutual learning was thus related to the method, to the agency of the business analysts, and to the boundaries between business and IT. Technology was also discussed, since a central question during the workshops was how a new system might be constrained by the existing system. In addition the boundaries between business and IT set the limits with regards to who was allowed to talk about technology, and in what way, during the workshops.

Gendered Division of Labour

According to the business development method the business analysts were not supposed to care about technical issues and thus the method constituted the business analysts as being disinterested in technical issues. In discussions among the business analysts the administrative officers (Sonja and Maria) repeatedly cited the division of labour in the project that was based on boundaries between business and IT. In this Sonja and Maria were constituted as being uninterested in technical issues. When working with the prototypes Jacob, the graphical user interface (GUI) expert, appeared to be constituted as an IT expert. Thus it might have

appeared as though they were reiterating gendered divisions of labour in which the women were users and the men were technological experts. It is however important to highlight that this reiteration was produced by the method. The method defined and limited the agency of the administrative officers to regard only business perspectives and not technical perspectives.

During the workshops with the business analysts and the IT representatives this gendered division of labour was reconfigured. When the business analysts met and discussed with the IT representatives, boundaries were constituted between the two groups – instead of between the administrative officers and the GUI expert. In the transcripts above Hans, the method expert, John, the client, and Maria, an administrative officer constituted a 'we' (the business analysts) as opposed to 'you' (the IT representatives). My agential realist reading of this is that gendered divisions of labour were not reiterated but reconfigured. Thus gendered divisions of labour were reconfigured as a result of the reconfiguration of the method – and this happened in the meetings with the IT representatives.

Entanglements and Co-Dependencies

All in all there were many entanglements, co-dependencies and mutual constitutions in this story, and these appeared to confirm that it is impossible to separate the configuring agencies from the bodies that are configured. It appeared as though the agency of the business analysts, mutual learning and gender were all related to the business development method through the formulation of roles and the divisions of labour in the project, to technology, and to the boundaries between the business department and the IT department. They were also related to each other. The desire for mutual learning was a result of a wish by the business analysts to extend their limited agency. Furthermore the agency of the business analysts constituted an important prerequisite in discussions between the business analysts and the IT representatives that constituted the arena for mutual learning. Between the business analysts the reiterations of gendered divisions of labour had to do with the business development method, and thus with their agency. When the business analysts met the IT representatives in the workshops all the business analysts were constituted as users. Previously boundaries between users and IT representatives had been constituted between the business analysts. In agential realist terms the gendered divisions of labour were reconfigured due to the change in material-discursive practices. The workshops in which this happened were situations of mutual learning in which the agency of the business analysts was performed. An agential realist analysis thus shows how agency, mutual learning and gender were entangled with each other and with the identified apparatuses (see above). That they were entangled with each other means that they cannot be separated; take away one and the others will be lost or changed. It seems as though the becoming of these was dependent on each other. In other words these categories were produced through one another (Barad, 2007, p. 241).

CONCLUSION

In this paper agential realism has been used as an analytical approach in order to obtain a rich and nuanced understanding of a local IT design project. The purpose of the paper was to explore entanglements of agency, mutual learning, and gender in a business process analysis. I have argued that these issues were inseparable from each other, and from the sociomaterial relations of which they were part, and produced. In agential realist terms agency, mutual learning and gender were entangled with each other and with the material-discursive practices which intra-acted to produce them. The story is also about the possibility of exerting agency and making changes. In an agential realist account, agency is about the

possibility to intervene in the world's becoming, and the story told here is about how the business analysts changed and expanded their roles in the project. The business analysts realised that they faced the risk of being excluded from mattering. They decided to act in order to prevent a situation arising in which their suggestions risked being excluded. Workshops in which mutual learning between the business analysts and the IT representatives could take place were initiated. During these workshops gendered divisions of labour were reconfigured. This became visible through using agential realism as an analytical approach. An agential realist analysis also highlighted how this choice of analytical approach (along with other research practices) was part of the contextual conditions which produced a specific result. It appears that agential realism offers a very rich analysis, which highlights how various intertwined (material-discursive) agencies intra-act to produce certain results.

An agential realist approach is not obvious, or easy to understand and use for an analysis of this kind. It requires use of a rather complicated terminology, and a fundamental rethinking of many aspects often taken for granted, such as the pre-given existence of entities such as humans or IT systems. It might take some effort and time to do this rethinking, and to translate the terminology into something concrete, but once this is done, an agential realist analysis appears to offer several benefits. It highlights the genealogy of concepts; that entities such as gender and mutual learning do not appear from nowhere but have a history. The analysis here also showed how these concepts are not isolated from contextual conditions, but instead deeply situated in, and produced by these. The analysis showed how this genealogy is sometimes a matter of reiterations and sometimes a matter of reconfigurations, and thus how nothing is simply reproduced in a simple or mechanical way. One such reconfiguration was the gendered divisions of labour, which were reiterated in one setting, but reconfigured as the business development method was reconfigured. Another reconfiguration occurred when the business analysts realised their limited agency in the project and decided to intervene in the business development method in order to widen their agency, and did in fact succeed in this intervention. Agential realism also offers the possibility to make visible how deeply the researcher, the research methods and practices are embedded in the results of research. Thus it can be one way of taking responsibility for "what we learn how to see", as Donna Haraway writes (1991b, p. 190).

Agential realism appears to be quite the opposite of reductionism, and implies instead a thoroughgoing contextuality and situatedness. This kind of analytical richness invites an understanding of the world as an intricate and dynamic sociomaterial web of interdependencies and mutual constitutions, instead of as a number of related, predefined entities. Perhaps this might counteract the kind of simplified understandings that sometimes lead to uninformed and short-sighted technoscientific practices, resulting in problems such as those discussed in the introduction of the paper (not to mention nuclear weapons and global warming). This becomes even more important in an increasingly complex world where locally accessible commodities and services are part of global sociomaterial webs of production with far reaching consequences of social, environmental and economic character. In this kind of world, it might at the same time be harder to foresee the consequences of interventions. Thus the need for responsible and sustainable ways to understand and act is more important than ever.

ACKNOWLEDGMENT

Thank you to the *GLIT Research Network* for the opportunity to of presenting an earlier version of this paper at the *Symposium on Gender, Learning and IT*, in Helsingborg, August 2007. This network and symposium received support from *the KK-Foundation (The Knowledge Foundation of Sweden)* and its research programme *LearnIT*.

REFERENCES

Aull Davies, C. (1999). *Reflexive Ethnography – A Guide to Researching Selves and Others*. London, New York: Routledge.

Barad, K. (1998). Getting Real: Technoscientific Practices and the Materialization of Reality. *A Journal of Feminist Cultural Studies, 10*(2), 87-128.

Barad, K. (1999). Agential Realism – Feminist Interventions in Understanding Scientific Practices. In Biagioli, M. (Ed.), *The Science Studies Reader* (pp. 1–11). New York: Routledge.

Barad, K. (2003). Posthumanist Performativity: Toward an Understanding of How Matter Comes to Matter. *Signs: Journal of Women in Culture and Society, 28*(3), 801–831. doi:10.1086/345321

Barad, K. (2007). *Meeting the universe halfway – quantum physics and the entanglement of matter and meaning*. Durham, NC: Duke University Press.

Beck, E. (2002). P for Political – Participation is Not Enough. *Scandinavian Journal of Information Systems, 14*, 77–92.

Bjerknes, G., & Bratteteig, T. (1995). User Participation and Democracy: A Discussion of Scandinavian Research on Systems Development. *Scandinavian Journal of Information Systems, 7*(1), 73–98.

Bødker, K., Kensing, F., & Simonsen, J. (2004). *Participatory IT Design, Designing for Business and Workplace Realities*. Cambridge, MA: The MIT Press.

Boivie, I. (2005). *A Fine Balance, Addressing Usability and Users'Needs in the Development of IT Systems for the Workplace.* Published doctoral dissertation, Uppsala University, Sweden.

Bossen, C. (2008). How to analyze IT. Strategies, Methodologies and Challenges. Presentation at PhD workshop 2nd-4th June 2008, Aarhus, Denmark.

Bratteteig, T. (1997). Mutual learning. Enabling cooperation on systems design. In Kristin Braa & Eric Monteiro (Eds.), *IRIS Conference '20: Proceedings* (pp. 1-20). Oslo, Norway: Dept. of Informatics, University of Oslo.

Bratteteig, T. (2004). *Making Change, Dealing with relations between design and use.* Published doctoral dissertation, University of Oslo, Norway.

Bruun Jensen, C. (2004). *Researching Partially Existing Objects: What is an Electronic Patient Record? Where do you find it? How do you study it?* Working Papers from Centre for STS Studies, Department of Information & Media Studies, University of Aarhus, Denmark.

Butler, J. (1993). *Bodies that Matter. On the Discursive Limits of "Sex".* London, UK: Routledge.

Butler, J. (2006). *Undoing Gender.* New York: Routledge.

Elovaara, P. (2004). *Angels in Unstable Sociomaterial Relations: Stories of Information Technology.* Published doctoral dissertation, Blekinge Institute of Technology.

Elovaara, P., Igira, F. T., & Mörtberg, C. (2006, July 5-August). Whose participation? Whose knowledge? – Exploring PD in Tanzania-Zanzibar and Sweden. In Proceedings of *Participatory Design Conference: Vol. 1,* 31, Trento, Italy.

Foucault, M. (1991). *Discipline and Punish: the Birth of the Prison.* London: Penguin.

Fraser, N. (1992). Introduction. In Fraser, N., & Lee Bartky, S. (Eds.), *Revaluing French Feminism: Critical Essays on Difference, Agency and Culture* (pp. 1–24). Bloomington, IN: Indiana University Press.

Greenbaum, J., & Kyng, M. (1991). *Design at Work: Cooperative Design of Computer Systems.* Hillsdale, NJ: Lawrence Earlbaum Associates.

Gulliksen, J., & Göransson, B. (2002). *Användarcentrerad systemdesign.* Lund, Sweden: Studentlitteratur. [*User centred systems design*]

Haraway, D. (1991a). A Cyborg Manifesto: Science, Technology, and Socialist-Feminism in the Late Twentieth Century. In Haraway, D. (Ed.), *Simians, Cyborgs and Women – The Reinvention of Nature* (pp. 149–181). New York: Routledge.

Haraway, D. (1991b). Situated Knowledges: The Science Question in Feminism and the Privilege of Partial Perspective. In Haraway, D. (Ed.), *Simians, Cyborgs and Women – The Reinvention of Nature* (pp. 183–201). New York: Routledge.

Haraway, D. (1997). *Modest_Witness@Second_Millennium. FemaleMan©_Meets_OncoMouse™. Feminism and Technoscience.* London: Routledge.

Haraway, D. (2000). *How Like a Leaf – Interview with Thyrza Nichols Goodeve.* London: Routledge.

Haraway, D. (2004). Cyborgs, Coyotes, and Dogs: A Kinship of Feminist Figurations and There Are Always More Things Going on Than You Thought! Methodologies as Thinking Technologies. An interview with Donna Haraway in two parts by Nina Lykke, Randi Markussen, & Finn Olesen. In Haraway, D. (Ed.), *The Haraway Reader* (pp. 321–342). London: Routledge.

Henriksen, D. L. (2002). Locating virtual field sites and a dispersed object of research. *Scandinavian Journal of Information Systems, 14*(2), 31–45.

Kyng, M. (1991). Designing for Cooperation: Co-operating in Design. *Communications of the ACM, 34*(12), 65–73. doi:10.1145/125319.125323

Löwgren, J., & Stolterman, E. (2004). *Thoughtful interaction design. A Design Perspective on Information Technology*. Cambridge, MA: The MIT Press.

Marcus, G. E. (1995). Ethnography in/of the World System: The Emergence of Multi-Sited Ethnography. *Annual Review of Anthropology, 24*, 95–117. doi:10.1146/annurev.an.24.100195.000523

McNay, L. (2003). Agency, Anticipation and Indeterminacy in Feminist Theory. *Feminist Theory, 4*(2), 139–148. doi:10.1177/14647001030042003

Mörtberg, C. (2003). In Dreams Begin Responsibility – Feminist Alternatives to Technoscience. In C. Mörtberg, P. Elovaara & A. Lundgren (eds.) How do we make a difference? Information Technology, Transnational Democracy and Gender (pp. 57-69). Division Gender and Technology, Luleå University of Technology, Sweden.

Newman, S. E. (1998). Here, There, and Nowhere at all: Distribution, Negotiation, and Virtuality in Postmodern Ethnography and Engineering. *Knowledge and Society, 11*, 235–267.

Oudshoorn, N., Rommes, E., & Stienstra, M. (2004). Configuring the User as Everybody: Gender and Design Cultures in Information and Communication Technologies. *Science, Technology & Human Values, 29*(1), 30–63. doi:10.1177/0162243903259190

Parkins, W. (2000). Protesting like a Girl: Embodiment, Dissent and Feminist Agency. *Feminist Theory, 1*(1), 59–78. doi:10.1177/14647000022229065

Suchman, L. (2002). Located Accountabilities in Technology Production. *Scandinavian Journal of Information Systems, 14*(2), 91–105.

Suchman, L. (2007). *Human-Machine Reconfigurations – Plans and Situated Actions* (2nd ed.). New York: Cambridge University Press.

Wajcman, J. (2007). From Women and Technology to Gendered Technoscience. *Information Communication and Society, 10*(3), 287–298. doi:10.1080/13691180701409770

Wajcman, J. (2009). Feminist theories of technology. *Cambridge Journal of Economics Advance Access*. First published in January 8, 2009, doi:10.1093/cje/ben057.

KEY TERMS AND DEFINITIONS

IT System: An IT system is a system consisting of for instance artifacts such as various computers, software, cables, practitioners who use it, administrators who administrate the system, user manuals, administrative manuals, use and / or organizational practices.

AgentialRrealism: A philosophical approach to understanding reality on an ontological and epistemological level. The approach was developed by the US researcher Karen Barad, who has a doctorate in theoretical particle physics.

Feminist Technoscience: An approach which uses feminist research as a resource in order to critically analyse and intervene in problematic technoscientific practices.

Participatory Design (PD): A research approach concerning IT design, which is particularly influential in the Scandinavian countries. The central focus in PD is that the users of IT systems and services should participate in the design of these.

Apparatuses: Material and discursive conditions and relations which produce specific phenomena such as for instance gender and IT systems.

Material-Discursive Practices: Specific instances of apparatuses.

Intra-Action: These take place in material-discursive practices. The term means that human and non-humans come into being in their encounters with each other, and that they are inseparable from the material-discursive conditions which produce them.

Cut: A cut is a specific moment in time in which something comes into being in the intra-actions of material-discursive practices. At the time of the cut the world is temporarily frozen.

ENDNOTES

[1]   Other attempts which are relevant for techno-scientific practices and information systems design come for instance from ethnography (see e.g. Suchman, 2002, 2007, Newman, 1998, Marcus, 1995, Henriksen, 2002, and Bruun Jensen, 2004).

[2]   All names mentioned are fictitious.

[3]   The client was one of the higher directors in TIA but he was not very active in this phase of the project. Instead his tasks were delegated to a representative, a delegated client (John).

[4]   It is worth noticing that on TIA the IT department consisted of sixty individuals, and of these 28 were women. Thus the IT department was rather gender balanced, if you disregard the top four positions which were held by men. However, the IT department was not much involved in the business process analysis, so the gender and power distribution on the IT department is not relevant in this paper.

[5]   But it can also be seen as part of the larger tradition of feminist science studies.

[6]   Suchman (2007) uses the similar concept *sociomaterial*.

[7]   Economical feasibility could also prevent the business requirements from being implemented, but here I will focus on technical issues.

[8]   The discussion was translated from Swedish to English (this was done by the author).

Chapter 5
Attaching People and Technology:
Between E and Government

Christina Mörtberg
University of Umeå, Sweden & University of Oslo, Norway

Pirjo Elovaara
Blekinge Institute of Technology, Sweden

ABSTRACT

The Swedish public sector is involved in an overwhelming change process aiming towards creating a good-service society based on information technology. Rationalisation, efficiency and effectiveness are the leading signs in the dominating discourse of Swedish society of today. This discourse is silent about public sector employees, their agencies, their participation, and how the public sector is the dominant labour market for women. Alternative stories of women's presence in the creation of a good-service society are presented with a focus on performances of gender, skills, learning and technology. The empirical material was collected in municipalities in the south east of Sweden. Methods sensitive to everyday practices in order to create space and time for women and their stories were developed and used. The methodological approach, feminist technoscience, provides opportunities to move beyond the dominating IT discourses in order to make visible other discourses where women are present.

BACKGROUND

Since the dawn of the new internet era, from the middle of the 1990s, information technology has become a strong political actor of change. One of the main visible areas of this change in Sweden, among many other countries, is the public sector. This overwhelming change process is aiming towards, with strong political hopes spiced with ingredients from

the New Public Management ideology (see e.g. Pollit and Bouchaert, 2004), to creating a good-service society based on information technology. The transformation process is united under the overall concept of e-government, with its two dominating aspects of e-administration and e-services. This is characterised as a modernisation process with the use of the concepts of rationalisation, efficiency and effectiveness as its leading signs.[1] This is the grand narrative or the dominating discourse of Swedish society of today.

DOI: 10.4018/978-1-61520-813-5.ch005

The very same discourse, however, is silent about public sector employees, their agencies, and their participation in the development of the service-society based on information technology. Consequently, this also means that the discourse does not speak about how the public sector is the dominant labour market for women, and that the modernisation and implementation of IT will probably radically change their working conditions and practices. Just how the experiences, knowledge and skills of these employees could provide valuable bits and pieces for the process of developing IT-based work practices and also a good service environment for citizens is not articulated in the dominating discourse.

We also know from the context of the gender equality and information technology debate in Sweden, that the official story emphasises the absence of women when talking about information technology. Women are the minority when investigating fields of the labour market labeled under the umbrella concept of the IT-sector, and the same is also true when looking at the numbers of women students within the so-called IT-field. Of course, if the emphasis is limited to the computational aspects of IT, such as systems development and programming, the story of absence is not far wrong. The connection to the silence about public sector employees and the IT-based public sector development, as identified in the dominating IT-discourse, is clear if one accepts that information technology is, above all, concerned with issues such as software engineering and information architecture. However, gender and technology researchers provide other stories where the meaning of IT is extended and thus opens up new spaces for action and agency. (see e.g. Mörtberg, 1997; Karasti, 2001; Elovaara, 2004; Tuuva-Hongisto, 2007).

We are tying together this silence in the dominating IT-discourse with alternative and contrasting stories of women's presence in the creation of information technology. Further, we pay particular attention to, and are conscious of, the fact that working life experiences and skills are valuable components in the design of IT systems and solutions. We also want to include the observation that the introduction of new technologies is intertwined with people's working conditions and work practices. Using this weave as a starting point, we focus on asking questions about e-government, gender, skills, learning and technology. How gets e-government done in day-to-day activities in a Swedish municipality? How do the civil servants learn and enhance new skills? What does it actually mean to be skilful in everyday administrative work? Finally, what is the agency of technology in work and change?

In this chapter we discuss performances of gender, skills, learning and technology, starting with our questions above and the stories based on the research project From government to e-government (2005-2007)[2] We will invite contemporary feminist technoscience scholars Karen Barad, Donna Haraway, and Lucy Suchman along as our main weaving companions to support us in our story telling and analysis. Their methodological approaches provide opportunities to move beyond the dominating IT discourses, in which women are excluded, in order to make visible other discourses where women are present. In conclusion, we gather together the threads and discuss our findings and the (hoped for) consequences.

METHODS IN USE

We take our departure from the above mentioned research project From government to e-government (2005-2007) and describe what methods we applied while working with the project. By our rather detailed method story we want to emphasise that research methods, both in general and specifically in our context, do matter. If tuned to hear sensitive waves, even the very silent and silenced voices and sounds can first of all be heard and even more important, heard more clearly and distinctly and not only as a part of loud but nonspecific noise (Law, 2004). Our goal has been to work with seemingly modest methods, but our intention has been that they will tell us complex and also, we hope, new stories about the contemporary everyday where knowing about and doing gender and technology are interwoven.

The empirical material has been collected within four municipalities in the county of Blekinge, in the south east of Sweden. In the autumn of 2005, working groups were established of 2-3 civil servants who participated in three workshops with various topics. Participatory design (PD) and its dialogic methods (Bødker, Kensing & Simonsen, 2004) together with feminist pedagogy (hooks, 2000) were starting-points in the decisions about the methods to be used. We have however developed the methods in order to situate and locate them to our chosen setting and participants: women with a long working-life experience and without higher education; women with long experience and with higher education; and women with a relatively short working-life experience and with higher education. In between

the three workshops we conducted informal interviews.

We have used a range of methods, such as cartographic maps, scenarios, walking through their workplaces with disposable cameras, in-situ interviews, informal interviews (group and individual), and digital story telling. In the first workshop the participants conducted a cartographic exercise. The topic was: "I, my workplace, and my work". The intention was to create trust through a non-formal and open dialogue where the civil servants were able to talk while simultaneously doing things. These activities resulted in maps of their work and workplaces, of familiar objects and subjects, relations within and outside their office and so forth. The creation did not require preparation in advance and the tools were simple, cheap and familiar for all participants: coloured paper, images, tapes, scissors, catalogues with pictures of desks, computers, printers, faxes, telephones, post-it notes, binders etc see Fig. 1.

In-situ interviews were also conducted during the mapping activities: sometimes in order to clar-

Figure 1. An example of a cartographic exercise.

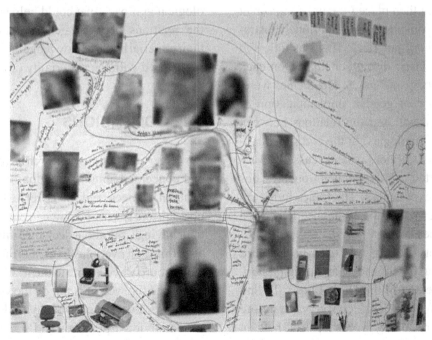

ify things, other times to complement their maps. The participants werc able to talk in an informal and uncomplicated way about various issues and topics in their day-to-day work. The cartographic exercise also demonstrated the most important relations in their workplaces with their fellow colleagues, other employees at the municipal offices, citizens, politicians, representatives various service deliverers and also with non-human actors (printers, computer, faxes, telephones, mobiles, wastebaskets, web pages, and so forth). The sessions ended with scenarios of hypothetical situations where we (Pirjo and Christina) acted as citizens who contacted the municipality through phone calls, personal visits, web inquiries etc. These scenarios were created in advance by the researchers and were used as role-play between the participants and the researchers (citizens). Disposable cameras were handed out at the end of the first workshop. The aim was to reinforce the civil servants' involvement and also encourage them to explore their day-to-day practice; an ethnographic study of their work.

In the second workshop, the participants had a fresh look at the maps, then they showed the photos taken in their own ethnographic exercise. They chose and then placed the most important ones on the map in order to add additional illustrations of their work practices. This was followed by specific thematic discussions based on each site on the participants' maps. The themes were: the performance of gender, implementation of the digital assistant, and the relations between humans and technologies. In the end some conceivable future e-services were discussed. Every workshop started with reflections on previous activities and experiences. The topics in the informal interviews were the 24-hour authority and future e-services.

Digital Story Telling was used in the third workshop. It was based on ideas about digital story telling documented in the Digital Story Telling Cook Book[3]. We visited the civil servants before the digital story telling workshop was held in

order to inform them about the method and also to practice story telling. The exercises were based on events and experiences from their day-to-day work. The participants were also asked to prepare a story based on their working life experiences to be used in the digital storytelling session. Three researchers familiar with the method were responsible for the workshop, which was held in October 2006. It started with an introduction to the method and the software. Then the participants started the exercise to record the story, including images and music. At the end of the workshop the civil servants shared their stories with each other. They also reflected upon the method. In the final meeting, in June 2007, we discussed the civil servants' experiences of the digital story telling session, the present situation and also their visions of the future.

All these activities provided a huge number of threads for our further analysis. As we indicated in the introduction of this chapter, our core research concern was to face seriously the question of women's absence and silence in dominant IT discourses and public IT-discussions. In order to find unexpected and unforeseen entrances to work with the empirical material, we needed a methodological approach that could help us re-consider the relations between gendered humans, with their material bodies, knowledge and experiences, juxtaposed with the materiality of technology.

THE COMPANIONS

For a long time feminist research has been troubled and concerned about the notion of agency. This concern has been, and still is, related mostly to the position and space of women in public arenas and their having a say about decisions influencing and affecting their everyday lives, and the possibilities and resources accessible to them. When agency is discussed the weight is put on the very activity – the power to act, the "capacity to determine and act…individual practices and social processes"

(Messer-Davidow, 1995, p.118). Today, much of the inspiration for the discussions and problematisation of the notion of agency comes from feminist technoscience because it challenges many of the present understandings, interpretations and even experiences of technology, agency and participation, and thereby proposes essential re-thinking. Border transgressions can consist of traditional feminist issues of knowledge and power, but the real challenge is that there are no given answers and solutions to serious current problems, present wherever we live or to wherever we move (See Haraway, 1997). The question of agency is still under consideration, but the choices are no longer either-or but more multifaceted and multidimensional because, today, we humans share the world and co-exist with a complex network of diverse hybrid creatures. Agency and participation is no longer the privilege of humans, but a shared skill and experience, together with our co-habitants, and co-operation, collaboration, communication and participation often operate in networks of humans and non-humans. New experiences, possibilities and also limitations of participation are possible, which indicates that further thinking about agency is also needed, here and now.

Karen Barad, professor of Feminist Studies, Philosophy and History of Consciousness at the University of California, Santa Cruz, puts forward a challenging notion: "Agency is not an attribute but the ongoing reconfigurings of the world" (Barad, 2003, p. 818). She elaborates this in her epistemological and ontological approach of agential realism, where her main focus in on matter and how matter matters (Barad 2003, 2007). Barad underscores the ongoing entanglements of meaning and matter. She is thus one amongst other feminist researchers who pay particular attention to materiality (see also Haraway, 1994, 1997; Wacjman 2004; Suchman 2007). Various feminists have thus problematised materiality, but in Barad's agential realism it is more obvious how materiality matters and how subjects and objects emerge out of enactments that take place

in boundary-making practices/actions/doings or in the world's becoming (Barad, 2003, 2007).

In agential realism "reality is sedimented out of the process of making the world intelligible through certain practices and not others." (Barad, 1999, p. 7). Separate subjects (humans) and objects (nonhumans) come into being at specific moments, that is, moments when agential cuts are enacted. Consequently subjects and objects are not pre-given, but constituted in performances in a world of becoming. In a scientific experiment, for example, a cut is made when a measurement is performed, that is, "a particular practice is being enacted" (Barad, 2007, p. 155). Hence the cut is made in a specific moment and, thereby, subjects and objects are constituted or sedimented out of a material-discursive practice. However, the cuts in which the subjects and objects emerge are not only applicable in experiments but also in other practices to help us to explore the constitutive role of what is included and what is excluded in various material-discursive practices. For example, in our project a number of cuts were made by us, both during the data collection and also in the analysis. The questions we (Christina and Pirjo) asked (in in-situ interviews) during the cartographic exercises created cuts in the processes or ongoing entanglement. The resulting subjects and objects are thus dependent on the cuts. June's story about invoices, presented in the later sections, is also unfolded through a cut that is where it starts and where it ends. Dependent on our enactments in a specific moment, particular subjects and objects came into being. Further, cuts were made within June's story, e.g. the telephone calls that created cuts in her day-to-day work or intra-actions. The agential cut is thus one important notion in agential realism. Performativity is another.

Judith Butler (1990) discusses how gender is "a kind of becoming or activity" (p. 112); gender does not pre-exist but emerges out of enactments where norms and values are cited through repeated activities or iterative actions. Butler underscores also that "[i]f gender is performative, then it follows that the reality of gender is itself produced as an effect of the performance" (Butler, 2004, pp. 218). Butler's notion of performativity pays particular attention to the materialisation of bodies. Although Barad starts from Butler in her exploration of performativity, she claims that Butler's (and Foucault's) use is limited as they stop at the surface of the body without any considerations of its materiality. Barad pays attention not only to the materialisation of human bodies, but to all bodies; humans and nonhumans. That is, the focus is both on discursive and material practices or material-discursive practices. Performativity, following Barad, is then intra-actions or entanglements with inseparable entities.

Intra-action is thus important in how subject and objects obtain their meaning. We bring in Lucy Suchman (2007) to explain the notion intra-action and how it differs from interaction. Suchman (2007) writes: "Whereas the construct of interaction suggests two entities, given in advance, that come together and engage in some kind of exchange, intra-action underscores the sense in which subjects and objects emerge through their encounters with each other" (p. 267).

The subjects and objects are constituted in particular boundary-making practices/doings/ actions. Further, the emergence is dependent on where the boundaries are drawn or what is included and excluded in the practices, because the enactment takes place in intra-actions with various intertwined apparatuses. Barad writes, in a discussion about causality; "[Indeed], intra-actions iteratively reconfigure what is possible at a given moment and what is impossible – possibilities do not sit still. One way to mark this might be to say that intra-actions are constraining but not determining." (p. 234). Apparatuses are not only instruments (nonhumans) but also humans. In the re-configuration of the world (practices) some apparatuses are included and others excluded. Those apparatuses at work in a specific case constitute the specific enactment where the boundaries are drawn or where, for example, experts, non-experts,

or gender are constituted. Knowledge and understandings are also produced in these intra-actions due to the realities that are made visible in the specific intra-actions.

Agential realism, with its concepts of performativity, apparatuses, intra-action and agential cuts, invites us to discuss the workshops and the work practices presented in this chapter as performances of material-discursive practice. Specific apparatuses are involved or excluded in the boundary-making practices that took place in the workshops and in the civil servants' day-to-day doings. Boundaries have real material consequences that became obvious in how the dominant Swedish IT discourse excludes employees in the development of the service society and ignores the gendered division of labour in Swedish society. Boundaries are necessary for making meanings, but this does not make them innocent. This moves us to accountability and how to draw the boundaries in order to make a difference with an intention to produce stories other than those told within the dominant IT discourse. In agential realism accountability is related to the world's becoming, produced in boundary-making practices, thus in ongoing intra-actions with a range of apparatuses. Barad underscores accountability as she moves to Donna Haraway's diffraction[4] figuration. Haraway (1999) argues for diffraction and not reflection; both are optical phenomena, she writes "Diffraction does not produce 'the same' displaced, as reflection and refraction do. ... A diffraction pattern does not map where differences appear, but rather maps where the effects of differences appear" (p. 320). The effects of differences will be the focus in our diffractive reading of stories produced by the civil servants.

Further, knowledge is also something that is produced in performance or in intra-actions. Knowledge is not objective; it is not comprehensive but is generated in particular material-semiotic practices (Haraway, 1997). Knowledge builds on the past, is always partial, located and situated somewhere. Haraway (1991) uses the notion of situated knowledges to characterise production of knowledge and its heterogeneity. Consequently it is not possible to isolate knowing and being because they are implicated in the practices; they are not stable but are becoming in the doings and actions; in intra-actions (Barad, 2003; 2007). The conducted workshops with the civil servants' activities in their everyday life are material-discursive (or sociomaterial)[5] practices where both knowledge and being are produced. In the following sections we present four vignettes or material-discursive practices created in the workshops and interviews.

ENTANGLEMENT OF GENDER, SKILLS, LEARNING AND TECHNOLOGY – THE MESSY STAGE

We entered the municipal department, we saw photo copiers, printers, files, ceramic angels, green plants, cleanliness and order, computers, notice-boards, cinnamon buns, piles of paper, people walking around in corridors, people standing in doorways, locked doors, thermos jugs, cables, recycling boxes, people cleaning their offices, print outs. We heard people laughing, talking, printers printing, the sound of a photo copier at work, phones ringing. "What a place!" we thought "So many things going on. How do we find our way into this places, relations, practices?" we wondered. For us, outsiders with other experiences than those of the employees at the department where we were going to conduct our study, this was just a messy and complex place and space; an unknown and strange stage.

We had our initial concerns: the silence created by the dominating discourse of IT about the change in the public sector, the concerns of skills, gender, technology and learning. But is the silence actually that silent when you enter into it? The very first, perhaps a naïve, impression was that, of course, a work place is not silent. You hear voices of people and you hear sounds of machines. But

what do people say, how do the machines work? How do gender, skills, learning and technology intersect in activities in this specific municipal department?

Let's move to Ann's, June's and Kate's stories told during the workshops and interviews. Ann, June and Kate were colleagues in the municipal offices where the research was conducted. The first four stories told in the workshops and interviews are presented. The presentation is followed by a genealogical analysis and diffractive reading of them.

Remaking Of The Room: A Story About Computer Training

As stated, Digital Storytelling was used in the third and last workshop, held in October 2006 at the Blekinge Institute of Technology. There were pre-meetings before the workshop to explain the foundational principles of digital storytelling. The aim of the meetings was, in addition to introducing the method, to practice storytelling, and to start thinking about a work-related story to bring with them to the actual workshop, to be translated into a digital story. In the workshop the participants recorded their stories, used illustrations and created their digital story with the use of particular software. The workshop ended with reflection on what they had experienced and all shared their story with each other.

In the instructions for the workshop the participants were told to think further about their work and especially in relation to the use and introduction of information technology. Kate chose to create her story about an occasion that had occurred in 1999. The municipality where she is still employed had purchased a new IT-based accounting system. The staff was in need of training in order to get acquainted with this new system and Kate was in charge of organizing and conducting a training session for 15 people. She had booked the computer training room, a room designated for computer courses, in good time and also ordered coffee for the break. When the actual day came and the training session started, with every person who had registered for the session in place, Kate went around and switched on the computers, and checked that everything was in order. She also distributed the necessary passwords. The workshop got started. The participants (women) had a quick look at the system as a whole and then picked up invoices that they had brought with them. It was time to test the system by entering information from these invoices. At the same moment they heard someone knocking on the door. Two carpenters (men) entered and announced that they were going to re-make the room. Kate and the participants protested by saying that the carpenters must have the wrong room. But they found out that it was indeed the computer training room that was going to be re-constructed and their protest was in vain. Kate and her colleagues had to collect their files and papers and the workshop was cancelled. Later on, Kate had to re-organize the training in her own office with small groups of two participants. It became seven training sessions instead of one.

Ceramic Angels: A Story about Paying a Fee

June chose to create her digital story about an incident that happened during the annual summer festival of the municipality. The whole town was filled with people, music, market stalls and sellers. June explained that the sellers had to pay a fee for the stall which they were going to hire during the festival to sell their products. The municipality had sent the invoices in beforehand so that the payments would arrive in the municipal bank account before the festival started. "If some invoices were sent too late or if the seller came from abroad, it was ok to pay in cash. We fixed it", June commented when we ask how and if the system really worked. In practice this procedure was not without complications and exceptions. For example, if somebody had received and paid her/

his invoice so late that it was not registered in the municipal accounts system, they could just show the receipt to the civil servant in charge to prove that the payment was indeed in order. June went on to talk about a couple coming to the festival from Lithuania. For many years, without success, the same couple had applied for a market stall and this specific summer their application was finally approved. According to June their stall was located in "the cheap street", slightly apart from the heart of the festival, which meant that the fee for the stall was not that high. There were no problems with their fee and payment; they had received the invoice within a good time margin before they started their trip to Sweden. But a couple of days before the festival started a stall became available in "the expensive street", at the very heart of the festival activities. The Lithuanian couple was very happy, satisfied that they could be located in a place where they probably could sell more of their handicraft products. They just had to pay the difference in the fee between the two stalls. June's colleague, in charge of hiring the stalls, was supposed to go and meet them and collect the rest of the fee. "But the problems started", June adds. The colleague made a mobile phone call to June: "June, you have to help me! I cannot explain. Come here. She hardly speaks any English and he doesn't speak any English at all." So June sat down and wrote down the whole situation "in her best English", as she expressed it, in order to be prepared before meeting the Lithuanian couple, and to be able to explain the problem. The Lithuanian woman took June's text, and read it slowly and carefully and explained to her husband what was written on the paper, which took quite a long time. Finally, they understood what was needed and they paid the difference. So everything was organised and fixed. The municipality got their money and the Lithuanians a good stall in the festival. "And in the end, as an expression of their gratitude they gave me a huge hug and two wonderful ceramic angels", June finishes her story. And the angels she got this summer day, June still keeps in her office, on her desk.

The Ordeal: A Story about Invoices

We conducted an informal interview in June 2007 with June. At the time of the interview June had worked in the municipal accounts office. June was responsible for the invoice process and related tasks. She had worked in the accounts department for more than 20 years. Consequently June had experience of various transformation processes that had taken place in the municipality due to implementations of new technologies or new governance regimes.

The dialogue started with a reflection on the digital story she had created in the earlier workshop. We then moved to questions about how her experiences and knowledge are made visible in her office and among her colleagues. We, the researchers, related June's embodied knowledge and her thoughtfulness to today's discourses where the citizens should be at the centre, and that the municipality's aim is to offer good service to the citizens. June then told us a story about 1500 invoices that were sent out to caretakers with children in the municipal daycare system. These paper-based invoices had printed information on two pages. Usually, such an invoice consists of a single page. On the second page there was additional information about a new service, a direct debit system, that the municipality offered to the citizens and the invoice also included a demand for an extra fee of 160 Swedish crowns (SEK). June explained to us that the inclusion of this fee was a mistake. Also on the invoice was June's telephone number. What happened then was that the citizens who received the invoices with incorrect information phoned June but she also started to make phone calls on her own initiative to the people who had received these invoices. June had to deal with 400 phone calls during a single day. Some of them were not even related to the wrong information but because her phone number was

on the invoice. June told us that usually it is the number of the main switchboard that is given, but she preferred to give the direct line.

An ordeal was how June described the result of the mistake. It was a bit troublesome during these days, she continued. But the story does not end here. June's intention was to identify the source of the mistake; the two page invoice with incorrect information. What she found out was that one of her colleagues had made some changes to the text which, being longer, was thus divided into two pages. When we asked if they could have made a test print to check if the modified invoices were correct, June explained that it was not possible as the printing of the invoices was outsourced to an external company. All the invoices were stored in a file and then submitted to the company responsible for the printing, which June and her colleagues could not control.

Double Work: Stories about Learning

The first workshop was conducted in October 2005, when the participants created their maps of their work places, relations within and outside their organisation and their everyday tools. Ann, June and Kate started to talk about the extensive project they had started five years ago to move from paper based invoices to electronic invoices. As a transitional stage, they were scanning existing paper invoices. There had been a lot of discussion about the costs connected to this project; a proper scanner, for example, would cost over 60,000 Swedish crowns (SEK), and, in their decentralised organisation, they would need to purchase a large number. The local team had, however, found a cheaper solution: to use the scanning function of the photo copier. "And each department already had a photo copier" said Kate. She explained that this is the way they work: they find, by discussing with each other, local solutions to technical problems. Problems do occur even "…if there are people who think that today's technology is so advanced that there no obstacles, but there are hindrances that you have to jump over all the time", was Kate's comment.

The introduction of new systems demands acquisition of new knowledge and skills. Learning is done as a part of everyday work, but it does not necessarily mean that there is special time reserved for training and learning. Learning is added onto the existing practices and becomes just a new layer. Kate took an example from 1994, when they started to use a local server. This change meant that the routines were changed and, compared to the old way of working, everything was new. Kate told us that she even had to work during the evenings and try to find out the implications of the new system:

There was so much new – something you never done before – so you had to learn...Sometimes I had to go the office in the evenings to have a look and ask myself, well, what is this all about.? And there were times when I even sat during the night and tried to put my thoughts together...

She also explained that their organization is slimmer; all new tasks have to be done and fixed alongside the existing work tasks. No new staff will be employed.

During the discussion we asked about more formal ways of learning, such as, for example, attending courses. Ann started to explain to us that a municipality is a politically-steered organisation, consequently the priorities are made by the politicians. And the amount of money available is not endless. The core activities in which the politicians have been willing to invest money have been, and still are, school, care and health care, said Ann. And she added that the economic situation of the municipality has not been that good and this means, according to her, that a support function such as theirs cannot stick its neck out to claim that they need hundreds of thousands of crowns. "We have to set a good example", Ann stated.

As the dominant Swedish IT policy is silent about civil servants' participation in the transformation of government to e-government, as well as

the development of e-services, we want to make a difference, with a diffractive reading of the presented stories, by paying attention to various boundary-makings where diffractive patterns help us in "displaying shadows in "light" regions and bright spots in "dark" regions" (Barad, 2003, p. 803). Or in Haraway's (1997) words: "What we need is to make a difference in material-semiotic apparatuses, to diffract the rays of technoscience so that we get more promising interference patterns on the recording films of our lives and bodies." (p. 16). A diffractive methodology is also to be tuned to a lower frequency or here, to civil servants' practices and doings rather than to the dominating IT discourse. What did these stories tell us about the encounter between humans and nonhumans?

A FABRIC OF SKILLS, GENDER, LEARNING AND TECHNOLOGY

Agential realism is used in the analysis and with this framework the stories can be understood as intra-actions in which meaning and matter are entangled (Barad, 2003, 2007). We have combined a genealogical analysis with a diffracted reading of the presented stories in order to identify the involved apparatuses and intra-actions that took place in the civil servants' activities and doings. The focus has been on Barad's understanding of how matter and meaning are entangled in intra-actions. Hence intra-actions are ongoing entanglements until an agential cut is enacted, whereby humans and nonhumans come into being and obtain their meaning. We are also aware that we created cuts in the ongoing entanglements that took place in the interviews or in the workshops. Dependent on the cuts enacted in a specific moment, particular bodies came into existence. Gender performance focuses on practices where norms and values are cited, resulting in materialisation of human bodies or sexed bodies (Butler, 1993, 2004). Agential realism underscores, however, the necessity to pay attention to the materialisation of all bodies. That is, bodies that are constituted are not only human but also nonhuman. It is not only what is included but also what is excluded that has a constitutive role "in the enactments of knowledge-discourse-power practices" (Barad, 2007, p. 57). Further, subjects and objects do not pre-exist but are inseparable: they obtain their meaning when a cut is constructed. The becoming or the realities that are made visible are dependent on where the boundaries are drawn, i.e. what is included or excluded in the intra-actions. The materialisation, or when bodies achieve their meanings, takes place in ongoing reconfigurations performed in ongoing intra-actions with a range of apparatuses. Apparatuses are not just the human but are all bodies that encounter in iterative material-discursive practices.

We start with June's story about invoices. It consists of at least two iterative performances or intra-actions (Barad, 2007). The first was when the invoices were produced. The second was the reconfiguration of June's day-to-day work because of what came into being in the first iteration. We have identified a range of apparatuses included in the intra-action, such as incorrect invoices, paper, printer, software, fees, file, time, direct debit system, day-care, children, caretaker, telephone number, outsourcing, the physical distance between the civil servants and the printing office, division of labour, good service, grievances, governance regimes. The first telephone call, one among the 400 hundred, created an agential cut and without this the ongoing intra-action would probably have continued without disturbance.

The invoices and the telephone calls are the obvious apparatuses that became visible through the agential cut of the ongoing entanglement (Barad, 2007). Good service, annoyance at the demand, calls not related to the incorrect demand of 160 SEK, division of labour, new public management (governance regime) were not self-explanatory but also came into being through the cut. All apparatuses of the bodily production that came into being mattered in the performance that reconfigured June's day-to-day work as well as that of the citizens.

1500 invoices with two separate pages instead of one and, moreover, a demand for 160 SEK was what emerged out of the entanglement of meaning and matter (Barad, 2007). In addition, June's colleague who made the changes became visible, as well as an inflexible IT system that does not have a functionality to check registered changes in order to avoid mistakes.

400 telephone calls, to locate the problem that constituted the incorrect invoice and to adjust it, were the reconfigurations that mattered in June's doings. Further, knowledge and understandings were also produced in the intra-actions (Barad, 2007). June had to use her knowledge and experiences from previous performances to deal with citizens' grievances and indignation at the demand, in order to offer them good service. This is an example of how possibilities are opened up in intra-actions – they "do not sit still" (Barad, 2007, p. 234). We also refer to Haraway to explain June's doings and actions. Haraway (1994) writes: "The point is to get at how worlds are made and unmade, in order to participate in the process, in order to foster some forms of life and not others" (p. 62). June figured out what went wrong and solved it; that is, she both considered what was made and unmade. She also dealt with all the 400 telephone calls and thus took responsibility (even if she had not caused the problem), and offered good service despite grievances; she "fostered accountable forms of life".

Festival, stalls, additional costs, Lithuanian couple, language, standardised routines, flexibility, cash payment, non-English speaking colleague, being prepared, writing explanation, hugs, angels, offering good service, accountability (helping the colleague, explaining, dealing with cash), were apparatuses identified in the festival story. Cash payment was not accepted as a standard routine in the municipality (see Mörtberg, Stuedahl & Elovaara, forthcoming, for a discussion of sustainable design) but during the festival cash payment was an exception. That is, in the ongoing reconfigurations of possibilities, cash payment was an apparatus included in the material-discursive practice (the festival story) and, thereby, flexibility came to matter in the doings and actions. Consequently, where the boundaries are drawn, or what is included and excluded in intra-action, effects "what is possible at a given moment and what is impossible" (Barad, 2007, p. 234).

The governance regime was not entangled in Kate's story but the gendered division of labour in Swedish society became obvious: male carpenters and female civil servants, and also who has the preferential right of interpretation about defining the most important activity. Further, the physical distance as well as the social between groups at the office became visible through the agential cut of the ongoing entanglement. The physical and social distance mattered; Kate was constituted as a non-informed employee. Care and consideration were also materialised through the coffee ordered. Users, passwords, computers and software were also included in the intra-actions that took place in Kate's story.

The materalisation (bodies) of technologies and the bodies (materialities) of Ann, June and Kate emerge out of the intra-actions. And most of all, these materialisation processes produced positive opportunities for learning but also pressure and the stress of having to learn. Because what on the one hand opens up opportunities for ongoing learning means, on the other, that learning is something that is forced upon Ann, June and Kate. In the reconfigurations of their realities, thus in the on-going intra-actions, they learn, but the involved governance regime, the new public management, matters in such a way that they also have to manage this on top of their ordinary work tasks; hiring new employees is not an option. Learning costs – it takes time, it means extra work, it means that more has to be done with unchanged resources. Learning is not a package which smoothly delivers knowledge, but is a constant negotiation of possibilities and pressure. Learning is, to a high degree, a material and bodily practice (See e.g. Law, 2006).

The apparatus involved in the material-discursive practices presented in the stories show Ann, June and Kate demonstrating technological skillfulness as well as being innovative and creative problem solvers. Knowledge and qualification, such as how to fix the layout for the printed invoices and find cheaper scanning solutions, get their value in the day-to-day activities. They were constituted as problems because the boundaries were drawn in such a way that they have to do it. That is, boundaries are not innocent, they reconfigure practices, and come to matter (Barad, 2007). Layers of fluency were important contributed apparatuses in the material-discursive practices, that Ann, June and Kate talked about. Fluency also achieves its important meaning in everyday work, or in the making of Ann's, June's and Kate's realities. Fluency thus became a prerequisite in all encounters (intra-actions); with themselves, colleagues and citizens.

Cuts of ongoing entanglements were created when technology created problems, for example when the functionality did not allow for a print preview of changes in the invoice layout. Matter and meaning entangled in intra-actions continue without any cuts when the IT-systems in use work. This also means that the service for citizens works. Ann, June and Kate know from the past intra-actions that problems have been, and in most cases can be, solved. Possibilities (and constraints) are not given once and for all but they are "reconfigured and reconfiguring." (Barad, 2007, p. 234). Good, loving and caring governance, and non-technical experts also came into being through iterative intra-actions among civil servants (Ann, June and Kate) and other apparatuses identified in the analysis of the stories (Barad, 2007).

Innovation is often related to specific individuals but Lucy Suchman (2005) argues that: "[a] central strategy in recognizing [those] labors is to decenter sites of innovation from singular persons, places and things to multiple acts of everyday activity, including the actions through which only certain actors and associated achievements come into public view" (pp. 1-2). Innovation and creativity were also what was constituted in the materialisation in Ann's, June's and Kate's stories. Further, it was also evident how both were produced in the ongoing doings and actions where a range of apparatuses were involved. If we bring together the dominant IT discourse with its linearity and technical determinism and the situated everyday e-government practice, as told in Ann's, June's and Kate's stories, we notice that they have similar trajectories. The dominant discourse talks about effectiveness, efficiency and modernisation. These were also constituted in the intra-actions that took place in the stories. E-government emerges out of both material-discursive practices.

At the same time as there are similarities between the e-government that comes into being in the policies and the everyday practices, there are also differences. When e-government travels from the policies to a municipal office, it also means that it changes its shape (Akrich, 1992). The boundaries get drawn differently and the apparatuses included are not the same. As we have previously stated, the dominant IT-discourse draws boundaries in a way that excludes the local doers of e-government, the public sector employees. In the local stories, the identified apparatuses are situated in local practices. The apparatuses are not constant (e.g. inclusion or exclusion of cash payment) but are dependent on boundary-making practices in which some are included and others are excluded (Barad 2003, 2007). The local stories make the boundaries in the way that previous lessons are enfolded within future ones and the importance of including the knowledgeable and caring employees is demonstrated. At the local level, e-government is emerging, in intra-actions between a range of apparatuses: human and non-human. The diffractive reading of the employees' stories showed the need to have efficient IT-systems, but they also emphasise that technology does not get done by itself; it gets constituted in encounters with humans. The employees also know that e-services do not get done by technology alone, but in practices in which the participation

of humans is compulsory. The linearity expressed within the dominant discourse is not an apparatus included in the civil servants' stories but what was constituted in them was local, situated and complex everyday work.

CONCLUDING THOUGHTS

In more innocent times, long, long ago, such desire to be wordly was called activism (Haraway, 1994, p. 62).

In order to investigate the silence within the dominant Swedish IT discourse about the role of employees, and in particular, women, we have conducted a diffractive reading of some civil servants' stories using Karen Barad's agential realism. The approach, together with its notions, makes visible the materialisation of subjects and objects but also how it is impossible to separate them; how they are woven together in the practices.

Agency has been one of the key concepts in the feminist theorising and practices over the last two decades. Barad now expands the idea of agency to involve even non-human actors. She writes: "Agency is not an attribute but the ongoing reconfigurings of the world" (Barad, 2003, p. 818). Does this mean we have to say goodbye to the old dreams of empowerment? Is Barad's use of agency in conflict or is it a way to re-think agency? Our reading and understanding of Barad's use of agency is related to accountability and responsibility. This is obvious in how Barad emphasises the world's becoming and what is included and excluded in the mattering, that is, how the boundaries are drawn have consequences for what comes into being, for example, the ones our civil servants were part of. The diffractive reading made visible the civil servants and their actions and doings – how it is impossible to separate people and technology – and it also shed light on the importance of paying attention to both human and nonhuman forms of agency.

ACKNOWLEDGMENT

We wish to thank LearnIT, the research programme on learning and IT of the Knowledge Foundation of Sweden, for funding the research on which this chapter is based, through its research network Gender, Learning and IT (GLIT). And thanks also to the GLIT network for being a forum for discussion, and to Heather Owen.

REFERENCES

Akrich, M. (1992). The De-Scription of Technical Objects. Shaping Technology/Building Society: Studies in Sociotechnical Change. In Bijker, W. E., & Law, J. (Eds.), *Shaping Technology Bulding Society Studies in Sociotechnical Change* (pp. 205–224). Cambridge, MA: MIT Press.

Barad, K. (1999). Agential Realism. Femininist Interventions in Understandings Scientific Practice. In Biagioli, M. (Ed.), *The Science Studies Reader* (pp. 1–11). London: Routledge.

Barad, K. (2003). Post-humanist performativity: Toward an understanding of how matter comes to matter. Signs. *Journal of Women in Culture and Society, 28*(3), 801–831. doi:10.1086/345321

Barad, K. (2007). *Meeting the universe halfway: Quantum physics and the entanglement of matter and meaning*. Durhamn, NC: Duke University Press.

Bødker, K., Kensing, F., & Simonsen, J. (2004). *Participatory IT Design. Designing for Business and Workplace Realities*. Cambridge, MA: MIT Press.

Butler, J. (1990). *Gender Trouble: feminism and the subversion of identity*. London: Routledge.

Butler, J. (1993). *Bodies that Matter: on the discursive limits of 'sex*. New York: Routledge.

Butler, J. (2004). *Undoing Gender*. New York: Routledge.

Elovaara, P. (2004). *Angels in unstable sociomaterial relations: Stories of information technology*. Doctoral Dissertation. Karlskrona: Blekinge Institute of Technology.

Handlingsplan för eFörvaltning (2008) [The Action Plan for eGovernment]. Stockholm: Näringsdepartementet. Retrieved February, 2008, from http://www.sweden.gov.se/content/1/c6/09/65/12/4ffd1319.pdf

Haraway, D. J. (1991). *Simians, cyborgs, and women: The reinvention of nature*. London: Routledge.

Haraway, D. J. (1994). A Game of Cat's Cradle: Science studies, feminist theory, cultural studies. *Configurations, 2*(1), 59–71. doi:10.1353/con.1994.0009

Haraway, D. J. (1997). *Modest_witness@second_millenium. Female man©_meets_oncomouse™: Feminism and technoscience*. London: Routledge.

Haraway, D. J. (1999). The promesis of monsters: A regenerative politics for inappropriate/d others. In J. Wolmark (Ed) Cybersexualities: a reader on feminist theory, cyborgs and cyberspace (pp. 314-366). Edinburgh, UK: Edinburgh Univ. Press.

Hooks, B. (2000). Feminism is for Everybody: passionate politics. Cambridge MA: South End Press.

Karasti, H. (2001). *Increasing sensitivity towards everyday work practice in system design*. Doctoral Dissertation. Oulu: Oulun Yliopisto.

Law, J. (2004). *After method: Mess in social science research*. London: Routledge.

Law, J. (2006). Pinboards and Books: Juxtaposing, Learning and Materiality. Retrieved February, 2008, from http://www.heterogeneities.net/publications/pinboardsandbooks.pdf

Messer-Davidow, E. (1995). Acting Otherwise. In Kegan Gardiner, J. (Ed.), *Provoking agents: gender and agency in theory and practice* (pp. 23–51). Urbana, IL: University of Illinois Press.

Mörtberg, C. (1997). *'Det beror på att man är kvinna-': gränsvandrerskor formas och formar informationsteknologi.* ['It's because one is a woman...' Transgressors are shaped and shape information technology]. Doctoral Dissertation. Luleå: Luleå tekniska universitet.

Mörtberg, C., Stuedahl, D., & Elovaara, P. (forthcoming). Designing for Sustainable Ways of Living with Technologies. In Wagner, I., Bratteteig, T., & Stuedahl, D. (Eds.), *Exploring digital design multi-disciplinary design practices.* London: Springer.

Pollit, C., & Bouchaert, G. (2004). *Public management reform. A comparative analysis* (2nd ed.). Oxford, UK: University Press.

Regeringens proposition (1999-2000):86, *Informationssamhälle för alla* [Government Bill 1999/2000:86, Information Society for All]. Stockholm, Regeringen. Retrieved February, 2008, from http//:www.regeringen.se

SOU 2003:55, *Digitala tjänster – hur då?* [Digital Services- How?]. Retrieved February, 2008, from http//:www.regeringen.se

Star, S. L., & Strauss, A. (1999). Layers of silence, arenas of voice: The ecology of visible and invisible work. *Computer Supported Cooperative Work, 8*(1/2), 9–30. doi:10.1023/A:1008651105359

Suchman, L. (2005). *Agencies in technology design: Feminist reconfigurations.* Retrieved February, 2008, from http://www.lancs.ac.uk/fass/sociology/papers/suchman-agenciestechnodesign.pdf

Suchman, L. (2007). *Human-machine reconfigurations: plans and situated actions* (2nd ed.). Cambridge, UK: Cambridge University Press.

Tuuva-Hongisto, S. (2007). *Tilattuja tarinoita: etnografinen tutkimus pohjoiskarjalaisesta tietoyhteiskunnasta.* [Negotiated stories of the information technology: en ethnographic study of the Northcarelian information society]. Doctoral Dissertation. Joensuu: Joensuun yliopisto.

Wajcman, J. (2004). *Technofeminism.* Cambridge, UK: Polity Press.

KEY TERMS AND DEFINITIONS

Agency: This has mostly been related to women's and men's positions and spaces in public arenas, their possibilities to influence decisions and how this affects their everyday lives, possibilities and resources accessible to them, and how asymmetrical power relations are intertwined in actions and doings. In (feminist) science and technology studies (STS), agency is no longer the privilege of human forms of agency but attention is also paid to nonhuman forms of agency. Agency is, then, ongoing reconfigurations of practices (worlds) with co-habitation, co-operation, collaboration, communication and participation taking place in intra-actions with humans and non-humans.

Agential Realism: An epistemological and ontological approach with a focus on the entanglement of meaning and matter and how specific intra-action comes into existence – becomes matter. The entanglement take place in ongoing intra-actions until an agential cut is enacted and breaks the entanglement. Subjects and objects are inseparable in intra-actions; they do not pre-exist but come into being and obtain their meaning when an agential cut is enacted. Material-discursive practices are used to pay attention not only to language (discourses) but also to materiality, how meaning and matter are entangled, and how they matter in doings and actions. In agential realism accountability is related to the world's becoming, produced in boundary-making practices, thus in ongoing intra-actions with a range of apparatuses (humans and nonhumans). Boundaries are not innocent but are discursively and materially enacted, and this includes or excludes apparatuses that meet in intra-actions. Performativity, in agential realism, is intra-action or entanglement with inseparable entities.

Cartography: A method of describing practices through cartographic exercises or mappings. The mapping produces a rich picture of all activities in a practice and results in maps of a practice, of familiar objects and subjects, cooperation and communication within and outside the practice and so forth. The method does not require preparation in advance. The tools are simple, cheap and familiar such as coloured paper; images; tapes; scissors; catalogues with pictures of desks, computers, printers, faxes, telephones, post-it notes, binders, etc.

E-Government: An overall concept used in the transformation process of the public sector based on information technology. e-administration, e-service, and e-democracy are three central aspects within the overall concept. Rationalisation, efficiency and effectiveness are leading signs in the process that is characterised as a modernisation process. Another is the aim of creating a good–service society.

Gender Performance: An understanding of gender. Gender does not pre-exist but is an activity or a kind of becoming. Gender comes into existence in actions and doings in which existing norms and values are cited in repeated activities. Norms and values are reproduced or questioned in the performances (citational practices) resulting in materialisation of human bodies or sexed bodies.

Intra-Action: A central concept in agential realism and is used to underscore the inseparability between subjects and objects, humans and machines, the social and the material. The inseparability is an example of how human-nonhuman entanglements have implications for how we understand subjects and objects, or, rather, how they come into being or are reconfigured in encounters. Intra-actions reconfigure possibilities and constraints in particular boundary-making practices, doings, or actions.

Knowledge: Not objective but is created in particular practices (material-semiotic, material-discursive or sociomaterial). Situated knowledge is to characterise production of knowledge, its heterogeneity, and instability, and also how knowledge builds on the past, is always partial, located and situated somewhere. Knowing and being intersect in knowledge-production practices; they are not stable but come into being in doings and actions – in intra-actions.

Learning: Takes place in formal settings, in day-to-day activities and doings, and in reconfigurations of practices (realities). It is a kind of becoming that emerges out of material-discursive practices or in entanglements of meaning and matter. Learning is also a material and bodily practice.

ENDNOTES

1. See for example SOU 2003:55, RegProp 1999/2000:125, Handlingsplan för eFörvaltning, 2008

2. The research project was part of GLIT-network, funded by the Foundation of Knowledge and Competence and LearnIT

3. http://www.storycenter.org/memvoice/pages/cookbook.html

4. Karen Barad has developed and elaborated the notion diffraction in her book Meeting The Universe Halfway Quantum Physics and The Entaglemant of Matter and Meaning (2007).

5. Karen Barad uses material-discursive, Lucy Suchman sociomaterial and Donna Haraway material semiotic to underscore the entanglement of humans and nonhumans.

Chapter 6
Against All Odds, From All-Girls Schools to All-Boys Workplaces:
Women's Unsuspecting Trajectory into the UK ICT Sector

Marie Griffiths
University of Salford, UK

Helen Richardson
University of Salford, UK

ABSTRACT

The trend for women to be severely under-represented in the UK ICT (information and communication technology) sector persists. Girls continue, year in year out, to excel in academia whilst initiatives are put in place to challenge the gender employment gap in ICT[1] professions. As part of a larger research study of women in the ICT labour market, over 500 women were asked about their initial routes into ICT; this included educational backgrounds, influential factors and perceptions of that transition. In analysing the findings we attempt to explain the tendency for women in our sample group to come from single-sex schools and to have a predilection for mathematics and the sciences, then move into male dominated educational and work environments. Our findings report on the personal experiences of women's unsuspecting trajectory into the UK ICT sector.

INTRODUCTION

There is a declining minority of women taking ICT and technology related subjects at school and University in the UK and the numbers of ICT professionals in the labour market are similarly at an all time low comprising around 15% (EOC 2004). Women ICT students are commonly a small minority and experience similar isolation in higher education. Often

excluded, facing direct and indirect discrimination, stereotyping, with barriers to advancement (Adam et al 2006), research indicates that women leave the ICT profession in disproportionate numbers (Platman and Taylor 2004) vowing never to return (Griffiths et al 2007). So an interesting question remains: why do women study and work in ICT at all? This chapter draws on empirical work from six research projects completed during 2004-2006 that investigated the severe under-representation

DOI: 10.4018/978-1-61520-813-5.ch006

of women in ICT professions[2] Research has suggested that the backgrounds and entry routes of women ICT professionals are diverse and unpredictable (Webster 2005) and include women who excelled in maths and science or those with support from parents or a particular teacher. Accidental encounters with computers have often been the root of a passionate interest and rather than being alienated from technology many have been attracted to the opportunities of analytical problem solving and the creativeness of the work (Webster 2005). Faulkner (2005) discussing the entry routes of women engineers found them to be often 'unusual' women, rebellious, remarkable, those who were seeking a challenge but always with a story to tell.

In this chapter we tell the stories of the experiences of 14 women of the 500 plus ICT professionals in the UK who participated in our research. Against all odds many developed a passion for working with computers often stemming from experiences at home and in single-sex education. Their routes into the ICT profession are varied and generally involve experiencing a shock when moving to University classes or workplaces where for the first time they experience themselves as one of very few women. We examine studies that have advocated all-girls schooling as a counter to the 'masculine domain' of technology education (Clegg 2001), yet the 'jury is still out' (Speilhofer et al 2002) on whether this is a significant factor informing gendered career choices. In this chapter we present rich descriptions of women's trajectories into the ICT labour market and an opportunity for interesting stories of – in our view - remarkable women to be heard. We firstly outline the situation of women in the UK ICT labour market and introduce some issues related to technological education and single sex schooling. We then develop specific themes from our case study research informed by social and structural influences (Adya and Kaiser 2005) that have shaped women's career trajectories. Social influence for example involves gender stereotyping and the influence of teachers, families and media. Structural influences include institutional support and access to technology and opportunities.

WOMEN IN ICT IN THE UK LABOUR MARKET

Employment in the ICT sector has continued to grow significantly in recent years and e-Skills UK (2008) have predicted that it will grow at 2.5% per annum, which is five times faster than the average employment growth of the UK. However this growth has not led to a parallel increase in women's participation in the ICT labour market. Women's employment figures in ICT are in decline, despite twenty years of continuous efforts and concerns of policy makers and gender equality practitioners (Webster 2005). Given that there have been decades of equal opportunity and related policies as well as many government initiatives designed to address the gender imbalance in ICT employment patterns, sex segregation in ICT occupations and a gender pay gap in the ICT sector, we could be forgiven for assuming that these initiatives have had a beneficial effect on the position and number of women in the ICT workforce. However, although we cannot make any comment on the success or failure of any specific initiatives the statistics continue to highlight that women are hemorrhaging out of the UK ICT workforce (Platman and Taylor 2004). The so-called 'leaky pipeline' for women in technology employment (Sanders 2005) is contributed to by various factors. There is often a requirement for 24/7 (24 hours and 7 days a week) presenteeism (a phrase meaning the social/peer pressure to be seen to be at work beyond the call of duty and beyond contract stipulations, possibly to improve promotion prospects) raising issues about work-life balance for women (Tattersall and Keogh 2006). Women can also experience hostility and isolation at work (Adam et al 2006) and significant events can trigger an exodus (Griffiths et al 2007).

Concerns are also being raised regarding gender diversity in the ICT sector given that the percentage of women in ICT has fallen, from around 27% in 1997, 21% in 2004, to about 16% in 2006 (e-Skills 2008, Platman and Taylor 2004). An associated concern is that 61% of those women working within the ICT industry are clustered at the lower end of the salary scale with limited promotion opportunities (e-Skills 2008). In the UK, the Office of National Statistics (ONS) statistics indicate that women accounted for 30% of ICT operations technicians, but a mere 15% of ICT Managers and only 11% of ICT strategy and planning professionals (EOC 2004). This is a classic case of vertical gender segregation with women more strongly represented in lower level ICT occupations than in higher status and higher paid arenas (EOC 2004). Clegg (2001) describes how feminists have been trying to untangle the knots to understand why, when women were the first programmers, they became marginalized as low-paid end-users and massively under-represented in Higher Education. She discusses how schools and universities help shape the meanings of technologies and reproduce gendered expectations about their use and capacities; concluding that 'gender is the key dynamic in understanding the present educational meanings of computing' (Clegg 2001 p313). In the next section we discuss key aspects of technology education and the debates around impacts of single sex schooling.

Technology Education and Single Sex Schooling

Single-sex schooling continues to stimulate intense discussions: by parents and educators regarding current practices and choices for their children and by those who have experienced single sex education first hand and have conflicting opinions. Regardless of the actual educational dichotomy - single-sex versus co-ed[3] - this issue also questions the social implications of gender separation and the long-term effects this may have on individuals whether negative or positive. It is generally accepted that single-sex education is thought to reduce sexually stereotyped subject choices and to be academically advantageous for girls (e-Skills 2008, Curtis 2009, DfES 2007). Out of a total population of 3.5 million school age children only 221,000 girls and 160,000 are educated in single sex state secondary schools in the UK (Curtis 2009).

A recent analytical study conducted by the Good Schools Guide (in Curtis 2009) of over 700,000 UK state sector educated girls' GSCE scores, reinforces an existing body of research suggesting that girls progressed better in single sex schools (Speilhofer et al 2002, Sullivan 2008, Curtis 2009). Findings from the study show that girls' who attended single–sex schools, all attained better results than their predicted outcomes and 20% of the girls who took their GCSEs in co-ed schools achieved worse than was expected. Further analysis also suggested that girls at the lower end of the ability range benefited most from single sex education. Recent research found that girls with the lowest test scores at the start of their secondary education made the greatest improvements in single-sex schools.

The polarisation of physics and languages between the sexes in comprehensive schools[4] is greater in mixed-sex schools than single-sex schools (Sullivan 2008). Girls in single-sex schools were more likely to study 'resistant materials' and single subject science courses and less likely to study 'food technology'; which appears to counter traditional stereotyping. In the same study girls from single-sex schools had a greater chance of being entered for higher tier key stage 3 maths and science exams than peers in mixed comprehensives. The greatest difference was in science examinations, with girls in single-sexed schools having a 40% greater chance to be entered into higher tier examinations. There is some evidence to show that boys and girls in single-sex schools are less likely to hold gender-stereotypical views about science subjects compared to children attending co-educational schools. Some supporters of single sex schooling say gendered norms of behaviour are more strictly enforced in mixed schools – it is therefore harder for girls to show interest and ability in maths in mixed schools. Advocates of single sex schooling for girls suggest that girls self esteem is better fostered in a single sex environment because boys dominate the class-room in a mixed environment especially in maths and science subjects (Sullivan 2008). We now turn to more specific themes raised by social and structural influences on women's career trajectories in ICT.

Social Influences

Early experience of the use of information and communication technologies in the home and school shapes attitudes towards them (Richardson and French 2002), representing what Clegg (2001) describes as a 'love affair between men and machine'. When computers entered the home they were targeted at boys and males hobbyists (Kirkup and Abbot 1997). Evidence today suggests that boys still have more access to home computing than girls and that parents favour boys over girls in issues of access (Habid and Cornford, 2001; Na 2001). It has been suggested that males using a computer in the home thus become primed at an early age to believe that 'computers constitute a naturalised part of male heterosexual identity' (Clegg 2001 p314). Research continues to suggest that this introduction to computing has led to teenage boys and girls having different attitudes to computing: Na (2001) suggests boys view it as a toy whilst girls view it as a tool; an indication perhaps of why boys may be more attracted to computers.

A reluctance by girls to embrace the computer was perceived as a problem of girl's confidence or alternatively boys behaving badly rather than rooted within the technology (Clegg 2001). It is rarely understood fully and taken into account that social issues may contribute to attitudes

to technology in schools. As Clegg suggests, 'ICT's in the curriculum needs to be examined in terms of their social meaning and contribution to pedagogy rather than in the way it is currently being deployed in the rhetoric of the information society' (Clegg, 2001 p319). The continued lack of women lecturers and teachers may serve to reinforce the idea that technology is not for girls, (Richardson and French 2002). Evidence suggests that children perceive their mothers and female teachers to be less competent with technology than their male counterparts (Sanger et al, 1997). This may relate to what Green and Adam (1998) refer to as the gendered social relation of domesticity, which surrounds the use of ICTs. Moreover, Richardson and French (2002) suggest that women view computers in the home as a shared family resource; they don't prioritise their own use or access to them; whereas men are more likely to see a computer as belonging to them and therefore prioritise their access in the home. Although currently there are often many different devices situated in the domestic setting nevertheless the home remains an arena where scarce resources have to be competed for.

Earlier research conducted over twenty years ago identified gender differences in attitudes and use of computers of children at this time, these children are now part of the current workforce. Siann et al. (1988) found that boys were more positive towards computers and were more confident in using computers than girls. It was estimated that 80% of home computers in the UK were bought for boys (Hoyles, 1985) and it was acknowledged at that time in both the UK and in the USA that computer clubs at schools were dominated by boys. Siann et al (1988) also found gender differences even at the age of 6 and 7 years old. They found that girls were less interested and more prepared than boys to accept direction and help from others in their use of computers. Boys were consistently found to use home computers more frequently and for more applications (Siann et al., 1988; Mumtaz, 2001) with boys' level of use of home ICT remaining fairly constant with age whilst girls' use steadily declined as they got older (Comber et al 1997). In the 21st century there are more devices in UK homes and uses of ICT has changed, nevertheless the pattern of male and female participation remains unequal. In the Oxford Internet Survey 2009, for example, about Internet use in Britain more males than females are active in all the reported areas including checking emails, using instant messaging, gaming, downloading music and videos, reading and writing a blog, participating in chat rooms and using Skype. The only area that females matched their male counterparts was in participation in social networking (Dutton et al., 2009).

Structural Influences

Education often perpetuates issues in the home and plays a part in gendering our social worlds (Evans, 1994). Schools, according to Clegg (2001) become a primary site for the reproduction of gendered meanings in society. Social relations in the home can be transferred to the school environment. Early school computers were usually bought and controlled by male teachers in the maths and science subject areas. This positioning of computing alongside science and maths, areas dominated by boys, has disadvantaged girls. As Clegg (2001) suggests, girls as a result are 'already ideologically positioned as outsiders' (2001 p314). Thus we further marginalise girls' position in school in relation to gender and technology and the shaping of the curriculum. Teachers of ICT were often male hobbyists from the science and maths subject areas and despite computing now being seen as a communication tool embracing different media and ubiquitous in the office this perception of a computer as a scientific problem-solving machine remains. This shaping of computer education continues after schooling. As Clegg (2001) suggests universities are key sites where the meaning of computing as a discipline was forged. They placed a strong

emphasis on formal and mathematical methods, artificial intelligence and computer science. This perhaps is one explanation why girls are a much larger proportion of students taking ICT A level compared to computer science A level with a perception that ICT also involves communication and more social and collective skills and activities. Selby et al. (1997) suggest that computer orientated careers have an image of being nerdy, geeky, anti-social, machine-orientated, and solitary. This message that computing is not a place for girls is then perhaps transferred from school to university, to career choices.

Siann (1997 p120) suggests that women and girls are saying 'I can, but I don't want to'; they are choosing to opt out of ICT study and careers. So as Clegg (2001) points out, women are marginalized not because of lack of confidence but because their generally preferred way of working with computers is marginalized and what is presented to them is unattractive. Although clearly not a global experience, nevertheless our research concurs with the work of Newmarch et al. based in New South Wales in Australia who, investigating the male culture of ICT, suggested that it is not necessarily computers and technology per se that girls avoid but the competitive male environment of the field (Newmarch et al., 2000). Many UK girls today enjoy using the Internet, playing adventure and simulation games and using email and other communication tools. Numbers of girls studying computing in schools are also increasing, but in post secondary education and in career choices UK girls are still not interested in IT. The Australian study found similar experiences to the UK with sex-role stereotyping, cultural influences and the image of the industry as 'blokey' and 'nerdy', so putting girls off (Newmarch et al., 2000). Furthermore, teachers are significant in shaping pupil's early perceptions so the presentation of the subject in schools is an issue as is poor teacher knowledge of the ICT industry. Research studies conducted in the UK involving primary school teachers reflect these concerns. One study of 36 teachers observed a lack of integration in using ICT to support teaching and learning across the curriculum, with heavy use of word processing which was considered boring by the pupils (Mumtaz (2001). Dunn and Ridgeway (1991) add to this the notion of the *silo* approach to teaching ICT; in other words ICT was not integrated into the curriculum but was taught as a rigidly separate discipline in their study of 137 student teachers and their observations of ICT exposure in the classroom. 'A depressing picture begins to emerge of a 'Noah's Ark' style of teaching, where children go two-by-two for their weekly dose of computing, which is an activity isolated from the rest of their work' (Dunn and Ridgeway, 1991 p238). A consideration from this study is that these school children in 1991 would now be new entries into the workforce.

What then are the consequences of this teaching approach to ICT in primary education? Recent research shows that girls do better than boys at GCSE by nearly 10 percentage points (e-Skills. 2008). In mathematics, there has been a shift since 1991 from male advantage to a slim female advantage. Girls are more likely to take arts, languages, and humanities whilst boys take geography, physical education and ICT - but even boys are showing reluctance to study ICT. So although girls surpass boys in the UK in educational attainment, gaps in what is studied in higher education evidences the persistence of gendered self concepts. At Advanced level[5] study in schools girls' most popular choice is English whilst boys' is maths (DfES, 2007). Girls are significantly under represented on ICT A-level courses but they consistently out performed males in terms of results (e-Skills, 2008).

There has been a 50% reduction in applicants to computer related degree courses in the UK over the last 5 years while the total number of applicants on to all UK degree courses has increased by 12% over the same five year period (e-Skills, 2008). The drop off in numbers of students studying A-level computing is reflected the

numbers doing computing degrees where there has been a 45% decrease from 2004-2008. This falling student interest in computing - a subject area that has strategic importance to the overall economy - and a continuing gender imbalance needs further consideration by educators, future employers, and government agencies. e-Skills (2008) argues that there is a confusion, that needs addressing, regarding subject matter and terminology with students believing wrongly that the GCSE curriculum somehow reflects ICT-related university courses and also ICT careers. We now describe our research which reflects on women's experiences in education that have shaped their career choices in the UK ICT sector.

CASE STUDY – METHODOLOGY AND DESIGN

As part of the gender and ICT research carried out at the at The University of Salford (UK) over 500 women contributed to six research projects via three online questionnaires and in-depth interviews. Generally, the sample was self-selected as the women contacted the research team through news releases, a websites (www.iris.salford.ac.uk/GRIS/) and word of mouth. The projects ran from January 2004 until December 2006 and were partially funded by the European Social Fund (ESF). A broad range of research instruments were adopted, including online questionnaires, life history interviews, blogs, sketches and life history calendars. For the purpose of the chapter, we will be extracting data from the life history interviews where women spoke of their educational experiences prior to entering the ICT sector. It was understood from the outset of the research process that the women who volunteered usually had a story to recall about some event or period of time that they considered worthy to be heard by others. One interviewee referred to the process as 'cathartic' and many of the women became emotional (including on occasions the interviewers) when recalling painful episodes from their past. The interview approach we adopted was not a 'search and discovery mission' and the women involved were not perceived as mere repositories of knowledge for the taking (Jarvinen, 2000) but rather the interviews were understood as the interviewees' constructions of knowledge in association with the interviewer. Wagner and Wodak (2006 p392) note that biographical narratives are almost episodic interviews in that when an interview stimulates memories it acts to construct 'significant episodes' which can illustrate how certain events contributed to the shaping of personal biographies.

Part of our interview strategy for all the projects was to ask women participants prior to the interviews to reflect upon their ICT careers. We suggested that participants recall events in their work-life histories in a chronological manner, usually starting from their educational background to the present day. Such a structured process helps establish meaning for both the interviewee and the listener. A (visual) sketch of the interviewee's life history was also requested, a pre-interview task which initiated the recalling of past events for these women. Other women were asked to complete life-history calendars. Some interviewees commented that this was the first time in years or ever that they had 'returned' and plotted the career trajectories invoking painful memories for some. Throughout the interview process certain events were probed and then explored in more detail and in some instances the women were encouraged to elaborate on what they had highlighted as key events in their ICT careers. There was a tendency for domestic events to be used as markers of time to order the recall of work related events; the women constructed their work histories alongside or intermingled with their life stories, talking of events such as pregnancy, change in job roles, periods of illness, geographical relocations and so on. Customarily each of our interviewees started the interview process off by recalling their educational background including secondary school, college or university.

As part of the autobiography interview process women were asked to explain first their educational history, what type of schools they attended and if they studied A Levels, in what subjects. Higher education was also a key topic as the majority of the women included in the study attended university at some stage, either straight from school or once they had had their families. We were also interested in their educational decision processes: who or what influenced them on their trajectory of a career in ICT? We found that the majority of our interviewees had attended single-sex schools. These findings correspond to those of the WWW-ICT project which notes, 'In the UK a considerable part of women with careers in ICT come from all female secondary schools' (WWW-ICT 2004 p52). The women in our sample range from 25 years old into retirement age and we acknowledge that the UK educational system has radically altered over the past fifty years. Their educational circumstances are also diverse ranging from attending fee-paying single sex schools to mixed sex comprehensives. However, interestingly comparable educational experiences were recalled by both young and older women who work in the UK ICT sector.

What Influenced Study and Career Choices – Stories From the Field

Adya and Kaiser (2005) have produced a useful research review of the social and structural influences that can affect career choice positively and negatively. Social influences can include gender stereotyping with teachers influencing the shaping of roles and choices through their interaction. In this way role models can influence choice as can the way women are represented in the media (Blomqvist, 2007; and see also Blomqvist chapter in this book) where research shows rampant gender stereotypes about people in technical roles. Parents and families are important influences with factors including whether both parents are working and educated to degree level being important. Structural influences include the institutional support available from teachers and careers advisors for example, and access to technology at home and in school. Within structural influences the issue of same-sex versus co-educational schooling plays a part. In this section we reflect on these influences and describe the experiences of some of the women who participated in our research. Names have been changed to ensure anonymity.

Social Influences

Despite computing and ICT involving a range of knowledge and skills, its roots and origins as a mathematical based discipline persists and a majority of our participants became ICT professionals after a grounding in and passion for mathematics. Gail absolutely loved maths and exams for her *'were like a gladiator going into combat and I loved it'*. Although research finds a marked tendency 'to view maths as a symbolically male domain' (Brandell and Staberg, 2008 p495), nevertheless many women noted a passion for maths from an early age. Parvinda said *'I always loved maths from about 3 or 4 years old, it just one of those things it was my favourite subject always.'* Lisa decided where to start with her story about going into ICT, *'Well let's go all the way back to when I was about eight or nine. I liked maths. Maths was my favourite subject'.* Dana recalls, *'erm at school I was always really really good at maths, very logical, good at maths it was just understood and expected that Dana would set the maths world alive in some way'.* Sometimes however participants felt they should temper their passion. Gail the 'gladiator' continued *'I loved it but I learnt to shut up because most people didn't'.*

Adya and Kaiser (2005) found that that parents, particularly fathers, are a key influencers of girls' choice of ICT careers and also that early access to computers may reduce intimidation towards technology. Our study certainly has echoes of these trends as Gloria's father was a computer science teacher, Gail's parents were both maths

teachers, Laila had a computer at home from an early age that was used for gaming and Meredith also had a father who was a scientist. Chloe's parents were both software engineers. Sometimes fathers wanted daughters to follow in their footsteps. Parvinda's father was science orientated but never had a chance to pursue science as a career and he wanted her to be a doctor so she *'just let him rave and I came up with this idea, I said 'oh I need to know about computers for work so if I come down every week could you give me tuition you know so I can keep abreast of things'.*

When trying to establish what career direction she should take Juliet looked towards her family for guidance - her father was an electrical engineer and she had expected to follow in his footsteps as this area had also interested her *'I was more influenced by what I thought my family had done'.* ICT was not an option at this stage, the family had a computer *'a BBC Acorn something like that'* at home but it was viewed in an entertainment role rather than a career option. Kay was encouraged throughout her childhood by school teachers but especially her father to pursue a degree in mathematics. She considered herself to have a logical mind and enjoyed that aspect of maths. Carole noticed that her own daughter viewed maths as *'a boy thing'* but as a child she grew up with four brothers *'so frankly I was as good as them as far as I was concerned'* and didn't find the mathematical attribution of ICT as a barrier.

Many of the women remember computers at home and for Mosa her interest in computing began as a hobby and she changed her career from Medical Lab work to ICT *'I was just doing it [computing] as a hobby, it just fascinated me but what I began to realise in work was that computers were beginning to take a very important role in medical labs. I'd finished my fellowship and the only option at that point for me to do was to go on and do it was some kind of managerial laboratory management course. I just had no interest in that whatsoever and I approached my sort of Head of Department and said would you fund me to go to college and do computing'*. Lisa remembers computer gaming at home *'we had a computer at home, playing games on it, did a bit of messing about....my brother used to play lots of games but it just wasn't there for me really.... and then the first job I got...that's when I first started to use computers for anything other than playing games really'*.

For one of the women in the study: Freda - at the time of the research enjoying a successful career in a rapidly expanding telecommunication company - computing was not the first choice of degree. Educated at an all-girl's fee-paying school her parent hoped she would continue the family tradition and become a doctor but poor exam results stopped these aspirations. Her parents encouraged a vocational degree so ensuring employability at the end of the course but Freda hated the first year from an academic point of view because it was so technical. As the course progressed the business and strategy aspects interested her much more but she was at a loss to know how these skills could be transferred into the workplace. This reiterates research findings regarding the inefficiencies in presentation and application of ICT and career opportunities. However in Freda's case this confusion or serendipity guided her decision to join a graduate scheme at a multinational ICT consultancy with a view to sample different aspects of ICT.

Structural Influences

Same-sex schooling could be described as an arena comparatively devoid of male-female comparisons and so where there is less pressure to conform to gender role stereotypes. However sex-segregation can also reinforce stereotypes and 'squander opportunities to address issues of gender equity' (Adya and Kaiser, 2005 p238). Given that the majority of women (more than 90%) we spoke to attended single sex schools there was little evidence of the reinforcement of sex-stereotyping regarding what subjects were

taken. Rather many women recalled a distinctive 'can-do' ethos. ICT, mathematics and the sciences were not framed as 'masculine' subjects but sat equally alongside English, Languages or History as Lola illustrates *'I went to a girls' school. ICT wasn't seen as a boys' subject, science wasn't a boys' subject. There weren't boys' subjects, they were just subjects.'* Further confirmation of this countering attitude against sex stereotyping in single sexed schools is given by Gloria who adds, *'I was fortunate, in that I went to a selective, independent girls school...and I went there from the age of 11, and when I was there it was, basically, anything you wanted to do you could do. There were no blockers or anything, and we were pretty much taught that all the way through'*. This she explained contributed to her continued passion for computing. Anita experienced something similar *'we were taught I think that basically anything you could do you could do.....because we taught by women you know'*. With many of the women attending single-sex schools it often was a surprise for them when they studied maths or computer science at University: Dana made the observation *'I had gone out with boys in my private life you know had relationships with boys but to actually have one next to me in class was a real shock. It took me about a month to get over it'*. Kay found herself as one of only two women *'in a sea of men'* at university. Rhonda also recounts how she found herself amongst *'a sea of young male kids in leather jackets'*. Lisa found it *'a bit of a surprise going from an all-girls'* school to being one of only two girls in a hundred students in engineering. *'But it never fazed me. I was a Venture Scout so I was used to being in a minority there, so no, it didn't faze me'*.

Another theme in the stories of some women in our interview sample is that of determination to pursue an interest and love of computers and ICT, often in the face of negative and dismissive attitudes from others when in the ICT sector, whether from more senior male colleagues, line managers, teachers, careers advisors or by their parents before they entered the sector. Juliet was discouraged from pursuing a career in ICT right from an early age. She says, '*It was a pretty circuitous route, well, how I got here. I didn't join IT straight from school. I was interested in IT at school but at that time it was a very new industry and I was strongly steered away from it by all concerned, by my careers advisor, my father, everybody*'. Anita joined a small maths department and was surprised how few women students there were - by the end of the course she was the only one left '*in those days people tended to be rather formal to students, so all the men were just called by their surname whereas women were 'Miss Something' you know, so obviously there was that difference and I actually find my supervisor looking back, I had a very bad experience though I didn't realise at the time. I had a supervisor who would rather I hadn't been doing his subject*'. Maxine was interested in ICT at school but was not encouraged '*the image presented at careers conventions were white coats and that IT was a technical, masculine sphere*'. Careers advisors often act as 'gatekeepers' and discourage women. As Ayisha described: '*I remember going into a careers interview when I was at University... this man telling me that doing mathematical physics in industry [the obvious thing for me]...I would not be happy in industry, I ought to be a teacher. I shouldn't even think of it, I ought to be a teacher, it was my bounden duty or something [laughter]*'. It was also assumed Charlotte was going to pursue a teaching career, '*So I went into teaching experience, which again girls could do, they could teach, and I absolutely hated it. I just wanted to get into IT somehow*' which is the career direction she eventually took.

However positive experiences at school were encouraging. A number of women entered the ICT sector as a result of serendipitous events at school. Parvinda said: '*I went to a girls grammar school....it was quite a science based and I found that everyone else was going to university......so I followed, I followed everyone else*'. Charlotte recalls '*so maths was my subject and I was going to go into teaching and basically it was at school and I remember you could go on one of these career days and I went, it was literally the very start of IT, and I went into this company... and I thought wow, this looks different, you know it looked really nice*'. Bel was also guided through school and encouraged to attend a '*2 day course on an Elliot 803 Computer (at a local firm) .... well it goes back a long way..... it was one of those machines with valves and it sort of needed people with white coats in attendance.....my head mistress asked was I interested in going on this course so I thought why not so I went and I found it absolutely fascinating*'. Bel ended up as a senior manager in a major software house. Our 'remarkable women' therefore reinforce the research highlighted by Adya and Kaiser (2005) reflecting the social and structural influences that can affect career choice.

CONCLUSION

Our research focused on women moving in, moving on and moving out of the UK ICT sector. Some of the women followed a direct route in whilst others took a more indirect route. However for the purpose of this chapter the focus is primarily upon women 'moving in'. Interesting common themes emerged from this self-selective sample of women regardless of their demographical backgrounds. Significantly each woman had an early and earnest passion for maths, science or technology and a tendency to excel in that subject area at school. This passion and proficiency was mostly encouraged by parents, sometimes teachers and the younger of the women recall using computers in their domestic settings. The majority of the women also attended single-sex schools and a 'can-do' ethos prevailed. Many of the women mention it was only on entering University that they realised that they had become the minority in a 'sea of men'. An obvious common theme was that the majority of the sample group had not been either discouraged from studying ICT or their passion had not yet waned before they entered the ICT sector. However this is in stark contrast to a recent report where a majority of teachers, careers advisors and parents participating in a large European study still regarded ICT study and careers to be more suited to men (Gras-Velazquez et al., 2009).

We do not make claims that these findings, from one part of a much larger project on women in the UK ICT sector, to be conclusive. This chapter is intended only to highlight specific themes in women's entry trajectories into the ICT sector that continue to emerge decade after decade. We note with dismay the wealth of research contributing to debates on gender and technology and experiences of girls at home and throughout their education and yet little has been acted upon and little positive change is evident. Research conducted ten, twenty and even thirty years ago about children and the educational system is now being realised in the workplace - those children are now employers and employees. Clearly government and policy makers need to review research conducted over the past 30 years to enable a rich review of the educational environment and familial settings that the current workforce stemmed from. This review should act as a guide to a significant UK wide reflective longitudinal study. Paying lip-service to educational deficiencies in the way ICT is studied at school and University and impacts of continued sex stereotyping of subject areas will continue to reproduce the status-quo and the absence of women in the ICT labour market.

REFERENCES

Adya, M., & Kaiser, K. (2005). Early determinants of women in the IT workforce: a model of girls' career choices. *Information Technology & People*, *18*(3), 230–259. doi:10.1108/09593840510615860

Blomqvist, M. (2007, June 27-29). Working conditions in the ICT sector mediated by newspapers *Gender, Work and Organisation 5th biennial international interdisciplinary conference*, Keele University, UK

Brandell, G., & Staberg, E. (2008). Mathematics: a female, male or gender-neutral domain? A study of attitudes among students at secondary level. *Gender and Education*, *20*(5), 495–509. doi:10.1080/09540250701805771

Clegg, S. (2001). Theorising the machine: gender, education and computing. *Gender and Education*, *13*(3), 307–324. doi:10.1080/09540250120063580

Curtis, P. (2009). Girls do better without boys, study finds, *The Guardian*. Retrieved March 18, 2009, from http://www.guardian.co.uk/education/2009/mar/18/secondary-schools-girls-gcse-results

DfES. (2007). *Gender and Education: the evidence on pupils in England*. Department of Education and Skills.

Dunn, S., & Ridgeway, J. (1991). Naked into the World: IT experiences on a final primary school teaching practice: a second survey. *Journal of Computer Assisted Learning*, *7*(4), 229–240. doi:10.1111/j.1365-2729.1991.tb00254.x

Dutton, W., Helsper, E. J., & Gerber, M. M. (2009). *The Internet in Britain 2009 Oxford Internet Surveys*. UK: University of Oxford.

EOC. (2004). *Occupational Segregation, gender gaps and skills gaps*, Occupational Segregation Working Paper Series No.15.EOC e-Skills(2008). *Technology Counts IT and Telecoms Insights 2008*. Retrieved February 10, 2009, from http://www.e-Skills.com/Research-and-policy/Insights-2008/2205

Evans, T. (1994). *Understanding learners in open and distance education*. London: Kogan Page.

Faulkner, W. (2005). Becoming and Belonging: Gendered processes in engineering. In Archibald, J., Emms, J., Grundy, F., Payne, J., and Turner, E. (Eds.) *Women into Computing (WIC) Conference Proceedings: The Gender Politics of ICT* 15-25. Middlesex, UK: Middlesex University Press.

Gras-Velazquez, A., Joyce, A., & Derby, M. (2009). *Women and ICT, why are girls are still not attracted to ICT studies and careers?* European Schoolnet Brussels, Retrieved August 20, 2009 from www.eun.org

Green, E., & Adam, A. (1998). On-line leisure. Gender and ICT's in the Home. *Information Communication and Society, 1*(3), 291–312.

Griffiths, M., Moore, K., Burns, B., & Richardson, H. (2007). *The Disappearing Women: North West ICT Project Final Report.* University of Salford.

Habib, L., & Cornford, T. (2001). Domestication and Gender:Computers in the Home. Global Co-operation in the New Millenium. *ECIS 2001 9th European Conference on Information Systems,* Bled, Slovenia.

Hoyles, C. (1985). *The learning machine: The gender gap.* BBC1 on 9 May 1985.

Kirkup, G., & Abbott, J. (1997). *The gender gap. A gender analysis of the 1996 computing access survey. Milton Keynes, PLUM Paper number 80.* Programme on Learner Use of Media, Open University.

Mendick, H. (2005). A beautiful myth? The gendering of being/doing 'good at maths'. *Gender and Education, 17*(2), 203–219. doi:10.1080/0954025042000301465

Mumtaz, S. (2001). Children's enjoyment and perception of computer use in the home and the school. *Computers & Education, 36*(4), 347–362. doi:10.1016/S0360-1315(01)00023-9

Na, M. (2001). The Home Computer in Korea: Gender, Technology, and the Family. *Feminist Media Studies, 1*(3). doi:10.1080/14680770120088909

Newmarch, E., Taylor-Steele, S., & Cumpston, A. (2000). *Women in IT – what are the barriers.* New South Wales: Department of Education, Training and Youth Affairs.

Platman, K., & Taylor, P. (2004). *Workforce Ageing in the New Economy: A Comparative Study of Information Technology Employment,* Cambridge, UK: University of Cambridge. Retrieved from http://www.wane.ca/PDF/Platman&TaylorSummaryReport2004.pdf

Richardson, H., & French, S (2002, November). *Exercising different choices – the gender divide and government policy making in the 'global knowledge economy.* 6th International ETHICOMP conference. Lisbon, Portugal.

Sanders, J (2005). *Gender and technology in education: a research review.* Retrieved March 10, 2009, fromwww.josanders.com

Selby, L., Young, A., & Fisher, D. (1997). *Increasing the participation of women in tertiary level computing courses: what works and why.* ASCILITE'97.

Siann, G. (1997). We Can, We Don't Want to: Factors Influencing Women's Participation in Computing. In Lander, R., & Adam, A. (Eds.), *Women in Computing.* Exeter, UK: Intellect.

Siann, G., Durndell, A., Macleod, H., & Glissov, P. (1988). Stereotyping in relation to the gender gap in computing. *Education Research, 30,* 8–103.

Speilhofer, T., O'Donnell, L., Benton, T., Schagen, S., & Shagen, I. (2002). *The impact of school size and single-sex education on performance.* Local Government Association. National Foundation for Educational Research (NfER).

Sullivan, A. (2008). (forthcoming). Academic self-concept, gender and single-sex schooling. [Routledge]. *British Educational Research Journal.*

Webster, J. (2005a). Why Are Women Still So Few in ICT? Understanding the persistent under-representation of women in IT professions. In Archibald, J., Emms, J., Grundy, F., Payne, J., and Turner, E. (Eds.) *Women into Computing (WIC) Conference Proceedings: The Gender Politics of ICT*, 3-14. Middlesex, UK: Middlesex University Press.

WWW-ICT. (2004). *Widening Women's Participation in ICT: Synthesis Report of the European Project.* Brussels, Belgium: European Commission.

KEY TERMS AND DEFINITIONS

Education: The process of acquiring knowledge through teaching and learning at a school, college or university.

Single-Sex Schooling: The process of acquiring knowledge through teaching and learning at a school exclusively for an all-female cohort or an all-male cohort.

ICT: Information: Communitarian Technology a broad term that includes Information Technology and Information Systems.

ENDNOTES

1. ICT has been used through this chapter when referring to the employment sector except when direct quotes by interviewees use related terms, for example IT (Information Technology)

2. Acknowledgement here goes to Alison Adam who also directed the projects and researchers Claire Keogh and Angela Tattersall (WINWIT, DEPICT and GATE projects), Karenza Moore (WINIT and Disappearing Women projects) with Frances Bell and Beryl Burns (KAN project). See www.iris.salford.ac.uk/GRIS/ (accessed 10/03/09)

3. Co-ed is short for co-educational and is the UK term used for mixed sex schools

4. Comprehensive education is state run and funded through taxes.

5. Examinations taken in England Wales and Northern Ireland usually at the age of 18

6. Private sector run schools

Section 3
Representation in Media

Chapter 7
Challenging Gender Stereotypes Using Virtual Pedagogical Characters

Agneta Gulz
Lund University, Sweden

Magnus Haake
Lund University, Sweden

ABSTRACT

This chapter explores motivational and cognitive effects of more neutral or androgynous-looking versus more feminine-looking and masculine-looking virtual characters. A user study is presented, in which 158 students, aged 17-19, encountered four virtual characters that were visually manipulated to represent gender stereotypicality versus androgyny. On the one hand we explored students' attitudes towards the different characters as seen in how they ranked them as preferred presenters and articulated their arguments for doing so. On the other hand we looked for patterns as to which character(s) influenced female and male students most positively with respect to their attitude towards a university level computer engineering programme. Results from the study are presented and discussed. We conclude by pointing towards future research and potential within the area.

INTRODUCTION

A long-standing issue in higher education in engineering and other technical fields has been that of recruitment and retention of female students. The arguments for this are many, and here we will restrict our interest to recruitment with the support of virtual coaches. Baylor and collaborators demonstrated (Baylor & Plant, 2005; Baylor, Rosenberg-Kima, & Plant, 2006) that the use of

virtual coaches portrayed as young and attractive females can increase the willingness of female students to chose technically oriented courses and help increase their belief in their own ability in technical domains. Processes of role modelling and identification (cf. Bandura, 1977, 2000) seem to be involved. The female students could more easily match these coaches with their personal identity compared to a virtual coach portrayed as a "typical male engineer" (see Figure 1).

When the results of Baylor and collaborators are analysed in detail it appears, however, that the

DOI: 10.4018/978-1-61520-813-5.ch007

Figure 1. Example of two alternative engineering coaches (young, attractive female versus "typical" male engineer) in Baylor et al. (2006). (© 2006, State University of Florida. Used with permission.)

increase in their belief in their own abilities partly stems from a conception of a "female, feminine, young and attractive" engineer as *less competent* than a "real, typical male engineer". The prejudice that females, and in particular females with a strongly feminine appearance, are less competent in technical domains seems to spill over to the virtual area, generating increased self-efficacy of the kind 'If she is able to do it, I can do it!'.

Now, this implies a potential conflict between a *short-term* pedagogical goal of recruitment and boosted self-efficacy in female students, and a *long-term* pedagogical goal of changing rather than reproducing gender prejudices and stereotypes. Attempting to avoid this conflict, the present study explores motivational and cognitive effects of more neutral- or androgynous-looking virtual characters versus more typically feminine-looking and masculine-looking ones – in a recruitment context. A multimedia presentation was developed, featuring four different virtual presenters of a university programme in computer engineering. The characters (presenters) were *visually* manipulated – and pre-validated during the design process – to represent a young feminine woman, a more androgynous young woman, a more androgynous young man, and a young masculine man. (The characters are depicted and described in detail later in the article.)

Participants encountered one of the four characters in the role as presenter (see Figure 2) and were afterwards asked whether and how the presentation had affected their attitude towards the computer engineering programme as well as what they thought of the presenter. Finally they were presented with all four characters and asked to rank them in terms of which one they themselves would prefer as the presenter of the computer engineering programme, and to motivate their ranking.

Issues in Focus

We wanted to:

1a) Explore students' attitudes towards the different characters, as seen in how they *ordered* them as preferred presenters of the computer engineering programme: Would the more neutral, androgynous characters be preferred to the more gender typical characters, or vice versa? Would the rankings of female students differ from those of male students?

1b) Explore how students *articulated* their attitudes towards the four characters: What reasons would they give for their first and last choice?

Figure 2. Screenshot from the multimedia presentation with the "more androgynous young woman" presenting the programme in computer engineering at Lund University. (© 2007, Magnus Haake. Used with permission.)

Additionally, we wanted to:

2) Explore which character(s) *influenced* female and male students most positively with respect to their attitude towards the computer engineering programme.

It should be emphasized that it was not assumed in advance whether or not there would be a concordance between the character(s) that the students *explicitly chose and argued that they preferred* most as presenters, and the character(s) that had the most *positive influence on their attitudes* to the educational programme presented. Many studies have shown that perceptual gender-related stimuli can have a considerable impact on peoples' non-conscious cognitive processes that is not necessarily in accordance with what the same

people are aware of and consciously report (e.g. Reeves & Nass, 1996; Brave & Nass, 2005).

Therefore the study was designed to collect *both* conscious, articulated responses in the format of preference rankings and arguments, *and* responses that reflect less conscious influences and processes.

STUDY

Participants

Eighty-six female and 72 male 17-19 year old students at four different high schools in two cities in southern Sweden participated.

Figure 3. The four virtual presenters used in the study. (© 2007, Magnus Haake. Used with permission.)

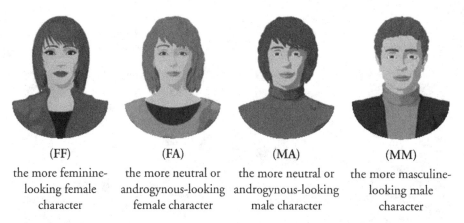

(FF)	(FA)	(MA)	(MM)
the more feminine-looking female character	the more neutral or androgynous-looking female character	the more neutral or androgynous-looking male character	the more masculine-looking male character

The Virtual Characters

Visual Appearance

The design aspect manipulated in the four virtual characters (see Figure 3) was their *visual appearance*. This was done by one of the team members (educated in visual arts) according to *gender schemes* used in design practice.

The two more neutral or androgynous-looking characters, *FA* (female androgynous) and *MA* (male androgynous), were developed out of an identical bust, differing in:

- the length of their hair
- the eye brows (with FA having more regular and slightly plucked eye brows)
- the clothing (somewhat neutral as to fashion but gender specific)
- FA having short eye lashes accentuating the eyes
- MA having a somewhat darker colour scheme, producing slightly bigger and more pronounced shapes

A more *feminine-looking* female character, *FF*, was developed from the bust of MA and FA by using feminine attributes such as rounded head shapes, bigger eyes and smaller nose, make-up,

long, dark eye lashes, the mouth modelled with fuller lips and the cheeks lifted and slightly more pronounced.

A more *masculine-looking* male character, *MM*, was designed by using masculine attributes such as broader, angular and more pronounced head shapes (especially the shape of the jaw), broader shoulders, a distinct Adam's apple and pronounced eyebrows.

Gender Stereotypical and Androgynous Visual Appearances

The focus on both conscious and articulated and more non-conscious responses to the characters, with respect to visually represented gender, set some constraints on the visual designs.

Over-explicit visual gender stereotypes had to be avoided. A feminine female character who looks like Pamela Anderson, and a masculine male character who looks like Arnold Schwarzenegger (cf. Figure 4), would probably initiate *conscious* reflections on gender and gender stereotypes, the purpose of the study, "politically correct" answers, and so on and dominate or rule out more immediate and non-reflected responses. Thus, FF and MM were not designed as *pronouncedly gender stereotypical* in their looks, and in particular, we sought to avoid the bimbo stereotype for FF.

Figure 4. Examples of visual gender stereotypes in digital media. Left: two characters from the console game Ninja Gaiden® Sigma that reflect parts of the computer game domain's action/fantasy-genre. (© 2008, Tecmo, Ltd. Used with permission.) Right: two characters designed by members in the online world Second Life™ Showcase. The characters could be found in a collection of examples (showcases) directly in the main menu of the home page (secondlife.com/showcase/).

FA and MA, in turn, are not *pronouncedly androgynous* in their looks, even though only a few visual parameters differ between them. In an early design phase, they were actually more similar to one another, and in particular FA appeared as more clearly androgynous. This, however, evoked negative responses in the validation process. In a pre-test a number of participants declared that they were at first uncertain whether the FA character was female or male, and that they found her – they all finally decided it was a girl – rather unattractive.

This was undesirable given the aim of the study. We wanted to explore the potential in using more androgynous in comparison to more strongly gender-differentiated visual characters. But such a comparison presupposes that all characters are comparable in the sense that none is perceived as particularly unattractive, irritating, strange or unusual, since this may otherwise take away the focus from the central variables.

However, the need to avoid strange or unusual characters is also a dilemma. Not being able to decide whether someone is a man or a woman is known to induce insecurity and unease in many people (Brave & Nass, 2005), and this constrains the possibility to explore more pronounced androgynous-looking characters. In order to progress here, our next step will be to use less naturalistic-looking, more cartoonish characters – more of this in the section on future research.

Character Features other than the Visual Appearance

Since we wanted to explore possible effects of visual appearances, we strived to keep all other character variables constant, or at least comparable, between the four characters. The slide show behind the characters was identical, as well as the information communicated by the characters. The characters' facial expressions followed the same animation scheme. As to voice, one and the same recording – originally a woman's voice – was digitalized into a female and a male voice. In this way features such as dialect and tone were well controlled for. It was also important to choose a female voice that would work with *both* the female characters, and a male voice that would work with *both* the male characters since mismatches between look and voice, like other inconsistencies in virtual agents, are known to disturb or irritate people (Nass, Isbister, & Lee, 2000).

Procedure

The computer program was run on four laptops. The 158 participants all used headphones to ensure that they were able to hear well and concentrate.

After filling in demographic data on the screen (see Figure 5a), the participants read brief texts about seven university level educational

Figure 5. Screenshots from the multimedia presentation. Left (5a): Demographic data form. Right (5b): Evaluation of the seven university programmes. (© 2007, Magnus Haake. Used with permission.)

programmes and were asked to what extent they could imagine themselves as students on these different programmes. For each programme they were asked to check one of the following alternatives: <never>, <unlikely>, <perhaps>, <yes> or <absolutely> (see Figure 5b).

Thereafter they were told, in the digital environment, that a new presentational media was being developed, which they were invited to help evaluate. It would concern the computer engineering educational programme (from their perspective seemingly randomly chosen among the programmes they had just evaluated).

At this instance the virtual presenter appeared (see Figure 6) and spoke about the educational programme for 2 minutes, with an accompanying slide show presentation. Parts of the presenta-

tion had been pre-validated as to its content and style by other students in the same age group in a previous and related study (Altmejd & Vallinder, 2007).

When the presentation was finished and the presenter had thanked the listener, a number of questions were posed. All were presented on-screen and filled out on the computer. First, the students were asked to evaluate on a 6-step Likert scale whether the presentation had influenced them in their attitude towards the computer engineering programme: in a positive or negative direction and to what extent. Thereafter they were asked *why* they had been influenced in this way (see Figure 7a).

The next question regarded their view of the presenter they had encountered. Thereafter

Figure 6. Screenshot from the slide show with the virtual character presenting the university programme in computer engineering. (© 2007, Magnus Haake. Used with permission.)

Figure 7. Screenshots from the multimedia presentation. (© 2007, Magnus Haake. Used with permission.)

all four alternative presenters were shown, and the participants were asked to rank them from 1 to 4 in order of preference: 'Who would they prefer as presenter of the computer engineering programme?' (see Figure 7b). Following this, the virtual character they had ranked as number 1 appeared and they were asked why this was their first choice. Thereafter the character they had placed as number 4 appeared and they were asked why this was their last choice. Finally, the participants were thanked on screen for their participation and asked to speak to one of the experiment leaders for debriefing and to receive a lottery ticket for cinema vouchers.

Ten groups of participants, in total about a fifth of the participants, also took part in focus group interviews after they had completed the session just described. These interviews centred around masculinity and femininity in appearance, behaviour, style, and occupations – as well as on the topic of androgyny.

RESULTS AND ANALYSIS

Character Choices

First and Fourth Places in Rank

The female participants most frequently chose MA and FA as favourite presenter with 29 and 28 choices respectively, versus 21 for FF and as few as 8 for MM. As many as 32 female participants put MM last and 24 put FF last. Only 16 and 14 put FA and MA, respectively, in fourth place. In other words, the two androgynous characters were clearly preferred. (See Figure 8.)

The first choice of the male participants was much more even (see Figure 9). As to the fourth place, the pattern was, on the other hand, very pronounced with 28 votes for FF, 25 for MM, and only 9 and 10 for FA and MA. In other words, also the male participants showed a preference for the androgynous characters, although primarily seen through their fourth place ranking (see Figure 9).

Two other choice patterns are particularly interesting from a gender point of view: (i) the extent to which participants ranked the *two female characters* or the *two male characters* in the two first places, and (ii) the extent to which participants put *the two more androgynous characters* in the two first places.

Same-Gender Characters in the First Two Places

Thirteen female and 12 male students, corresponding to random distribution, ranked the two female characters in first and second place (see Figure 10, leftmost bar). Ranking the two male characters in first and second place occurred much less often. Ten male and only 6 female students

Figure 8. Female participants' first and fourth place ranking of the virtual presenters.

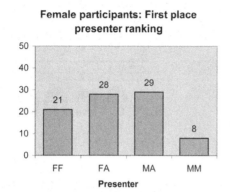
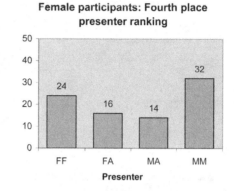

clearly correspond to less than random distribution (see Figure 10, second leftmost bar). In other words, even though computer engineering is an education and professional field with strong male dominance, students and in particular female students, tended not to place two male characters in first and second place.

The Two Androgynous Characters In The First Two Places

As many as 28 female and 18 male students, 46 in total (see Figure 10, second rightmost bar), put *the two more androgynous characters* as their two first choices of presenter. This is significantly above what is expected by chance. Placing the two more gender stereotypical characters in first and second place, on the other hand, was a little less common than what is expected by chance.

Arguments and Reasons for Character Preferences

We now leave the ranking preference data and move to the participants' arguments and reasons for their character rankings. The issues focused on in analyzing these are: (i) participants' referring to the *gender of the characters* in arguing for a placement of the character, (ii) comments and arguments about the *attractiveness of characters*, and (iii) *the nerd* as appearing in arguments and comments. These issues are presented below in due order.

Referring to the Gender of Characters in Arguing for Ones Preferences

On 35 occasions the gender of characters was brought up in motivating a first or last choice

Figure 9. Male participants' first and fourth place ranking of the virtual presenters.

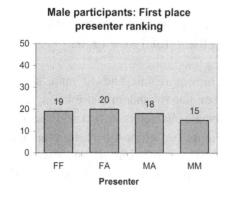
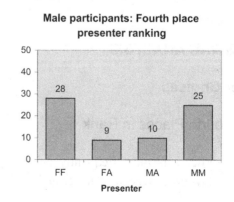

Figure 10. Distribution of the different combinations of the two top ranked (first and second) virtual presenters ($\chi 2$[total distr.] = 23.595; p = 0.000).

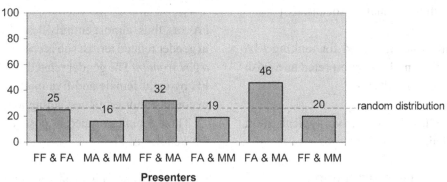

of presenter: by female participants in 22 cases and by male participants in 13. This difference in number may reflect a more pronounced gender consciousness in women compared to men (e.g. Hirdman, 2003). Below we look in more detail at the content of participants' comments when referring to characters' gender. This material gives indications both of ways of reasoning, and of how the different characters afford or mediate – or perhaps even trigger – different types of gender related arguments.

MM: Gender Related Arguments

The character that is *least* – only four times – referred to in gender terms in choice/non-choice arguments is MM. For instance, one male and one female student chose him since:

- 'it is suitable for a boy to talk about technical things'
- 'this is a guy, and I think that this [the computer engineering programme] is for guys'

MA: Gender Related Arguments

Nine participants raised gender related arguments concerning MA. Arguments for choosing MA as presenter were, for example:

- 'it is a guy, and it is a computer education'
- 'he looks like a *computer-guy*'
- 'he looked nice, and in many contexts, many people find it more reliable when it is a man speaking'

An example of an argument for the ranking of MA in the *fourth place* is:

Figure 11.

Figure 12.

- 'since he is a guy, and "the typical kind of guy" for this kind of education' [In this female student's further reasoning it was clear that she thought it would be good to break with the "usual" associations.]

One female student argued for ranking MA first in a way that might be interpreted as a wish to avoid gender typicality:

- 'because he did not have typical short "boy's hair"'

FA: Gender Related Arguments

Turning to the female characters, eight female and two male students came up with gender related arguments concerning FA. All argued *for* their choosing FA in terms of her *being female*. They said for example:

- 'I think it is good that girls are more visible'
- 'I think it is important that it is a women speaking since that can make more girls realize this can be for them'
- 'she seems young and looks nice, and I think she would make more girls interested'
- 'I like to see that also girls can be profiles for an engineering education, in particular one involving computers, which has many male students'
- 'because she was good – and a girl'
- 'I think women too ought to have influence in speaking for such programmes, so that

girls can see that there are also female students here'

FF: Gender Related Arguments

FA was, thus, almost entirely described positively in gender related terms: she is *chosen/preferred as a girl/woman*. The gender related arguments about FF, by eight female and five male students, were in contrast more split and ambiguous.

Three females argued in positive terms about their choice of FF:

- 'when one thinks about computer educations one thinks, at least I do, mostly of males – to hear a woman present is really a good thing'
- 'because she was the best-looking and seems more conscious of what women want'
- 'she looks like a focused woman, who knows what she wants =) ha-ha'

The other five females as well as the five males put FF in last place. Several of them seemed to defend this by saying that they *do* want women presenters in this context, but not *this* woman, not FF. The female students commented:

- 'it could perhaps be good to have a female presenter, but perhaps not her' [She placed FA as number 2.]
- 'I cannot say straight on that she would not be good as presenter but she just does not seem competent' [She placed FA first, with the motivation that she finds it important to have a woman as presenter.]

Figure 13.

Figure 14.

- 'she is a kind of woman I don't like' [She ranked FA first.]
- 'I am not against her really but I think it should be mixed between women and men when it comes to influencing' [She placed FA first.]
- 'males are usually good at presenting these things' [Nevertheless she ranked FA first, saying that FA was good.]

The males reasoned:

- 'women are, on the whole, less interested in computers, and this one looked less motivated than the other woman'
- 'she looked the least like someone dealing with technology'
- 'she was a woman on a computer education and she did not seem to belong there'
- 'she doesn't give the feeling of being as serious as the man, doesn't seem to have the same working experience as the man'
- 'as I said, a woman feels more welcoming than a man, but she looked so styled, which I don't like'

Summing Up

In summary there is a considerable difference between *ten* arguments (five by girls and five by boys) *against FF* as presenter in terms of her being a woman – or as being 'this kind of woman' – and *no* argument *against FA* as presenter in terms of her being a woman. On the other hand, *ten* participants (eight female and two male students) argue *for FA* as presenter since she is a woman, but only *three* (three females) argue *for FF* as presenter since she is a woman.

Arguments Involving the Attractiveness of Characters

In general, it appears to be crucial for young peoples' educational choices that they can find adequate role models (Kessels, 2005; Rommes, Overbeek, Scholte, Engels, & de Kemp, 2007).

One of the parameters known to influence the strength of a role model is *attractiveness*, If a role model is perceived as attractive the behaviour of the model is more often imitated (Rommes et al., 2007). Therefore, we wanted to analyse our material to see to what extent attractiveness and non-attractiveness was brought up in evaluating the characters as presenters of the computer education.

Indeed, comments on attractiveness were quite frequent in arguments for choosing a character as first place presenter, while comments on non-attractiveness were quite frequently involved in argument for placing a character in fourth place.

There were no large differences in the number of comments on attractiveness made by male students (52) and female students (67). The number of comments was relatively evenly distributed among the four characters with the exception of FF who received one third of the attractiveness/ non-attractiveness comments. Notably, there was quite considerable divergence in students' opinions regarding *all four* characters in terms of their attractiveness/non-attractiveness. Firstly, this is positive in view of the study design. If one character was found particularly attractive or non-attractive this might have interfered with the factor we intended to study, namely the influence of gender stereotypicality in visual appearance. Secondly, the divergence in opinions reinforces the notion that tastes differ.

Another appearance aspect relatively frequently commented upon was that of looking 'plain' or 'common'. Also here *all* four characters were commented on as looking (most) 'normal'/'plain'. That the perception and evaluation of who looks 'normal' and 'common' differ among participants is interesting since such perceptions as well can play a role in an identification process.

The Nerd in Arguments and Comments

The topic of attractiveness/non-attractiveness leads us to the topic of *the nerd*. An elaborate analysis of this issue, based on a rich empirical material from the Netherlands, is provided by Rommes et al. (2007). Using several methods, including focus group analyses and pictures drawn by young students, they pinpoint the Dutch cultural image of a computer scientist: male, unsociable, "married to his computer", wearing unfashionable clothes and glasses, has a bad haircut, is overall unattractive and basically asexual – that is, *a nerd*.

Also organizers of computer engineering programs in Sweden mention a problematic image of the computer engineer student: a male student, constantly in front of his computer, drinking large amounts of coca-cola (Kihl, 2003).

Given that the image or prototype of a person studying a certain subject or belonging to a certain professional group seems important for young peoples' educational and career choices (Hannover & Kessels, 2004) a nerd image associated with computer engineering is a major obstacle for young people who might potentially apply to such programmes. The nerd is not somebody to identify with or aspire to be, but someone extremely non-attractive and non-glamorous. Furthermore, relationships and sexuality are important during adolescence, and thus the risk of being associated with the "asexual" nerd image can be extremely threatening (Lippa, 1991; Rommes et al., 2007). Baylor and collaborators (Baylor & Plant, 2005; Baylor et al., 2006) also touch upon these issues, in calling for virtual role models, who are knowledgeable about engineering and simultaneously stand out as attractive and as affirmative in their sexuality.

Rommes et al. (2007) suggest that it is the nerd prototype of the computer scientist, rather than ideas of what is actually involved in studying or working in the field, that makes many young Dutch females – and males – refrain from applying to computer related programmes. Thus, not least given the student recruitment context that our study took place in, we were interested to see whether we would find "the nerd" in our material when subjects motivated why they chose or did not choose a certain presenter.

The Swedish Nörd

The Swedish language has the word "nörd", pronounced very similar to "nerd", along with the specific word *datornörd* (*computer nerd*). In the logged material (we do not include the focus group interviews here) the word *nörd* was used twelve times, primarily by female participants. Additionally fifteen other arguments can be associated with the "nerd" concept, even though the word *nörd* was not used.

Figure 15. A nerd. (© 2009, Magnus Haake. Used with permission.)

Six participants ranked MM last as a presenter because he was – explicitly or implicitly – a *nörd,* writing for example: 'because I think he looked like a computer-nerd (*datornörd*) with his very ugly hair', 'he looks a little dull, and a little nerdy (*nördig)*', 'because he looks like a proper computer-person (*äkta datamänniska*), no one you can recognize yourself in', 'he looks a bit dull and stiff, a typical computer-guy'. The last participant placed MA first since: 'he is cool, and I got the impression that cool people study this educational programme'.

On the other hand, a student who had previously said that he was very interested in the computer engineering programme and later on declared that he had become even more positive after having heard the presentation by FF, argued *for* MM as his choice 'because he looks nerdy (*nördig*) ☺'. Another male student wrote that he chose MM: 'because he looks like a genuine computer-guy'. (The word *äkta* (*genuine*) used here has a positive connotation in Swedish in general.)

Such variation in value ascribed to nörd recurs when turning to MA. Some participants chose MA and argued about the look of 'computer-people' and of 'the nerd' in positive terms: 'he looks like a handsome computer-guy', 'he looks good, and looks like a computer-nerd (*datanörd*)'. On the other hand, one female ranked MA as her number one presenter, motivating this by MA *not* seeming like a nerd: 'he looks good and not too nerdy *(nördig)*'.

Both male characters, then, were at some occasions held to be a *nörd.* However, none of them really fits with the description of the nerd offered by Rommes et al. (2007), and both were held to be good-looking by at least some participants. MM was slightly more often associated with a nörd than MA and more frequently said to look dull and boring. However, MA received many more comments than MM of the sort that 'he fits in with this education'. Thus there is no support for the notion that *the nörd* is tightly connected to this education.

In connection with the female characters, *nörd* comments occurred more rarely. Yet one female student put FA in the fourth place 'because she looks dull and nerdy (*nördig*)', and put FF first, 'because she is no nerd (*nörd*)'. Another female student chose FA 'because she does not seem nerdy (*nördig*)'.

Summing up, what emerges from this material is not an equally strong cultural image as the one that emerged of *the nerd* as the typical computer scientist/engineer (Rommes et al., 2007). Perhaps *nörd* has a partly different meaning and use than the English *nerd*, with a less tight association to an unattractive appearance or look.[i]

Attitude Influences

We have come to the part of the analysis that is not based on participants' explicit rankings and arguments about the characters, but instead on changes in participants' attitudes towards the computer engineering programme after they had listened to the presentation by one of the four virtual presenters.

Before the presentation they had been asked to what extent they could imagine themselves as a student on some different educational programmes. After the presentation of the computer engineering programme they were asked to mark on a Likert scale the extent to which their attitude towards this programme had been influenced: very negatively, negatively, a little negatively, a little positively, positively, or very positively.

Eighty-six participants answered 'a little positively', and four answered 'a little negatively'. In our analysis we do not include these two middle positions but only 'negatively' and 'very negatively' that were given the values 2- and 3-, and 'positively' and 'very positively' that were given the values value 2+ and 3+. In Figure 16 the added values character by character are presented.

Overall more male than female participants reported a clearly positive influence from the presentation. The total sum of positive values

Figure 16. Attitude influences from the multimedia presentation.

Added positive (+) influences only

	FF	FA	MA	MM
Males	54 +	38 +	21 +	58 +
Females	31 +	36 +	36 +	36 +

Added negative (–) influences only

	FF	FA	MA	MM
Males	8 –	11 –	14 –	0 –
Females	0 –	4 –	15 –	5 –

Added total (positive and negative) influences

	FF	FA	MA	MM
Males	46 +	27 +	7 +	58 +
Females	31 +	32 +	21 +	30 +

for the male participants was 171 (+) and for the females 139 (+). However, the values were overall relatively high. The negative influence, measured in negative values, was considerably smaller, with 33 (-) for males and 24 (-) for females.

When it comes to the presenters involved when participants reported a strong positive change in attitude towards the education, the results were as follows. For female students, the positive influence was evenly distributed over the characters. This is not in line with the results of another study (Baylor et al., 2006) where female students' attitudes towards engineering classes were considerably more positive if the virtual coach was *female*. What must be borne in mind is however the difference in contexts. Baylor investigated students' encounters *over some time* with a pedagogical coach, directing a tutorial. In our study there was *one brief* encounter with a presenter.

Also the very evenly distributed positive influences from the characters on the female participants was not in accordance with their strong preferences for the two androgynous characters indicated through their *explicit* ranking and reasoning about the characters.

With the male participants the contrast between their explicit ranking and reasoning about characters, and the positive and negative influences from characters, was even more striking. In explicit rankings and reasoning, the androgynous characters were preferred but the positive influence values were low for these characters. Furthermore, the character the male participants ranked lowest and argued most negatively about was MM. But the positive influence on attitudes among male participants was clearly strongest from MM, followed by relatively strong positive influences from FF.

Analyses in the Pipeline

When circumstances allow we would, first of all, want to analyse the material from the focus group interviews where participants discuss androgyny, masculine and feminine professions, etc. Furthermore, we would like to pursue a more focused analysis from the perspective of recruitment of young females to computer engineering programmes. It would also be interesting to pursue culture comparative studies. In what ways do countries, such as the Netherlands and Sweden, differ as to whether computer engineering is an unattractive or attractive discipline – and can differences, if found, be related to different cultural images of the computer engineer and of "the nerd"?

TENTATIVE CONCLUSIONS

It has long been acknowledged that there are close symbolic associations between information technology, and masculinities and femininities (Cockburn & Ormod, 1993; Faulkner, 2003). Here, we suggest, virtual agents or characters, with their properties of interactivity and human-likeness, constitute a particular form of information technology endowed with a particular (re)constructive power with respect to gender. The presented study used virtual characters for presenting a university programme on computer engineering, but they could be used to present all kinds of educational domains, and may be of particular interest when aiming for less gendered occupational choices. Studies by Baylor and her collaborators (Baylor & Plant, 2005; Baylor et al., 2006) provided important background and a point of departure for our study in highlighting the importance of images and alternative cultural role models for engineering students. Also other researchers have suggested that more physically attractive and glamorous female role models might change the negative prototypes of computer scientists (Coltrane & Adams, 1997).

But Baylor and collaborators also pointed out problems of stereotype reproduction in using such characters and images. The aim of our study was to look for an alternative to the explicitly feminine female characters used in Baylor's studies (Baylor & Plant, 2005; Baylor et al., 2006), and thus a means to reconcile the *short-term* pedagogical goal of recruitment and boosted self-efficacy in female students, and the *long-term* pedagogical goal of changing rather than reproducing gender prejudices and stereotypes.

Using More than one Character?

For the female participants in our study, the following could be seen with respect to the two virtual female characters. In explicit rankings and arguments FA, with her in a relative sense more androgynous look, was clearly preferred to FF. In attitude influences no difference between FA and FF was seen on female participants.

A central result comes from the analysis of arguments that refer to the *gender of the character*. Here we found that a whole group of ten participants argued *against FF* as presenter in terms of her being a woman – or as being 'this kind of woman' – whereas *no* participant did so *against FA*. And vice versa, a considerably larger group of participants argued *for FA* as presenter *as being a woman* than correspondingly *for FF*. Our interpretation is that the more androgynous female character has more positive affordances in gender terms. The FA character was more frequently and more consistently used in positive reasoning and arguments about women in this computer technological context. Female students who already have thoughts about a positive role for women in the computer science domain, or in technical domains in general seem more satisfied with picking the FA-character than the FF-character. The FF-character, on the other hand, seems to mediate or afford, or lend herself more easily, to arguments about women not fitting in this context.

But two things concerning divergence and multiplicity should be pointed out. First, it should not be neglected that there was one group of female participants for whom the FF character appeared to be valuable, as reflected in comments such as: 'she looks as if she also knows what a woman wants', 'she has a chic look', 'she looks like a focused woman who knows what she wants'. Likewise, it should be remembered that opinions on attractiveness/non-attractiveness, as well as on commonness/plainness, diverged for all four characters. In all, this points towards the possibility of using not just one virtual character, in this case one presenter, but two or several that take turns and interact with each other.

Second, it is important to situate the results of the present study in a cultural context. Virtual characters, which might function well and be adequate in Sweden, are not necessarily the ones that ought to be chosen in another country. For instance, we observed that *the nörd* seems to have less impact and be more modulated than *the nerd* in some other cultures – which might decrease a need to introduce attractive, sexy female and/or male characters as a counter balance.

Further Potentials

On a broader scale the results from this and other studies indicate a possibility to exploit virtual characters to support identification and formation of identities in young people while avoiding the reproduction of undesired stereotypes. Smartly used, this kind of technology could, to borrow from Rommes (2007), be developed into tools that may increase the freedom for young people to create their personal "gender identity cocktails".

There certainly exist information technological applications that to the contrary reproduce and even reinforce gender stereotypes, (compare Figure 4). But there is reason to focus also on the strong constructive potential for *changing* and *broadening* cultural images. For one thing, we have quite a different room in which to manoeuvre in virtual worlds than in the real world. As Brave and Nass (2005) reason: 'Rapidly increasing the number of female teachers in stereotypically male disciplines (or vice versa) seems difficult. But technology provides a wonderful opportunity to […] "staff" educational software to counter stereotypes.' (p. 29).

Furthermore, within computer game communities where members continually contribute to game development, we see a growing diversity in characters – not least new kinds of female heroines. In the wordings of Pinckard (2003) '[…] in MUDs and MOOs, one can often create a third sex and

invent a pronoun and refer to oneself always with that pronoun (and insist others do the same). In these science-fiction and fantasy-themed online worlds, it's perfectly plausible that ungendered, ambiguously gendered, or bi-gendered races could exist.'. Examples of gender busting characters can also be found in existing ready-made programs, such as: *Nights into Dreams* with the magical, androgynous character *Nights* whose identity can be assumed by both the female and male characters, *The Legend of Zelda* with gender ambiguity around all main characters, or *Metroid* with the gender bending action heroine *Samus Aran*.

SOME BROADER ISSUES & FUTURE RESEARCH

We regard the presented study as a first step in a larger programme of exploring the pedagogical potential of virtual characters that challenge stereotypes, with several different paths to follow and to explore. In this section we discuss some that have high priority on our agenda: (i) exploration of perceptions and attitudes towards androgyny in virtual characters and the pedagogical potentials herein, (ii) education and gender with respect to educational programmes where men are in the minority, and (iii) development of dedicated gender pedagogical digital tools involving virtual environments and characters.

More Imaginative Androgynities and their Pedagogical Potentials

The first study would explore perceptions and attitudes towards androgyny and how androgyny in virtual characters can be used pedagogically, focusing on more stylised and imaginative characters. As related earlier in the text, *visually naturalistic* characters like those from the presented study constrain possibilities of exploiting more pronounced androgyny, since naturalistic androgyny induces insecurity in many people.

But with more imaginative characters, the design freedom and potentials appears wider (see Figure 17) while there is still evidence that *identification processes* with respect to visually less naturalistic characters can function well (GameGirlAdvance, 2003; Gulz & Haake, 2006a, 2006b; Haake & Gulz, 2007; McCloud, 1993).

Attractiveness, mentioned above, would here be an issue, since it seems of importance for positive and well-functioning role models and cultural images. We will therefore look for and explore *non-gendered, attractive characters*. An implication is a need to avoid androgyny in the sense of in-between: greyish, neither feminine nor masculine, average.

In the context that we are dealing with, androgynous attractiveness could be a gain over gender-stereotypical attractiveness, and in particular over *feminine attractiveness* of the kind that Baylor and collaborators work with. By turning towards androgynous attractiveness, one may get away from associations of attractiveness and women and femininity leading to conceptions like 'a woman's primary role or function is not competence but to be good-looking and to attract'.

Our approach to androgyny is overall optimistic. We consider it a large space with many possibilities for combinations of characteristics – those classified as feminine and those classified as masculine. Other researchers who express an optimistic view on the boundary widening potential in digital world with respect to gender are Haraway (1991), Turkle (1995), Gilmour (1999), and Chess (2006). They all argue, in various ways, that androgyny in the digital world is a rich continuum with many possibilities for femininity, masculinity, both or neither.

Programmes with Male Students in the Minority

The second study would focus on a domain with under-representation of male students, in contrast to the presented study which has focused on images of computer engineering, a domain where women are under-represented.

The underlying issue regards the possibility to influence such situations by offering examples that differ from culturally dominant prototypes of engineers, nurses, etc. We wish to explore the potential in virtual worlds to offer a broader range

Figure 17. Androgynous and visually less naturalistic virtual characters. (From left to right, top to down: Two avatars from Second Life™ (secondlife.com); Illustration by Magnus Haake, © 2009, Magnus Haake; Illustration by Johnny Scharonne, © 2008, Johnny Scharonne (scharonne.wordpress.com); "The androgyne face", a painting by artist Klaus Hausmann © 2008, Klaus Hausmann (www.arsvenida. de);Illustration by Magnus Haake, © 2009. All copyrighted images used with permission.)

of styles and identities than in the real world. Can this be a place where cultural images are constructed, with potentials to countering other cultural representations of gendered technology? A number of researchers discuss or propose this (e.g. Reeves & Nass, 1996; Rommes, 2007), and we find it highly interesting. Not the least given the dynamics and interactivity of these novel digital media, which might make them even more powerful in mediating cultural norms than traditional media.

Dedicated Gender Pedagogical Tools

Going one step further, there is a potential for a third study, constructing dedicated digital tools based on virtual characters to support gender perspectives in teaching/education. Already we see tools used for experimentation with simulations and virtual role-games, and toolboxes for designing virtual characters, such as *SitePal* (www.sitepal.com), *PeoplePutty* (www.haptek.com), and *Meez* (www.meez.com).

The use of such tools imply that a number of design decisions must be made: 'What is this judge, this police officer and this arrested person going to look like and speak like?', 'Which gender, age, ethnicity, clothing, voice, and dialect shall we assign to them?'. Educationalists interested in discussing and challenging prejudices and proposing alternatives now have an opportunity to use such a situation as a basis for reflection and discussion: 'Why did we choose this character in this role?', 'Whose appearance is exposed and whose voice is heard, in terms of gender, age, ethnicity, class, regional subgroup, etc?', 'What features did we combine with one another and which not?'.

Notably, *various* alternatives may be suggested and *tried out*. Such an active and dynamic situation can provide a natural basis for reflection and discussion – in contrast to a more disconnected classroom discussion on stereotypes.

This is perhaps particularly important in the academic context, where language and other ab-

stractions often have a strong position compared to a more tangible visual tradition. Yet we know that visual, and other perceptual, stimuli and codes have a subtle but powerful influence on us all (Schneider, 2003). It is therefore unlikely that real success in attempts to reconstruct gender structures can be reached by too much focus on language. Perhaps virtual characters can help in the endeavor.

ACKNOWLEDGMENT

Thanks to the KK-Foundation (The Knowledge Foundation of Sweden), its research programme LearnIT, and GLIT, its network for research on Gender, Learning and IT, for financial support. Also thanks to Adam Altmejd and Aron Vallinder for conducting a pre-study, to Betty Tärning and Thérèse Deutgen for collaboration in the study, and to Else Rommes for sharing valuable manuscripts!

Not least, thanks to all student participants and to helpful teachers and school leaders at the participating schools.

REFERENCES

Altmejd, A., & Vallinder, A. (2007). *Betydelsen av en virtuell agents sociala förmåga* [*The Significance of the Social Skills of Virtual Agents*]. Student research paper, Lund University, Lund, Sweden. Retrieved May 31, 2009, from http://www.lucs.lu.se/Agneta.Gulz/selected_student_works/AA-AV_StudReport_2007.pdf

Bandura, A. (1977). *Social Learning Theory*. Englewood Cliffs, NJ: Prentice Hall.

Bandura, A. (2000). *Self-efficacy: The Foundation of Agency*. Mahwah, NJ: Lawrence Erlbaum.

Baylor, A., & Plant, A. (2005). Pedagogical agents as social models for engineering: The influence of appearance on female choice. In Looi, C. K., McCalla, G., Bredeweg, B., & Breuker, J. (Eds.), *Artificial intelligence in education: Supporting learning through intelligent and socially informed technology* (*Vol. 125*, pp. 65–72). Amsterdam, The Netherlands: IOS Press.

Baylor, A., Rosenberg-Kima, R., & Plant, A. (2006). Interface agents as social models: The impact of appearance on females' attitude toward engineering. In CHI'06 Extended Abstracts on Human Factors in Computing Systems (pp. 526-531). New York: ACM.

Brave, S., & Nass, C. (2005). *Wired for Speech*. Cambridge, MA: MIT Press.

Chess, S. (2006). *Working with Sex, Playing with Gender: Locating Androgyny in Video Games*. Retrieved December 12, 2007, from http://www.shiraland.com/Work/gender_media.pdf

Cockburn, C., & Ormod, S. (1993). *Gender and Technology in the Making*. Thousand Oaks, CA: Sage Publications.

Coltrane, S., & Adams, M. (1997). Work-family imagery and gender stereotypes: Television and the reproduction of difference. *Journal of Vocational Behavior, 50*, 323–347. doi:10.1006/jvbe.1996.1575

Faulkner, W. (2003). Teknikfrågan i feminismen [The technology issue in feminism]. In B. Berner (Ed.), Vem tillhör tekniken? [Who Owns Technology]. Lund, Sweden: Arkiv förlag.

GameGirlAdvance. (2003). *It's Time for Androgyny, It's just Vaan!* Game+Girl=Advance Weblog. Retrieved May 31, 2009, from http://www.gamegirladvance.com/archives/2003/12/02/its_time_for_androgyny_its_just_vaan.html

Gilmour, H. (1999). What Girls Want: The intersections of leisure and power in female computer game play. In Kinder, M. (Ed.), *Kids' Media Culture* (pp. 263–292). Durham, NC: Duke University Press.

Gulz, A., & Haake, M. (2006a). Pedagogical agents – design guide lines regarding visual appearance and pedagogical roles. In Méndez-Vilas, A., Solano Martin, A., Mesa Gonzalez, J., & Mesa Gonzalez, J. A. (Eds.), *Current Developments in Technology-Assisted Education (2006)* (*Vol. III*, pp. 1848–1852). Badajoz, Spain: FORMATEX.

Gulz, A., & Haake, M. (2006b). Visual design of virtual pedagogical agents: Naturalism versus stylization in static appearance. In *Proceedings of the 3rd International Design and Engagability Conference @ NordiChi 2006*.

Haake, M., & Gulz, A. (2007). Virtual pedagogical agents: Stylization for engagement. *Interfaces, 70*, 12–13.

Hannover, B., & Kessels, U. (2004). Self-to-prototype matching as a strategy for making academic choices. Why high school students do not like math and science. *Learning and Instruction, 14*, 51–67. doi:10.1016/j.learninstruc.2003.10.002

Haraway, D. (1991). A cyborg manifesto: Science, technology, and socialist-feminism in the late twentieth century. In Haraway, D. (Ed.), *Simians, Cyborgs and Women: The Reinvention of Nature* (pp. 149–181). New York: Routledge.

Hirdman, Y. (2003). *Genus* [Gender]. Stockholm: Liber AB.

Kessels, U. (2005). Fitting into the stereotype: How gender-stereotyped perceptions of prototypic peers relate to liking for school subjects. *European Journal of Psychology of Education, 20*(3), 309–323. doi:10.1007/BF03173559

Kihl, M. (2003). *Välkommen i LTH? – en studie av D02:s och C02:s första år på Teknis* [*Welcome to LTH? A study of the first year at the Lund Institute of Technology for computer and information & communication engineering students*]. Sweden: Report. Lund Institute of Technology, Lund University.

Lippa, R. (2001). On deconstructing and reconstructing masculinity-femininity. *Journal of Research in Personality, 35*, 168–207. doi:10.1006/jrpe.2000.2307

McCloud, S. (1993). *Understanding Comics*. New York: Harper Perennial.

Nass, C., Isbister, K., & Lee, E.-J. (2000). Truth is beauty: Researching embodied conversational agents. In Cassell, J., Sullivan, J., Prevost, S., & Churchill, E. (Eds.), *Embodied Conversational Agents* (pp. 374–402). Cambridge, MA: MIT Press.

Pinckard, J. (2003). *Genderplay: Successes and Failures in Character Designs for Videogames*. Game+Girl=Advance. Retrieved December 3, 2007, from http://www.gamegirladvance.com/archives/2003/04/16/genderplay_successes_and_failures_in_character_designs_for_videogames.html

Reeves, B., & Nass, C. (1996). *The Media Equation: How People Treat Computers, Televisions and New Media like Real People and Places*. New York: Cambridge University Press.

Rommes, E. (2007). *Images and Identities; Sex, Sexuality and Soaps*. Invited speaker manuscript at The 3rd Christina Conference in conjunction with The 4th European Gender & ICT Symposium, Helsinki, Finland. Retrieved May 25, 2007, from www.helsinki.fi/kristiina-instituutti/conference/pdf/rommes.pdf

Rommes, E., Overbeek, G., Scholte, R., Engels, R., & de Kemp, R. (2007). 'I'm not interested in computers': Gender-based Occupational Choices of Adolescents. *Information Communication and Society, 10*(3), 299–319. doi:10.1080/13691180701409838

Schneider, D. (2003). *The Psychology of Stereotyping*. New York: Guilford Press.

Turkle, S. (1995). *Life on the Screen: Identity in the Age of the Internet*. New York: Simon & Schuster.

ENDNOTE

[i] An anecdotatl observation in the context is that the Swedish "James Bond like" master spy Carl Hamilton (from books and films) has an alias as a computer expert.

Chapter 8

Absent Women:
Research on Gender Relations in IT Education Mediated by Swedish Newspapers

Martha Blomqvist
Uppsala University, Sweden

ABSTRACT

This chapter presents a study on the use of research based information on gender and IT education disseminated by Swedish newspapers between 1994 and 2004. The predominant content of the newspaper articles concerns the lack of women, and refers mostly to reports presenting statistics. A gender-blind discourse is almost nonexistent in the articles, meaning that the small proportion of women in IT education on the whole is understood as a problem. A masculinity-connoted discourse – assuming a close relationship between masculinity and technology – and a feminized discourse – based on the idea that women have qualities and skills important in the area of IT – are both given a significant voice, so that the link between masculinity and technology is strengthened and that a gender dichotomy is confirmed. However, a differentiated discourse, which acknowledges gender variations among women as well as men, has had little impact in the newspapers.

INTRODUCTION

Some ten years ago, somewhat surprisingly to most politicians, gender researchers, and educators, the proportion of women studying IT started to decrease. The decline started several years before the dot.com crisis, which therefore cannot explain it, and it occurred at about the same time in several countries in Western Europe (Valenduc et al., 2004)[1]. Different interpretations of the decline have been suggested, e.g. that young women find IT boring and are not interested in training for an IT job, or that young women believe that women are treated badly in the sector and therefore do not want to be part of it.

Media as Constructers of Social Reality

Television and daily newspapers are two of the main sources of information about the IT sector

DOI: 10.4018/978-1-61520-813-5.ch008

available to most people outside the sector. They do not, however, innocently reflect some kind of reality, but are influential producers of social reality, such as gender relations. Like all of us, the media participate in the everyday business of doing gender. The contributions of newspapers and television journalists, however, are the most widely spread, and their constructions of gender thus have an impact on a larger public. Television, making use of pictures as well as sound, is of course a more powerful medium than newspapers. Though younger persons read newspapers less often than elderly persons do, there is reason to believe that the traditional newspapers do have an influence also on young women.[2]

In order to discover what kind of information is disseminated about the ICT sector, the project *Gender relations and working conditions in the ICT sector*[3] has conducted a systematic analysis of contents of Swedish newspaper articles between 1994 and 2004 as they discuss the ICT sector and women.

THE NEWSPAPERS

Four Swedish national newspapers were selected for the analysis: Svenska Dagbladet (SvD), Dagens Nyheter (DN), Aftonbladet (AB) and Computer Sweden (CS). Two of the newspapers – SvD and DN – are traditional morning papers, though both have lately changed to a tabloid format. AB, a traditional tabloid, used to be an evening paper, but is now published in the morning. CS is a newspaper explicitly covering IT-related information and is published three times a week. DN is politically liberal, SvD is politically conservative, AB is social democratic and CS is 'politically neutral'. On the whole, SvD is the morning paper preferred by conservatives, DN has readers all over the political spectrum, while AB is the evening paper preferred by social democrats.[4] The political leanings of these newspapers have an impact mainly on the edito-

rial page; the news desks of the papers make a point of being autonomous.

Database Searches

The *Presstext* database comprises all articles published in DN since 1994, the *Mediearkivet* database comprises articles from SvD and AB, also since 1994, and the *Affärsdata* database contains all articles published in CS since 1992. These databases have been used for article searches in the papers for a ten-year period, from 1994 to June 2004. The search criteria used were 'wom* and IT' (in Swedish 'kvinn* and IT'). The Swedish kvinn* captures kvinna (woman), kvinnor (women) as well as kvinnlig (female) and kvinnlighet (femininity).

More than 7,000 articles in the four newspapers matched the search criteria. In quite a few of these articles, the 'IT' hit did not refer to information technology at all, but, for example, to post-*it* notes or, more often, to '*it*' in English song texts such as '*It*'s a man's world' or '*It*'s raining men'. These articles were excluded. A number of articles mentioning 'wom*' and 'IT', but in different contexts and without any connection, were also excluded.

The remaining 1,280 articles (201 from DN, 224 from SvD, 300 from AB and 555 from CS) connect the terms in a meaningful way and have been subject to analysis. Figure 1 shows the distribution of these articles in the four newspapers over the ten-year period.

We see that the distribution of articles follows a similar pattern in the four newspapers. Articles on 'wom* and IT' increased in the four newspapers during the second half of the 1990s, reached a peak in 2000 and then dropped to a low level by 2004. The small number of articles during the early years is not surprising, as the IT concept became established in Sweden only in the mid-90s, gradually replacing the concept of computer (in Swedish 'dator' and derivations of that term). But the reason for the decrease from

Figure 1. Articles discussing wom* and IT in DN, SvD, AB and CS between 1994 and 2004.

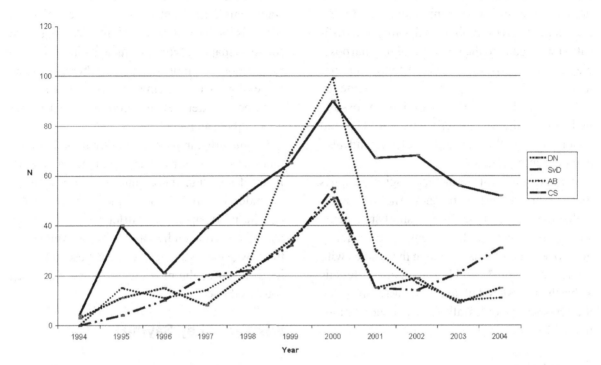

the year 2000? It coincides with the dot.com crisis. The research data suggest that the sector's economic decline then became the focus of media attention, and did so at the expense of questions about gender relations, which in the late 1990s received considerable media attention, but later dropped into the background.

A study of IT policies in the Nordic countries, conducted by Christina Mörtberg and Beathe Due (2004), shows that equal opportunity issues were common in policy texts during the years of IT expansion, but were left out of later policy documents. The researchers pose the question of whether we can afford equal opportunity issues only in times of expansion, thereby suggesting that equal opportunity matters are emphasized only in times of prosperity (Mörtberg & Due, 2004, p. 14). Our results support their findings; the daily newspapers' interest, especially the tabloid AB's, in gender relations in the IT sector seems to be extremely sensitive to economic fluctuations.

SUMMARIES OF ARTICLES

The article search was swiftly finished, reading the articles to decide whether they were relevant to our study took more time, but most time-consuming was summarizing the articles. As a tool for this, we used a modified version of Kenneth Burke's 'dramatistic pentad' (Burke, 1969). The pentad, comprising the elements act, scene, agent, agency and purpose, provides a method for analysis and critique of texts, and offers a systematic way of analysing situations, statements and courses of events narrated in, e.g., newspaper articles. The questions to be answered in the pentad are similar to the news reporter's questions: who, what, when, where, why. Like the journalist's questions, Kenneth Burke's pentad gives us a way to look at a topic from different angles.

The pentad is very useful for capturing different statements about the IT sector and it was interpreted and adapted to serve the purposes of the research. As the research is more interested in the 'outcome' and in the 'consequences' of the act than in its stated or implied goal, a major modification was made to the pentad: and the 'purpose' element was substituted with an 'outcome' element. In applying the pentad to the statements, the text is read very closely, avoiding the possible inclusion of the researcher's personal ideas and conclusions at this stage of analysis, and also avoiding interpretations.

One advantage of this methodological design is that it assures some transparency. Another benefit is that the result, in the form of short statements summarizing the article contents, gives a fairly good overview of what is said in the articles with reference to wom* and IT. The method offers us a shorthand way to talk about the ways in which the newspaper articles talk about gender relations in the IT sector.

Statements

In every article, at least one, often more than one, statement or claim is identified. A total of 3026 statements were identified. In each of them the elements 'scene', 'agent', 'act', 'agency' and 'outcome' were distinguished. Although all statements do not comprise all elements, many of them do.

The numbers of statements cannot be used as absolute measures of the amount of information, and it is important not to overemphasize their meaning. However, information about the sources of the statements and about their contents is given below and can be used as rough indicators of which sources are given a voice on different issues and how the issues are assessed. In a second step, a voice is attached to each statement.

Who's Talking?

Many articles make use of more than one source. This is not the case at the statement level; behind one statement there is principally only one source.

The uncontested main source for newspaper statements turned out to be the IT sector itself, which is the basis for every third statement in all four newspapers. Women managers in the IT sector are most common as sources, whereas women professionals and men managers occur as sources to an equal extent, each accounting for five per cent of the statements.

Studies, researchers, research, authors or books make up sources for 17 per cent of the statements. In the following, these categories are summed up under the label research/studies. SvD and AB are the newspapers that differ most as regards use of research/studies as a source. Among all the newspapers studied, SvD uses research/studies as a source the most, whereas AB uses such sources the least.

What are They Saying?

The outcome element in the statements were categorized as positive, negative or neutral/ambivalent as regards gender relations in the IT sector. Two persons independently conducted these estimations, reaching a level of agreement of more than 90 per cent. Where the estimates differed, the statements were examined again.[5] Typical positive outcomes are inclusion of women, improved equal opportunities in ICT professions or in technological education and training. Typical negative outcomes are exclusion of women, increased or stable male domination, discrimination of women, the shortcomings of women and women being disinterested in technology.

There are more statements presenting positive outcomes than negative ones, in all newspapers except in AB, where negative outcomes predominate. In SvD, positive outcomes outnumber negative ones more than in the other newspapers. My interpretation of these differences is that AB, the social democratic tabloid, takes a more sceptical and distanced stance to the IT industry than does SvD, the conservative newspaper, with its very close connections to trade and industry.

The statements from the IT sector comparatively often present positive outcomes, whereas research/studies as sources account for more than an average amount of statements with negative outcomes. This difference can be understood as an expression of different viewpoints. For sources that are part of the IT industry, it is more natural to present a positive picture of the industry – 'You don't bite the hand that feeds you' – whereas the role of researchers is different, and allows and encourages critical comments and observations.

Research and Studies

605 research-based statements were found: 88 in DN, 93 in SvD, 124 in AB and 300 in CS. Six major themes were recognized in the statements: Use of computers/Internet, Education, Equal opportunity, Management, Wages and Work environment. Table 1 shows the number of statements identified on these themes. As themes are overlapping in some statements, one statement may include more than one theme, e.g. Equal opportunity as well as Management themes.

Statements on the themes listed in the table make up 61 per cent of all research-based statements in DN, 73 per cent of statements in SvD, 72 per cent of statements in AB and 77 per cent of statements in CS.

The table shows that the theme of 'Management' is the one paid most attention to by DN and, especially so, by SvD. In AB, information

on 'Use of computers/Internet' is predominant, and in CS, the 'Management' and 'Use' themes are given the same amount of attention.

Under the theme of 'Education', there were research-based statements in 62 of the articles – 9 in DN, 16 in SvD, 8 in AB and 31 in CS. Most of these statements are negative. At this point, a reservation is appropriate. There are more research-based statements in the newspapers that discuss computer education, but without mentioning the concept 'IT'. These articles are not included in the analysis below.

In the following sections, the contents of the articles are presented, followed by an examination of the data supporting the statements. Finally, different understandings of reasons for the (small) number of women in IT education expressed in the articles are explored.

WOMEN AND IT EDUCATION

The predominant content of statements on women and education concerns the lack of women. Most discussions of this lack rely on quantitative research.

Statistics on the Distribution

A good half of the articles – 33 of 62 – present statistics on the representation of women and men in IT courses, also covering applicants or those

Table 1. Major themes in statements based on research/studies, n (%).

Themes	DN	SvD	AB	CS
Use of comp./Internet	11 (13)	11 (12)	43 (34)	74 (25)
Education	10 (11)	16 (17)	11 (9)	49 (17)
Equal opportunity	15 (17)	12 (13)	9 (7)	21 (7)
IT sector:				
Management	22 (25)	36 (39)	15 (12)	71 (24)
Wages	5 (6)	6 (6)	12 (10)	31 (10)
Work environment	2 (2	6 (6)	7 (6)	20 (7)

admitted to the courses. In DN's and SvD's articles, the statistics are always commented on, in AB and CS; they are sometimes left without comment. There are three main producers of statistics on IT education: the Swedish Agency for Economic and Regional Growth (Nutek), the Gender Equality Council for Transport and IT (Jämit) and the National Agency for Services to Universities and University Colleges (VHS).

In 1998 and 1999 statistics from a study conducted by Cecilia Sjöberg (1998), of Nutek, are presented. The study shows that the proportion of women graduating from IT programmes at most made up 37 per cent in 1986, and ten years later, in 1996, it was halved to 19 per cent.[6] The same figures from the study are reiterated in the newspapers, though not in SvD, where there is no reference to this study.

In 2000, Jämit steps in and becomes the main source of statistics on the gender distribution in IT education. Readers are again informed of decreasing proportions of women graduating from IT programmes (SOU 2000, p. 58). Figures from this report are presented in all four newspapers. In SvD they are found in a debate article, signed Görel Thurdin, the chairperson of Jämit, but not in the news sections.

In 2002, VHS becomes the most used source of educational statistics. Readers are informed of falling proportions of women admitted to technology- and computer-related education programmes.

In 2004, CS is the only newspaper still reporting on the statistics produced by VHS. At this time, the number of applications on the whole to the IT educational area had been decreasing for many years and it seems as if the newsworthiness of the proportion of women admitted was overshadowed by the dramatic decrease in the number of applicants of both sexes. Where women earlier had hit the headlines – Raset för kvinnor extra dramatiskt (Fall for women extra dramatic) (CS 20020909) and Svårt stoppa kvinnoraset (Hard to stop fall-off in women) (CS 20030711) – they

are now, though their numbers are still falling, found only in the article text. Below the headline "Katastrofläge – Antagningssiffrorna för IT och teknik de lägsta någonsin" (Catastrophic situation – admissions figures for IT and technology lowest ever) CS in 2004 reports:

According to statistics from VHS, the drop in number of applicants has been 30 per cent yearly from 2000 to 2003 prior to autumn admissions. This year's drop is only 10 per cent, which means that the decline is now levelling out. This has previously been explained by the drastic decrease in the number of women applicants, but this explanation no longer holds.

– The dramatic decline has ceased, but we can hardly claim that it is particularly popular. The figures just continue to go down. This applies to both male and female applicants, even though it is highest among women, says Per Nyholm, who works with admissions statistics at VHS. (CS 20040813)

The characterization of the situation as catastrophic seems to be motivated by the fact that the decline can no longer be explained only by the decrease in the numbers of women, but also applies to men.

As the figures from Nutek, Jämit and VHS are not fully comparable, it is not possible, relying only on the article contents, to follow in more detail the development over the ten years. The overall picture is, however, very obvious. The proportion of women in courses leading to work in the IT sector decreased during the period. It is no wonder that the negative accounts in the statements on the IT educational theme are much more frequent than the positive ones. But has there been anything other than gloomy statistics on admissions and applicants to report on?

There were only three articles containing statistics pointing in a positive direction in the batch on articles in the sample. The first is from 1995 and deals with a new engineering programme developed in Linköping:

40% women got into the IT Programme, a new 180-credit civil engineer programme at the University College of Technology in Linköping.

– The goal is a civil engineer programme that attracts women and that provides a somewhat broader perspective on computer technology, says Ingemar Ingemarsson, Professor of Information Technology and the man behind the programme.

The IT Programme is based on problem-based learning, PBL. This means that the starting point is a real-life problem and that, on the way to solving that problem, students acquire the knowledge they need. Students work in small project groups with a supervisor. Ingemar Ingemarsson is pleased with the results.

•

– It has gone very well. So far, this is still our honeymoon and everyone is very enthusiastic. We didn't really know what the response would be like, but less than 25% would not have been good. (CS 19951117. Fler tjejer vill bli dataingenjörer (More women want to become computer engineers))

In the article, the people responsible for similar courses at Chalmers and KTH also comment, saying that they too foresee, or already have noticed, an increase in the number of women applying. It is reasonable to assume that the newspaper coverage offers a chance for the universities to further promote their new initiatives.

Five years later, optimistic reports come from Uppsala University.

The penetration of the Internet has increased women students' interest in IT programmes, although men still predominate. The proportion of women in the Computer Science Programme increased during the mid-1990s from 10 to 20 per cent. (SvD 20000316. IT på tvären växer i längden (IT growing across the sexes in the long run))

Shortly thereafter, there is a report on a KTH effort, financed by the Ministry of Education, to employ women researchers and doctoral students.

These efforts gave immediate results. In only four years, the proportion of women postgraduate students and doctoral candidates increased from 10 to 25 per cent.

This trend would seem to have rubbed off on students, among which the proportion of women has increased from 22 to 27 per cent since 1993. (DN 20000603. Mästare i mansdominans (Masters of male dominance))

Thus, of the 33 articles presenting statistics on IT education, only three contain some optimistic accounts. Two of these concern educational endeavours explicitly aiming at increasing the recruitment of women.

The next section takes a closer look at the articles which are not based on statistics.

Distributions Discussed Without Numbers

There were 15 articles that, though not based on statistics, relate to the small numbers of women in IT training. Three of them also contain positive statements. Two of these are about a labour market education effort called the SwIT programme. The aim of this programme was to provide skills training for occupations within the IT area that had a shortage of labour. The commission, to train some 10,000 persons, most of them unemployed, was given to Industriförbundet (The Association of Swedish Industries) and the trade association IT-företagen (Swedish IT Industries) (Martinsson, 1999, Johansson & Martinsson, 2000). One of the articles, including partly positive information, was published in SvD in 1999.

With regard to the gender distribution among SwIT participants, following the training, the per cent of women finding employment is higher than that of men. 70.5 per cent of women and 66.6 per cent of men have found employment after completing a SwIT course. (SvD 19990408. Risad IT-satsning ger många jobb (Criticized IT programme gives many jobs))

A second article containing the very same information was published simultaneously in CS. (CS 19990409. 70 procent får jobb efter Swit-utbildning (70 per cent find a job after SwIT course)). In both articles, it is pointed out that, though the proportion of women is lower than in other labour market education programmes, women finishing this training more often get a job than do men.

At Luleå University of Technology an IT programme, Datateknisk ingång för kvinnor (Preparatory Programme in Computer Science and Engineering), was developed in order to attract women. The outcome of this effort is reported on by Christina Mörtberg:

– We had an incredibly small proportion of women in the computer technology programme. But the proportion of women has increased dramatically through admissions to the Preparatory Programme, says Christina Mörtberg (CS 20010307. "Kvinnor har samma tekniksyn som män" ("Women have the same outlook on technology as men"))

One of these articles containing optimistic statements about women in IT education thus

concerns programmes specially developed to recruit more women.

Other Aspects of IT Education

Only 14 of the articles in the educational theme did not take their point of departure as the lack of women in IT education. Three of these deal with an investigation of IT companies conducted by JämO (The Equal Opportunities Ombudsman) (JämO 2000). DN presents JämO's report in a news article:

One reason often given for the skewed gender distribution [in IT companies] is that it is difficult to find women with technical expertise. But considering the measures taken in higher education to encourage women, JämO does not accept these excuses. (DN 20000203. JämO ger IT-företagen bakläxa (JämO rebuffs IT companies))

In AB, the report is mentioned in one item:

IT companies' claims about the lack of women with technical expertise do not correspond with reality. On the contrary, according to JämO, it has become easier to recruit women with IT qualifications during recent years, thanks to targeted programmes. (AB 20000630. 21 IT-företag får bakläxa av Jämo (IT companies rebuffed by Jämo))

In SvD, the report is criticized in an editorial column:

In the report presented on the outcome of the witch-hunt, the politically correct is applauded. Companies making known that special competence programmes and training will be established are emphasized, despite the fact that they confirm the picture of a lack of women with the desired qualifications in the IT industry. Companies attending to a problem that JämO denies the existence of receive praise. (SvD 20000805. Grötmyndigheten slår till (Pomposity strikes))

The quote makes very clear that the question of women in IT, the interpretation of the issue, and suggestions on how to handle it are indeed political. SvD, the conservative newspaper in opposition to the social democratic government policy, here seizes the opportunity to mock JämO, a government authority.

The remaining eleven articles deal with various issues, and do not have any common contents. Only two of them, both published in 2004 by CS, report some optimistic news:

- Women between 30 and 40 have shown the greatest interest in university studies over the Internet. (CS 20040806. Kvinnor mest intresserade av nätstudier (Women most interested in Net-based studies)).
- Although male upper secondary school teachers are much more likely to have access to their own computer at school than are female upper secondary school teachers, female teachers generally have more positives attitudes towards using IT in teaching than do male teachers. (CS 20041001. Kvinnliga lärare utan skoldator – men de har en positivare attityd till IT i undervisningen än män (Women teachers lack computers at school – but have a more positive attitude towards IT in teaching than men do)).

All in all, the picture of women and IT education presented by the newspapers during the ten-year period is a very pessimistic one. In 62 research-based articles, there were only eight optimistic accounts. Without doubt, women in the context of IT education are constructed as a problem.

DATA SUPPORTING THE ACCOUNTS

As is already evident from the examples above, the lion's share of the statements based on research/ studies refer to reports presenting statistics. A smaller number of the newspaper accounts are based on other kinds of research or studies.

Surveys

There are three surveys referred to, all of them in CS. The first one is a questionnaire directed to men and women, who had been admitted to the IT programme in Linköping, asking about their *motives* for applying to the training.

The second survey mentioned is a yearly investigation, conducted by the IT department at Telia, reporting that women employed at Telia do not think the IT training they get is good enough (CS 19970516. Internt missnöje med datasupport på Telia (Internal dissatisfaction with IT training at Telia)).

The third is an attitude questionnaire directed to upper secondary school teachers and asking about their access to computers. (CS 20041001. Kvinnliga lärare utan skoldatorer – men de har positivare attityd till IT I undervisningen än män (Women teachers lack computers at school – but have a more positive attitude towards IT in teaching than men do.))

Researchers

Two articles, both published in CS, quote researchers, but without specifying the research or publications as a source. In the first (quoted below under the heading: 'Understandings of gender in IT education as an example of a differentiated discourse'), Christina Mörtberg objects to the idea that women and men have different outlooks on technology. (CS 20010307. "Kvinnor har samma tekniksyn som män" ("Women have the same outlook on technology as men"))

The second is a debate article written by Inger Stjernqvist, a PhD student at KTH, who urges her (fictitious) daughter to demand IT training that does not require that one has had the computer as a hobby from boyhood and that does not one-sidedly attach importance to the technology. (CS

20030115. Några ord om IT till min dotter – om jag hade någon. (A few words about IT to my daughter – if I had one))

Qualitative Studies

Only five articles provide references to qualitative studies and research. The first one is found in AB in 1996. It refers to *Women and Computers* by Frances Grundy (1996), who teaches computer science at Keele University.

[Frances Grundy] considers that boys have an early advantage. In spite of all the debate, computer training in the schools easily becomes the boys' department. The girls are interested enough, but they have a social pressure they must fight against. It is assumed that they should actually be interested in other things. (AB 19960403. Klart att tjejen ska ha en dator (Of course the girl should have a computer))

The citation corresponds with some of the content of the book, though the book (of course) gives a thorough overview of previous research and knowledge in the area of gender and technology.

In 1997, SvD reports from a seminar for young unemployed women held by the pedagogue Ann Steenberg.

The pedagogue calls for more fighting spirit among girls, but also for more formal competence.

– Look around you and see what's happening. Adjust to the demands of the market and complement with IT and computer skills, which is what everyone says we need. (SvD 19970515. Tjejer måste lära sig att säga JAG (Girls have to learn to say "I")).

The article refers to a popular science publication by Steenberg (1997) in which she advocates

teaching boys and girls separately for shorter periods. Her arguments are based on her own teaching experiences in the compulsory school.

In an editorial column, DN cites a chapter by Anna Kamjou (1998), researcher in media and communication.

The preconception that women have a hard time mastering science and technology is deeply rooted. To be sure, few women choose to study or work in these areas, but that can be traced to stereotypical ideas that women should choose "soft" occupations, such as nursing and teaching. Men, on the other hand, are more technically inclined and suited to becoming physicists or computer programmers. These sociocultural misconceptions still affect young people's career choices to a great degree, despite the fact that we know they are untrue. (DN 19980323. IT-samhället ger kvinnor möjligheter. (IT society gives women opportunities))

Kamjou's chapter gives an overview of mainly theoretical writings in the area of gender and technology, and it seems to be a very relevant reference in the context.

Also in DN, a doctoral thesis by Maria Udén (2000) is referred to, more or less in passing:

It is still taboo for women to talk about power. [ ] Despite ten years of propaganda trying to attract women to technical training programmes, women's values and outlooks have little scope in technical programmes and the number of women who choose IT training is in constant decline. (DN 000604. Avhandlingen (The doctoral thesis))

The research material for the thesis consists of interviews with women engineers. As the thesis does not focus on gendered values and perspectives, the conclusions presented in the article seem to me to be somewhat beside the point and do not do the thesis real justice.

The fifth reference to a publication is found in SvD in a debate article, written by Görel Thurdin, who cites a doctoral thesis by Minna Salminen-Karlsson (1999).

For decades, male teachers have provided technical training for male students. Female students encounter male dominance both in their daily lives and in education. Male behaviour patterns, values, language usage and the male drinking culture are predominant and normative – the female is deviant. Women and men have different values regarding use of technology and different attitudes towards military technology and environmental problems. (SvD 20001106. Nyansera debatten om globaliseringen "Pedagogik skrämmer kvinnor" (Nuance the debate on globalization. "Teaching methods scare women"))

The empirical findings presented in Minna Salminen-Karlsson's thesis are based on observations and tape-recordings of planning meetings for new computer engineering programmes, and on interviews with academic staff taking part in the reform work.

Thus, none of the statements in the Education theme in these articles stem from research or studies on women who are actually taking part in IT education.

UNDERSTANDINGS OF GENDER IN IT EDUCATION

In the articles in the sample, the small number of women in IT education is often commented on as being troublesome, worrying, alarming or just gloomy. Why it is a problem, and for whom, is not always made clear. It probably does not seem necessary to develop thoughts on the issue; the texts are all written during a period of an all-embracing equal opportunity discourse in Swedish society. According to this dominant Swedish discourse, the equal distribution of women and men is always good, an uneven distribution is always bad, and the more uneven it is, the worse the situation.

The predominant equal opportunity discourse, however, does contain sub-discourses.

In Norwegian discussions of women in IT training, Hilde Corneliussen (2003) has identified three discursive understandings of the small numbers of women.

The *gender-blind* discourse does not focus on gender, and it understands technology as gender neutral. The fact that more men than women choose an IT education is seen as an expression of the fact that men happen to be more interested. A statement like 'women can manage if they want to and if they dare' fits into this discourse. The understanding does not call for a change in the situation. Women and men are treated the same, and we should not worry about the fact that less women than men get an IT education. According to Corneliussen, this non-problematizing attitude prevailed until the numbers of women started to decline, i.e. until the mid-90s. At that time, it became more common to problematize the gender and technology issue also outside the research community.

The *masculinity-connoted* discourse is based on an understanding of a close link between masculinity and information technology. Thus, it constructs gender in relation to information technology in a way that makes women deviant, thereby putting them in an inferior position in IT training. A reasonable strategy to counter the disadvantage of women is through re-organization, e.g. creating women-only groups in courses, or through support measures directed at women. The statement 'women can make it, if they comply with the masculine norm' fits into this discourse.

The *feminized* discourse brings about a twist in the masculinity-connoted discourse, without challenging the link between masculinity and technology. Instead, the definition of IT skills is widened and comes to include also social and communicative skills, which are ascribed to women. Women, thus, receive a room of their own within IT, and their own relation to information technology. Men are still ascribed technological skills and the connection between men and technology is not questioned. The gender dichotomy is thereby confirmed.

Hilde Corneliussen calls for a discourse that embraces gender and also gives space for variations among women as well as men, a *differentiated* discourse, that allows women to take an interest in programming and men to be socially talented.

A closer look at the contents of the articles in relation to the understandings of gender in IT education as defined by Corneliussen proves interesting. As I do not wish to over-interpret the data, I have refrained from categorizing articles that do not connect with the discourses in an obvious way.

I have identified only one article which connects to a gender-blind discourse. The article stems from the editorial column of SvD and comments on measures suggested by Jämit.

There are extremely few women in management and on the boards of IT companies. This shows the extent to which men and women follow traditional patterns when choosing their occupation and education. (SvD 20000630. Jämit vet bäst? (Jämit knows best?))

This editorial is in line with another editorial from SvD in 2000, quoted above (SvD 20000805. Grötmyndigheten slår till (Pomposity strikes)). Both reject any measures taken by the government to change the status quo as regards women in IT. As the writer in no way suggests that the traditional educational choices should be worrying, or worth changing, I argue that this article belongs to a gender-blind discourse.

The masculinity-connoted discourse is the most common one in all the newspapers. It is in many cases spelt out to explain the small number of women in IT training, also when the person expressing it does not necessarily embrace it. In connection with publication of the above-mentioned report from Nutek (Sjöberg, 1999), the author of the report states:

– Young women see IT as a male profession, which was not the case ten years ago. With the advent of the hacker culture, IT has been taken over by men. (CS 19981106. Allt mindre andel kvinnor på IT-utbildningarna. (Increasingly small proportion of women in IT programmes))

With reference to the small number of women students in the SwIT programme, Margareta Winberg, the Swedish social democratic Minister for Equality, who had promoted measures to attract women, makes following statement:

– [...]The explanation I've heard is that the first courses were not very well adapted to women, but that the upcoming courses will be more female directed, says Margareta Winberg, the current Minister for Equality [...]

– Even in elementary school girls are given less room at the computers than boys are. I support teachers who instruct boys and girls separately.

The article ends:

Ingemar Ingemarsson's three best reasons why girls and IT belong together:

1. Girls often have better prerequisites to get through the programme. It requires patience, precision and an ability to see the whole.
2. IT technology is not "inhuman". On the contrary, such technology is just as close to human beings as our good old telephone.
3. Both sexes are needed to create technology that is adapted to human beings of the future.

(AB 60 19981115. Tjejer nobbar grabbarnas IT. Ny larmrapport: färre kvinnor väljer datautbildningar. (Girls reject guys' IT. A new alarming report: fewer women choose computer programmes.))

Because Winberg presupposes that women are in need of special treatment – 'female framing' of the courses – in order to take part in IT training, and that training in girls-only groups is necessary to help girls dare to use computers in school, her statement belongs to the masculinity-connoted discourse. Ingemar Ingmarsson's points are, however, closer to a feminized discourse. This is also common in our articles. In an article on IT training, tailored to fit women, the person in charge of the training states:

Women don't grab at opportunities and maybe don't dare apply to the same extent to regular IT programmes, which is why these kinds of alternatives are good.

– We need to make women understand that IT is not just for techno-freaks and hackers, but that female traits are just as important, says Krister Bergman, in charge of operations at the Technical IT College for Women (CS 19999115. IT-utbildningar för kvinnor möts av fördomar (IT programmes for women met with prejudice))

A letter to the editor in SvD states:

Less than one-third of those admitted in the areas computers and technology are women. And this proportion has decreased markedly since last year. If this negative trend continues, it will become more than an equality issue, it will become a severe threat to Swedish IT development in general.

Women with technical training often possess a perspective that men lack, and naturally vice

versa. (SvD 20021010. Sverige hotat som IT-nation (Sweden threatened as an IT country))

It is the unique perspective ascribed to women, a perspective judged to be important to the development of Sweden, that positions this statement in a feminized discourse. The message is not compatible with previously quoted editorial comments in SvD and shows that the newspaper's political position does not govern contents of letters to the editor.

Expressions of a differentiated discourse are not common. I have identified only three. The first is found in DN in an editorial article referring to a research publication by Anna Kamjou (1998) and quoted above under the heading Publications. In the article, beliefs about women being suitable for care work and educational work and men for technical work are pointed out as misconceptions (DN 19980323. IT-samhället ger kvinnor möjligheter. (IT society gives women opportunities))

In an article, in CS in 2001, two understandings of gender and technology are confronted – a feminized and a differentiated understanding:

– Women and men have different experiences and therefore different frames of reference from which to begin. This means that women deal with technology in a different way than men do. The industry is missing out on an important dimension when the female outlook on technology isn't allowed to influence developments. Sweden can't afford this, says Görel Thurdin, on International Women's Day. [...]

But Görel Thurdin is met with opposition from several well-known researchers who claim that there is no difference between how men and women understand technology. One of these is Christina Mörtberg, Doctor of Engineering in Gender and Technology at Luleå University of Technology. She has also served on the board of Jämit.

– Before I started doing research, I worked 20 years in the computer industry. Of course I developed systems in the same way men did then and of course women in IT usually have more in common with their male colleagues than with women who work at preschools, she says

According to her, there are many gender equality projects trying to get girls interested in using technology, not in the technology itself. She feels that this is the wrong way to proceed.

– Of course girls are interested in the technology itself, she says. (CS 20010307. "Kvinnor har samma tekniksyn som män." "Women have the same outlook on technology as men do.")

Christina Mörtberg's assertion about sameness as regards men's and women's technological work, and her dismissal of equal opportunity measures that assume that young women are not interested in technology per se, place this statement in a differentiated discourse.

The third example is also found in CS. The person in charge of the IT programme at Chalmers University of Technology lets us know:

To broaden the perspective, the IT Programme has something called the Culture Project, which is run by teachers and students. All students in the programme have to take courses in Swedish and English as well as an environment course. [...]

It is sometimes said that male students take over easily and that women are pushed aside.

— The drop-out figures don't show that women are unhappy once they've been admitted, says Erik Eliasson.

— When students do exercises in pairs, it is easy for the more capable of the two to take over, but that does not mean that men are always taking over. (CS 20030711. Svårt stoppa kvinnoraset (Hard to stop fall-off in women))

The *masculinity-connoted* and the *feminized discourses* are thus given much more voice than the differentiated discourse. This means that the link between masculinity and technology is being strengthened and that the gender dichotomy is being confirmed.

CONCLUSION

Between 1995 and 2004, the Swedish newspapers under study have mediated research results that in the main describe IT education in very negative terms as regards women's participation.

Studies reporting statistics are shown to have a great impact and make up more than half of the studies referred to. Qualitative research is more seldom used as a source. Numbers seem to have newsworthiness per se, and are sometimes presented without any comments or analysis. Qualitative research, mostly much more theoretically informed, without doubt requires more work if it is to be transformed to an article text. Furthermore, statistics pour in regularly, from well-known producers of statistics, often government authorities, whereas qualitative research has to be looked for. All this taken together means that statistics are more accessible to journalists and much easier to use as a source in an article. Nick Davies (2008) found that the lion's share of stories in the British press are directly derived from press releases or taken straight from the main British news agency, the Press Association (Davies, 2008, pp. 90f.). Davies understands this as a result of commercial pressure on costs. Stories need to be cheap, meaning 'quick to cover', safe to publish; they need to 'select safe facts' preferably from official sources (ibid., p. 114, p. 118). Statistics produced by government authorities must be the ultimate 'safe facts', and the dominance of statistical information in newspaper articles can thus be understood as a reflection of journalists' working conditions.

The gender-blind discourse is nearly absent in these articles. This means that the decreasing proportion of women in IT education on the whole is understood as a problem in the articles using research as a source. An assumed close relationship between masculinity and technology is used as a point of departure in several articles, but the idea that women have other qualities and skills important in the IT area is also common. A differentiated discourse, however, has not had an impact in the newspapers. My guess is that a masculinity-connoted discourse and a feminized discourse are much more worthwhile to popularize in a newspaper article than is a differentiated discourse, which presupposes problematizing the gender stereotypes to some degree, and that differentiated understandings therefore are given less voice. Again, the commercial pressure on journalism, resulting in the favouring of stories based on 'safe ideas' that do not contradict loved and prevailing wisdoms, can be seen as partly responsible for the reproduction of the traditional simplified discourses (Davies, 2008, p.125)

What the newspapers have mediated about research on gender and IT education is that masculinity and technology are closely connected, and that women are thus oddballs in the world of IT, that IT education programmes have not been adapted to women, and that women, though they are not skilled in technology, have other qualities that are important in the area of IT. Most of the statements based on research are about the absence of women in IT training. In the articles, we find very little information based on research or studies on women actually taking part in IT training. The research mediated by newspapers thus focuses on women's non-existence, not on their presence.

These research-based statements on IT education do not portray IT education as an attractive

choice. In as much as the information given in newspapers has some impact on young women's thinking and on their choice of educational paths, newspapers do not do much to interest women in IT. The main responsibility for this, however, does not fall on the media. Most of the coverage seems to be in good accordance with the research reported. In the media reports covered here only one case of reformulation. In all the other instances the research findings seem to be reported fairly accurately. Can researchers be held responsible for the message communicated about women being absent in IT training? Such an attribution of responsibility will no doubt be met by immediate objections like 'I cannot report about women being present, when they are not'. However, the analysis presented here suggests that researchers could change the way their work is reported. One way to do this would be to put more effort into the press releases – to make sure that the accounts of women in IT training are nuanced enough that they do not invite unjustified interpretation of gender stereotypes. Also, speculation or discussion about what might change the present situation, indicating possible ways forward, would shift the one-dimensional focus on absence to a focus on change. As part of demonstrating the value of their work, it is becoming increasingly important for researchers to play an active role as sources of news material (Hammersley, 2006). In that role, it is also essential that they take an interest in how media report on research results.

ACKNOWLEDGMENT

Thank you to the *GLIT Research Network* for the opportunity to of presenting an earlier version of this paper at the *Symposium on Gender, Learning and IT*, in Helsingborg, August 2007. This network and symposium received support from *the KK-Foundation (The Knowledge Foundation of Sweden)* and its research programme *LearnIT*. I gratefully acknowledge the contributions of

Kristina Eriksson and Agneta Helmius, my co-researchers in the project. Thanks also to the anonymous reviewers for comments and to the editors of this anthology for support.

REFERENCES

Burke, K. (1969). *A Grammar of Motives*. Berkley, CA: University of California Press.

Corneliussen, H. (2003). Konstruksjoner av kjönn ved hoyre IKT-utdanning i Norge. (Constructions of gender in higher ICT education in Norway) *Kvinneforskning 4*.

Davies, N. (2008). *Flat Earth News*. London: Chatto & Windus.

Grundy, F. (1996). *Women and Computers*. Exeter, UK: Intellect Books.

Hammersley, M. (2006). *Media bias in reporting social research*. London: Routledge.

JämO(2000). Rapport från en granskning av 22 IT-företags jämställdhetsplaner. (Report on survey of 22 IT companies' plans for gender equality)

Johansson, P., & Martinsson, S. (2000). Det nationella IT-programmet – en slutrapport om SwIT. (The national IT programme – final report on SwIT) [Uppsala, Sweden: IFAU.]. *Forskningsrapport, 2000*, 8.

Kamjou, A. (1998) "Han, hon, den, det" ("He, she, it") in Westerberg, Bengt (ed).

Martinsson, S. (1999). *Det nationella IT-programmet – en delrapport om SwIT. (The national IT programme – interim report on SwIT)*. Uppsala, Sweden: IFAU.

Mörtberg, C., & Due, B. (2004) "Med IT och kön som prisma i studier av nordiska IT-policies" in Mörtberg, C. & Due, B. (ed) (2004) Informationsteknologi och kön som prisma i analyser av nordiska IT-policies. (Information technology and gender as prisms in analyses of Nordic IT policies) NIKK Småskrifter nr. 9.

Nordicom–Sveriges Mediebarometer. (1998-2006). (Nordicom – Sweden's Media Barometer) Retrieved February, 2008, from http://www.nordicom.gu.se

Salminen-Karlsson, M. (1999). *Bringing women into computer engineering. Curriculum reform processes at two institutes of technology. Linköping studies in education and psychology*. Linköping, Sweden: Linköping University.

Sjöberg, C. (1998). *Utbildning och arbetsmarknad för IT-specialister. (Education and the labor market for IT specialists)*. Stockholm: Nutek.

Steenberg, A. (1997) *Flickor och pojkar i samma skola. (Girls and boys in the same school.)* Solna: Ekelunds Förlag.

Udén, M. (2000). *Tekniskt sett av kvinnor. (Women technically speaking.)* Luleå: Tekniska högskolan. Institutionen för Arbetsvetenskap.

Valenduc, G. (2004). *Widening Women's Work in Information and Communication Technology*. Namur, Belgium: European Commission.

Westerberg, B. (1998). *Han, hon, den, det. Om genus och kön. (He, she, it. About gender and sex.)*. Stockholm: Ekerlids Förlag.

KEY TERMS AND DEFINITIONS

Gender: The social dimension of being male or female.

Newspaper Articles: Pieces of journalistic writing appearing in the press.

Research-Based: Using research to inform the development of something.

IT Training: Skills based education which uses information technology to deliver aspects such as content and assessment.

Quantitative (Research): Research which obtains and analyses data which can be numerically analysed.

Qualitative (Research): Research which deals with unstructured information that is not readily analysed by numerical techniques and is more often used in the social sciences to get access to human understanding and motivation.

Discourses: A communication, usually entailing a narrative with meaning.

ENDNOTES

[1] Interestingly enough, the situation is very different in some non-Western countries, like Malaysia. (See, e.g., Ulf Mellström's chapter in this anthology.)

[2] In the age group 15-24 years in Sweden, 55 per cent read a morning paper and 29 per cent an evening paper (Nordicom–Sveriges Mediebarometer 1998-2006).

[3] The project is financed by the Swedish Council for Working Life and Social Research. Researchers also participating in the project are Kristina Eriksson and Agneta Helmius.

[4] A competing evening paper, not included in this analysis, is Expressen, which is politically liberal.

[5] In this context, the terms positive and negative are not equivalent to good and bad, and the categorization does not imply an assessment of the research sources.

[6] During these years the total numbers of graduated increased from 1301 to 2097, meaning that there was a decrease of women in absolute numbers as well.

Chapter 9
Heteronormativity Revisited:
Adolescents' Educational Choices, Sexuality and Soaps

Els Rommes[1]
Radboud University, The Netherlands

ABSTRACT

The aim of this chapter is to explore to what extent heteronormativity, the norm that man and woman are attracted to each other because of their presumed difference and complementarity, can offer an explanation for the persisting association between masculinity and technological/computer competence. Two aspects of heteronormative gender relations, namely sexual attractiveness and the heteronormative division of labour are particularly explored. The main focus in this chapter is on how technological competence and the gendered division of labour and of sexual attractiveness are represented in mass media. Along with this, some examples of the consequences of these heteronormative imaginaries and ideology for people's lives will be given. Amongst youth popular soap operas, stereotypical images are repeated of technologically competent men and socially competent women. For some women, this image also seemed to dominate in their personal lives, where they seemed to want to stay away from technologies as soon as there was a man around. Being (hetero)sexually attractive and being computer competent did not go well together in several block buster movies. The adolescents included in this study clearly shared this notion. These two aspects of heteronormativity do seem to strengthen the understanding of why it is so hard for women to choose a career in technology and particularly in computing science.

INTRODUCTION

In most Western (oriented) countries, like the USA, Japan and some European countries, the gender-segregation of Science, Engineering and Technology

DOI: 10.4018/978-1-61520-813-5.ch009

(SET) education and professions continues to exist. Especially in the Netherlands, girls hardly ever want anything to do with what they see as science or 'technology', nor do they imagine themselves in a career in SET. The European project 'Motivation' studied pupils of around 15 years in Germany, France, Slovakia, Austria, Sweden, Spain and the

Netherlands. Interviews with around sixty pupils in these countries showed that the Dutch pupils and especially the girls were least interested in SET. Only 21 percent of the Dutch girls in the study were interested, whereas 80 percent of Slovenian young women seemed interested (Els Rommes & Schönberger, Forthcoming). Indeed, in academic studies, the percentage of female Dutch students in technological subjects is 17, which is only half the number of other European and OECD-countries (Buis, 2003). Similarly, a recent European study shows that of pupils in the countries France, UK, Italy, Poland and the Netherlands, the Dutch pupils and especially the Dutch girls are least interested in a study Information and Communication Technologies (ICTs). Only 8 percent of Dutch girls expressed an interest, whereas these numbers were for instance 48 percent for the UK and 43 percent of the girls in Poland indicated they were interested (Gras-Velazquez, Joyce, & Debry, 2009). Indeed, only 12 percent of computing science students is female in the Netherlands, which is again the lowest number in the EU.

There are some possible explanations for why these numbers are particularly low in the Netherlands. A majority of the Dutch women has part time employment rather than full time, making paid part time work by women in the Netherlands by far the highest in the world. Only recently, child care provisions have picked up in quantity and quality. As SET and ICT work is usually regarded as having long working hours and a bad work-life balance, these bad child care provisions and a culture which encourages women to stay (part time) at home to care for their children may offer one explanation for why Dutch women lag behind in choosing SET as a career. On the other hand, the same notions of bad work-life balance exist in other professions such as medicine, which is particularly popular amongst young women nowadays. Another consequential difference between countries can be found in their educational systems: If girls are obliged to follow SET subjects

until a later age, they are more likely to develop a stronger interest in SET (Langen & Vierke, 2009). Again, this may offer only a partial explanation, since there are more countries in which children are given the choice to drop SET subjects at a younger age, and which do not have as low numbers of girls in SET as the Netherlands. Finally, the comparison between (post)capitalist and (post)communist countries offers additional explanations: The presence of a political system enforcing careers for women, providing child care and offering non-sexist education has been identified as a main factor in explaining the higher numbers of women in SET in (post)communist countries than in countries with a capitalist background (Blagojevic et al., 2004). This does, however, not explain why the numbers in the Netherlands of all (post)capitalist countries are so particularly low.

The main explanation for adolescents' gendered occupational choices, underlying other explanations, seems to be that masculinities and technologies have become intertwined, so that being technology or computer competent is 'gender inappropriate', or 'gender inauthentic' behaviour, as Wendy Faulkner has called it, for women (Faulkner, 2000).[2] This 'inauthentic'ness is closely connected with the notion that 'in our culture heterosexuality is posited on an ideological attraction of opposites' (Faulkner, 2000: 782). Hence, the aim of this chapter is to explore to what extent sexuality, or the more encompassing term heteronormativity, the invisible and underlying force behind gender relations (Butler, 1999; Rich, 1993; Warner, 1991), can offer an explanation for the persisting association between masculinity and technological/computer competence. What does heteronormativity, as an analytical lens, add as explanation for the continuing disassociation between women and technology/ IT? I will particularly focus on two aspects of heteronormative gender relations, namely sexual attractiveness and the heteronormative division of labour.

As heteronormativity is as much an ideal which forms part of our symbolic environment (e.g. in fairy tales, stories and dreams) as it shapes our daily lives, I will use two kinds of data. On the one hand, I will describe images of gender, technology and heterosexuality in amongst youth popular media contents, particularly some Dutch soap operas and Hollywood movies, to map some of the 'heterosexual imaginary' that Ingraham described as 'underlying heteronormative structures', because this imaginary makes heteronormativity invisible through normalization (Ingraham, 1997). On the other hand and as a way to show how heteronormativity can play a part in girls' and women's lives, I will use examples from material I have gathered in the course of time during various kinds of research. In various interviews and focus group interviews I have done in the past years with adolescents and adult women I encountered stories which were interesting but hard to interpret. Only by using the concept of heteronormativity, their stories about their images of technology and about what they find attractive in their (future) partner seem to make sense. I will use some gathered material of (focus group) interviews with adolescents and particularly focus on the stories of Judith, a middle aged heterosexual woman, and Tina, an 18 year old early user of the Internet, as heteronormativity seemed to play a particularly interesting role in their relationship with technology, particularly ICTs. All of the informants used for this study have a white, middle class, Dutch background. It may very well be that heteronormativity has a very different shape for men and women with other backgrounds.

Heteronormativity is all the more relevant for teenagers' occupational choices as adolescents are in the middle of the project of being seen and seeing themselves as no longer a child but as an adult-in-the-becoming. One of the crucial aspects of the negotiation and building of an adult identity includes a sexual identity and coming to terms with a body that is shaping itself along gendered lines. As Linda Stepulevage wrote: 'negotiating and building an identity in childhood and adolescence includes a sexual identity, in which the

desire or need to attract, please, spend time with, and invest in a sexual relationship with a male or another female is intertwined with learning.' (Stepulevage, 2001). Part of this identity building process and the vulnerability and insecurity that belongs to it, is that adolescents are heavily involved in the project of being (seen as) normal, as belonging to a group. It is not coincidental that some researchers found that thinking in stereotypes is at its peak during early adolescence (Hill & Lynch, 1983).

A word of caution is clearly in place here. By writing about the (hetero)normative, I make invisible the many women who love computing and technologies, sometimes even for the same reasons as for which many women do not feel at home in these professions. Katherine Landström and Linda Stepulevage, for example, wrote about lesbian women who may feel attracted to computing science for the same reasons that hetero women may feel disinterested in this field (Landström, 2007; Stepulevage, 2001). Moreover, in writing about heteronormative gender and symbolic associations of masculinities and technologies, I run the risk of not only repeating, but also reinforcing the same old stereotypes of men and women, masculinities and femininities. As Knut Sorensen and various others have warned, by repeating these dichotomies, gender and technology studies analysts run the risk of enlarging or even creating the stereotypes that we want to break down by analyzing them (Gansmo, Lagesen, & Sorensen, 2003). The modernist approach of bringing mechanisms into the light in the hope that by showing their construction they will lose their effect may be too optimistic. This disclaimer may, for the same reasons, also have no effect.

The Concept of Heteronormativity

So what do I mean when writing about heteronormativity? I follow Stevi Jackson in saying that heteronormativity "defines not only a normative sexual practice but also a normal way of life', meaning that 'in their daily lives women are frequently identified and evaluated in terms of their sexual availability/attractiveness to men and their presumed 'place' within heterosexual relationships as wives and mothers', what she calls the (heterosexual) domesticity (source). Judith Butler (1999) adds to this the relevance of hierarchies and power relations, when she wrote that "[gender] emerges as the congealed form of the sexualization of inequality between men and women (....) sexual hierarchy produces and consolidates gender" (Butler, 1999).

In a paper on the construction of gender identities, Dorte Marie Sondergaard gave an excellent example of how inequality can be sexualized at an individual level, when she quoted one of her research informants 'Henrik' talking about his ideal partner: "In reality maybe she should be a little bit below me for it to be, you know, ideal. But not too much below. That's what I feel. (…) So it's really my project to try and find a lover that I can be a man with. Without feeling that this is someone I control." (Sondergaard, 2002) What makes this sexualized inequality interesting is that there is a delicate balance of being unequal, but not too unequal: it does not make sense to love someone whom you look down upon too much, or whom you feel you 'control', as Henrik calls it, nor would it be healthy for the self-esteem of the underlying partner, I would add. Although Henrik talks about inequality in general terms, there is of course a more common way of sexualizing power difference whilst preserving a power balance. Henrik would probably not mind if his partner is 'bigger' in e.g. caring for children, the household or in being more attractive. So if each of the partners can be 'on top' or 'bigger' than the other in their own domain, they can both feel powerful and appreciate the other for their strength in their own domain, a way of dealing with each other in relationships which is implied by the concept of heteronormativity.

Maybe the most interesting point about heteronormativity is that it shows what men and women have to gain by continuously (re)constructing gender differences. The popularity of fairy tales, books such as 'Men are from Mars, Women are from Venus' and of soap operas and romantic novels may serve as testimonies for this. Firstly, there is the comfort and security people experience as they perceive their partner and themselves, man and woman, as 'naturally' needing each other, as being complementary to each other and meant to live happily ever after. And secondly, by splitting humans up in two categories, we at least do not have to compare and compete with people from the other sex, or worse, with our own partner, but can assume to be better in our own themes (and sometimes just a bit better). The obvious pleasure which some feminist strands and especially many of my students display in emphasizing the ways and arenas in which women do better than men shows some of these advantages. Similarly, girls have often been observed in feeling better than boys, whom they consider to be immature and childish. This way of feeling 'better' than boys often continues into adulthood, when women talk fondly about their husband as being still so 'boyish': for women, it seems there is a real feeling of empowerment in feeling motherly in some ways, even or especially about their partner, as men will probably feel a similar kind of empowerment by being the provider of their family. One of the problems with heteronormativity is that even though complementarity seems to imply 'of equal value', in modern western society in practice the masculine half of the values is usually given a higher value than the feminine.

To cut it short, we could say that heteronormativity is about the norm that man and woman, as ideal types, are attracted to each other because of their presumed difference and complementarity. This societal norm also affects homosexual couples. In many western societies, homosexual relationships are not given the same value as heterosexual, which shows for example in that they do not have the same marital rights or the same rights for fertility treatments as heterosexual couples. Moreover, the norm of being heterosexual is used to reinforce the norm of having a proper heterogender. Boys who behave 'too feminine' are policed by their peers by being called 'poofter' or 'gay' (Frosh, Phoenix, & Pattman, 2002). Similarly, girls who display masculine connoted interests are warned against this behaviour by being called 'lezzie'. The question remains to what extent lesbians and gay men are influenced in their 'heterogender' by these norms or whether they, because they are already deviating from the heterosexuality norm, have somewhat more freedom in performing their genders. Can they, to some extent 'do' different kinds of gender than heterosexuals (West & Zimmerman, 1987)? Monique Wittig goes so far as to state that lesbians are not even women, as "'woman' has meaning only in heterosexual systems of thought and heterosexual economic systems" (Wittig, 1993). Several researchers did find that non-heterosexuals do have some freedom or specificity in playing with or performing signs of attractiveness of the opposite sex as a way of being attractive to someone of the same sex as themselves, although at the same time they also (have to) relate to traditional notions of masculinities and femininities (Bolsø, 2002; Esterberg, 1996). Similarly, there are some indications that homosexual men and women have a somewhat larger freedom and variety in their division of labour, for instance it seems like a higher proportion of men in feminine connoted jobs is gay and of women in masculine connoted jobs is lesbian (Castell & Bryson, 1998), although research in this area is sorely underfunded and underdeveloped. Nevertheless, lesbians and gay men live in the same heteronormative society as heterosexuals, surrounded and maybe even invested in the same heteronormative values which will shape their gender as much as their sexuality will, hence, their freedom of performing mixed gender identities is limited. Although the question of how heteronormativity works differently or the same for non-heterosexuals is highly interested, in the context of this chapter there is neither place nor time to further investigate these questions. So

the remainder of this chapter is on how the aspects division of labour and being sexually attractive of heteronormativity may work on the relationship between women and technologies.

As there is, in present day western societies, the norm that having a relationship based on romantic love is one of the main ways to get happy, the importance of heteronormativity for gender relations is hard to overestimate. Indeed, various authors have paid attention to the relationship between gender, technology and sexuality. Most notably Flis Henwood emphasized the importance of studying 'gender segregation at work (…) not simply in terms of gendered power relations but in terms of the power relations of heterosexuality as well' (Henwood, 1998). Authors like Holloway, Reilly, Jenson and de Castell have looked at 'schools as important site through which gender and sexual identities are reproduced' and among others Stepulevage warned us not to 'conflate gender with heterosexuality' in studying students, gender and IT (Holloway, Valentine, & Bingham, 2000; Jenson, De Castell, & Bryson, 2003; Reilly, 2004; Stepulevage, 2001). But how can we do that? What becomes visible if we turn the lens of heteronormativity/sexuality on the relation between gender and technology?

Following the definition of heteronormativity that I mentioned earlier by Stevi Jackson, heteronormativity is about sexual attractiveness, but also about the domestic and extra-domestic division of labour (Jackson, 2005). In short, heteronormativity is about 'who buys the sheets, who washes them and what goes on between them'. Heteronormativity focuses on specific elements of gender dichotomies: on dichotomies like being attractive through looks versus being attractive via being active and pretending that you do not care about how you look (Frosh et al., 2002). Dichotomies concerning the division of labour are equally important, such as carrying the main responsibility for domestic versus extra-domestic work (which maps on the private/public dichotomy) and in being interested in things versus people e.g. in job choice or in the division of domestic chores like repairing or keeping in touch with family. Another common dichotomy regarding division of labour concerns the goals behind working; those main driving forces behind a career differ along lines that mirror a heteronormative division of tasks (Schein, 1987). In earlier research among high school students, Remke Bras and I have found that for some boys and for none of the girls, earning money is still one of their main drivers in choosing one job over another (Bras-Klapwijk & Rommes, 2005). Such findings indicate that despite emancipation, men are still seen as the main breadwinner in a family. For many girls, 'doing good for society' was their main driving force for working, they had what I would call 'Lady Di Syndrome'. With regard to the topic of this chapter, computer science is much more associated with earning money than with 'doing good for society'; so it seems that this aspect of heteronormativity does indeed offer a partial explanation for girls' reluctance to choose CS.

Importantly, how gender is dichotomized and which aspects of this dichotomization are seen as most relevant depends on the context. In poor families, earning money will be the main motivation for women as well as men to work and 'doing good for society' is clearly less relevant. Similarly, which division of tasks is seen as fitting with a heteronormative gender order will also be class and ethnicity dependent, as will also be signalled in the last section of this chapter. Even in comparing some Dutch and British women who followed a course to become a computer professionals, we found that their attitudes towards computers were different: the British women, who also were more often of lower classes, did not feel a strong conflict between their own femininity and being computer competent as the Dutch women (E. Rommes, Faulkner, & Slooten, 2005).

In the remaining part of this chapter, I will explore how a focus, on the one hand, on heteronormativity in the analysis of a gendered division of labour and, on the other hand, on the notion of

'being sexually attractive to the opposite sex' may clarify the relationship between women, men and technologies. Heteronormativity is expressed and normalized in culture, so each of the two sections will start with an analysis of how heteronormativity and technologies are expressed in mass media. This is the core empirical material of this chapter. This analysis will be followed by illustrations of the importance of heteronormativity for two older women with whom I had in-depth interviews: Judith, who was 44 when I first met her, and Tina, who was 18 when I first met her. I will show what kinds of effects heteronormative norms had on the relationships of these women with computers. I will also draw on focus group interview material that I gathered for a previous study (Els Rommes, Overbeek, Scholte, Engels, & Kemp, 2007). In these nine focus group interviews, fifty-one boys and girls between 14 and 18 years old were asked, among other things, about their perceptions of computer scientists. I will start with analyzing how the division of labour regarding technology is played out and playing into the heterosexual imaginary underling heteronormative structures, in soap operas popular amongst youth.

MEDIALIZATION OF THE DIVISION OF LABOUR AND TECHNOLOGIES

Movies, television series, music clips and commercials not only mirror social reality, they also contribute in constructing culturally dominant images which, in turn, affect social behaviour. A multitude of mostly quantitative and experimental studies shows that television series influence the thoughts and behaviour of adolescents. These effects can be in areas as diverse as smoking and drinking behaviour, acceptance of violence or perceptions of single motherhood and sexuality. The effects can be short-term (e.g. shown in observational studies where boys who watched movies in which actors drank alcohol literally imitated every sip taken by the actors (Engels,

Hermans, Van Baaren, Hollenstein, & Bot, 2009), or long-term (as shown in a correlational study which I did together with colleagues and students). In this particular study, we asked over 2,000 adolescents to fill out questionnaires about their drinking behaviour and about how often they watched the two soap operas that are most popular among Dutch youth (Engels et al., forthcoming). After counting the number of alcoholic drinks that were taken in these soap operas in the six weeks before the questionnaire was filled out (in which significant differences were found between the two soap-operas) and comparing them with the answers of the adolescents to the questionnaires, we found that girls who regularly watched soap opera series in which large quantities of alcohol were consumed drank more alcohol than those who watched soaps in which less alcohol was drunk.

Soap operas also influence teenager professional choices. In Belgium, van den Bulck and Beullens (2007) found that studies for professions recently shown in docusoaps received a larger influx of first year students. Similarly, a 'CSI effect' has been noticed in various countries, where the popularity of forensic science, particularly among girls, suddenly grew after the popular Crime Scene Investigation (CSI) series was shown on television. The Australian series 'MacLeod's Daughters' has also had a similar effect among girls regarding the popularity of becoming a farmhand in the outback areas of Australia (Mercer, 2008). In interviews with pupils and students about the reasons behind their study choices, they themselves mentioned this effect of popular television series as well (Jones, 2006; Kitzinger & Barbour, 1999; Whitelegg, 2006).

The explanations for this effect of soaps can be found, among other fields, in social learning theories with particular reference to adolescents, who are developing a sense of their personal identity as they no longer want to be seen as a child, but certainly don't want to be like their parents and are looking for role models. According to the social learning theory, behaviour is more

often imitated if the role model is more attractive, more glamorous and/or more realistic and similar to oneself (Spijkerman, 2005). In other words, actors in soap operas offer good role models. Sometimes, the behaviour of these role models is directly imitated (e.g. when young people copy the dress code of famous pop stars or as shown in the sipping experiment). In other cases role models have a more indirect effect when adolescents partially identify with, and pattern, their behaviour after these norms. It may be expected that if the behaviour is shown as normal (e.g. in the background as part of the scene, not as a topic under discussion), this will have a different effect than if it is the topic of a scene. In the former case, clearly, behaviour does not need an explanation anymore and it is assumed to be 'norm-al'; in the latter case, the behaviour is more visible, therefore, potentially even more influential. The context in which the behaviour is displayed becomes all the more relevant, and that explains the focus on content analysis of these scenes.

We[3] analyzed 35 episodes of the four soap operas that were the most popular among Dutch adolescents between 10 and 18 years old. This does not mean, however, that these soap operas were particularly made for adolescents, or that older people did not watch them. Interestingly, Dutch soaps, i.e. originally Dutch soaps or soaps from other countries which were adjusted and rewritten to fit the Dutch culture, were much more popular among Dutch adolescents than imported soaps. We analyzed episodes of four Dutch series: episodes of the two most popular soap operas 'Goede Tijden, Slechte Tijden' and 'Onderweg naar Morgen' and, in addition, we analyzed some episodes of 'Zoop', a soap opera which targets a somewhat younger audience of 10 to 14-year-olds, and 'Baantjer', which can strictly not be called a soap opera but rather a detective series, but which is more popular among boys. By making this selection, we tried to create some diversity in target groups of these series. We started by selecting all fragments in which some sort of technology was visible, no matter whether it was a mobile phone, a washing machine or a toolbox. In 119 fragments in these soaps, 'technologies' were present; in 62 fragments this technology was not merely a piece of the scenery but was actively used in the foreground. We analyzed all 119 fragments quantitatively and studied more closely the 62 fragments in which the technology was not merely a part of the scenery but also generated meanings around them. In this latter analysis, we paid particular attention to the role technologies played in the relationship between men and women.

Which technologies were displayed, and how? While the results were hardly surprising, they were even more stereotypical than we expected. Men were significantly more often seen in connection with technology: in 64 percent of the times that technology was shown, it was connected with a man and per fragment they were given more time (about 30 seconds per fragment as opposed to only shown 21 seconds per fragment for women). In addition, male use of technology was more visible: in 71 percent of the cases that men were visible with technology they were displayed in the foreground of the scene, whereas with women this was only the case in 44 percent of the fragments. Thus technologies were clearly more easily associated with men than with women.

What follows below are results of the analysis in which every kind of technology was taken into account, where it obviously made a difference whether a man was shown in connection with a drilling equipment or washing machine. Some technologies were related to the feminine realm of the heteronormative division of tasks; others to the masculine. In the soap operas, we could distinguish technologies that are related to domestic work and technologies that are related to the extra-domestic or public sphere. Some technologies are related to the people versus things dichotomy, to caring values versus virtuoso values: when technology is regarded as a toy or when the technology itself is the topic (e.g. in repairing or constructing (Pacey, 1999). Using these criteria,

we regarded household equipment (iron, hoover, sewing machine, coffee maker) to be female connoted technologies. Male connoted technologies were, for instance, audiovisual equipment (film/camera, ghetto blaster, music equipment); electronics (light bulbs, wires); (repairing) tools (saw, measuring tools) and technologies such as a stopwatch, leaves blower or megaphone. 'Neutral' connoted technologies, which could not easily be related to a heteronormative division of tasks were, for instance, communication technologies (e.g. mobile phone), information technologies (computer, laptop, monitor, printer) and technologies like the television.

Only 4.5 percent of the shown technologies in soap operas were female connoted, 29 percent had a male and by far most technologies were neutral, ICT especially had an abundant presence, perhaps mirroring its pervasiveness in the modern world. In no case did we observe a man using or touching female connoted technology, whereas the women hardly used any male connoted technology (5 percent). Women used mostly neutral technologies (83 percent), men used neutral (57 percent) and male connoted technologies (43 percent). Soap operas clearly give an indication that technology is related to a division of tasks between men and women, i.e. having a gender connotation, or indeed should not be used by the opposite sex.

Perhaps even more interesting than this statistical summary is what men and women did with and around the technologies. Again, the soap operas could not have been more stereotypical. Women use technologies. On the contrary men not only use them, but also construct them (for instance, an audiovisual set), discover how to use more complicated technologies (such as how to use a professional video-camera), repair them (such as a broken light bulb or a cold storage room). In virtually all of these scenes women are admiring, and sometimes being the impatient bystanders, offering both verbal and material support in the form of cups of coffee, assistance or verbal encouragements. Clearly, the men in these scenes feel at ease with technology, show interest in them and almost seem to have 'magical hands' as they succeed in everything they do with the technology. Even when men were obviously being introduced to what was for them new technology, they would be presented as the expert with magical hands. For example, after glancing in a manual and holding the video camera for 30 seconds, the guy who is supposed to learn how to operate a professional video camera states that he 'almost understands everything, except for the progressive scan modus' and the person who successfully repairs the broken cooling equipment of the cold storage room says that he does not need the blueprint that his female partner so helpfully holds up for him.

Whereas the technology in all these cases is clearly a 'man's thing', even if the objects they repair or build are sometimes 'meant for a woman', her task in most of these scenes in which both a man and a woman appear is to help him with his relationships and feelings, e.g. for his mother, partner or colleague. He silently and expertly deals with technology; she initiates a conversation and is grateful for his help. In most scenes he gives only short answers to her direct questions and does not initiate conversation himself, nor does he show any gratitude for her help in bringing coffee, cleaning the house or helping with relationships. In this way, not only a complementary task division is constructed, but also a hierarchical difference between the ways of helping each other. This hierarchical difference is well known in society as a whole (one only need compare the amount of money that is paid for which type of work) and apparently played out in relationships. This might mean that men have more to gain by maintaining the heteronormative gender order than women. Such scenes create a direct association between technology and masculinity and, as far as women are concerned, an incomprehensible or even magical expertise and also non-communication. The same kind of non-communication was found when we looked more closely at the use of computers in the scenes: both

men and women used their work at the computer in various cases to avoid conversation, albeit in gendered ways. Men, for example, would use their work at the computer as an excuse for not wanting or being able to talk about emotions, whereas women would use it more often as an excuse for avoiding an argument. Only in one other fragment did we see a technology that was mainly used as an excuse not to talk, which was a vacuum cleaner. So, even feminine connoted technologies are associated with 'things, not people', looking at how technologies were used to not communicate. As a whole, these soaps are giving a clear message to adolescents: certain technologies are for girls, other technologies are for boys; in general,: boys are into technologies and girls are into people - a heteronormative division of tasks.

Mirroring the Division of Labour in Girls' and Women's Lives

The messages from soap operas about the gendered division of labour regarding technologies are mirrored in what female adolescents tell about their occupational choices. Technology, and especially computer science, is related to being 'anti-person', being non-communicative and into things rather than people. Heterosexual girls are supposed to be interested in people and relationships, whereas boys are expected to be more interested in things, in repairing and building (Faulkner, 2000). In a recently published article, I showed that it is not the activities, but rather the identity of a computer scientist that girls reject (Els Rommes et al., 2007). Accordingly, though girls in many cases, in fact, do like to sit behind the computer, to be seen as a computer person is something else and definitely not a desirable identity for girls, especially not around men. Nor is it a desirable identity for adult women as the story of Judith shows. Identity construction is particularly interesting around computers because as they do not have a strong gender connotation to start with. But how they fit into the heteronormative division of tasks seems to result from a combination of the kind of tasks that are done with it, in which context it is being used, and how specific tasks are distributed between men and women.

One of the women I encountered while studying the role of ICTs in women's lives was Judith. She was a 44-year old heterosexual mother of two sons, whom I met at a basic introductory course in "Computers for Absolute Beginners." I interviewed Judith for the first time during the course, when it soon became clear that she was anything but a beginner, yet her self perception as a beginner had everything to do with the role the computer played in her life. Although the computer was introduced in Judith's household for her job as a translator, her husband soon took it over, causing her to retreat from it - something which Marja Bakardjeva has also observed elsewhere (Bakardjieva, 2005). Judith hated the computer. Also, according to her, she could no longer communicate with her husband because of it. In fact, after she divorced her husband, the meaning of the computer, which she now called 'communication centre', changed completely for her. In her own words:*'The computer 'suddenly changed meaning. It has now become a sort of communication centre for me; I do everything on it (...). I am so amazed at myself (seeing), that I am now so enthusiastic about it!'*

She described and showed the many ways in which she now uses the computer: she plays music and creates a file for her music on it; she does her administration on it which 'cleaned her house up nicely', as she puts it; she uses it to communicate; she does her banking on it and spends evenings enjoying herself by surfing the net. This is the time when she also did the course for beginners and I also interviewed her. A year later I went back and interviewed her again. She now had a new boyfriend, Danny, and, once more, the computer had changed meaning:

Danny is the one who plays most with the boys on the computer and who keeps them in check, also

because he might like it better to play. And maybe I would also like to play, really, but then I am so 'dowdy, frumpish' (ER: 'truttig') that I then go and wash the dishes, instead of playing along.

Although it is clear from this quote that she did not go back to hating the computer again, as she did with her former husband, it is evident that her relationship with the computer was much more distanced as she even left the supervision of her sons' use of the computer to her boyfriend while she washed the dishes. I think Judith's story shows forcefully how the heteronormative division of tasks between Judith and the men in her life had a clear impact on her pleasure and feeling of competence with the computer. In her heterosexual relationships, the computer changed meaning and became increasingly male territory.

Judith, and girls and women in general, have every reason for not wanting to be associated with this heteronormative masculinity since it contradicts directly one of the main precepts of heteronormative femininity: to be social and people oriented. Norwegian researchers Bente Rasmussen and Tove Hapnes found this aspect to be particularly important for the self image of adolescent girls (Rasmussen & Hapnes, 2003). Violating this rule may have some serious consequences for women. For example, Flis Henwood, quotes a female engineer who had experienced that every time she mentioned her profession to a man, he would immediately stop the conversation, it was a real 'conversation stopper' (Henwood, 1998); Ulrike Kessels shows that 'girls with very good grades in physics considered themselves to be particularly unpopular with boys' (Kessels, 2005) and Holloway (Holloway et al., 2000) observes that girls would rather not work on technological projects at school together with boys because, according to Holloway, 'despite misgivings about [the boy's] maturity and attitudes towards women, [the girls] want to appear [both socially and physically] attractive, and being shown to struggle with technology in front of a group of boys apparently hampered it. In a similar vein, Stepulevage shows that female students did not want to promote themselves and their technological skills in front of male group members, for fear of being considered unfeminine or even lesbian (Stepulevage, 2001). Clearly, as Epstein and Johnson (1998) also observe, young women have a very good insight into 'the underlying effects of sexuality on gendered interactions' and employ these insights mainly to structure interactions with boys 'in ways that please and pacify (...) their male cohorts' (Epstein & Johnson, 1998; Reilly, 2004).

At this point it is relevant to reiterate the original question: why is it so particularly gender inauthentic for women to be technologically competent? After the material presented above, one of the reasons is that masculinity and technology have become intertwined in several dimensions and that girls who are technologically competent threaten the heteronormative order. Not only are certain technologies associated with masculinity directly, but they are also (and this is especially true for computers) being associated with 'anti-sociality', with not communicating, whereas being people and communication oriented is a pivotal aspect of 'good femininity'. Last but not least, dealing with technology is a core aspect of the heteronormative division of tasks. Technologically competent women may run the risk of 'transgressing into a male domain' and disturbing the heteronormative division of tasks which might be regarded as indicating that they do not need a relationship (after all, they are anti-social as well) and they do not need men to do these things for them. Indeed, there are indications that technologically competent women are associated with independence and perceived as independent, assertive, women who might very well be feminist, even lesbian, an image which several female engineers are seen to consciously struggle against.

So, this explanation may offer an insight into Judith's refusal to sit behind the computer as soon as she was with a male partner again, or why the female engineer that Cockburn wrote about put away her tools as soon as she came home and left all the repair work in the household to her husband (Cockburn, 1985). By transgressing into the male domain and disturbing the heteronormative domestic division of tasks, they might signal themselves to be anti-social and not in need of a man. This aspect of heteronormativity may very well be an important factor behind occupational choices of adolescents.

Tina, who has been an active MOO user since she was 14 and one of the first women on her MOO, is 18 years old. She describes herself as follows:

A girl of eighteen, I am not really pretty but also not very ugly (...) I try to come across as adult but I also sleep with cuddly toys, and with men. (...) I can do a lot, I don't know that I can do a lot, I started typing it but what follows I have forgotten, that might come later.

In her description of her experiences with the MOO during the interview I had with her, it became clear that her main pleasure of being on the MOO was to meet men who helped her overcome her sense of insecurity, especially about her looks. After a couple of years, she became more secure to the level that she felt she could even feel some 'power' over men.

Tina: Technologically, I am really bad in these things. I always let these things be done for me (with sweet, childlike voice): Picture, please, could you make it for me? And that's still the way I do it... (laughs) hopeless...

ER: you don't like doing it that way?

Tina: on the one hand, yes, 'cause I always feel a bit stupid if I don't know something. But, I know enough important people that can do this for me. And I also enjoy it a bit to misuse my power?

ER: What kind of power do you have?

Tina: Power is maybe not really the right word, but in several MOOs I know practically all wizards, and those are just people with most power, they can do practically everything. So, if I can't do something, I just look at a wizz and (sweet childlike voice) ah, could you please do this for me? And yes!

Even if the men could not see Tina on the MOO, which she initially experienced as a relief, she is also playing with a combination of childlike innocence and sexual seduction. Tina is clearly buying into, enjoying and feeling a sense of empowerment from a heteronormative division of tasks, showing that such a division of tasks is not only to the disadvantage of women. The advantages men and women may have from this division of tasks helps to keep heteronormativity in place. At the same time, it may obscure the disadvantages that women such as Tina may have from it: by relying on men to help her with what she perceives as 'technological' tasks, Tina will not learn how to do these jobs herself, nor will she develop a sense of self efficacy regarding technology. And by keeping the heteronormative gender order in place, Tina also does not challenge what made her feel bad and insecure about herself in the first place: the importance of having good looks for women.

Following this analysis of a heteronormative construction of tasks around technologies and the computer in soap operas and in the lives of Judith and Tina, I will now focus on the importance of sexual attractiveness and its potential consequence for women's relationships with, and ambitions about, computers.

MEDIALIZATION OF SEXUAL ATTRACTION AND COMPUTING SCIENTISTS

The computer was by far the most often shown technology in the soap opera fragments we studied: in 60 percent of the fragments with technology in it, technology was a computer. This may result from the fact that the computer is a multipurpose device which fits both in domestic and in extra-domestic settings. It also shows the extent to which the computer is diffused in society and has become a normal, almost invisible, technology, particularly so perhaps in the lives of adolescents. We have a strong suspicion that the Apple Company has engaged in product placement in one of the soap operas. In that opera Apple computers appeared very often, even in scenes in which computers seemed anything but relevant to the storyline and the Apple trademark was very visible each time. Interestingly, this product placement happened in the soap particularly popular among girls. It seems as if Apple is collaborating in its own image as a 'women's computer'.[4] That computer use is seen as a more or less gender-neutral activity was also visible: men and women were equally often displayed with, or working on, the computer. Small differences were however still visible, for men more than women were often seen in the foreground with a computer. Besides, the kinds of use men and women made of it, in as far as we could observe, were slightly different. Though both used it for administrative work, women seemed to use it more as a sophisticated typewriter, whereas men were more engaged in making graphics.

In no single fragment did we see a computing scientist and only in one case did we see a police officer trying to break the password of the computer of a suspect. The gender division of tasks in this fragment was clearly gender stereotypical. The officer's female colleague observed his attempts and would rather like to give up. As soon as a male colleague enters, the officer who is attempting to break the password uses some technical term to describe why he has difficulty breaking the password. Yet another male colleague finally guesses the right password. In no other fragment were actors repairing a computer, building a computer, or programming software, but they were building or repairing some other technology. I must add that scientists and technologists are not often shown on television in other countries or, if they are, they are shown in rather stereotypical ways (Whitelegg et al., 2008). In Germany, Michel and Pelka found that only 1.5 percent of the shown professions were technical even though it was 6.6 percent for the population (Michel & Pelka, 2004).

Indeed, in movies and serials, in general, computer scientists don't appear often. If they do, they are generally more of a 'hacker' type: miraculously breaking into main frames, breaking passwords, evading security systems, etc. Not only do their competences and actions match the hacker stereotype, but also their looks and lack of sexual attractiveness as well as problems in getting relationships with women. These aspects have become almost the defining characteristics of the 'hacker' or 'nerd' stereotype - a notion confirmed by reality television shows like 'Beauty and the Nerd', or the Dutch off-spring show in which nerds are taught how to be heterosexually attractive and successful in getting a woman and maintaining a relationship with her.

Some of the main female hackers in movies and television series, at least until five years ago, are Sandra Bullock posing as Angela Bennett in 'The Net' and Alyson Hannigan as Willow in 'Buffy the Vampire Slayer'. Again, like their male counterparts, these 'female nerds' are not examples of successful heterosexuality. Whereas 'Angela' initially fails even to have any kind of relationship in 'the world out there' (e.g using a pizza delivery service) and ends up living with her old mother. 'Willow' starts off as a shy and childlike person and when she later develops into a more mature, strong and sexual character, she has her 'coming-out' as a lesbian. "Terry" Doolittle, the

main character in the movie 'Jumpin' Jack Flash' is, as a bank employee, not a typical example of a female computer scientist. Nevertheless, her character (being quite competent on the computer, lonely and 'not fitting' in her office) and the fact that it is played by one of the few openly lesbian actresses, Whoopi Goldberg, makes her similar to the other two characters mentioned earlier. The fear of being seen as a 'lezzie', which I described in the introduction, seems to have some grounding, or is mirrored in some of these movies. Similarly, in one of the few instances I found of an advertisement in which a woman is displayed who (tries to) install a computer network, I found that the woman looked very differently than women in other advertisements.[5] She was not shown in as sexy a way: her blouse was buttoned up such that hardly any skin or breast was showing, she wore glasses and had a facial expression which was not a classical smiling 'I am available' look. Her hair was pushed back and her make up was hardly present, so her femininity, in comparison with other advertisements, was clearly not made as visible. It seems as if this picture shows that traditional heteronormative attractiveness and being engaged with computers do not go together. This overview of how the media presents female nerds or nerdettes is not exhaustive and it does seem like the last years the nerd/ette stereotype may undergo some changes and is less directly connected with computing competence. Nevertheless, the examples given do represent some of the main examples of nerdettes in movies up till five years ago. If this is true, then the dominant image of computer scientists in mass media has been that they do not go together with looking and being sexually attractive.

Mirroring Sexual Attraction of Computer Scientists in Adolescents' Lives

Whether or not the mass media presents an image of computer experts as sexually unattractive, adolescents do clearly have this image (see figure 1). When asked to 'draw someone working with computers', adolescent boys and girls all made drawings which looked remarkably similar. The outcomes of these drawings look a bit like other 'Draw A Scientist' or 'Draw an engineer' kinds of research (Fralick, 2008; Whitelegg, 2006). However, if we compare these drawings with those the Dutch adolescents made of computing scientists and the comments they gave to these drawings, it seems that the looks of computer

scientists are regarded as even less attractive than those of 'scientists' in general. In their descriptions of these drawings as well as the discussion in in focus group when we asked them to describe a computer scientist, they made it clear that they thought these were persons that wear unfashionable clothes, have ugly haircuts, wear glasses and are, overall, unattractive.

It seems that being in computer science does not fit in with hegemonic masculinity, in other words, the culturally dominant ideal of masculin-

Figure 1. Examples of drawings made by adolescents when asked to 'draw someone working with computers'

ity, associated with e.g. strength/physicality, paid work, heterosexuality and authority (Connell, 1987). This view became clearer during our focus group interviews with adolescent boys and girls. When asked to name masculine professions, they named a multitude of professions, which related to physical strength, power and competence (e.g. an athlete, a car mechanic or a road-paver. Only when we asked them what they considered CS to be did they indicate that this was – of course – a profession for men. Computer science can be seen as fitting with complicit masculinity as defined by Connell: it does have some of the characteristics of hegemonic masculinities to some extent, hence some of the advantages associated with hegemonic masculinity, but it definitely is not the culturally dominant ideal of masculinity.

The above discussion makes computer science a less attractive discipline for girls as well as boys. In our focus group interviews this notion clearly emerged: none of the adolescents expressed an interest in studying computer science, and a popular boy who considered a profession involving computers gave up this idea rather quickly when he found out that the group and he himself thought of computer scientists as nerds. One girl even started crying in a focus group discussion because she felt sorry for her brother for being into computers. Although computer science is clearly an unattractive discipline for boys, there are still some ways in which they can relate to technology without being 'unmasculine': it is to some extent still connected to making money, which several boys indicated was the main relevant thing they wanted from a profession, and boys can gain some power by being seen as a technological expert. Moreover, the pressure to look attractive is somewhat less for boys than for girls. Boys, however, may experience pressure to be sexually active and take action to seduce women. This is not necessarily incompatible with being a nerd as seen in movies such as 'Weird Science' or 'The Revenge of the Nerds.'

For girls, it is even more unattractive to become a computing scientist. This is not to say that girls cannot imagine themselves in traditionally masculine professions. Some of these professions, especially those related to hegemonic masculinity, are even given erotic associations, as is the case with female directors or building constructors. This seems to be so especially if these professions have an erotic attraction to start with, for example, if they are related to being in control or physically involved, in which case these cases girls may be able to play with signs of masculinity such as being erotic. Indeed, when we asked what a girl in a 'technological profession such as computing science' would look like some examples were given of female car mechanics and women in other 'male' professions, but it seemed hard or even impossible for them to imagine what a nerdette would look like. Being interested in an a-sexual profession (or, as one of the adolescents said: 'he is married to his computer') which is related to physical unattractiveness, seems too far removed from heteronormative femininity.

That being physically attractive is so relevant, especially for adolescent girls, became clear both in the other projects and in the focus group discussions. In Irish role-model experiments in high-school girls, it became clear that role models who were glamorous and attractive were most successful in influencing girls' educational choices. After a particularly attractive, longhaired female pilot had told about her job, the enthusiasm of girls to choose science-subjects rose considerably (MacKeogh, 2003). Similarly, the Dutch 'Technica 10' project, which was intended to get young adolescent girls to go to after-school projects, where they play with technology, was only successful in attracting girls if the girls displayed on the PR material had long hair, hence looked attractive in the 'proper' feminine way (Eck & Volman, 1999). In focus group interviews, both boys and girls were convinced that what boys were most interested in was the physical attractiveness of girls and that they should be girly-girls to be attractive.

HETERONORMATIVE IMAGINARY AND ITS CONSEQUENCES

Heteronormativity, which one could loosely describe as being about who buys the sheets, who washes them and what goes on between them, seems to be crucial in constructing 'proper', heteronormative genders, based on a heteronormative complementary division of tasks (taking care of things versus taking care of relationships) and a heteronormative basis of attraction (women need to be physically attractive, men need to be sexually active). In a study on prototypical masculinity and femininity, the dominance of these perceptions of 'typical' femininity and masculinity became clear from a long list of characteristics of femininity: 'being critical of own appearance' and 'concerned with outward appearance' are on first and second place, 'being object of desire' also scores fairly high, as does being 'nurturing' and being 'family oriented'. Masculinity is in the first place related to being 'career oriented', and in the eight place of most clear characteristics we find 'interested in technology', a feature which does not even appear on the list of characteristics of femininity (Visser, 2002).

The heteronormative division of tasks and of attractiveness may not have equal relevance nor equal effects on the popularity of technology and computer science among boys and girls. More importantly, the notions of which tasks or personal characteristics belong to which gender can be different depending on other aspects like culture and class. In Malaysia and in parts of rural Scotland, for instance, computing science is seen as belonging to women in the division of tasks. In Malaysia, one of the reasons for this is that it is indoor work that can easily be combined with caring for children and the household (Mellstrom, this book). In rural Scotland, computing is compared with heavy machinery and outdoor work and is hence delegated to the women's realm of non-physically heavy work (Faulkner & Kleif, 2004). Similarly, Herman has shown how

in some Eastern European countries previously masculine connoted professions were given new meaning by connecting them to the feminine part of the heteronormative task division: e.g. by comparing chemistry to cooking (Herman, forthcoming). Moreover, there might very well be a class and culture difference associated with the understanding of heteronormativity already described: Marijke Naezer found, for instance, that low class boys from ethnic minority backgrounds were much clearer in expressing their fear of being associated with homosexuality than white boys following a higher level of education, hence, they were 'policing' each other much more heavily than other boys. These examples show that the precise understanding of heteronormativity can be different in different groups. It also shows that there is no biological necessity behind a heteronormative division of tasks or characteristics, and that its division and its consequences are dynamic. Could the heteronormative imaginary or its influence on pupils' lives and choices related to technology in the Netherlands be stronger than in other countries and, more specifically, be strongly related with middle class white adolescents? It seems a good idea to do more internationally comparative research on this topic and study adolescents (and adults) who are from other classes and cultures than the majority studied for this chapter.

Also in the Netherlands, there are of course many women who have no problem with being technologically competent. The effects of a heteronormative division of tasks and of physical attractiveness are not just dependent on the cultural context. Being technologically competent may also be contextually dependent on a smaller scale; it may not be considered as breaking the heteronormative division of tasks if there are males around, (father, husband or colleague), who are even more competent or, as Henrik whom I quoted in the introduction said, 'it is ok as long as I am slightly better.' Moreover, as Landström also wrote (2007), some women may be less interested in following the rules for proper heterogendered behaviour (Landström, 2007). Nevertheless, I hope this article has given some additional suggestions as to what may be behind the difficult relationship between femininity and technology and particularly between femininity and computing science by pointing at sexuality as a major underlying mechanism for the gendering of men and women. I have shown some of the heteronormative imaginaries in present-day Dutch society, how men, women and technology relate to one another and why the relationship between femininity and technology is so hard to imagine. Through heteronormativity, technologically competent women become masculinized in various dimensions: they are no longer associated with being good for society, with being social and people oriented, with being interested in heterosexual relationships or with being sexually attractive to the opposite sex. Of course, they also gain something by being technologically compe-

Figure 2. 'Screen Goddess Sharon', part of the 'IT Screen Goddesses Calendar 2006-2007' which was launched in Australia to present 'beautiful photos of real women working in the IT industry' (http://www. itgoddess.info/) © [2007] ThoughtWare (2007). Used with permission..

tent, most notably they gain self-confidence and pride in a profession that is perceived to be very difficult, especially for women.

If the focus shifts to underlying mechanisms of heteronormativity, this also implies some new ways of changing stereotypical occupational choices. Firstly, this study suggests the importance of the age at which adolescents make their occupational choices. Studies of child development show the importance of identity development and of sexuality as crucial for teenagers: the younger they are, the more stereotypically they will choose. At later ages, sexuality and 'fitting the teenage norm' seem less relevant as children become more secure in their identities and display a wider variety of gender identities. Statistical data in the Netherlands have indeed shown that the number of girls choosing to study in a technology field has indeed dropped after the age at which pupils make their choices for school subjects was lowered, resulting in more gender segregation in the Netherlands (Langen & Vierke, 2009).

Secondly, this chapter has shown the importance of the heterosexual imaginary: cultural images of gender, technology and heterosexual attraction and division of tasks. These images in soap operas are not the result of any malicious intent on the part of the soap producers to replicate stereotypes and keep women away from technology, rather they are accidental replication of the unquestioned norms by soap producers, and the stereotypes they engender are not a key-line in the stories but rather a side effect. That producers might be willing to change the images they convey has occurred in the past. After a study of the Dutch soap opera 'Goede Tijden, Slechte Tijden' showed that alcohol intake in that soap was much higher than what can be considered 'normal', the alcohol intake by the soap characters was and still is drastically reduced. Perhaps soap opera producers might be willing to rethink some of the gender stereotypes their series convey. They could start by introducing images in which masculinity and femininity on the various dimen-

sions of heteronormativity are mixed, such as the Australian calendar of women computer science experts in figure 2 has tried to do. Of course, it would be even better if stereotypical ideas of what is an attractive woman might become more diversified and masculine features such as (technological) competence, muscles or even body hair are regarded as sexually attractive rather than as a sign of failed heteronormative femininity.

Most importantly, it might be good if both in the imaginary realm and in heterosexual relationships the division of tasks would be left open. There are certain advantages to a complementary division of tasks in society and in relationships. If this division of tasks could be more the result of individual preferences, talents and negotiations rather than the result of upbringing, societal pressure and pressure of heteronormativity, both men and women would gain greatly.

REFERENCES

Bakardjieva, M. (2005). *Internet Society. The internet in everyday life*. London: Sage Publications.

Blagojevic, M., Bundule, M., Burkhardt, A., Calloni, M., Ergma, E., & Glover, J. (2004). *Waste of talents: turning private struggles into a public issue. Women and science in the Enwise countries*. Luxembourg: European Commission.

Bolsø, A. (2002). *Power in the Erotic; feminism and lesbian practice*. Trondheim, Norway: NTNU.

Bras-Klapwijk, R. M., & Rommes, E. (2005). Voorbij de twee seksen: inspelen op uiteenlopende loopbaanoriëntaties van middelbare scholieren. In M. v. S. Z. e. Werkgelegenheid (Ed.), De Glazen Muur. Essaybundel over beroepensegregatie. (pp. 53-68). Den Haag: Ministerie van Sociale Zaken en Werkgelegenheid, Directie Coördinatie Emancipatiebeleid.

Buis, T. (2003). *Technomonitor 2003. Een kwantitatieve analyse van het technisch onderwijs en de technische arbeidsmarkt*. Nijmegen: Kenniscentrum Beroepsonderwijs Arbeidsmarkt.

Butler, J. (1999). *Gender Trouble, Feminism and the Subversion of Identity*. London: Routledge.

Castell, S. D., & Bryson, M. (1998). From the Ridiculous to the Sublime: On Finding Oneself in Educational Research. In Pinar, W. F. (Ed.), *Queer Theory in Education* (pp. 245–250). Mahwah, NJ: Lawrence Erlbaum Associates.

Cockburn, C. (1985). *Machinery of Dominance; Women, men and technical know-how*. London: Pluto Press.

Connell, R. W. (1987). *Gender and Power, Society, the Person and Sexual Politics*. Oxford, UK: Polity Press.

Eck, E. V., & Volman, M. (1999). *Techniek. Leuke hobby, saaie baan?* Amsterdam: SCO-Kohnstamm Instituut.

Engels, R. C. M. E., Braak, D. T., Eyndhoven, S., Overbeek, G., Scholte, R. H. J., & Kemp, R. A. T. d. (forthcoming). The Impact of Alcohol Portrayal in Soaps on Adolescent Drinking. *Psychology & Health*.

Engels, R. C. M. E., Hermans, R., Van Baaren, R. B., Hollenstein, T., & Bot, S. M. (2009). Alcohol portrayal on television affects actual drinking behaviour. *Alcohol and Alcoholism (Oxford, Oxfordshire)*, *44*(3), 244–249. doi:10.1093/alcalc/agp003

Epstein, D., & Johnson, R. (1998). *Schooling Sexualities*. Buckingham, UK: Open University Press.

Esterberg, K. G. (1996). "A Certain Swagger When I Walk": Performing Lesbian Identity. In Seidman, S. (Ed.), *Queer Theory/Sociology* (pp. 259–279). Cambridge, UK: Blackwell Publishers.

Faulkner, W. (2000). Dualisms, Hierarchies and Gender in Engineering. *Social Studies of Science*, *30*(5), 759–792. doi:10.1177/030631200030005005

Faulkner, W., & Kleif, T. (2004). Included women, excluded men: users and nonusers of rural community resource centres. In N. Oudshoorn, E. Rommes & I. v. Slooten (Eds.), Strategies of Inclusion: Gender in the Information Society, Vol. III: Surveys of Women's User Experience (pp. 137-166). Trondheim, Norway: NTNU.

Fralick, B., Kearn, J. Thompson, S., & Lyons, J. (2008). How middle schoolers draw engineers and scientists. *Science education technology*, *18*, 60-73.

Frosh, S., Phoenix, A., & Pattman, R. (2002). Policing young masculinities. In Young masculinities. Palgrave: Handmills.

Gansmo, H. J., Lagesen, V. A., & Sorensen, K. (2003). Forget the hacker? A critical re-appraisal of Norwegian studies of gender and ICT. In Lie, M. (Ed.), *He, She and IT Revisited. New Perspectives on Gender in the Information Society* (pp. 34–68). Trondheim, Norway: Gyldendal Norsk Verlag.

Gras-Velazquez, A., Joyce, A., & Debry, M. (2009). *Women and ICT. Why are girls still not attracted to ICT studies and careers?* European Schoolnet.

Henwood, F. (1998). Engineering Difference: discourses on gender, sexuality and work in a college of technology. *Gender and Education*, *10*(1), 35–49. doi:10.1080/09540259821087

Herman, C. (forthcoming). *Re-engineering gender? Public discourses and private lives of women SET professionals in East and West Europe*.

Hill, J. P., & Lynch, M. (1983). The Intensification of Gender-Related Role Expectations during Early Adolescence. In Brooks-Gunn, J., & Petersen, A. C. (Eds.), *Girls at Puberty; Biological and Psychosocial Perspectives* (pp. 201–228). New York, London: Plenum Press.

Holloway, S. L., Valentine, G., & Bingham, N. (2000). Institutionalising technologies: masculinities, feminities, and the heterosexual economy of the IT classroom. *Environment & Planning A, 32*(4), 617–633. doi:10.1068/a3238

ICM. (2001). *IT Technology Tracker.*

Ingraham, C. (1997). The Heterosexual Imaginary: Feminist Sociology and Theories of Gender. In Seidman, S. (Ed.), *Queer Theory/Sociology* (pp. 168–193). Malden, Oxford, UK: Blackwell Publishers.

Jackson, S. (2005). Gender, Sexuality and Heterosexuality. The Complexity (and limits) of Heteronormativity.

Jenson, J., De Castell, S., & Bryson, M. (2003). "Girl talk": gender, equity, and identity discourses in a school-based computer culture. *Women's Studies International Forum, 26*(6), 561–573.

Jones, R. B. A. (2006). The CSI effect. *Science scope.*

Kessels, U. (2005). Fitting into the stereotype: How gender-stereotyped perceptions of prototypic peers relate to liking for school subjects. *European Journal of Psychology of Education, 20*(3), 309–323. doi:10.1007/BF03173559

Kitzinger, J., & Barbour, R. S. (1999). The challenge and promise of focus groups. In Barbour, R. S., & Kitzinger, J. (Eds.), *Developing focus group research: politics, theory and practice.* London: Sage.

Landström, C. (2007). Queering feminist technology studies. *Feminist Theory, 8*(1), 7–26. doi:10.1177/1464700107074193

Langen, A. V., & Vierke, H. (2009). *Wat bepaalt de keuze voor een natuurprofiel? De invloed van de leerling, de school, de ouders en de peergroup.* Den Haag: Platform Bèta Techniek.

MacKeogh, C. (2003). Women in Technology and Science Role Model Project. In M. Lie & K. Sorensen (Eds.), Strategies of Inclusion: Gender in the Information Society. Vol. 1: Experiences from public sector initiatives (pp. 401-418). Trondheim, Norway: NTNU.

Mercer, P. (2008). *Cattle farms lure Australia women.* BBC News.

Michel, L. P., & Pelka, B. (2004). *Die Darstellung von Berufen im Fernsehen und ihre Auswirkungen auf die Berufswahl - Ergebnisse einer Pilotstudie": Dream jobs for all? Representation of jobs on TV and consequences for job choices - results of a pilot study.* MMB Institut für Medien- und Kompetenzforschung.

Oldenziel, R. (1999). *Making Technology Masculine; Men, women and modern machines in America 1870-1945.* Amsterdam: Amsterdam University Press.

Oost, E. V. (2000). Making the computer masculine. In Balka, E., & Smith, R. (Eds.), *Women, Work and Computerization, Charting a Course to the Future* (pp. 9–16). Dordrecht, The Netherlands: Kluwer Academic Publishers.

Pacey, A. (1999). *Meaning in Technology.* Cambridge, MA: MIT Press.

Rasmussen, B., & Hapnes, T. (2003). Gendering technology; Young girls negotiating ICT and gender. In Lie, M. (Ed.), *He, She and IT Revisited; New Perspectives on Gender in the Information Society* (pp. 173–197). Oslo, Norway: Gyldendal Akademisk.

Reilly, C. A. (2004). Sexualities and technologies: how vibrators help to explain computers. *Computers and Composition, 2004,* 363–385.

Rich, A. (1993). Compulsory Heterosexuality and Lesbian Existence. In Abelove, H., Barale, M. A., & Halperin, D. M. (Eds.), *The Lesbian and Gay Studies Reader* (pp. 227–254). New York: Routledge.

Rommes, E., Faulkner, W., & Slooten, I. V. (2005). Changing Lives: the case for women-only vocational technology training revisited. *Journal of Vocational Education and Training, 57*(3), 293–317. doi:10.1080/13636820500200288

Rommes, E., Overbeek, G., Scholte, R., Engels, R., & Kemp, R. D. (2007). 'I'm not interested in computers', Gender-based occupational choices of teenagers. *Information Communication and Society, 10*(3), 299–319. doi:10.1080/13691180701409838

Rommes, E., & Schönberger, M. (in press). *Report WP 4 Motivation*. Wuppertal, Germany. *EU Coordinated Action Motivation.*

Schein, E. H. (1987). Individuals and careers. In Lorsch, J. W. (Ed.), *Handbook of Organizational Behavior* (pp. 155–171). Englewood Cliffs, NJ: Prentice-Hall.

Sondergaard, D. M. (2002). Postructuralist Approaches to Empirical Analysis. *Qualitative Studies in Education, 15*(2), 187–204. doi:10.1080/09518390110111910

Spijkerman, R. (2005). *An Image to Die For; Prototypes of Smoking and Drinking Peers and Adolescents' Substance Use*. Nijmegen, The Netherlands: Radboud University Nijmegen, Stepulevage, L. (2001). Gender/Technology Relations: complicating the gender binary. *Gender and Education, 13*(3), 325–338.

Van den Bulck, J., & Beullens, K. (2007). The Relationship between Docu Soap Exposure and Adolescents' Career Aspirations. *European Journal of Communication, 22*(3), 355–366. doi:10.1177/0267323107079686

Visser, I. (2002). Prototypes of gender: Conceptions of feminine and masculine. *Women's Studies International Forum, 25*(5), 529–539. doi:10.1016/S0277-5395(02)00312-6

Warner, M. (1991). Introduction: Fear of a Queer Planet. *Social Text, 9*(4), 3–17.

West, C., & Zimmerman, D. H. (1987). Doing Gender. *Gender & Society, 1*(2), 125–151. doi:10.1177/0891243287001002002

Whitelegg, E. (2006). *Invisible witnesses? How scientists, technologists, engineers and mathematicians are represented on UK television*. Paper presented at the British Educational Research Association Annual Conference.

Wittig, M. (1993). One Is Not Born a Woman. In Abelove, H., Barale, M. A., & Halperin, D. M. (Eds.), *The Lesbian and Gay Studies Reader* (pp. 103–109). New York: Routledge.

KEY TERMS AND DEFINITIONS

Complicit Masculinity: Concept coined by Robin Connell. Form of masculinity of most men, comprising some elements of hegemonic masculinity and so getting some of the advantages of being associated with it.

Hegemonic Masculinity: Concept coined by Robin Connell. Culturally dominant ideal of masculinity, not attainable by most men but something men strive for as it is associated with the kind of manhood associated with men that are in power

Heteronormativity: The norm that man and woman are attracted to each other because of their presumed difference and complementarity.

ENDNOTES

[1]   The author is very grateful for the helpful comments of the anonymous reviewers and the editors of this book.

[2]   Although this association between masculinity and specific kinds of technology have become persistently intertwined, it has been otherwise in the past, as the research on how technology became masculine by Ruth Oldenziel and on how computers gained their masculine connotation by Ellen van Oost has shown (Oldenziel, 1999; Oost, 2000)

[3]   The author would like to acknowledge the invaluable work of Master's student Mariska Schönberger in collecting and analyzing the data on soap operas.

[4]   Apple probably has this image as the result of its attention to the looks of the computers. Whatever the reason, Apple is indeed by far the most well-known computer brand amongst women (whereas Dell is the most familiar amongst men) (ICM, 2001).

[5]   Unfortunately, the Dutch company (KPN that was responsible for this picture did not give permission to reprint it.

Section 4
Adult Education

Chapter 10
Approaching Higher Education:
A Life-World Story of Home-Places, Work-Places and Learn-Places

Shirley Booth
University of the Witwatersrand, South Africa & University of Gothenburg, Sweden

Eva Wigforss
Lund University, Sweden

ABSTRACT

The chapter tells of two women with low educational qualifications who embark on a journey into higher education by taking a distance course to introduce them to and induct them into academic practices, under the auspices of their trades union. In order to analyse and describe their learning, we look more closely at their contexts for learning, their life-worlds, using the conceptual framework of life-world phenomenology. Learning, in this case, means learning to find their place in higher education, and we place this against a background of the variation of ways in which the whole cohort of students was found to conceptualize the university. Grounded in an analysis of two interviews and written course assignments, we find superficial similarities and deep differences in their journey into higher education, and we give consideration to this from a gendered perspective.

INTRODUCTION

In this chapter we will be looking at two women who undertook the challenge offered by their trades union, to take a distance course that would not only give them some insights into being a student at university, but would even count as credit towards a degree if they decided to move forward in that direction. We will look at their experiences and the outcomes of their venture in the perspective of their life worlds – home-places, work-places and learn-places – and the role their new-found prospects played there.

We did not start out to study the experiences of women, and did not ground our work in a feminist or gender perspective. Rather we were interested in the learning that took place during the course, which one of the authors (Eva Wigforss) developed and ran, in contrast and comparison with other distance learning enterprises that the university was supporting. In distance courses directed to three different non-traditional groups of university

DOI: 10.4018/978-1-61520-813-5.ch010

students, and which embodied high degrees of flexibility in different dimensions, we wished to examine how the study impacted on the lives of the course participants in their lived context. However, having studied interviews with these two women in one data collection, and preparing to make another more life-world oriented interview, we noted not only that their lives had both superficial similarities and deep differences, but also that the course played different roles for them. It thus became a challenge to consider their lives from a gendered perspective, the importance of which was supported when we read:

A striking example of the difference made by applying a gender perspective in [distance education] is the area of students' private lives. This is usually seen as something which does not concern the [distance education] institution (other than granting the occasional dispensation due to family commitments interfering with the meeting of deadlines). It is strictly the student's responsibility to fit his or her distance studies into their work day. [...] It is inevitable, given the structural differences between the private situations of men and women, that men have less of a problem setting up a conducive study system for themselves (von Prümmer, 2004).

Given that, as we will elaborate below, the course was initiated by a trades union and pedagogically designed to offer good support to the distance learners, we needed to research the consequences for their approach into higher education, and in particular as it relates to their private lives, or as we choose to term it, their life-worlds.

THE BACKGROUND TO THE STUDY: THE DISTANCE COURSE

The distance course was designed as a collaboration between Lund University and the Municipal Labour trade union (Kommunal) in Sweden. It could be seen from the trades union side as a move towards their members taking the inevitable step into more qualified work, and from the university's side as a move to a more diversified student population (Wigforss et al., 2004). The full course had the goal of introducing the adult students, often with poor educational background, inadequate for entrance to further studies, to higher education as well as inducting them into its academic practices as a concrete complementary workplace for lifelong learning.

The course had three main attributes:

- it was totally off-campus with telephone conferences and IT-communication as the medium that linked participants, teachers and subject matter;
- it was highly flexible in time, in that as soon as four union members declared a commitment to taking the course, they were brought together in a conference mode and a course was started just for them;
- It was problem oriented and group-based, in that the course was focused around 5 problems, or cases, which the group of 4 could work with in order to meet the goals of the course.

The five problems that comprised the learning objectives of the course took up different critical aspects of academic practices: Studying in higher education; What is a university?; Learning and researching in higher education; Academic language and its practices; and Critical information literacy. The analysis we are presenting here is based on the papers written as one of the assignments and on two interviews with two successful course participants, one year apart (Wigforss & Booth, 2006).

The principal of problem-based learning was adopted in order to hand the adult learners some autonomy from the start. While the five themes were chosen in advance, and ways of tackling them were sometimes suggested and other times

Figure 1. The task given for the second session, Task 2, "What is a university?"

> Task 2. Formulate a study goal on how the university or university college is organised, what kind of workplace it is and how you picture yourself studying at a specific university. Choose a university near to you, contact a student counselor and arrange to make a personal study visit. Your written assignment (not longer than 1-2 pages) on "What is a university?" should take into account the experience of the study visit, written information that about that university including home pages and books, and the specific course material on the CD-ROM: *What is a university*? It should also contain a personal reflection on further study at a university or college.

prescribed, the course participants were free to handle them in their own ways. For example, for the theme of *what is a university*? The students were given the task as shown in Figure 1.

Task 2. Formulate a study goal on how the university or university college is organised, what kind of workplace it is and how you picture yourself studying at a specific university. Choose a university near to you, contact a student counsellor and arrange to make a personal study visit. Your written assignment (not longer than 1-2 pages) on "What is a university?" should take into account the experience of the study visit, written information about that university including home pages and books, and the specific course material on the CD-ROM: *What is a university*? It should also contain a personal reflection on further study at a university or college.

To give the reader an idea of the Swedish system of higher education that these students were engaging with, we can start by saying that the difference between a university and a university college is that the former have education at undergraduate and post-graduate levels as well as research, potentially in all the disciplines and areas of professional work, while the latter focus on undergraduate education and have only limited areas with post-graduate education and research. Study at university or university college can take one of two forms: the student can either enroll into a three or four year programme of studies which is generally prescribed in the first year and

offers increasing freedom of relevant choice as the programme progresses; or the student can enroll in individual courses which in time make up a degree with a major and two minor subjects.

The model that the course adopted complies with the three constitutive concepts for distance education for adults that Peters (1998) following Moore (1993), designed, when applied in different degrees, to reduce the transactional distance of the distance learning situation. The elements are dialogue, structure and autonomy, and the idea of transactional distance is described thus:

Transactional distance depends on whether students are left alone with their distance education materials or whether they can communicate with their teachers. The transactional function is determined by the extent to which teachers and students can interact ('dialogue'). At the same time, it is influenced by the extent to which the learning path is determined by pre-planned teaching programmes ('structure'). Accordingly the transactional distance is greatest when teachers and students do not communicate with one another at all and when the teaching programme is pre-planned and prescribed down to the last detail, so that individual learning needs cannot be taken into account. And it is therefore shortest where the teaching programme is open, i.e. not determined and with frequent dialogues in which the prior knowledge, interests and desires of individual students have an effect and are able to influence the learning and teaching. Peters, 1998, p. 28)

By dialogue he means "direct and indirect oral interaction between teachers and students, in other words, actual dialogue", in contrast with conversations and correspondence of the virtual IT-classroom (p. 33). Peters makes another point that underpins the importance of dialogue in distance education of great relevance to the project of this course: "In a dialogue, speech turns into a social act, whereas this is not the case with the isolated reading of printed material", or of the isolated writing of essays one might add. In undertaking the task, the four students and the tutor decided, in dialogues conducted by telephone and internet, on how they would go about getting the information and access they were asked for.

The second of Peters' constitutive concepts is structure, in our case not of the heavy and restrictive kind found in the principles of programmed instruction, but in the structures of writing and communication, on pragmatic grounds. This is brought about by the repeated structure of task discussion, report writing and seminar. Having decided on a meaning for the problem and discussed ways of going about the tasks, the students worked on their tasks individually, they met in virtual meetings with their tutor and with one another during the problem solving period, and finally presented their written report in a seminar with telephone and internet communication.

The third constitutive concept is that of autonomy, not merely in the sense of doing things in one's own way at one's own pace, but "a state of affairs in which a person is no longer the *object* of educational guidance, influences, effects and obligations, but the *subject* of his or her own education" (Peters, p 48), in line with the Kantian concept of *bildung*. The mode of work is autonomous both in the usual sense of being carried out according to the students' interpretations and the individual student's own will, and in the sense of Peters, in

that they are in the course as a whole determining their own future higher education as subjects of that education rather than as having it imposed and becoming objects of higher education.

We would add a fourth constitutive aspect of this distance pedagogy: collaboration and sharing. When the four students meet in an initial problem-solving meeting or in the final seminar, they are bringing their own understandings and experiences to the table and sharing them. Initially they are coming to joint understandings of what the problem involves and demands, and finally they are reading and critiquing one another's written reports.

The course was attended by a total of 42 Municipal labour union members from all corners of Sweden. This labour union covers more than 200 branches of work, from churchyard caretakers to fire-fighters, from day care givers to school cooks, and from nursing to occupational therapy assistants; 27 passed the course, 7 formally resigned and 8 are in abeyance. Their ages spanned from 24 to 60. Of the 42 who started the course, 35 were women, predominantly from the care sector, and 7 were men, from care and paramedic sectors as well as the fire service. This imbalance is in keeping with the general observation that women learn while men earn (McGivney, 1999); it also reflects the general pattern in Sweden in which women tend to participate more in higher education than men[1].

Learning in such a course can be seen merely as the difference between passing and gaining credits in higher education, or failing or non-completion. Learning can be seen in the extent to which the students have gained new knowledge and insights into the subject matter, academic practices in higher education. In contrast, learning can be seen as the ways in which the lives of the students have been touched by the course and in what ways it has had a lasting effect on their lives. In order to grasp this last, and more fundamental form of learning, we need to analyse and describe the ways in which individuals have been affected, and to understand that we need to understand individual contexts for learning.

CONTEXTS FOR LEARNING: HOME, WORK- AND LEARN-PLACES

The Theoretical Framework of Life-World Phenomenology

In research on the experience of learning and teaching in higher education, the context for learning is generally taken for granted, in that there is an assumption of more or less homogenous groups of young adults spending time on campus over an extended period, in face-to-face contact with their teachers and with one another. In distance education for adults, the situation is not at all clear and the context for learning becomes much more significant.

We have turned to Alfred Schutz' phenomenology of the everyday life-world (Schutz and Luckman, 1974, Bengtsson, 2004) in an attempt to capture more closely the context in which these students are studying and learning. As members of the labour union, they can be assumed to be in a state of transition between the working life in lesser qualified jobs in the knowledge society, where more and more qualifications are necessary to ensure continued employment, and taking a leap into the life of higher education with the possibility of raising their qualifications. The distance course that they have embarked on, with the encouragement and support of their trades union, is not only a *ground* for deciding whether or not to take that leap, and in what direction to take it, but it is also *in* the world of higher education, so they are both introduced to practices of higher education while being inducted into those practices through the seminars and written assignments demanded by the course.

The assumption that underpinned the course was that the student already has an indirect relation to university – it belongs to their *Mitwelt* – the world within potential reach – where the university and its objects and people and practices are in a "they-relationship" to the student, as types. The course was seen as offering an opportunity to concretize these types, so that the university would be drawn more into the – the world within actual reach – of the student, into a we-relationship of actual presence. Here we are following the description of the life-world put forward by Bengtsson (2004), commenting on Schutz, and by Schutz and Luckman, (1974):

In the Umwelt we stand face to face with other people and have direct contact with their lives. This direct contact can be separated into a you-attitude and a we-relation. In the you-attitude I am one-sidedly aware of another person's lived presence. In the we-relation, on the other hand, the parties involved are mutually aware of one another and participate in one another's lives. We only have indirect relations to people in our Mitwelt. They are known to us only as general types. Therefore, we have a they-attitude to them and they are experienced as more or less anonymous. But when persons from the Mitwelt enter my Umwelt, there is a possibility to concretize and modify the types." (Bengtsson, 2004, p. 27. Our translation)

Thus Bengtsson describes three relationships between the individual and the world, and in our situation the first of these, in reverse order, can be described as the they-relationship of the outsider who looks at the world of higher education and sees there only "they", categorised as general types of academics in the *Mitwelt*, possibly stuffy professors and super-clever researchers. The second is the you-attitude of the *Umwelt*, where the world of higher education is peopled by other individuals but they are not known or understood, while in the we-relationship these people of the *Umwelt* are in direct contact, colleagues in the project of higher learning.

In the everyday life-world where our adult students go about their business of work and home life, removed from higher education, its practices are generally unseen, unknown. Taking the step of applying to the course offered, they are reaching out to an attainable goal, of entering higher education and a – possibly parallel with its retained they- or you-attitude, possibly integrated with its we-relationship – life-world of higher studies. Meeting the course involves introducing into the everyday life-world a new world of future possibilities, but it also re-introduces a past world of study in school and all that that entails. The restorable past, the attainable future and the lived present constitute the time-related context for learning.

The phenomenon we are attempting to grasp is the context for learning that is constituted in the meeting with that world of higher education, not in an abstract way but as it might affect the learning of the adult students taking the course. While people only have one life and they live in one world, for our purposes of analysis and achieving better understanding, we will regard their everyday life-world as constituted of their places of work, home and learning, qualitatively different life-worlds that nonetheless constitute the one lived world. The everyday-world is the most real of all, while the delimited worlds that we visit in our trajectory through life can be seen only as modifications of this real world, mediated by social and physical contexts. Whether at home, or at work, or at a place of study, the everyday life-world is present to the individual and the individual is present to that life-world.

Each and every one of these worlds constitute delimited and consistent areas of experience with their own style and character of reality. The transition between these worlds demands a leap, since we cannot leave the superior everyday world we have natural attitude to just like that. But even so, we people make this leap all the time and land in the enchanted world of the story as soon

as we begin to read fiction, in the magical world of the child when we start to play with her, in the theatrical world when the curtain rises, and so on. (Bengtsson, 2004, pp 28-29. Our translation)

While we have taken a turn to phenomenology to analyse and describe the context for learning, the study was conceived in a phenomenographic framework (Bowden & Walsh, 2000; Marton & Booth, 1997), which takes human experience as the object of research, in common with phenomenology. Also in common with phenomenology, phenomenographic research takes an epistemological standpoint that knowledge is relational – knowing is a relation between the knower and what is known, and learning is developing the capability to shift that relation, and consequently coming to know (or understand, or see, or experience – the choice of verb depends on the nature of the phenomenon) something in a distinctly new way which is contextually flexible. However, phenomenography is an empirical research movement within the discipline of pedagogy whereas phenomenology is essentially a philosophically grounded movement with empirical offshoots, and phenomenography gives priority to analysing and describing the variation of the experience of the students at a collective level (Marton, 1981). The theoretical understanding of learning which underpins our study of the context for learning is that which has emerged from phenomenographic studies, now known as variation theory (Marton and Booth, 1997). Here, learning is characterised as the learner becoming able to discern new qualities in some focal phenomenon or aspects of that phenomenon, which demands opening dimensions of variation in awareness, becoming able to see that that which has been taken for granted could be otherwise (Marton and Pang, 2006; Runesson, 2006).

Phenomenographic research studies generally focus on what is learned, or how the tasks of learning are approached, or how learning in a particular situation is experienced. In this study, as we have described above, we are more interested in the context for learning in relation to what is learned, and the mutual dynamic between them. This dynamic is inevitable in that the students are being inducted into (not only introduced to) the practices of higher education. Thus the context for learning, which inevitably includes a course emanating from an institution of higher education with its practices embedded, is changing as the students are introduced to and discuss those practices.

The data that this study rests on, as a whole, is the collected reports to two of the tasks, a series of interviews with 8 of the course participants within some six months of completing the course, and two in-depth interviews with the two women participants, who we will now call Agneta and Britt[2], one year later. The first interviews were lengthy and very open, and focused around themes intended to explore the course participants' understanding of the course and of higher education. The second interviews, with only Agneta and Britt, were intended to return to some of the issues of their first interviews and to follow up what has been attained and what changes have occurred. What was addressed in both interviews was the everyday work life, the everyday family life and the everyday study life, and in so doing the interviews extended to the future, to what might be in reach, and they looked back at how things were in earlier times. In this chapter we are referring only to the two interviews with each of Agneta and Britt, and the responses of the whole course to Task 2 (see Figure 1).

The Everyday Life-World: Home-Place and Work-Place at the Time of the Course

In this study we see people who have their everyday lives as the starting point for their meeting with the world of higher education, and we study the leap they make (or could fail to make) to that new life-world. Is it a leap that is necessary, or

are there ropes and bridges to help them make the transition? In the case of Agneta and Britt whom we have chosen to study as a case of similarities and contrasts, we see some obvious factors that characterise their situation in the light of the gender literature, including the tendency for women to study when change is in the air (McGivney, 1999; Wännman Toresson; 1999). The most significant aspects of their everyday-worlds are those of work and home, a work-place and a home-place, as Gouthro calls it (Gouthro, 2005), and the first tentative steps to enter a place of higher education, a learn-place, has now begun.

For these students, with a full working life and studying in their spare time from their homes, the concept of home-place is significant. Gouthro (2005), writing from a critical theoretical perspective, offers this:

An easy, single definition cannot be provided for the term 'homeplace'. Its meaning is different for each person, depending upon his/her unique life circumstances. A person defines her homeplace based upon personal lived experience and her family and cultural background. The homeplace may fit into a larger socio-cultural context than an individual residence, inclusive of community, neighbours, and larger cultural setting. The homeplace is located in both tangible and non-tangible realms, and may be linked with a specific geographic location. (p. 9)

Agneta and Britt were initially chosen as two of the group to be interviewed directly after the course ended as members of a subset which was representative of the variation of people in the course as a whole. They have similar backgrounds, both being middle aged women working in the health care sector as assistants with low formal qualifications, but in positions with responsibilities and having a good deal of work experience. As mentioned previously they are both union members and have work that does not require university qualifications. Thus they could be considered potential "class travellers" – this is a Swedish term that attempts to capture the changes in life and cultural practices that follow the movement through social classes. They appeared to address the course and their future study in rather different ways, and were thus singled out for a more detailed study through a second interview one year later. We will analyse their everyday life-worlds, as described in their first interview, in terms of their home-places and work-places, and how they interact in relation to their ambitions to enter higher education.

How would these two women define their home-places? Agneta, who is married with teenage children and lives in a large city, told us that she came from a family with little formal education and virtually no experience of higher education. Her parents had the minimum of education when young, but they continued their studies as adults, her mother in order to get work when the family moved from a small town to the city, her father in order to further his own business. She tells that her mother regrets that she didn't push her children to continue their studies after school. Her brother, however, has had some experience of higher education, and Agneta has talked about it with him. He, like his mother before him, had to improve his educational credentials when he moved to another part of the country, in order to get work and has just, after some time, received his degree.

Her family, both husband and children, respect what she is doing, give her the time she needs to be by herself and study, and one of her children helped her over the hurdle of her writing difficulties by reading all her written assignments. She describes that she has the use of a study and has taken the best computer in the house for her own use; but she also likes to sit in the kitchen and read, and then her children take care not to disturb her. Her husband will prepare dinner if she has studying to do, and her children accompany her to the library to find her literature. She has a strong expectation that her teenage children will

go to university, looking into the future and seeing there the need for more than the basic education of school. Agneta, in her home-place, then, has a they-attitude to higher education but in a we-relation to studying in general, the university is in her *Mitwelt*, but not to the extent that she is totally foreign to it, while study is in her *Umwelt*.

Britt is also married with teenage and young adult children, living not in the city but in a small and rather isolated town. She comes from a family with no experience of higher education at all – it was never even considered that she might continue to study after the end of compulsory school, but it was straight into a job. Her older child is the first person in her family to enter higher education and in her first interview Britt tells how she is counselling him not to give up because of difficulties with a particular subject. She looks back on her own home and wishes she had had the opportunity to have similar talks with her own mother, but she did not. Her other child is younger and while being proud of her mother studying, doesn't make allowances for the time she needs to read in peace and quiet. She says that she understands that for the family it is a huge change in situation, and that her husband is actively opposed to her studies, especially when on one occasion it meant her being away from home for two days at a time. She expresses in several ways that she has experienced a vacuum, which she appears to fill with study, initially egged on by a friend who was taking a distance course.

For Britt, both higher education and study are in her *Mitwelt*, she is in a they-attitude to higher education seen from her home-place of everyday life, with occasional excursions into the *Umwelt* of discussions with her older child, saying that when such discussions take place, it is a sort of exclusive discussion, when "we talk about our studies".

After the home-place, the work-place is the most significant aspect of the everyday life-world, for the purpose of this study at least[3]. Agneta's working life started as an assistant in the health care system but circumstances prevented her from continuing in her original job. As a result she moved into an academic environment, and at the time of the first interview she was working with clerical duties in a research group, collecting and organizing data for them, but also doing some more qualified work in connection with courses they held. She describes her relations with her colleagues as good, but that she sometimes has difficulties in understanding how they are thinking, ascribing it to the fact that they have studied at university, that they assume that she also knows what they are doing and planning to do. At the same time, she learns from them, has gained new insights and ways of thinking, and is prepared to take initiatives without waiting to be told what to do. So in the everyday life of the work-place higher education is in her *Umwelt*, she can take a you-attitude to most of the activities and people she associates with higher education, and has a burgeoning we-relationship with them. However, when it comes to them as academics, their assumptions and ways of thinking, they appear to remain on the periphery, in her *Mitwelt*.

Britt told us that she had had a number of different jobs, working as shop assistant for periods, though most of her work had been as assistant, and now head of a team, looking after severely disabled children. In her job she had a lot of responsibility, and described herself as "taking her work home with her" and "taking some children home with her", though only figuratively. She took on the role as team leader partly because she wanted to, partly because she was asked to, but mainly because no-one else wanted to – and she seemed to give priority to the last of these three reasons, as if she doubted her ability to take on the role. But she wanted to take charge of dealing with information in her team and was pleased with her work there. She got on well with her colleagues, but they had no ambitions with regard to higher education and did not understand her repeated participation in distance courses.

There was an exception in that a former colleague who had since left was the one to introduce her to distance courses in higher education, as mentioned earlier, and Britt described how being away at a course over a weekend really encouraged her to get started on studying; it gave her the opportunity to study in peace, which she appreciated. Since then she had taken a number of courses at a distance but at the time of the first interview had not completed them. Though they no longer worked together, she still had some contact with this person and they talked over their respective study experiences.

Seen against the background of the broad study, both Agneta and Britt can be seen as successful students. For example, in their final essays they both focused on extending and elaborating the subject matter of the course while in the course as a whole a variation of topics was seen, focusing on personal family issues, workplace issues and general interest in life. The course can be said to have given them different experiences of both the university as a place of study and distance education as a facility for learning. Agneta's purpose with taking the course is to test her ability to go further now, move on from being on the sidelines of the academic practices of her workplace to being more active participant in them, while Britt is taking the course in order to help her succeed with her ongoing studies, rather than to test her ability as Agneta described.

The Learn-Place of Higher Education

This study is basically about how adults face entering the world of higher education and how the world of higher education enters into relation with their life-world. We have now described how the two women we are focusing on here experienced home and work in relation to higher education, and now we will attempt to analyse and describe how they experienced higher education in itself, in terms of the university and university college as institutions of higher education and of higher learning. First we need to shed light on how the adults in the course experienced higher education across the board, then we can return to Agneta and Britt and how they have, after one year, moved on in their relation to higher education.

The task referred to earlier and outlined in Figure 1 has been subject to a phenomenographic analysis of the resulting written reports on how the students experienced institutions of higher education after their visit and discussions. The empirical material consisted of the 42 reports that the students wrote in completion of the task. The categories that are presented are not categorisations of individual students and what they reported, nor are they thematic categories that describe the salient aspects that were reported on. They are phenomenographic categories that lie at the collective level of the data, which emanate from the whole body of material, which are both empirically and logically related, and which cover the whole material as succinctly as possible (Marton, 1981; Marton & Booth, 1997, p. 125; Bowden & Walsh, 2000; Akerlind, 2005).

Five distinct ways of seeing the university were revealed, recounted in more detail in Wigforss and Booth (2007). These were:

(A) The university is a statutory organisation, referring to the institution as formulated by law, to conduct higher education in line with the needs of society, against an historical and cultural background;

(B) The university is an organisation of buildings, referring to the spaces for educational activities that are seen on visiting the university;

(C) The university is a knowledge-based organisation, referring to the ways in which the university is structured around the knowledge that comprises its teaching and research activities: faculties and departments, programmes and courses;

(D) The university is an organisation for study, referring to the various kinds of activities

that take place in which the students and teachers are involved: for example, lectures, projects, problem-based learning, practical work; and

(E) The university is a social organisation, referring to the relationships between teachers and students, the atmosphere of the place, and the advantages and constraints for the individual student.

These are categories derived inductively from the descriptions offered by the course participants; of course, scholars of higher education might offer descriptions that are both more extensive and more elaborate. This set of categories describes, in its totality, where these course participants were coming from as they approached higher education. Learning, seen in one light, would imply coming to see more facets of the university as a result of the visit, the readings, the Task 2 and the discussions in seminar form. However, the fuller picture revealed in the task reports and the interviews shows another view of learning, in which the already known and identified takes on a richer hue due to the experience of the course and interactions that take place there. There is a trajectory from the known and experienced in one way to the known and experienced in another and richer way.

An important dimension to these somewhat basic ways of understanding the total institution of higher education is that of the relationship between people and the state, or the system. There is a shift from seeing the university as an organ of the state in (A) divested of its social aspects, to an un-peopled site of buildings and artefacts in (B). An expression of either of these ways of seeing the world of higher education is essentially expressing it with the they-attitude of the *Mitwelt*, where universities are the business of others who are not seen at all. For example, an expression of (A) was

Universities and colleges are authorities which answer directly to the government. Sweden has 13 universities and 23 colleges directly under the government. *(5⁴)*

And (B) can be exemplified by:

When you walk round the college it feels like a young place, with a fresh atmosphere, good quality buildings and materials. (31)

In (C), people are implied but not specified, in that one can assume that the knowledge activities are implicitly peopled by academics and students. An expression of this sort brings in the people who populate universities and who deal with the knowledge and structures for learning to be found there, for example:

There is a library where anyone over the age of 18 with an identification document can borrow books. You can also ask the librarian things over internet, but then you have to be registered at the college (28)

In (D) and (E), people come into the picture explicitly, with students and teachers interacting in the cause of knowledge and in social settings. For example,

When you take courses, you can study them at your own pace and take them in the order you want to. (23)

Exemplifies (D), where the writer identifies with the subject of the sentence, and

Older students said they find it hard to get started, and have to put 50-60 hours work in for the first year, to get going with their studies properly (20)

Exemplifies (E), where the student who wrote this has the interests of similar students in mind.

It has to be borne in mind that no student expressed a view of the university entirely in any one of these categories, nor did any one category come entirely from a single student. The categories are idealised ways of understanding higher education that come from an analysis of the meanings expressed in the entire pool of written reports. These five categories of understanding or experiencing "the university" constitute the collective understanding or experience of these adult students and here we see another potential trajectory for learning, as shifting one's own location with respect to higher education as external to the system in (A) to full participation in (D) and (E). From the they-attitude to a we-relation.

So, now we can place Agneta and Britt in this re-constituted experience of higher education, and ask how participation in the course has interacted with the everyday life-world of home-place and work-place to realise an experience of the university as "learn-place".

Seeing the World of Higher Education

Initially, for Britt the world of higher education is in her *Mitwelt*, and hardly there, in that, in her own words, "the university was only a word for me". She saw the university as "something huge", and expressed surprise that the course was a university course, that she expected a university course to be more research, this was more of a college course, she thought. Thus she was distinguishing between level of university, but her understanding that both sorts of establishment give similar undergraduate education at very similar levels was lacking.

She echoes this formalistic and external view of the university even in her project report for Task 2. Almost all of the report is written in an impersonal style of facts in the style of category (A). For example, she opens her report thus:

The difference that I can see between the university, which is generally bigger, and the university

college is that the university can give degrees at research level as well as at undergraduate level. The university colleges that have a disciplinary area have, however, the right to conduct research education and research. The main mission of the university and university colleges is to carry out education, research and to collaborate with the community.[5]

She goes on to describe the rules and funding that underpin higher education, giving references to websites to validate her facts. She had visited a small local university college, Z[6], and been shown round by the co-ordinator for collaborations with local industry and found a good deal of numerical information from him about Z. Some description of the buildings with their mixed history in the community and their current academic usages follows, as in (B). Finally, she reports on asking some students why they had chosen to study there, and she gives examples of their reasons; nowhere, however, does she relate a personal opinion or a personal reflection on the university she visits and the reports on how other students speak to her are in the "they" form.

Agneta says in the first interview that she is taking the course because,

one of the reasons is that I had thought quite a long time about university, but since it was such a long time since I went to school, and I can see my own kids in high school, how that has changed, so I realised that my knowledge about the university was very poor. ... I wanted to know more about what it actually is, the university, and how it works, what the structure looks like, and what you do there, and what an essay looks like, and how you write one.

Here the university is already on the fringe of the *Umwelt*; she is already identifying herself with its practices even while claiming not to know about them.

Her report for Task 2 opens thus:

On a fine spring day I packed my paper and pen and got into the car to travel to X university where I hoped to get answers to this question [What is a university?]. I had arranged to meet the study counsellor at X. To prepare myself I had been into their home page, and also to the home pages of the Swedish National Agency for Higher Education, and I had looked through the CD from Lund University.

Her report also takes up the formal rules that govern higher education in Sweden, as did Britt's, and a tour of the campus with a short chat with some students on why they chose the university. What strikes one is not only the livelier writing style of Agneta but also her interest in support for student health and well-being, and the social traditions that students uphold at X. Her report includes expression of the impersonal world of the institution but also engages in the social world of the university life. For example she wrote:

Student Health has courses in coping with stress, to support students. The churches have special priests who can offer confidential discussions and the student union has a counsellor who can help and give support.

If we compare Britt and Agneta at the time of the course and the first interview, we see that Britt started with, and had maintained, a greater distance from the world of higher education than Agneta had – even while narrowing the gap. Britt began with, apparently, the vaguest understanding of what she had started to go into, while Agneta saw her immediate working context as an opening to higher education. Britt was apparently trying to fill an emptiness in her life and to reach an imagined better success at work, while Agneta was aiming to take on more of the qualified work of her workplace. Britt had a much greater leap to make from her everyday life-world of home and work than Agneta had, if she was to enter the world of higher education without harming herself. While Britt started out with higher education in her *Mitwelt*, with hardly any point of contact with the we-relations of her *Umwelt*, Agneta has bridges between her everyday life-world, especially her work-place, and the world of higher education. Britt is moving towards the you-attitude of the *Umwelt* in her relation to higher education, while Agneta has access to the we-relation to higher education.

By the second interview, one year after the first and some 18 months after the course ended, Britt had formulated a goal for her studies, and said that she would complete the unfinished courses, take two more and then fill her goal of becoming a pre-school teacher. This was not mentioned in the first interview, when her interest was more on rising in her current workplace and becoming successful. In fact she contradicted herself on a number of points in the second interview. She recalls her family as being supportive, which is not at all in accord with the first interview. However, it has to be told that she has experienced a drastic and tragic change in family life since the first interview, and her recall might well be coloured by that. Change has characterized her life since the first interview. Her family has changed and even her workplace life has been restructured, though to her advantage with a better position in sight. This demands that she completes her studies, which can account for the greater degree of goal orientation and meaning in the studies. Her studies are no longer a way to fill empty time, to bring success in a vague way, rather they have become more meaningful.

Agneta, in the second interview, has achieved her study goals, in that she has been accepted into a distance programme at a university at quite some distance from her home, which she will visit for intensive periods and successful completion will qualify her for more responsible work in her group. Her goals at work are being fulfilled and she has already taken on more active part in their

work as an academic practice. She is even taking on a theme at work that no-one else can take, thanks to her studies in that area. She is pursuing a line of independent study that is clearly fulfilling her immediate goals and promising well for the future.

The trajectory that Agneta has embarked on has led her to the university programme and the success at work that she hoped for, helped along the way by work-place colleagues and supported by family. Her life-worlds had integrated both intellectually and in time, as her place of work gave her time off for her intensive periods at the university; the university has fully entered her *Umwelt*. Britt's trajectory has not taken her as far, but has led her to consolidate the ground she stands on, by completing hitherto unfinished courses, and it has helped her to mould her future ambitions in higher education. It seems as if during the year between interviews Agneta has moved confidently on, while Britt has re-considered her life and tells a different story about her life-world. Her life-worlds are still separate, but getting closer to one another. The university is impinging on her *Umwelt*.

ADOPTING A GENDER PERSPECTIVE

When challenged to consider the work we have described here in a gender perspective we, as is typical of researchers, searched for new literature in the field. And we found very little that could engage us in a discussion of adult women entering the world of higher education through a distance course intended to support just that. And so we have turned to three seminal works on the student's entry into the world of higher learning and their development thereafter.

William Perry (1968/1970/1999) set the scene in his book "Forms of ethical and intellectual development in the college years: A scheme" (Perry, 1968/1999), by following students at his university over the four years they studied there, with interviews of an open nature on their studies and experiences of studying. His analysis resulted in a complex developmental schema in which we can see four basic stages or positions: Duality, Multiplicity, Relativism and Commitment, each constituted primarily of a view of knowledge and relations to knowledge, and concomitant views of the roles of people and activities of higher education[7]. He offers definitions of these terms:

Dualism: A bifurcated structuring of the world between Good and Bad, Right and Wrong, We and Others.

Multiplicity: A plurality of "answers", points of view, or evaluations, with reference to similar topics or problems. This plurality is perceived as an aggregate of discretes without any internal structure or external relation.

Relativism: A plurality of points of view, interpretations, frames of reference, value systems, and contingencies in which the structural properties of contexts and forms allow of various sorts of analysis, comparison, and evaluation in Multiplicity.

Commitment: An affirmation of personal values or choices in relativism. A conscious act of realization of identity and responsibility. A process of orientation of self in a relative world. (Perry, 1968/1970/1999, p. 287)

If we put this into our framework of life-world phenomenology, we see immediately that Dualism is in line with a situation where a student has distanced him- or herself from the world of knowledge and higher learning, that it is others who make the pace, and the student stands in a they-attitude to the university at large which is in his or her *Mitwelt*. Commitment, at the other extreme, describes a view of knowledge that is owned, that is valued and identified with. The student has entered the world of higher learning and taken his or her rightful place there with the responsibilities that are implied. He or she has assumed the we-relationship, or the I-relationship of the *Umwelt*.

However, Perry's research was located at Harvard College and his research subjects were all men of a rather high social class and generally from a well-educated background. Not in contestation with Perry, but nonetheless in stark contrast when related to his work, Belenky, Clinchy, Goldberger and Tarule published *Women's ways of knowing* in 1986 (Belenky et al., 1986/1997), a study of American women, from a range of ages and educational backgrounds, and their relation with learning and intellectual competence. They state from the outset that:

... we believe that conceptions of knowledge and truth that are accepted and articulated today have been shaped throughout history by the male-dominated majority culture. Drawing on their own perspectives and visions, men have constructed the prevailing theories, written history, and set values that have become the guiding principles for men and women alike. Our major educational institutions [...] were originally founded by men for the education of men. [...] Relatively little attention has been given to modes of learning, knowing and valuing that may be specific to, or at least common in, women. (Belenky et al., 1987/1997, pp. 5-6)

They analysed four major stages or positions, covering similar dimensions to those of Perry, which they label Received knowledge, Subjective knowledge, Procedural knowledge and Constructed knowledge. The first of these they call the Received knowledge position, and relate it to Perry's Dualism:

Perry's dualist position describes men who hold an outlook that is similar to the received knowledge position we found in women's data: Dualism, the simplest way of knowing that Perry observed, was held only briefly, if at all, among members of his elite college sample. Perry's men particularly dichotomize "the familiar world of Authority-right-we as against the alien world of illegitimate-wrong-others (1970, p. 59)" [...] While some of the women we interviewed most certainly saw authorities as the source of the "right answers" and "truth" they did not align themselves with authorities to the extent Perry described occurring among men. The world of "Authority-right-we" was quite alien to many women. The women in our sample seemed to say "Authority-right-they" (p. 43)

This last statement can be reflected into the life-world analysis and point to the women that Belenky et al. speak of having a tendency to sustain a they-attitude to the authorities of higher education and its knowledge and values whereas, it is implied, men might identify with the authorities and thereby incorporate their identities in the *Umwelt* of high education more readily than women do.

It is more interesting from the point of this chapter that when it comes to Procedural knowledge, which is an objective relation to knowledge and implies seeking ways or methods of making sense. Belenky et al. make a distinction between Separate and Connected knowing, following the work of Gilligan (1982). The category of separate knowing emphasizes the critical thought that typifies traditional higher education, and Belenky et al. write that in their study: "Most of the women who leaned heavily toward separate knowing were attending or had recently graduated from a traditional, elite, liberal arts college." (p. 103) Connected knowers, in contrast, "begin with an interest in the facts of other people's lives, but they gradually shift the focus to other people's ways of thinking." (p. 115). Contrasting the two forms of knowing, they write:

Separate knowers learn through explicit formal instruction how to adopt a different lens – how, for example, to think like a sociologist. Connected knowers learn through empathy. Both learn to get out from behind their own eyes and use a different lens, in one case the lens of a discipline, in the other case the lens of another person. (p. 115)

Here, then, there are women who tend to the development scheme of Perry and his men, and women who have a distinctively different way of making sense of the world, more in line with our descriptions of Agneta and Britt. It can further be interpreted that the separate knowers need to approach higher learning through a they-attitude to those who already stand in a we-relation to knowledge, while the connected knowers need to make social contact with those in a we-relation in order to interact and empathise their way to knowledge. Their hovering on the fringes of the *Umwelt* of higher education has different characteristics, and to take the step themselves takes, one can suppose, different forms of responsiveness from the educational institution itself.

The results of the all-male study of Perry and the all-women study of Belenky et al. are echoed in a study of Marcia Baxter Magolda (Baxter Magolda, 1992), a Perry-like study of the development of students from a traditional liberal arts college in the mid-West of the Unites States, now taking a sample of traditional age students comprising half women and half men in order to look specifically at gender-related patterns of learning and knowing. Again, four main categories emerge from the data, which she calls: Absolute knowing, Transitional knowing, Independent knowing and Contextual knowing, and, again, they are generally in line with the four categories of our previous authors. In the first three of these, however, she identifies what she calls patterns of knowing which are loosely correlated with the sex of the participants. On the one hand, there are the Receiving, Inter-personal and Inter-individual attitudes of Absolute knowing, Transitional knowing and Independent knowing, respectively, and on the other hand, there are the attitudes of Mastery, Impersonal and Individual attitudes of Absolute knowing, Transitional knowing and Independent knowing, respectively. The first grouping, in which contact with other persons and sharing play significant roles, are more prevalent among the women students in the study while the second grouping, in which independence from others and self-governing are characteristics, are more prevalent among the men.

These patterns point, once again, to the importance of the social world in the learning of women in higher education, where the possibility to discuss, share, interact, and empathise, are considered valuable. And it is in contrast to the non-social world of self, which characterises the world of learning that is more valued by men.

CONCLUSION: REFLECTING BACK ON THE LIFE-WORLDS OF AGNETA AND BRITT AND ON THE COURSE

The three studies briefly and selectively outlined above lead one to re-consider the descriptions of the everyday life world that were offered earlier in the chapter, as they relate to this study. "In the *Umwelt* we stand face-to-face with other people and have direct contact with their lives", but it emerges that the standing face-to-face and the direct contact with the lives of others have distinctly different, and gendered, meanings. "When persons from the *Mitwelt* enter my *Umwelt*, there is a possibility to concretize and modify the types" (both quotations from Bengtsson, 2004, p. 27, our translation). But again, when persons from the *Mitwelt* enter my *Umwelt*, that entrance can too take on different forms of significance and they too are gendered.

Agneta's *Umwelt* is regularly entered by persons from the *Mitwelt* in the form of her work colleagues, and she wishes to empathise and become of the same type as them. This is one of her motivations in trying to enter higher educa-

tion – she wishes to think, act and be more like them. Britt does not share this good fortune and her *Umwelt* is rarely visited by persons from the *Mitwelt* of higher education. This difference can account for the different tones and contents of the written reports on the visit to a university or university college: Agneta can take on the persona of the student while Britt stands outside.

Our final consideration in this chapter concerns ways in which the course gave, and could have given better, support to these two women from non-academic backgrounds in coming to enter the world of higher education. At the start of the chapter we referred to the transactional distance function of a distance education course, with dialogue, structure and autonomy as its three constitutive elements in Peters' model of distance education (Peters, 1998), following Moore (1993), to which we added the element of collaboration. What can be said about the transactional distance of this course, as it affected the *Umwelt* of higher education for our two women students?

Certainly as we claimed earlier, these constituents were present to different extents in the course as it was conducted. The transactional distance was certainly not very great, in intent at least. The dialogues that took place were between a fully-paid up member of the *Umwelt* of higher education and the adult students and were designed to bring to their awareness the practices of higher education. But this was a person on the other end of a telephone line, or on the website of the course learning platform, or on a DVD introducing the course, rather than a person of flesh and blood whom they might bump into and chat with in the canteen, as on a campus: the transactional distance as in dialogue can never be as short as it can be on campus, but the different modes of dialogue can shorten it as far as possible. The structure of problem-based learning is less pre-ordained than traditional teaching approaches, in that a good deal of autonomy is given to the students, but in the interviews this did not appear to have presented problems to any of the adult students –

structure and autonomy seemed to have played well together. One possibility stands out for the support of students like Britt: the course could have included an on-campus element where the *Umwelt* of higher education would have presented itself for all and in the various ways that the students conceptualized it. Britt found not only the peace of being away from home helpful, but also benefited from the socialisation into the knowledge and learning of higher education that on-campus periods offered her. This could not have compensated for the on-going contact with higher education that Agneta enjoyed but could have gone someway towards bringing Britt closer to that world: the transactional distance would have for a short while been reduced to zero.

Finally, while this study is firmly rooted in Swedish traditions of distance education and higher education, with the life-worlds of two Swedish national participants as the object of study, we would suggest that it is relevant to similar situations world-wide where men and women are being recruited to higher education through such initiatives as induction courses to academic practices. The life-worlds of the students in terms of work-places, home-places and learn-places will differ in detail but the relations between the people and the knowledge that constitute higher education will be the same.

ACKNOWLEDGMENT

The authors wish to thank the Swedish Research Council, Committee for Educational Science, for their support for the research project "Learning in the ICT-mediated university: Experienced context and constituted meaning in ICT-supported outreach initiatives involving flexibility and diversity" from which this work originates. Thanks also to the research group that grew around that project. Shirley Booth wishes to acknowledge also the South African National Research Foundation for generous support while writing this chapter, and the support of the Gender, Learning and IT network of LearnIT.

REFERENCES

Akerlind, G. (2005). Variation and commonality in phenomenographic research methods. *Higher Education Research & Development, 24*, 321–334. doi:10.1080/07294360500284672

Baxter Magolda, M. B. (1992). *Knowing and reasoning in college: Gender related patterns in students' intellectual development*. San Francisco: Jossey-Bass.

Belenky, M. F., Clinchy, B. M., Goldberger, N. R., & Tarule, J. M. (1986/1987). *Women's ways of knowing: The development of self, voice and mind*. New York: BasicBooks.

Bengtsson, J. (2004). *Med livsvärld som grund (Grounded in the life-world)*. Lund, Sweden: Studentlitteratur.

Bowden, J. A., & Walsh, E. (2000). *Phenomenography*. Melbourne, Australia: RMIT University Press.

Gilligan, C. (1982). *In a different voice. Psychological theory and women's development*. Cambridge, MA: Harvard University Press.

Gouthro, P. A. (2005). A critical feminist analysis of the homeplace as learning site: expanding the discourse of lifelong learning to consider adult women learners. *International Journal of Lifelong Education, 24*(1), 5–19. doi:10.1080/02603704200031731 0

Marton, F. (1981). Describing conceptions of the world around us. *Instructional Science, 10*, 177–200. doi:10.1007/BF00132516

Marton, F., & Booth, S. (1997). *Learning and awareness*. Mahwah, NJ: Lawrence Erlbaum.

Marton, F., & Pang, M. F. (2006). On some necessary conditions of learning. *Journal of the Learning Sciences, 15*(2), 193–220. doi:10.1207/s15327809jls1502_2

McGivney, V. (1999). Men earn, women learn: Bridging the gender divide in education and training. Leicester, UK: The National Organisation for Adult Learning, NIACE.

Moore, M. G. (1993). Theory of transactional distance. In Keegan, D. (Ed.), *Theoretical principles of distance education* (pp. 22–38). London: Routledge.

Perry, W. G., Jr. (1968/1970/1999). Forms of ethical and intellectual development in the college years: A scheme. San Francisco: Jossey-Bass.

Peters, O. (1998). *Learning and teaching in distance education.* London: Kogan Page.

Runesson, U. (2006). What is it Possible to Learn? On Variation as a Necessary Condition for Learning. *Scandinavian Journal of Educational Research, 50*, 397–410. doi:10.1080/00313830600823753

Schutz, A., & Luckman, T. (1974). *The Structures of the life-world.* London: Heinemann Educational Books Ltd.

Toresson, G. W. (2002). Kvinnor skapar kunskap på nätet. Datorbaserad fortbildning för lärare. (Women create knowledge on the Net. Data-based further education for teachers.) Umeå: Umeå universitet.

von Prümmer, C. (2004). Gender issues and learning online: from exclusion to empowerment. In U. Bernath & A. Szücs (Eds.) Supporting the learner in distance education and e-learning. (pp. 474-480). Oldenburg, Denmark: BIS-verlag.

Walsh, E. (2000). Phenomenographic analysis of interview transcripts. In Bowden, J., & Walsh, E. (Eds.), *Phenomenography.* Melbourne, Australia: RMIT Publishing.

Wigforss, E., & Booth, S. (2006, April 10-12). Experiencing the University Context. In *Proceedings for the Symposium Research into Learning in Networked Outreach Initiatives at Networked learning 2006 – Fifth International Conference*, Lancaster, University, UK.

Wigforss, E., Nordin, L., Hylander, J., Badersten, L., & Johansson, K. (2004). *Rekrytering till universitet och högskolor via fria studier.* (Recruitment to higher education through free studies) Slutrapport till Rekryteringsdelegationen, Utbildningsdepartementet (Final report to the Recruitment Committee, Ministry of Education).

KEY TERMS AND DEFINITIONS

Life-World Pphenomenology: A research approach grounded in the phenomenological philosophy of Husserl, in which priority is given to the subjective experiences and perceptions of the individual (in contrast to the objective approach of the natural sciences), as elaborated by Alfred Schutz, among others.

Umwelt: The world within actual reach of the individual, peopled by other individuals and social groupings, with whom the individual identifies, in a we-relationship.

Mitwelt: The world within potential reach of the individual, peopled by types that lack concretization and stand in a they-relation.

Phenomenography: The empirical study of the variation of ways in which a particular phenomenon is experienced (or conceptualized, seen or perceived) across a group of people of interest, as elaborated in Marton and Booth (1997) among others.

Swedish Higher Education: The system of post-school education that is supported by the state and which is currently free, comprising universities and university colleges (see www. hsv.se → English).

Distance Adult Education: The whole system of educational activities that are offered to adults in all sectors of the education system which involving study that is primarily home-based.

Transactional Distance: A function of the dialogical, structural, autonomous and collaborative elements of a distance education course, following Peters (1998) and Moore (1993), which forms a continuum from the entirely stand-alone and pre-planned form of course to the highly interactive and flexible course.

Gendered Ways of Knowing: Empirical research results that indicate that the variation of ways in which people learn and relate to knowledge have a dimension that can be viewed as gendered, as typified by the writings of Belenky et al. (1986) and Baxter Magolda (1992).

ENDNOTES

[1] An inspection of the Swedish national statistics (www.scb.se) shows, for example, that participants in higher education in the age group 45-54 who had a school education normally considered inadequate for entrance to higher education, women outnumber men in the ratio roughly 5 to 2 in 2005, 2006 and 2007.

[2] These names are fictive, and we have removed geographical references throughout, if they could identify our interview persons. Permission has been obtained, however, to use their stories and to quote from their interviews and assignments.

[3] We can imagine that the "gardening-place" or the "cinema-place" of the everyday life-world could be more important for the individual, but such places are outside the scope of this study.

[4] The numbers in brackets refer to the different students' written reports, translated from the original Swedish by the authors.

[5] All quotations from Agneta's and Britt's interviews and written reports are the authors' translation from the original Swedish.

[6] We are making the visited university and college anonymous to avoid geographic identification.

[7] see Knefelkamp's Introduction to the 1999 edition of the book for a thorough breakdown of the scheme.

Chapter 11
Gendered Distance Education Spaces:
"Keeping Women in Place"?

Annika Bergviken Rensfeldt
University of Gothenburg, Sweden

Sandra Riomar
University of Gothenburg, Sweden

ABSTRACT

This chapter problematizes how gender is constructed and used in the arguments of flexible distance education. By using a gender and space analysis we destabilise the open, flexible and liberating features of distance higher education spaces, that are supposed to favour women. The questions are; How are the spaces of distance education gendered, and What power asymmetries are produced? The empirical material is Swedish education policies, mainly from the 1990s, concerned with the issue of creating new educational opportunities through a more open and flexible higher education. The chapter provides insights into the gender power asymmetries of these educational spaces through three lines of arguments: gendered technology use, off-campus studies and the home as place for learning. It is concluded that these spaces are characterized by enclosure and restrictions that risk "keeping women in place", and thus need to be questioned and challenged by feminist readings.

INTRODUCTION

Distance education as a form of organizing and distributing education more or less independently of time and space has been a recurrent feature in the Western world. Built on beliefs about the potential for widening access and enhancing learning opportunities, distance education has gained new interest and significance in modern society. More open and flexible ways of offering education have become a common rhetorical argument and the traditional places of learning have been challenged by, for example, IT-based study forms where dualities such as on-campus/off-campus, private/public are increasingly intertwined and blurred (Clarke et al., 2002; Edwards & Clarke, 2002; Edwards & Usher, 2007; Usher, 2002). The argument is that new opportunities for learning would be made available through such changes.

DOI: 10.4018/978-1-61520-813-5.ch011

Due to their supposedly strong commitment to the places and the inflexible circumstances of their lives, women are often put forward as a group who would gain from studying in a distance, flexible, mode of study. In this chapter we problematize how gender is constructed and used in the arguments of flexible distance education by using illustrations from Swedish education policy documents, mainly from the 1990s. As an opening example, the Swedish Ministry of Education and Science (hereafter SME, 1998b, pp. 80-82) argues, on the issue of "Women and men in distance teaching", as follows:

The fact that it is possible to combine studying at a distance with housework and childbirth has led to distance education sometimes being pointed out as especially suitable for women. (p. 81)

We consider this as a part of how gender operates in distance education practices, to produce traditional female and male positionings.[1] Women are assumed to be physically bound to certain activities and places associated with the home. Our point is that this gendered ordering is a part of a spatial politics of distance education which needs to be problematized because of the asymmetries and assumptions that are illustrated here. We are asking in what senses could distance education be regarded as a gendered space and whether there are implications of distance education that disadvantage or "keep women in place"? In this text, we elaborate on this spatial dimension of distance education in relation to Swedish higher education by using policy material from 1998 (SME, 1998a, 1998b, 1998c)[2]. We also relate these policy documents to Swedish education policies from other older and more recent epochs concerning the issues of distance and higher education reform (SME[3], 1962; Swedish Government Bill, 2002, 2005).

AIM, QUESTIONS AND APPROACH

We intend to analyse the spatial politics of Swedish distance higher education by using the feminist geographer Doreen Massey's (1994, 1999a, 1999b, 2004) conceptualization of space as articulated in relation to time, place and gender. According to Massey, space is more than merely physical localities and geographies. Rather, space is a construction, made up of relations with place and time. The approach challenges common understandings of space either as metaphorical and symbolic spaces or as concrete, physical places. Such constructions tend to fix meanings and our understandings of spaces. Instead, Massey argues, it is more relevant to elaborate on how aspects of space/place intersect and are co-produced. The spatial analysis contrasts with a more commonly used understanding of space as a physical container in which actions take place in time. For Massey (1999a) the concern is:

to understand space (and space-time) as constituted through the social, rather than as dimensions defining an arena within which the social takes place. (p. 262)

In our example, the open, flexible spaces associated with distance education are seen as metaphorical spaces that are shaped mutually with place connotations and gender. These together constitute particular, gendered spaces.

Clarke and Edwards (Clarke et al., 2002; Edwards & Clarke, 2002) have also used Massey's work when examining the "changing places" associated with flexible, lifelong learning. They problematize the metaphorical uses of open, liberating spaces in the context of British further education colleges that have been organized to be more flexible. Rather than relating to discourses of flexibility, students tend to desire traditionally enclosed educational places, above all the renowned campus, in which they can be firmly located on "the inside". We take their analytical approach further and elaborate on the space/place relation in terms of gender power asymmetries. Our aim in this chapter is to elaborate on the spaces produced in flexible distance education in relation to gender and possible implications of uneven educational access. By using examples from the Swedish education policies, our overall questions are: *How are the spaces of distance education gendered,* and *What power asymmetries are produced?*

Spaces are here regarded as non-static and are never fixed in relation to the dynamics of time, but they are shaped in relation to gender and place (Massey, 1994, 1999a). With this approach, space and time could never be separated analytically, but should be studied integrally. In the case of Swedish distance education, we can see how associations of an open, liberating space are reproduced over time in different policies, as are ideas of students being able to study independently of time and place. Similarly, Swedish efforts to achieve equity over recent decades have worked to increase women's participation in distance higher education. More recently, important contributions for enabling wider access and new extended spaces of flexible distance education have been made through the establishment of local learning centres and similar localities, as well as delivery through IT and virtual learning environments. These can be regarded as parts of a spatial politics that is heavily influenced by democratic and equity arguments. It can also be contended that space/place dynamics occur across a multitude of scales, which are discursively organized and formed, ranging from the virtual and open, to the place-bound, from the nation-wide to spheres of home. A place like the university, in this argument, could never be an authentic or "fixed" place, resting on a timeless, unproblematic identity; it is always inscribed with certain powers, relationally defined with other societal institutions and certain gendered privileges.

If spaces are considered relationally constituted with time, place and gender, they could never be finished or closed, they are always open for change and contestation, even in terms of gendered orderings. Massey (1999b) states that spaces and places "both reflect and affect the ways in which gender is constructed and understood" (p. 168). Space constructions in this sense are open to influences, and there is always a possibility of alternatives and a potential for other spaces and relations, suggesting different gender positions. Spatial orderings are also influenced by hegemonic struggles, where particular views come to dominate. It is in such struggles that gender power asymmetries are most surely produced, such that certain spaces or positions are made invisible or excluded, but that also give a potential for change (Laclau & Mouffe, 1985; Mouffe, 2005). With a feminist reading of the distance higher education policies, we use this as a departure for understanding how these particular spaces have become hegemonic and considered as democratic and gender equal, but also, how they produce inequalities and exclusions.

To clarify the relation of policy and the spatial dimensions, we can start by saying that space is not a simple effect of certain aims made concrete in policy but it is constituted and compromised in policy-making. Policies produce symbolic and discursive spaces that organise thinking and affect the limits of action. Therefore, our empirical material, the policy documents, are part of a spatial politics and orderings of significance where, for example, gender differentiations operate. For us, these policies, which often function in a rhetorical manner, offer one way of understanding the arguments of what distance education is or should be. They are a part of societal debates and controversies of education and learning.

Our approach is in line with the discursive understanding of how power and knowledge are spatially involved in discursive practices (Foucault, 1977, 1980, 2007) and the poststructuralist feminist understanding of gender (Butler, 1990[4], Massey, 1994). We therefore try to destabilize assumptions and essentialist descriptions of how women and men really are, how they use IT, or how they are bound up with fixed places and spaces over time. We refer to men and women, or preferably, male or female, positions, since men and women may be placed and place themselves in certain positions. With this approach we can point to some significant aspects of the spatial politics of distance education, expressed in Swedish education policies, which we argue have serious gender implications and may limit or make possible certain actions in regard to higher education access and equity.

STRUCTURE OF OUR ARGUMENTS

In our following analysis, we structure our arguments under three headings:

(1) Continuities and discontinuities of gendered spaces: "Female" flexible learning and "male" correspondence study?
(2) Academic spaces: Power and access in a differentiated university
(3) Challenging "home": Only a private, female place for learning?

In the first part we start with the recent arguments of flexible, IT-based learning and relate it to post-war correspondence study. In the second part we elaborate on the gendering of spaces of academic work and education, and in the third part, we analyze how home and private spheres of learning signify gender in specific ways. Finally, we summarize our arguments and conclude with a discussion of the gendered spatial dimensions of Swedish distance higher education.

Continuities and Discontinuities of Gendered Spaces: "Female" Flexible Learning and "Male" Correspondence Study?

A dominant purpose of Swedish distance education has been to offer compensatory access to higher education and to widen participation in it, built on the belief that an educated workforce leads to societal change and prosperity. This underpinned the ideas of correspondence study as part of the systematic post-war welfare development (e.g. SME, 1962), as well as contemporary emphasis on the need for a flexible, highly competent workforce (SME, 1998b, 1998c, Swedish Government Bill 2005). This might be seen as a continuity of how the spaces of distance education have been produced and the use of different distance technologies for distributing and controlling education. What we intend to examine under this heading is also the discontinuities of these spatial politics, starting with the policies of the late 1990s and the early 2000s.

In the Swedish education policies from the 1990s, IT can be related to gender in two different ways. On one hand, IT is depicted as a gender-neutral tool and enabler, on the other hand, IT is considered to enhance social communication and therefore considered as suitable for women.

In one of the distance education policy documents (SME, 1998b) it is argued that "technological support in all educational forms creates flexibility for the student" (p. 71). Moreover, the flexibility of distance education; "in time, space, pace and method, opens up for new possibilities of undertaking training at a university level." (Swedish Government Bill, 2002, p. 110) IT symbolises the possibility of a distributive expansion and flexible networking (Barry, 2001). This presumed liberation in time and space depicts a gender-neutral, boundary-free education, in which IT creates few limits. IT is thus constructed not only as a mediator for educational expansion and distribution, but also as a decidedly positive and flexible work tool.

In parallel to this technological rationale, IT is also depicted as a social mediator, a suitable tool for educational communication. In one of the policies from 1998 (SME, 1998a) where an evaluation was made of 100 distance education projects funded by the Government, the feature of IT-based communication is signified as an endeavour that will favour women:

There is no sign at all that women have had more difficulties than men in mastering IT [in the projects]. On the contrary, it seems to be the case that the written communication between teacher and student fits the women well. The experiences from campus education, on the other hand, usually tell us that men take all of the teacher's and student's attention at the expense of the women. (p. 153)

The dominating gender perspective, visible in this citation, is a popular version of the Belenky approach on "women's ways of knowing" (1986) and the fact that women seem to prefer a written and social mode of learning. This in turn could be understood as the asymmetries in a learning situation now could be ameliorated as this new mode of learning could overcome former gender asymmetries that traditionally have disadvantaged women or those who prefer this kind of learning. It alleges a potential challenge to old traditions of the gender asymmetries embedded in on-campus classroom spaces. However, the citation gives no idea of any short-comings of IT, how it might be unequally distributed (see Kirkup, 2001, p. 48) or how this gendered IT-use is constraining. This citation of a female IT use similarly illustrates a subordinate position;

While men seem to show interest in the technology per se and are prepared to invest resources in it, women's interest is mostly caused by motives from their life. It could have been changes at work or a need of helping the children in their schoolwork. (SME, 1998b, p. 82)

The female use of IT is ascribed to a private, caring and feminized function. It neglects the fact that IT already might be used in work life, not least in many female-coded professions, and also in domestic life. Male IT-use is also confined, and signified as more motivated and as "investment",

not caused by life circumstances as in the case of the female position. From a North American case, Waltz (2003) has argued that IT often maintains enduring social relations, and actually reproduces the socio-political configurations of the past. Even if IT is made to stand for the impending future, Waltz argues that technologies do not so much drive change as resist it. We relate his arguments to our specific example, describing how IT-use and even place commitments are traditionally gender-coded in the 1990s' policies. In the following, we will discuss how similar gender orderings operate in the Swedish post-war era of distance education, namely correspondence study.

In the systematic welfare development of the 1950s and 60s in Sweden, correspondence study was considered an important factor in educating the workforce and making possible upward mobility, based on an interlinked logic of occupational transferability and societal development (SME, 1962).

The mobility, which nowadays characterizes work life, is making great demands on the employees. The educational needs can change quickly in one and the same profession, and it has been proven that correspondence teaching has increasingly become a significant tool for those who wish to develop their knowledge in their professions. (SME, 1962, p. 16)

It is notable that the possibilities and tool metaphors of distance technology are similar to those in the earlier example. But is it a gendered technology in the same way? We rather see the technology, such as letter correspondence, as a part of a male-coded study form. The priority of correspondence study was above all the male workforce, studying outside work hours, solitary and strenuously, to become someone new, someone of value (Berner, 1996). The proposal was that they would engage in training, often in technical professions and often to become engineers. However, it was the men who did *not* attend who became the focus of many Swedish reforms at that time (see also Henning-Loeb, 2006). In spite of the fact that many women did attend education in the post-war era, it was the male contribution that became seen as progress and a contribution to the welfare state, and not the women's educational aspirations or their supportive housework, linked to traditionally female, unrecognised labour. We see this as an example of the politics of gendering at work in distance education, which has favoured the male workforce and their efforts as well as male technical knowledge. The male position is thus contested as we pay attention to the historical invisibility of female endeavours.

There are connections between the flexible, IT-based education of the late 1990s and the correspondence study of the 1960s in terms of spatial politics of distributed space, although their gender positionings are different. In contrast to the male positions of post-war correspondence study, the subject position of flexible, IT-based education of today seems to be the female. The rhetoric is that she is committed to an educational career as well as to the home sphere and family duties. It thus seems to be more complicated to relate the female subject of flexible learning to upward mobility as Walkerdine (2003) has argued. One explanation based on our case, might be that women are described as having a fragmented study trajectory, where they "more often than men, are studying part-time, in stages and at a later age" (Swedish Government Bill, 2002, p. 72). In regard to place and work commitments expressed here, there are gender differences in the possibilities of educational trajectories and careers in the different decades. At the same time, the arguments used in the flexible learning policies are in many ways similar to those in correspondence study, based on a fundamental assumption of education: if equally distributed and widely spread, education will contribute to societal and technological progress. One explanation for the similarities might be that distance education has been marked by neoliberal features and tightly connected to the

rationales and demands of working life (Jakupec & Garrick, 2000), as exemplified also by the 1960s' policy citation.

To use Connell's perspective (1997), we could regard these developments as "hegemonic masculinity" (p. 615), in which technological rationales and economic perspectives dominate. Connell relates this to recent discourses of flexibility where the demands for efficiency, productivity and ability to manage an unpredictable and uncertain future, increasingly have made flexibility – in the sense of flexible work forces, flexible learning and so on – appear necessary. According to Connell, a hegemonic masculinity will create gender power asymmetries, since it will exclude the incalculable activities connected to the home sphere and traditional female occupations of family. This in turn would counteract gender equity. Connell's writings are interesting in relation to what is said about studying in a flexible mode in our empirical material: flexible learning will open up for combinations of family duties, paid work and other activities as one is presumed to be freer in time and space (SME, 1998b, 1998c). Such flexibility could also counteract gender equity and strengthen ties to gendered places such as home. The "open, flexible" spaces instead become spaces of enclosure and gender restricted possibilities.

Jackson (2003), from a Marxist perspective, problematizes such inequalities in a similar way. She points to the diversities of women as a group, and also, the situation of working-class women. These women still, Jackson argues, share the experience of being "trapped in a cycle of life-long earning that centres on low-paid, low-status jobs" (ibid., p. 365). Jackson's contribution could be regarded as a part of an understanding of the formations described by Connell as hegemonic masculinity. However, Jackson and Connell have different perspectives on how the female subordination and other hegemonic imperatives are produced. With a poststructuralist approach, Connell & Messerschmidt (2005) emphasize the possibility of opening up such formations, due to their temporary fixations and mutual co-construction of space and power. Connell and Messerschmidt also argue that the female, subordinate position could affect both men and women.

Walkerdine makes a similar point when speaking of "the places of upward mobility through education and work as the feminine site of production of the neoliberal subject" (2003, pp. 238-239). Class and gender are still politically significant positions she argues, though the oppressive and exploitative features have changed and may affect both men and women. How does this relate to the case of distance education? It points to a break with the claimed spatial opportunities. Walkerdine's example of a feminine, flexible localization clearly has parallels with the Swedish flexible distance education and a more vulnerable subject position. To another extent, flexible learning relies on a self-responsible and self-manageable subject, as it is stated: "The perspective of the student has shifted from being an object of other's interventions to become an agent in his/her own development" (SME, 1998b, p. 96).

We have established that there are gender biases in our two examples from the distance education policies of the 1960s and 1990s. Both connect to economic rationales influencing and motivating these educational modes. In this way, and described in terms of a hegemonic masculinity, flexible distance education could be seen as a continuity of the modernist, rationalist project and similar to correspondence study. Even so, distance education is sometimes described as an industrial form of teaching and learning (Peters, 1994) or as "mass-individualization" (Lee, 2008). This image illustrates the viewpoint of distance education, as a production and delivery process of knowledge in large-scale systems, where universities become knowledge factories or diploma mills (Noble 1998), offering and facilitating learning services. As a part of this, flexible education maintains a construct of a progressive, (gender-neutral) universal subject, which does not consider gender asymmetries as problematic in terms of differenti-

ated access and spatially gendered confinements. We, however, question the alternative spatial distribution as a space of equal opportunities, as we will illustrate in the next section.

Academic Spaces: Power and Access in a Differentiated University

Swedish higher education has a long tradition of being a dual mode organization, where university institutions can offer both distance and on-campus education. However, distance education in the 1990s policies is seen as a marginalised and less legitimate educational form in relation to campus education. Distance teaching and planning has been given less status in relation to more prestigious campus activities. In the Swedish policy work this issue is expressed as follows:

The universities' administrators and teachers have prioritized research and campus education rather than distance teaching. And when distance teaching has been provided, it has seldom admitted the temporal and spatial freedom for the students, which is one of the main points in this educational form. The path to freedom in time and place is achieved by extensive work on educational planning and the use of technology in teaching, to bridge the gap between teacher and student. The general conclusion is that the university has failed in these regards. (SME, 1998b, p. 20)

The rhetoric here is blaming teachers and administrators on one hand, while pointing to the student as a victim on the other, and his/her freedom in time and space. This argument points to two important things. One is what Carr-Chellman (2005) has elaborated on. She makes a connection to how IT-based, and a more open, place-independent educational access, is presumed to challenge a democratic problematic of space/place in the academic world; "the idea of open access - the elimination of elitism as a function of place and prestige - holds the promise of equity" (p. 2). This kind of presumption neglects the asymmetries at work when academic space/place is co-produced. The emphasis on the flexibility that technology could make possible, seems to downplay the significance of campus life, connected as it is to more prestigious activities and places.

Morley's (2005) gender analysis of contemporary power asymmetries of academic work follows this line of thought. In a study of a group of British women academics and managers involved in quality assurance, she claims that academic work becomes differentiated by discourses of performance measures and accountability. A similar conclusion as Morley's could be made in our case as a second point; The neoliberal discourse makes the academic spaces highly gendered and influenced by hegemonic masculinities, which subordinates women and female-coded enterprises. We see such patterns of gendering in the dualities of on- and off-campus spaces, ordering university activities. As in Morley's (2005) argument, influential research might not be signified as a female enterprise to the same extent as the care of students, which rather would signify the endeavour of a female teacher (p. 413). Similarly, in our case, distance education and planning is devalued on the same terms, competing with the more influential and visible work of research and on-campus education.

The neoliberal agenda of performing and delivering education, as Morley's results point to, also creates a market relation based on student-customer needs and a short, just-in-time perspective on learning. In one of the policy documents (SME 1998b) it is stated that "extensive education planning" and "technology use" are "a path towards spatio-temporal liberation" (p. 20), as if spatial restrictions were possible to escape from. These are also problematic statements as they disregard other spatio-temporal alternatives such as non-linear or non-modularized learning and asynchronous social communication (some previously illustrated as features of women's learning). Another characteristic of working

at a distance, is that it is often made invisible; conducted privately and anonymously in virtual spaces. Working at home, in the extended higher education virtual space, at the "electronic frontier" (Bryant, 2000) could, of course, mean access to a publicly, technology-mediated space. However, working academically off-campus and perhaps also with a different time frame, will inevitably limit and exclude participation in certain activities. As a parallel, Kirkup (2002) has called it an irony that flexible learning becomes popular just as feminist perspectives have begun to get academic legitimacy (p. 11). If people are to be involved in, for example, university committees or in research groups, activities that generally are campus based, then being at a distance becomes a problem (Carr-Chellman, 2005). Therefore, in terms of academic influence and the spatial power asymmetries of off-campus activities, "real" influence is not yet achievable at a distance (see also Brown & Duguid, 2000); nor, we would claim, in a Swedish dual mode organization.

Taken together, and based on an assumption of distance education as a way of working for a more democratic and open educational system for both women and men, there is an issue of distance education being highly gendered. Therefore, not only the duality built into the separation of on- and off-campus academia, but other aspects, such as work tasks and educational activities, introduce an asymmetry of power in terms of gender, influence, prestige and access.

However, even if a masculine hegemony and a neoliberal discourse operate, they can never colonize distance education totally. There is always the potential for spaces of resistance or challenge, for students choosing to be off-campus, for virtual expansions and alignments of distance classrooms, research communities and networks. Similarly, given that several institutions now offer a wider range of study modes, which are even extended internationally, distinctions between on and off-campus learning are more difficult to maintain. If clearer convergence between on- and off-campus activities could be achieved in a Swedish distance education space, and if further social and scholarly activities could be distributed more equitably through IT, the gender orderings would most probably be destabilised and possibly change.

There is another spatial dimension of masculine hegemony operating in Swedish academic space today. If flexibility has been one key metaphor, it seems to be superseded by another spatial metaphor, namely mobility, to be clearly seen in the policies of the Bologna declaration and the idea of a unified, transparent system of European higher education (European Commission, 1999), where gender problematization is virtually non-existent. The idea is that it should be possible for a higher education student to be mobile, to study abroad and move globally, not being committed to place or territorial borders. But there is still a place, a Swedish nation and a Europe, which clearly define borders and participants for this higher education space. Massey (1994) has discussed the global spaces of movement and communication in the current era that seem to stretch out our social relations geographically. She argues that there are restrictions as well as possibilities associated with these new spaces of mobility and flexibility. It is not only an issue of who moves and who does not, according to Massey (1994), "it is also about power in relation to the flows and the movement" (p. 149). Her conclusion is that this "new" world order discourse of "space-time compression", IT-dependent flexibility and mobility, apart from being gendered, is ethnocentric and taken from the point of view of a relatively Western elite. In the Swedish case of higher education, similar questions arise: who is addressed, who is considered educable and who is supposed to be mobile? Should the discourse of mobility be considered as yet another move in favour of masculine hegemony in terms of the market logic of flexibility and gendering of spaces? We would argue that there are many similarities between the flexibility and mobility discourses produced in Swedish higher education policies in the 1990s

and early 2000s having to do with how the spatial imply gender power asymmetries.

We would like to continue to the next and final part of this chapter, challenging a dominant feature of Swedish education policy, namely, women's alleged preference for home and distance studies.

Challenging "Home": Only a Private, Female Space/Place for Learning?

As mentioned, women as a target group are foregrounded in Swedish distance education policy in the 1990s (e.g. SME, 1998a, 1998b, 1998c). As a part of the policy reform, and where 100 distance education projects were initiated and reported (SME, 1998a), some specific gender positionings are described. Here, the typical distance education student is exemplified as:

a 38-year-old woman, married or having a partner with 1 or 2 children. She worked full or part-time and had no academic family traditions. (SME, 1998a, p. 119)

This idealised woman is seen to be highly committed to place, to family, home and class ties. Similarly, traditionally female positions are viewed as not being mobile or movable as in the following policy example regarding women in rural areas in the north of Sweden:

Due to their family situation they do not consider moving to the university town as a realistic alternative. The long distances make commuting hard or impossible. (SME, 1998c, p. 121)

Similar research-based descriptions have been made regarding this group of students, who were often female adult learners with children, and therefore, it was supposed, that they had certain commitments to a local place, whether home or a learning centre (Roos, 2001; Wännman-Toresson, 2002). It is generally concluded in the policy work (SME, 1998a;1998b, p. 7; SME, 1998c, p. 71), that if there had not existed a local university, combined with the possibility of a local learning centre or study group, IT-support and some flexibility in time and space, they would probably not have entered higher education, and women professionals, e.g. nurses, teachers etc., would not have taken further training (SME, 1998a, p. 90). It is assumed that these women are confined to local places such as the home, the learning centre etc., which restricts their possibility to study in higher education more broadly. This is similar to how the essentialist, Belenky approach (1986) of women's proposed learning needs as mentioned earlier, is used in the policies.

In our empirical material, the close association of the home as a study place is implied, and according to von Prümmer (2000, p. 78) that is the most common place for distance studies. The responsibility for accomplishing flexible studies has been transferred to the learner, making education mostly a private concern as illustrated earlier. In line with what Walkerdine (2003, p. 241) has stated, the flexible subjects have become dependent on the ability to network and have the "right connections". In our case, this would favour those with educational experience and academic competence close at hand:

For the most part during a distance course the student spends time in his/her close context, at home, at work, among friends. Here it is the emotional connections which solve a lot of the problems related to studying, and perhaps also friends or family who have study experience, become important. In the informal arena there may be a person, or persons, who can confirm the success and development of the student. In a follow-up study where women with a low standard of education had achieved educational success, many of the factors which could explain their success were found to be in the informal arena. (SME, 1998b, p. 58)

Any conflict between studying and the private sphere would thus not necessarily be the univer-

sity's responsibility; rather problems should be solved and managed independently by the distance student him- or herself (see also Rose, 1999). There are several researchers who report on the difficulties many women face in the informal setting when trying to make space for learning (e.g. Moss, 2004; von Prümmer, 2000). The womens' studies are often in conflict with others in the household, which can result in lack of concentration and increased pressure (von Prümmer, 2000, p. 71). Moss (2004, p. 294) has also described how female higher education students have to struggle and negotiate their space and time for their studies in the household, as partners might see women's home study as private time off and leisure, and not as legitimate work-time. When it is in the powers of others to define and measure space and time for studying, simultaneous and emotional work is often dismissed or underestimated (Moss, 2004, p. 285). The negotiations and ambiguities of studying is thereby rendered invisible. This further emphasizes the need to challenge essentialist views of hegemonic identities of places, as in this case of "home". Or similarly, as analysed and discussed in this text, where specific sites are signified as female, i.e. close-family, emotional, private and informal. Rather, place should be conceptualized as "a site of negotiation" which is open for change (Massey, 1999b, p. 7).

What other implications might be at hand in the close association of woman-home-privacy in relation to distance education illustrated so far? Though distance education could be seen as an opportunity to gain access to education for those (women) whose life circumstances are to some extent inflexible, von Prümmer highlights the risks of the domestication related to women's distance studies. She argues:

There is, rightly, some concern over the possibility that Distance education could reinforce the traditional role of women being responsible for household and childcare and relegated to the private sphere. Home study, which can be pursued without entering the public sphere, could serve to "keep women in their place" and to "domesticate" them even further in accordance with traditional cultural values and social norms. (von Prümmer, 2000, p. 225)

The attempt to confine women to the domestic sphere has also been a way to limit the mobility of women historically, in terms of both identity and space (Massey, 1994, p. 179). We claim that this is highly relevant in our Swedish case. Similarly, the construction of home as "a woman's place" implies an idealization and adds a feminine coding and restrictiveness. We hold that the culturally embedded assumption of home as a woman's place also has an impact on the assumptions made about distance education, and that these influence the study modes made available. This would be equally valid for the claims of flexible learning where the freedom in time and space is seen as especially applicable and desirable for women. Moreover, these ideas are produced in line with a societal discourse of masculine hegemony and a female position of a new flexible workforce (Connell, 1997). In this perspective, the local is replaced by spaces of marketable social relations and by blurred boundaries of private and public life, where women and men are held responsible for their own sociability (Walkerdine, 2003).

With Massey's (1994) understanding of space, the identity of a place, such as "the home", is always and continuously produced and re-valued. It can never be an authentic or unmediated experience; it was and is open for contestation and new meanings. Wentzel Winther (2006a, 2006b) goes further, stating that the "old" conception of home has been undermined and needs revitalizing; she uses the term "homing" to describe how we inhabit territories in our home and transform space into place in new ways. In a time of movement and spatial transformations mediated by new technology, feeling at home might as well go beyond a physical place. She

concludes: "we are mobile and on the way out there – even if we are located in bed" (Wentzel Winther, 2006a, p. 25).

To sum up, we see the rhetoric of erasing boundaries between private/public, informal/formal spaces as also being a part of a spatially gendered politics of distance education. Different social groups and different individuals are placed in very distinct ways in relation to the possibilities of being flexible. This, we conclude, results in gender power asymmetries of distance education spaces, ordered and articulated in regard to female and male positions and constructions of masculinities and femininities.

CONCLUDING REMARKS

We have given some examples of how spaces of Swedish distance higher education are constituted in relation to gender. Our aim has been to outline and illustrate gender orderings, and also to relate them to possible implications of gender power asymmetries and uneven educational access. We have discussed how a masculine hegemony seems to be articulated in distance education policies, and how this hegemony is reproducing traditional female (and male) positions. Thus, the supposedly open, liberating spaces of distance flexible education are questioned and we sum up our lines of argument in the following way:

(1)   In both flexible IT-based distance education and correspondence study, arguments of societal and technological progress have been and still are emphasized. However, there are gender differences in the spaces of distance education, correspondence study being associated with a masculine gender and flexible learning with a feminine gender. Gender is also addressed in relation to social mobility, intertwined with a masculine hegemony, which seems to operate in both cases. The male correspondence study implies upward

mobility, while the female space of flexible learning is more of an enclosed and restricted space. This is a hanging indent.

(2) The gendering of Swedish distance education is at work in dualities between on- and off-campus spaces. To work invisibly in the private sphere, and to have little influence over high-prestige academic work, is associated with an off-campus mode. It is an open question whether an increased convergence between the two educational modes, or if alternative spaces such as learning centres and IT-based communities, could counter these dualities. Moreover, academic spaces are produced by, and produce, discourses of performance measures and accountability, attached to the hegemony of neoliberalism, but also that of masculinity, which subordinates female-coded enterprises.

(3) The spatial politics of distance education is making studying and education to a high degree a private concern and we highlight the risk of distance education being yet another way of domesticating women, suiting all too well a traditional female position. We hold a revitalized conception of home as promising, as it implies new possibilities for feeling at home in new spatial relations.

We are aware that our illustrations can only partly describe these spaces, and that we ourselves participate in these discursive formations through our choices of examples and approaches. We have chosen to see these developments of education as connected to overall developments in contemporary western society where public responsibility for different welfare areas is diminishing and transformed into individual self-regulation and self-responsibility (Rose, 1999). However, the hegemonic powers also show us the potential for counter-arguments in the spatial politics of distance education, for example in making education accessible in new ways and creating alternative, more gender equal spaces. Conceptualising the spatial in this way inherently implies the existence of a simultaneous multiplicity of spaces: "cross-cutting, intersecting, aligning with one another or existing in relations of paradox or antagonism" (Massey, 1994, p. 5). Culturally embedded assumptions, as well as other empirical research about women being tightly connected to specific places, needs to be complemented and destabilised, because this is not (only) a story of victimized women being trapped in a private space, to refer to Massey (1994). It is not our intention to dismiss flexible education, as generally counteracting gender equity. Instead, we have tried to illustrate and argue around some of the different articulations of these multifaceted and asymmetric spaces. We question one-sided references and essentialist views on women's learning and place commitment as being "natural", highly intertwined with a presumed IT-use, and considered impossible to signify differently. As we have shown, equal opportunities and a more open or flexible education as expressed in the spatial politics of Swedish higher education, should not be considered gender-neutral. Rather, these propositions, how benevolent they might be, could be strengthening traditionally female and male positions and thus work to "keep women in place".

Distance education probably will continue to offer women (and men) a satisfactory educational alternative and access to higher education studies. However, from a feminist and gender power perspective, the feminized, off-campus and home-based spaces illustrated in the policies here, should also make us question and continuously challenge the assumptions of a liberating and open flexible education.

ACKNOWLEDGMENT

We would like to thank Doreen Massey for comments on an earlier draft.

We would also like to thank the *GLIT Research Network* for the opportunity of presenting an earlier version of this paper at the *Symposium on Gender, Learning and IT*, organized in Helsingborg, August 2007. This network and symposium received support from *the KK-Foundation (The Knowledge Foundation of Sweden)* and its research programme *LearnIT*.

REFERENCES

Barry, A. (2001). *Political machines: Governing a technological society*. London: Athlone.

Belenky, M. F., Clinchy, B. M., Goldberger, N. R., & Tarule, J. M. (1986). *Women's ways of knowing: The development of self, voice and mind*. New York: Basic Books Inc.

Berner, B. (1996). *Sakernas tillstånd: Kön, klass och expertis* [The state of things: Gender, class and technical expertise]. Lund, Sweden: Carlsson.

Brown, J. S., & Duguid, P. (2000). *The social life of information*. Boston: Harvard Press.

Bryant, S. (2000). At home on the electronic frontier: Work, gender and the information highway. *New Technology, Work and Employment, 15*(1), 19–34. doi:10.1111/1468-005X.00062

Butler, J. (1990). *Gender Trouble: Feminism and the Subversion of Identity*. New York: Routledge.

Carr-Chellman, A. A. (Ed.). (2005). *Global perspectives on e-learning*. London: Sage.

Clarke, J., Harrison, R., Reeve, F., & Edwards, R. (2002). Assembling spaces: The question of "place" in further education. *Discourse: Studies in the cultural politics of education, 23*(3), 285-297.

Connell, R. W. (1997). The big picture: Masculinity in recent world history. In Halsey, A. H., Lauder, H., Brown, P., & Stuart Wells, A. (Eds.), *Education. Culture Economy Society*. Oxford, UK: Oxford University Press.

Connell, R. W., & Messerschmidt, J. W. (2005). Hegemonic masculinity. Rethinking the concept. *Gender & Society, 19*(6), 829–859. doi:10.1177/0891243205278639

Edwards, R., & Clarke, J. (2002). Flexible learning, spatiality and identity. *Studies in Continuing Education, 24*(2), 153–165. doi:10.1080/0158037022000020965

Edwards, R., & Usher, R. (2007). *Lifelong learning: Signs, discourses, practices*. Dordrecht, The Netherlands: Springer.

European Commission (1999, June 19). *The European Higher Education area: Joint declaration of the European Ministers of Education*.

Foucault, M. (1980). *Power/Knowledge: Selected interviews and other writings 1972-1977* (Gordon, C., Ed.). Brighton, UK: Harvester.

Foucault, M. (1991). *Discipline and punish: the birth of the prison*. Harmondsworth, UK: Penguin.

Foucault, M. (2007). Spaces of security: The example on the town Lecture of 11th January 1978. *Political Geography, 26*(1), 48–56. doi:10.1016/j.polgeo.2006.08.004

Henning-Loeb, I. (2006). *Utveckling och förändring i kommunal vuxenutbildning: En yrkeslivshistorisk ingång med berättelser om lärarbanor* [Development and Change in Municipal Adult Education. Life History Studies and Narrative Analysis of Teacher Trajectories]. Göteborg, Sweden: Acta Universitatis Gothoburgensis.

Jackson, S. (2003). Lifelong Earning: Working-class women and lifelong learning. *Gender and Education, 15*(4), 365–376. doi:10.1080/0954025031000161 0571

Jakupec, V., & Garrick, J. (Eds.). (2000). *Flexible learning, human resource and organisational development: Putting theory to work*. London: Routledge.

Kirkup, G. E. (2001). "Getting our hands on it": Gendered inequality in access to information and communications technologies. In Lax, S. (Ed.), *Access Denied in the Information Age* (pp. 45–66). Basingstoke, UK: Palgrave.

Kirkup, G. E. (2002*). ICT as a tool for enhancing women's education opportunities; and new educational and professional opportunities for women in new technologies*. Expert paper produced for a UN expert meeting, United Nations Division for the Advancement of Women (UNDAW), Seoul, Korea. Retrieved August, 2009, from http://www.un.org/womenwatch/daw/egm/ict2002/reports/Kirkup%20paperwith%20refs.PDF

Laclau, E., & Mouffe, C. (1985). *Hegemony and Socialist Strategy: Towards a Radical Democratic Politics*. London: Verso.

Lee, F. (2008). Technopedagogies of mass-individualization: Correspondence education in the mid twentieth century. *History and Technology, 24*(3), 239–253. doi:10.1080/07341510801900318

Massey, D. (1994). *Space, place and gender*. Cambridge, UK: Polity Press.

Massey, D. (1999a). Space-time, 'science' and the relationship between physical geography and human geography. *Transactions of the Institute of British Geographers, 24*(3), 261–276. doi:10.1111/j.0020-2754.1999.00261.x

Massey, D. (1999b). *Power-geometries and the politics of space. Hettner lecture, 1998*. Heidelberg, Germany: University of Heidelberg.

Massey, D. (2004). Geographies of responsibility. *Geografiska Annaler, 86B*(1), 5–18.

Morley, L. (2005). Opportunity or exploitation? Women and quality insurance in higher education. *Gender and Education, 17*(4), 411–429. doi:10.1080/09540250500145106

Moss, D. (2004). Creating space for learning: Conceptualising women and higher education through space and time. *Gender and Education, 16*(3), 283–302. doi:10.1080/09540250042000251452

Mouffe, C. (2005). *On the political*. New York: Routledge.

Noble, D. (1998). Digital diploma mills: The automation of higher education. First Monday, *3*(1), Retrieved August 2009, from http://www.firstmonday.org

Peters, O. (1994). Distance education and industrial production: a comparative interpretation in outline (1967). In Keegan, D. (Ed.), *Otto Peters on distance education: The industrialization of teaching and learning* (pp. 107–127). London: Routledge.

Roos, G. (2001). "Nya" studerande eller "gamla"? Rekrytering till studiecentra i Hälsingland ["New students" or "old"? The recruitment to study centres in Hälsingland]. *Pedagogisk forskning i Sverige, 6*(1), 1-18.

Rose, N. (1999). *Powers of Freedom: Reframing political thought*. Cambridge, UK: Cambridge University Press. doi:10.1017/CBO9780511488856

Statistics Sweden & the Swedish National Agency of Higher Education (2007, April 20). Higher education: Students and graduated students in undergraduate education 2005/06. Serie utbildning och forskning.

Swedish Government Bill. (2002). *Den öppna högskolan*. [Reforms in Higher education – A more open system]. Regeringens proposition. *Prop, 2001*(02), 15.

Swedish Government Bill. (2005). *Ny värld – ny högskola*. [New world – a new higher education]. Regeringens proposition. *Prop, 2005*, 162.

Swedish Ministry of education and Ecclesiastic Affairs. (1962). Korrespondensundervisning inom skolväsendet [Correspondence study in the school system]. *Brevskoleutredningen, SOU, 1962*, 16.

Swedish Ministry of Education and Science. (1998a). Utvärdering av distansutbildningsprojekt med IT-stöd [Evaluation of IT-supported distance education projects]. *Commission of Distance Education, SOU, 1998*, 57.

Swedish Ministry of Education and Science. (1998b). *På distans: Utbildning, undervisning och lärande* [At a distance: Education, teaching and learning]. *Kostnadseffektiv distansutbildning.* [Cost-effective distance education]. *Commission of Distance Education, SOU, 1998*, 83.

Swedish Ministry of Education and Science. (1998c). Flexibel utbildning på distans [Flexible education at a distance]. *Commission of Distance Education, SOU, 1998*, 84.

Usher, R. (2002). Putting space back on the map: Globalisation, place and identity. *Educational Philosophy and Theory*, *34*(1), 41–55. doi:10.1111/j.1469-5812.2002.tb00285.x

von Prümmer, C. (2000). *Women and distance education: Challenges and opportunities*. New York: Routledge.

Walkerdine, V. (2003). Reclassifying upward mobility: Femininity and the neoliberal subject. *Gender and Education*, *15*(3), 237–248. doi:10.1080/09540250303864

Waltz, S. B. (2003). Everything New is Old Again: Technology and the Mistaken Future. *Bulletin of Science, Technology & Society*, *23*(5), 376–381. doi:10.1177/0270467603259792

Wännman-Toresson, G. (2002). *Kvinnor skapar kunskap på nätet: Datorbaserad fortbildning för lärare* [Women creating knowledge on the Net. Computer-based further education for teachers]. Umeå, Sweden: Dissertation of the faculty of social science.

Wentzel Winther, I. (2006a). Kid's rooms as plus territory. *Interacções, 2*(2), 9-26. Retrieved August 2009, from http://nonio.eses.pt/interaccoes/artigos/B1%281%29.pdf

Wentzel Winther, I. (2006b). *Hjemlighed: Kulturfænomenologiske studier* [Homeness: Anthropological studies]. København: Danmarks Pædagogiske Universitets Forlag.

KEY TERMS AND DEFINITIONS

Distance Education: (DE) is often defined as a form of studying where the student and the teacher are separated in space and/or time, and where technologies (e.g. radio, TV, videoconferencing, computers etc.) are used to bridge the distance. In Sweden DE has a long tradition of offering compensatory and distributed educational opportunities, e.g. to rural areas or specific target groups such as women or those with inadequate educational qualifications. DE has been an integrated part of the Swedish higher education system since 1977.

Correspondence Study: An early version of DE, based on the correspondence letter as means for conducting studies at a distance or in rural areas. As a form of delivering education it had its peak in Sweden in the 1930s, with Correspondence Institutes such as Hermods, NKI and Brevskolan.

Flexible Learning: A late-dated term for DE and flexible study forms in space and time. The term is often used as a way to depict the need for a change in educational institutions to service provision and a new focus on the learner and her needs.

IT-Based Learning: or web-based learning etc., is often claimed to have made more flexible and communicative study forms available, e.g. flexible distance education. We highlight the inscriptions of IT and how it is used as a symbol, and thought of in terms of gender and as enabling tool.

Policy, or Policy Documents: Are the products of the processes of the Swedish government system, where commissioned material, proposals from the Ministries, and replies from different societal actors are negotiated and finalized in Government Bills. Swedish higher education is mainly State regulated and is free of charge. Policies make up the empirical material of policy analysis and should reflect the process around them; in the selection of documents, the character of compromise of the written proposals, as well as the overall ideas and presumptions produced in them.

Space: Here considered as the mutual shaping of space, place and time. 'Space' could be considered as the abstract-discursive dimension and 'place' as the concrete-material, i.e. specific geographies or localities bearing on certain values and inscriptions. Space and place are thus not simply opposed to time but rather formed through certain temporal and social relations.

Spatial Analysis: The spatial organisation of society is of interest here and especially: how spatial relations and conditions are expressed. The spatial is seen as constructed out of social relations and could cover different scales, through global information technologies, to national political power to the everyday spheres of the home and workplace. The arguments of a democratic Swedish higher education are analysed using a spatial analysis, meaning that the focus is on the discursive productions of spaces and how these are implicated in both history and politics. In recent poststructuralist debates (e.g. sociology and geography literature), the spatial has received increasing attention where time, traditionally considered as the dynamic, changeable dimension, has gradually lost its dominance in the space/time dyad.

Spatial Politics: 'The spatial' is seen as a dynamic dimension that is dividing and ordering people, resources, ideas etc. Politics is not limited to 'party politics' but used in the broadest sense of the word, connecting to power and uneven development and to the spatial organisation of society such as gender differentiations and male and female positionings.

Gendered Space: According to the feminist human geographer Doreen Massey spaces are co-constructed with gender definitions and gender relations (Massey: 1994). The gendered connotations of space/place in Western thinking implies that 'space' is attached to the universal, to the global and to freedom and thus coded masculine, while 'place' is seen as the locally place-bound, associated with dependence and the female gender. For instance, "the home" has been historically constructed as a female coded space and as a site for nostalgia, and thus has presumably limited women's mobility. These kinds of dualisms have been strongly criticized by feminists, as they are attached to the radical polarization of two genders. Massey problematizes the contrasting distinctions between space/place, global/local, public/private etc, as these dimensions are highly intertwined and each is part of the construction of the other.

ENDNOTES

[1] The high percentage of women participating in distance higher education, which from 1996 until 2006 has been around 65% (Statistics Sweden, 2007) also points to the relevance of considering gender and distance education.

[2] The material contains the Distance education commission's advisory documents (SME, 1998a, 1998b, 1998c). The commissioned material includes an evaluation of the governmental investment in 100 distance education projects (SME, 1998a), a research overview (SME, 1998b) and the Commission's final proposal (SME, 1998c).

[3] The correct title of the department at that time was The Swedish Ministry of Education and Ecclesiastical Affairs.

4   With Butler (1990), we argue that gender does not express some authentic inner core, but is produced by and maintained through discursive practices. Regulative discourses decide and reinforce what possibilities of gender are socially permitted to appear as coherent or "natural".

Chapter 12
Computer Courses in Adult Education in a Gender Perspective

Minna Salminen-Karlsson
Uppsala University, Sweden

ABSTRACT

In this study of computer courses in municipal adult education, 173 questionnaires from 10 Swedish adult education centres with students taking a basic computer education course were analyzed. The main findings were that men consistently reported greater computer competence, while computer interest or computer attitudes did not show gender differences. The gender differences in computer competence were significant even in the youngest age group. Young women were also the most distinctive group by being the most dissatisfied. The idea that gender issues in adult computer education mainly concern computer reticent middle aged women while young women attend computer courses on a more equal footing with men does not hold in this sample. The results raise some practical questions, particularly in assessing the differences in computer competence and women's feelings of inadequacy, taking advantage of women's computer interest, and coming into terms with young women's expectations.

BACKGROUND OF THE STUDY

A gender gap in computing—a digital divide between women and men (Cooper & Weaver, 2003; Wilson et al, 2003), even in western society—has been troubling researchers and policymakers; firstly, because women are seen as being at risk of being left behind in the new citizenship, and, secondly, because computer competence is essential in a well-qualified workforce. However, today 60% of Swedish women and 69% of Swedish men use a computer daily, either at home or at work (Statistics Sweden, 2006). The picture of women as not being interested in computers and computer competence does not hold true any more. Women do use computers, and they also enrol on computer courses. But how are these courses functioning for the students—men and women? Do women and men come to the course with similar interests and similar knowledge? What about different age

DOI: 10.4018/978-1-61520-813-5.ch012

groups? These are the questions that this study tries to answer.

This is a study of computer students in Swedish municipal adult education centres. The main focus is on the differences between men and women, and between women of different ages when it comes to their interest in and experiences of computers and computer education.

ADULT EDUCATION, WOMEN AND COMPUTERS

Women and Men in Adult Education

Few studies on adult education have been conducted from a gender perspective (Rogers, 2005) and the situation is not much better in Sweden. One exception is the work of Hägerström (2004), who conducted an observational and interview study in one municipal adult education centre.

There have been a number of studies of gender related to computer education, computer use, and attitudes to computers, but very few have been conducted in an adult education setting. One positive exception is the studies reported by the SIGIS group (Lie & Sörensen, 2003, Rommes, Faulkner & van Slooten, 2005). The studies made about gender and computer education have normally dealt with schoolchildren, adolescents and university students (for example, Upitis, 1998; Clift et al, 2001; Margolis & Fisher, 2002; Colley & Comber, 2003; Hartzel, 2003; Broos & Roe, 2006; Fuller & Meiners, 2005). They have repeatedly established that girls and women either are more reticent towards computers than boys and men, or they are perceived to be so by their teachers. Another way to interpret these findings is that women have other requirements than men on computers, computer education and the introduction of computers to their daily lives, but that their preferences are not respected by the male-dominated IT professionals, or male computing teachers, leading to a marginalization of women in computer education.

Adult education is different from other educational settings. Many students in adult education are middle-aged and have families. Women have often prioritized their family while men have prioritized employment (Ahrenkiel et al., 1998; Crossan et al, 2003). This extends even into the field of education. While the expressed aim of most students is to improve their qualifications or to get a job, men emphasize the qualification aspect and see the education in more instrumental terms while women tend to enjoy learning in itself and the social aspects of education. Hayes (2001) found that for women, education can bring new insights about their old roles and identities, and can thus involve much more profound changes than simply competence development.

For women studying computing, however, there often seems to exist an initial problem of self-esteem, and several authors (Hayes & Flannery, 2000; Green & Keeble, 2001; Lior, 2001; Faulkner & Kleif, 2003; Fuller & Meiners, 2005; Rommes, 2003) stress the importance of building up women's self-esteem to engage them in learning, both in general and with computer subjects in particular. Some of these studies (Green & Keeble, Lior, 2001, Faulkner & Kleif, 2003) have also found that female teachers are essential for the success of women learners.

Illeris (2003) divides students in Danish adult education into three age groups: those over 45–50 years of age, those between 25–30 and 45–50, and those under 25–30. In Denmark, as well as in Sweden, municipal adult education is both something you can engage in voluntarily, for example to improve your possibilities in the labour market, but also something that can be strongly recommended by the authorities if you are unemployed. According to Illeris, the oldest group sees education from a worker perspective: it is a shame to be without a job and to have to take to education instead; the teacher takes the place of the work leader and tells you what to do—and for doing what you are told, you get your salary/benefit. The middle group tends to think along the same lines, but can also see education as being something valuable as it can give you credits that you can use to get a better position in the labour market. For both groups, teachers are important authorities—and those who have the final responsibility for the students' learning.

Illeris (2003) found that young students are different, in that education itself is important for their identity-building; it is something that is naturally consumed but that has to suit their needs and interests if they are to partake. Ahrenkiel et al. (1998) compared women by age group and saw that older women are almost too satisfied with the education offered to them (while older men tend to be critical), but that younger women are different and more like young men in their attitudes to adult education. However, Hägerström (2004) found that even among the younger students, traditional gender roles prevail, in that women aim for traditional women's occupations in caring, while men aim for technical occupations. How all this translates to computer courses has not been studied. MacKeogh (2003) reported that younger women in computer courses in an adult education context appear to be less wary of computers than older women. However, studies carried out in secondary schools and among ordinary college students (Colley & Comber, 2003; Volman et al., 2005; Broos & Roe, 2006; Clift et al, 2001; Hartzel, 2003) have found that there is a difference between young women and men, in that girls and young women are less positive towards computers and less interested in them than men of the same age group.

Computer Anxiety or Masculinity of Computers?

Computer anxiety is a well-established concept (Marcoulides, 1989 and 2004; Weil & Rosen, 1995; Brosnan & Lee 1998; Bozionelos, 2001, Marcoulides, Stocker & Marcoulides, 2004), frequently used in the 1980s and 1990s when computer literacy came to be seen as a basic form

of competence for every citizen in the USA and Western Europe. Computer anxiety has been defined by Cooper & Weaver (2003) as "feelings of discomfort, stress or anxiety that people experience when responding to computers" (p. 13). Computer anxiety has been seen as a major obstacle to increasing the knowledge and competence level of the workforce, to respond to the demands of the new technological age. The concept of computer anxiety does not have the same cogency today. However, Marcoulides, Stocker & Marcoulides (2004) found that Marcoulides's original (1989) scale for measurement of computer anxiety was still valid; that is, computer anxiety is still a relevant concept when examining people's attitudes in confronting different aspects of information and communication technologies.

In many studies, women have been found to show a much higher degree of computer anxiety than men, which has fostered a perception of computer anxiety in the workforce as a problem that particularly concerns women. There have been numerous studies about the differences between men's and women's attitudes to computers and actual computer use (Lie, 1998; Fidishun, 2001; Cooper & Weaver, 2003; Corneliussen, 2003; Jenson & Rose, 2003).

However, the single concept of computer anxiety does not capture the full breadth of the gender dimension regarding computers. The differences that have been attributed to computer anxiety appear to stem from differences in interest. The perceived usefulness of computers in relation to one's own life situation appears to be of vital importance here. The gender labels of computers and different tasks associated with computers, affect both men's and women's interest and self-esteem in learning computer-related tasks but often in opposite ways.

Interaction with a computer happens in a cultural context, where artefacts are gendered in different ways. To use a computer is a gendered act. The association of computer technology with masculinity in different ways is well documented

(Ware & Stuck, 1985; Edwards, 1990; Jenson & Rose, 2003; Kleif & Faulkner, 2003; Lagesen, 2003; Cooper, 2006). Computers were for a long time primarily associated with science and mathematics, which were male-dominated fields. The first personal home computers became toys for boys, and what ordinary people heard about computer culture was male nerds and hackers. Home computer advertisements were directed to men. The middle-aged women of today got their first impressions of computers during this era.

With 60% of Swedish women using computers on a daily basis and 63% of them using computers frequently at home (Statistics Sweden, 2009a and b), the picture is not as clear-cut any more. Lie (1998) asserts that the computer as an artefact is not gendered, but that it is only gendered in relation to its context. For example, in an environment in which computers are connected to secretarial work, they may well be seen as feminine. However, just as women commonly summon a male partner for help if the car or even one of the household machines breaks down, it can be expected that the maintenance of the family computer is still a man's job rather than a woman's. For example, in 2000, 69% of men but only 42% of women had ever installed something (such as a printer or a modem) on their computer (Statistics Sweden, 2002).

Thus, it seems that computer use can be labelled as a masculine, feminine or gender neutral activity, depending on the context. However, when it comes to service or repair, computers are machines and, thus, predominantly masculine (Fidishun, 2001; Jenson & Rose, 2003).

On the basis of their study, Jenson & Rose (2003) suggested that individual competence is not always decisive for how much and how efficiently a person uses a computer, because gender and power relations (amongst other factors) may inhibit particularly women's use of computers.

Computer Use and Implications for Adult Education

In 2006, 60% of Swedish women and 69% of Swedish men used a computer on a daily basis (Statistics Sweden, 2009a), and 55% of women and 67% of men used the internet every day (Statistics Sweden, 2009b). Computer use at home was more frequent than computer use at the workplace for both women and men. During the whole period between 2003-2008, men have consistently used computers slightly more than women (Statistics Sweden, 2009b). However, the differences are small, between 5 and 11 percentages, the difference in use at home being slightly greater than that of computer use at work. These statistics indicate that the differences between women's and men's computer use are almost negligible. This also applies to what the internet was used for: men were more frequent users in the categories internet banking, and using the internet for fun, such as music, games, photos, magazines and radio/TV programs, but the differences between men's usage and women's usage were not large. However, men downloaded new programs more often than women (35% of men, 13% of women), which may indicate that the functioning of the computer was still a man's responsibility.

That women use computers less at home means that many of them come to a computer course with less experience. The combination of less experience and lower self-esteem means that it is important that enough time for practice is given during the course (Selwyn, 1997; Fürst, 2004). Both Selwyn (1997) and Andersen (1996) point out that the fact that computers sometimes behave in unexpected ways is much more disturbing for beginners, as they already feel that they are not in control of the situation. This emotional strain and feeling of totally losing control may make it quite difficult to turn to a printed manual for help (not to mention the help function of the computer itself). What is needed is help from a teacher or a fellow student who also can confirm that such problems are quite normal and can be handled in one way or another. Students helping each other may also alleviate those negative attitudes to computers that are based on the perception that sitting at a computer is very antisocial.

Co-operation appears to be particularly important for female students (Green & Keeble, 2000; Lior, 2001; Crossan et al, 2003; Rommes, 2003; Fuller & Meiners, 2005, Jubas et al, 2006). Besides the fellow students, the attitude of the teacher is important. Some researchers have found that a female teacher may be better for female students' computer learning (Lior, 2001; Faulkner & Kleif, 2003). It is important that women should be able to talk to each other, and to the teacher also, on issues relating to identity formation—and about finding practical ways of fitting studies into one's life (Lior, 2001; Fürst, 2004). This is not true of all female students, however, and not considering the diversity of women in this respect can cause protests from those who are more instrumentally oriented and want to focus on the subject matter of the course.

Even in adult education, as in higher education settings concerned with computer education (Wistedt, 2000; Zohar, 2006), women may be met with impatience on the part of the teachers for their need to "understand". Teachers in the studies by Corneliussen (2003) and Fürst (2004) talked about problems with women who wanted to understand what they were learning, and they asserted that some things just have to be taken in without questioning. In particular, women often feel that the rapid pace of instruction makes it difficult for them to gain the understanding they feel they need.

METHOD

The Setting

The educational settings of the respondents of this study were municipal adult education centres in Sweden, so-called "komvux" centres.

In addition to primary and secondary schools for children and young people, all Swedish municipalities are required to provide education for adults who want to complete or upgrade their primary and secondary education, and this is normally done through municipal adult education centres. Basically, a municipal adult education centre is a school for adults who want to acquire a secondary school certificate. (The centres also offer courses at primary school level, but the majority of students take secondary school courses). Traditionally, the courses are scheduled during daytime and the students either compose their own mix of subjects according to their needs, or follow a vocationally oriented secondary school study program (of which nurses' aid program is the most popular). Students at the centres are entitled to state study grants, though many who only take a couple of subjects work part time. In addition to their basic mission, the centres also take care of language teaching for immigrants. It has also become very common for Swedish secondary school graduates to upgrade their grades by taking a course at an adult education centre – the grades from the centres are fully comparable to ordinary secondary school grades when applying to higher education. This has lowered the median age of the students to around 30 years. Approximately two thirds of the students are women (Skolverket, 2006).

A basic computer course is included in most tracks in the Swedish secondary school, and most of those who take the course at the centres take such a course as part of their study program. However, the course is also an economically advantageous way for anybody who wants to acquire basic computer knowledge, either for a credit or for the skills, and thus there are students who only enrol on this single course. In addition, the centres are increasingly competitors in the educational marketplace, and computer courses can be marketed to employers as vocational development. Thus, some of the students take such a course during working hours, paid for by their employer.

The basic computer course is particularly popular among women: 71% of the students on this course are women, as compared to 66% of the students attending secondary school courses overall (Skolverket, 2006). This course includes basic knowledge of Microsoft Windows and Microsoft Office programs. The students answering the questionnaire in this study were enrolled in courses with classroom teaching, but computer courses are also provided as independent study, where the students are allowed or expected to use the computer lab of the school and advance at their own pace with the help of an instructor.

The Sample

Teachers giving computer courses in 43 municipal adult education centres were requested to ask their students to participate in the study. The centres were randomly chosen from the list of Swedish municipalities, and in most cases the e-mail addresses of the computing teachers were also found on the web – otherwise an e-mail was sent to a central administrator of the education centre with a request to forward it to teachers in computing. Those who did not answer were sent a reminder about a month later. Those centres who answered the mail and did not want to partake most often told that their students already answered a number of questionnaires, particularly in the end of the term. In the end, students from 10 centres answered the questionnaire. Two of the centres contributed the major proportion of the answers—55 and 38, respectively—while only a few students at a number of other centres answered the questionnaire. Most of the centres that were involved in the study are situated in small or middle-sized towns. The two centres contributing the most were very different: one of them is located in a middle-class municipality in the vicinity of Stockholm and the other in a small rural municipality in Southern Sweden. In the rural centre the dominance of women was striking – 52 of the 143 women in the study come from this centre, while the suburban

centre had a more even gender distribution with 32% men. One third of the older students (over 50 years) came from this centre.

As few of the centres that were asked finally took part in the study, it seems reasonable to assume that the answers came from centres with engaged teachers. This certainly contributes to the high appreciation of the teachers by the respondents, and does possibly affect the ratings even in other variables. However, how this affects gender aspects in the study is difficult to know.

There is no way of telling who answered the questionnaire and who did not—that is, how representative this sample would be of students taking computer courses in adult education centres in general. Eighty per cent of the respondents were women, which can be compared to the 71% women who were taking computer courses in municipal adult education in 2003/04 (Skolverket, 2006). The median age of the student sample was 40 years, which should be compared to the median age of 30 years for all students in municipal adult education in 2004/2005. (However, even though there is no figure for the median age of students taking computer courses, it could be expected to be somewhat higher).

About half of the 178 students reported having a male teacher and the other half had a female teacher (84 and 94, respectively). 24% of the women were in all-women groups, and 69% were in groups consisting of mainly women. Six per cent of the women reported gender-balanced[1] groups and 1% reported being in male-dominated groups. As women comprise 70% of the students in computer courses in adult education, the number of female-dominated groups is not surprising. [2] Whether the all-female groups were a result of a conscious strategy from the part of the centre or just a coincidence is not clearly indicated by the partaking centres or in the data. However, in the Swedish educational ideology, consciously using single sex groups is extremely rare and very controversial. None of the centres partaking in the study mentioned any such projects in their

Figure 1. Breakdown of the sample in terms of gender and age

Age (years)	Under 30	30–40	40–50	Over 50	Age not reported	Sum
Women	27 (19%)	34 (24%)	43 (31%)	37 (26%)	2 (1%)	143 (100%)
Men	19 (54%)	2 (6%)	8 (23%)	6 (17%)		35 (100%)
	46 (26%)	36 (20%)	51 (29%)	43 (24%)	2 (1%)	178 (100%)

communication with me or on their homepages. Thus, the most likely explanation is simply the composition of the student body, particularly the fact that about one third of the women came from a centre with hardly any male students.

Even though the sample was drawn from a number of municipal adult education centres, its representativeness can be called into question, because the numbers are small. This is particularly true of the men in the sample. Thus, it would be unreasonable to generalize the results to all students on computer courses at municipal education centres in Sweden. However, even as an exploratory study in a Swedish setting, it confirms some of the earlier research on women and computing, thus making it probable that similar mechanisms to those in other settings are also operating in Swedish adult education. And, more interestingly, when it does not confirm earlier research, new questions are awakened – to be researched in a more focused way with more focused samples.

The Questionnaire

The questionnaire consisted of 53 statements on a Likert scale and 11 questions of varying formats about age, gender, computer use at home and at work, occupation, study financing, course content, length of the course, the gender of the teacher and of the classmates, and what the student expected to gain from the course regarding computer use and employment. The Likert scale questions were 5-point with the end points marked "Very much true" and "Not true at all". In addition there was

space in the end of the questionnaire for general comments, not used by many respondents.

The 53 items were related to three different areas: (1) the course and the teacher, (2) being a student, and (3) being a computer user. A pilot questionnaire (the results of which are not included in the study) was answered by 44 respondents from one municipal adult education centre. The questionnaire was improved further based on the analysis of these answers. Some questions which did not substantially add to the analysis were deleted, and a few other questions on issues which were not covered in the pilot questionnaire, but which appeared to be relevant were added.

The introductory text on the questionnaire stated that the research issue was participants' experiences of computer courses, and the gender aspect was not mentioned. The questionnaire was filled in online. In some centres, this was done during class time while in others it was left entirely up to the student when and where it would be completed. The questionnaire was answered by the students in December 2006.

Fidishun (2001), Jenson & Rose (2003), Cooper (2006), and Hargittai & Shafer (2006) all found that women easily underrated their own computer skills—even when they were quite competent. For studies like this one, in which respondents evaluate their own computer proficiency, this is a problem—as women they can be expected to underrate their own competence, but it is unknown to what degree they do it. Thus, this study cannot present objective results about the actual computer competence of the sample, but only the respondents' culturally shaped perceptions and emotions about their own competence.

Analysis

Factor analysis was used as a heuristic device to discover patterns in the material. To start with, a factor analysis was run on all the single items (20 Likert items and 2 items on computer use) that in themselves showed significant gender differences, and another on the remaining 33 items. The items that had high loadings (greater than 0.5) for these factors were summed (reversing the scores when necessary) to form composite variables. This procedure resulted in 10 composite variables, 4 with significant gender differences and 6 with no significant gender differences.

To make it possible to find patterns, which included both gendered and ungendered items, three additional factor analyses were run—each with 24 randomly chosen items. Most of the factors produced by these analyses roughly echoed the factors already found and did not add to the analysis. Four new composite variables were created, however, using the same procedure as above.

In this paper, six of these composite variables—those most intelligible and most relevant in relation to previous research—are elaborated on. They are: computer competence, interest in computers, feelings of inadequacy, dissatisfaction, and two variables about teacher characteristics. The composite variables for interest in computers and dissatisfaction were adjusted by removing and adding items to increase the reliability. The Cronbach alpha levels of the composite variables after that were 0.64 (interest in computers and dissatisfaction) and higher. This is not totally satisfactory, but was deemed to be sufficient in an exploratory study such as this.

Gender and age differences in these variables and in the items included were studied using t-tests (gender) and one-way ANOVA (age). In addition, some single items not included in these composite variables were tested.

When comparing age groups between women and men, a division into three groups, below 30, 30–50, and over 50, was used. A stated difference between men and women or between age groups means a difference which is statistically significant at the $p < 0.05$ level.

THE RESULTS

Differences and Similarities Between Men and Women

Men used computers more both at home and at work. For home use, the alternatives ranged from "never" to "more than one hour every day", a six-step scale. The median alternative for women was "more than once a week" while for men it was "every day". The greatest differences in home use were on the alternative "more than one hour every day". However, as can be seen from figure 4, women stated more often that they would have liked to sit at the computer more, if only they had had more time.

Thus, almost all of the participants in the courses had previous computer experience—but the questions only concerned the amount of time spent at the computer, not what the respondents were actually doing. Men and women may well have different experiences of computers.

Computer competence was the factor which showed greatest differences between men and women. This factor measured computer competence, by simple questions on hardware ("I know at least four computer brands and "I can connect the parts of a a computer with cables"), free-time computer use, helping others with computer problems, enjoyment of computers (I enjoy doing things with a computer), and feeling of expertise (I could become a computer professional if I wanted to).

Figure 2. (a) computer use at home; (b) computer use at work

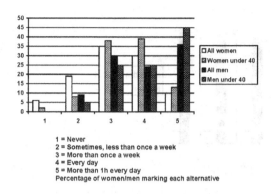

1 = Never
2 = Sometimes, less than once a week
3 = More than once a week
4 = Every day
5 = More than 1h every day
Percentage of women/men marking each alternative

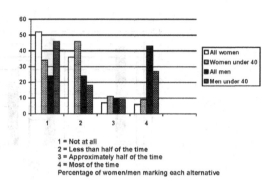

1 = Not at all
2 = Less than half of the time
3 = Approximately half of the time
4 = Most of the time
Percentage of women/men marking each alternative

The hardware questions were very elementary, but still, each question only got positive answers from 40% of the respondents. Among the men, however, 80% of the respondents gave a positive answer to each of these questions, while among the women only 24% knew computer brands and 29% could connect cables. Obviously, this knowledge must have been acquired outside the course in most cases, and it was the men who had acquired this knowledge.

The item "I could be a computer professional if I wanted to" also showed considerable gender differences. Eighteen per cent of the women and 66% of the men agreed with this statement. The difference in computer enjoyment was also significant, but much smaller.

The differences between men and women were also considerable when it came to helping others (28% of women and 66% of men agreed that they sometimes helped others with computer problems). Thus, there appears to be a difference in the social interaction surrounding computers and the competence that can be gained that way. While men agreed that they helped other people with computers more often than women, there was

Figure 3. computer competence[i]

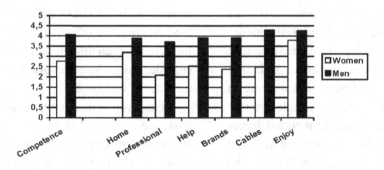

Home = At home I use the computer
Professional = I could be a computer professional if I wanted to
Help = I sometimes help others with computer problems
Brands = I know at least four computer brands
Cables = I can connect the parts of a computer with cables
Enjoy = I enjoy using the computer

---

[i] In each of the graphs the means of the variables included in the factor and the mean of the factor variable divided by the number of the included variables are given.

Figure 4. Computer interest

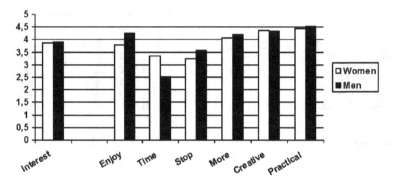

Enjoy = I enjoy using a computer
Time = If I had more time, I would use the computer more
Stop = When I'm using the computer I often find it hard to stop
More = I want to learn more after this course
Creative = The computer is a creative tool
Practical = The computer is a practical tool

no significant gender difference in asking for help. Looking at the single item about asking for help contradicts the impression of women being more helpless than men, but the meaning of the question may be different for men and women. For men, the items about asking for help and helping others had a positive correlation, which would imply a give-and-take interaction. For women there was no such correlation.

In contrast to computer competence, the *computer interest factor* did not show significant differences between men and women. There, the computer enjoyment item was combined with appreciating computers as being creative and practical, wanting to spend more time on computers, finding it engaging to sit at a computer, and wanting to learn more about computers. Thus, while reported computer competence, including reported spare-time use, differed significantly between men and women, interest in using computers did not. The difference in the item "if I had more time, I would use the computer more" may signal that the men to a greater degree might already have been spending all the time they wanted at the computer. Forty-eight per cent of the women would have used computers more if they had had more time, as compared to 24% of the men. Statistics Sweden's (2003) analysis of

women's and men's time use patterns shows that women's free time is more often split into short intervals between household chores, while men's uninterrupted free time is larger. Because it takes some time to sit down by a computer and turn it on, it is probable that women more often lack the possibility to integrate computer use in their daily life. Thus, women's answers of wanting to use the computer more could be interpreted in the light of women generally having less opportunity to sit at the computer, but it can also be interpreted in the light of the results of Gansmo et al. (2003)—that women prioritize other activities in their existing time frame, even though they say that they would consider using the computer more if the existing time frame was larger.

Thus, even in this group of adults studying the basic use of computers, the hardware, technology and expertise can be seen as being masculine. However, the fact that things have changed and that ordinary computer use is not gendered any more is mirrored in the computer interest factor, which did not show any difference between men and women.

Another factor with a significant difference between men and women was *the inadequacy factor.* It consisted of items indicating that the respondent had difficulty in following the course, difficulty in understanding the course content, and that the respondent felt stupid and lost courage when the demands became too high. In all these aspects, women scored higher. Thus, it seems that in computer courses, women feel more inadequate than men. This could be due to the special circumstances surrounding a masculine subject in an environment where men can show their competence and where male teachers adapt their teaching to masculine ways of approaching the subject. However, when comparing women's scores in this factor between women with male and female teachers, and between women in single-sex and mixed-sex groups, there were no significant differences. This indicates that the reasons for women's feelings of inadequacy lie somewhere else.

It is particularly interesting to note the difference between the items "I find it difficult to follow the instruction" and "Sometimes I find it difficult to understand what I'm learning", because it relates to the issue of women wanting to understand (Corneliussen, 2003; Fürst, 2004; Zohar, 2006). Even though both items showed significant gender differences, the difference was much greater in regard to the item about understanding. Thirty-three per cent of the women stated that they did not always understand, while 13% had difficulties in following the instruction. (The corresponding percentages for men were 9 and 3). Even in this sample, understanding appears to be an important concept. To elaborate the concept of understanding further, the statement "Sometimes I find it difficult to understand what I'm learning" was correlated with the statement "The time allocated for exercises on the course is sufficient for me", which did not belong to the inadequacy factor. This correlation was negative for women (Pearson, -0.232, $p = 0.05$) but not for men (Pearson, -0.188, $p = 0.280$). Thus, it is possible that the pace of instruction is important for women to get an experience that they understand, in a way that does not apply to men.

There were two factors measuring teacher ratings, *traditional teacher characteristics factor* and *student-centred teacher factor*. There were no gender differences in how teachers were rated. Both female and male students gave high ratings (means between 4.23 and 4.66) to their teachers in the traditional teacher characteristics factor (engagement, knowledge, ability to make the material interesting, and ability to make time for the students and care about them). They rated their teachers somewhat lower when it came to the student-centred teacher factor (having the students' knowledge as a starting point, mean 3.33, and encouraging the students to help each other, mean 3.28), but there were still no general gender differences. Some of the variables, but not others, were correlated to the teacher being male or female: female teachers were rated as being better at explaining, and being more knowledgeable and more engaged, while male teachers were perceived as being good at encouraging students to help each other more. There was no significant student gender-related interaction in these ratings; all these differences, though they existed, were not significant for the male students, but that may have been due to the smaller sample size. Thus, the hypothesis that women teachers are more appreciated by female computer students does not hold in this sample. Nor does the study confirm previous results regarding female teachers having difficulties in establishing their legitimacy among male students in computer-related subjects. However, the number of teachers involved in this study was not very large. Thus, the differences in teacher ratings are not a reliable result in themselves, but point to further questions regarding teaching styles in computer adult education.

The fact that women thought that nice classmates were important to a greater extent (mean for women was 3.76, and mean for men was 3.16) can be interpreted as women valuing the social aspect of just meeting people, but it could also indicate a wish to co-operate with classmates.

Figure 5. Feelings of inadequacy

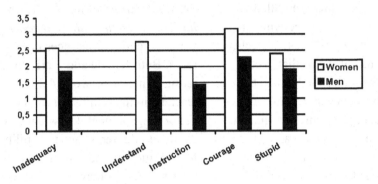

Understand = Sometimes I find it difficult to understand what I'm learning
Instruction = I find it difficult to follow the instruction
Courage = If the requirements are high, I easily lose courage
Stupid = I feel stupid when I make mistakes

Women also asked their classmates for help more often (mean for women 3.80, mean for men 2.94), thus indicating more co-operative behaviour. However, it is also possible that men did not report asking for help because they felt they had better computer competence, and thus did not expect their classmates to be able to help them with their questions.

Young Women are Different

Most of the factors did not show any significant differences when women in different age groups were compared. In a few respects, however, young women (under 30) were different from their older counterparts: they reported better computer proficiency and doing better on the course. They agreed to a higher degree that they could become computer professionals if they wanted to, they helped others with computer problems more often, they used computers more at home, and they knew computer brands better than the older women. However, there was no significant difference between young women and older women concerning the item about enjoying doing things with a computer; the means in the five-point scale were 3.9 for the young women and 3.8 for the older women. Thus, it was the actual computer use and the confidence (which may be connected to it) that was different between age groups, not enjoyment and interest.

However, in the *dissatisfaction factor* young women scored significantly higher than older women.

The dissatisfaction factor consisted of variables about the length of the work periods between breaks, the premises, the relevance of the issues presented, whether the respondent wanted to learn more after the course, and whether he/she enjoyed being in a classroom. This variable showed a l large difference between the youngest women and the older ones. Also, among the older women there was a correlation between dissatisfaction with the course and feelings of inadequacy (Pearson 0.31, $p = 0.00$), while this was not the case for the younger women (Pearson 0.02, $p = 0.92$). Thus, the young women might feel dissatisfied with their course even though they were doing fine on it. For the younger women, there was a positive correlation between dissatisfaction with the course and a factor denoting the easiness of the course (Pearson 0.47, $p = 0.01$), while there was no such correlation for the older women (Pearson -0.0 $p = 0.47$).

Figure 6. Dissatisfaction

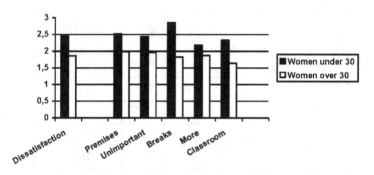

Premises = The premises are dreary
Unimportant = The course covers too much stuff that is unimportant
Breaks = The time between breaks is too long on this course
More = After the course I want to learn more (reversed score)
Classroom = Sitting in a classroom doesn't quite suit me

The differences between age groups in the single variables in the dissatisfaction factor were about finding the working periods too long, the premises dreary and in general not feeling at home in a classroom environment. It did not concern the subject content of the course and it could therefore be interpreted as general dissatisfaction with studying. There was no significant difference in dissatisfaction between younger and older men, only between women of different ages.

There were also differences between the oldest age group and the younger age groups: the oldest women (over fifty) found the course more difficult than women under fifty. However, they were also most satisfied with the course.

Feelings of Inadequacy are Evenly Distributed Among Women

It is interesting to note that in spite of these differences in perceived computer competence between women in different age groups, there were no significant differences in the inadequacy factor between the three groups of women: those under 30, those aged 30–50, and those over 50. Thus, in spite of their apparent computer competence, the young women did not feel that they understood better, they did not report being fast, and

they felt quite as stupid when making mistakes and as discouraged if the demands were high as the older women. The older women who found the course difficult still did not feel more stupid or lose courage. Thus, it seems that the feelings of inadequacy were not connected to measures of perceived difficulty and competence, but stem from some other source. The wording of the items refers to a study situation in general, and not only to the present computer course (even though the respondents had possibly interpreted the questions as referring to this particular course). The feelings of inadequacy may be connected to the ambivalent or resistant learner identities presented in the literature on adult education (Ahrenkiel et al, 1998; Crossan et al, 2003; Illeris, 2003, Assarsson & Sipos-Zackrisson, 2006). If the items were interpreted as concerning this particular computer course, the gendering of computers (Ware & Stuck, 1985; Edwards, 1990; Jenson & Rose, 2003; Faulkner & Kleif 2003; Lagesen, 2003; Cooper, 2006) may be of importance. In that case, women of all age groups would have had some problems perceiving themselves as competent computer learners.

Figure 7. Age and gender interaction

		Gender	Mean	*p*-value
Aged 50 or older Men (n = 6) Women (n = 37)	Computer competence	Men	3.17	.048
		Women	2.38	
	Inadequacy	Men	2.42	.352
		Women	2.85	
	Computer interest	Men	4.20	.139
		Women	3.71	
Aged 30–50 Men (n = 10) Women (n = 77)	Computer competence	Men	4.33	.000
		Women	2.74	
	Inadequacy	Men	1.60	.002
		Women	2.40	
	Computer interest	Men	3.97	.983
		Women	3.97	
Aged 30 or younger Men (n = 19) Women (n = 27)	Computer competence	Men	4.21	.001
		Women	3,57	
	Inadequacy	Men	1.83	.008
		Women	2,51	
	Computer interest	Men	3,79	.822
		Women	3,84	

Age and Gender

The age difference in the sample might explain some of the differences between men and women. For example, even though men report more home use, the differences are no longer significant when students are compared with others of the same age group. The difference between men and women in how much computers are used at work disappears in the youngest age group, though not among the older students. However, if one divides the sample into age groups, most of the differences persist—even among the youngest students.

The differences in computer competence were smaller but did not even out in the youngest age group, compared to the older students. The youngest and middle aged women also felt more inadequate than the men. This difference was not found in the oldest group, which was mainly due to men in this group also feeling inadequate. The one factor where there was no difference in any age group was that of computer interest.

Regarding the expected future effects of the course, there were some interesting differences between men and women in the different age groups. Women expected greater benefits from the course regarding their use of computers: 60% of the women and 43% of the men reported that they would use computers more after the course. However, in the youngest age group, only 20% of the men—as compared to 63% of the women—thought that they would use the computer more after the course. Considering that the existing use of computers did not show any gender differences in this age group, this is an interesting result. Both young men and young women expected that the course would broaden their use of computers: 74% of the young men and 70% of the young women expected to use their computers differently after the course. Thus, the frequent computer use of the youngest group may have been one-sided, and increased knowledge of office software probably enabled them to use the everyday potential of the computer more fully.

DISCUSSION

This study partly confirms and partly contradicts the results of previous studies on gender and computer education. The results of a number of previous studies are confirmed in that men even in this study reported more computer competence than women. In particular, they stated that they knew more about the hardware, which is in accordance with the gendering of technology as being masculine. The computer as a machine still appears to be more of men's area of interest, even though women can also be regarded as computer users. However, this study does not confirm earlier studies regarding men's greater interest in computers. Certainly, men reported that they used computers more at home—but more women than men answered that they would have liked to use the computer more if they had had more time. Thus, the fact that women spend less time using computers does not necessarily result from a lower degree of interest, but rather from other obligations and interests being given preference in their lives. Men reported to a greater extent that they enjoyed sitting at a computer. However, also women—and not only men—can become immersed in the computer.

What the women did reveal, though, was a kind of anxiety connected to the study situation. This may not be so strange as long as it is associated with finding the course difficult, but this was

not the case for the youngest women. And it can certainly be seen as a problem when one-third of the women students agree with the statement that they sometimes find it hard to understand what they are learning. Of course, this problem can be described—as a number of computer teachers evidently do (Corneliussen, 2003; Fürst, 2004)— not as a problem for the instructors but as a problem for the students who expect to understand while a basic computer course only can be about know-how.

It also seems problematic that 25% of the women felt that the time allocated for doing exercises was not sufficient, and that this also applied to the youngest women. This appears to be related to women's feeling that they find it hard to understand. If the time allocated for doing exercises is only intended to give the students a know-how, but a learner also wants to reflect on what she is doing, there may be a discrepancy. This lack of time might be due to external factors (a set curriculum), but it can also be due to teachers over-estimating the skills of the students. There were not many comments in the spaces provided for comments on the questionnaire, but a number of female students used this space to comment on the pace of the instruction and the importance of teachers understanding the difficulties of the learners.

Contrary to the recommendations that female students should be taught by female teachers, particularly in scientific and technological subjects, the problems described above were as prevalent for women who had a female teacher as for women who were taught by a male teacher. The reasons for this warrant further research. For gender inclusivity in computer teaching, it is interesting to note that the two aspects in which teachers were rated the lowest were those that previous studies have denoted as being particularly important for women: encouraging co-operation and taking the students' previous knowledge as a starting point. This means that even though computer teachers get high ratings from their students, there are areas in which they could improve, particularly for the benefit of women. However, in other respects that are also said to be important for women—such as caring about the students and having time for them—the teachers, both male and female, scored higher.

The descriptions by Ahrenkiel et al. (1998) and Illeris (2003) of the young generation of adult education students appear to fit the present sample. Ahrenkiel et al. and Illeris characterised young adult students as being consumers of education, who are interested only as long as the education suits their needs. Even in this study, the youngest students were those most dissatisfied with their course. For the young women, this was particularly significant. The results confirm Ahrenkiel's (1998) description of different generations of adult women learners, where older women are described as almost too docile and younger women are much more demanding.

In spite of all the dissatisfaction and the computer competence of the young students, however, the course seems to have been useful—especially since these students stated, more than others, that they would probably use the computer in new ways. Thus, although they might not increase the time spent on computers, which was already high, they would find new ways to benefit from the computer.

The differences between the young women and their male peers indicate that gender issues in computer education prevail also in this age group, even though there is no significant difference in the degree of computer use in the age group. Computers are still more foreign to young women than to young men, particularly when it comes to hardware and having, or using, the competence to help others. Young women do find a computer course more difficult than young men, and feel more uneasy on the course. Irrespective of whether these are "actual" differences or whether they depend on women and men using different scales to evaluate themselves, there is a problem indicating

that gender inequality regarding computers and computer education still prevails.

ACKNOWLEDGMENT

I want to thank the *KK-Foundation* (*The Knowledge Foundation of Sweden*), its research programme *LearnIT*, and *GLIT,* its *network for research on Gender, Learning and IT,* for its financial support of the research on which this chapter is based.

REFERENCES

Ahrenkiel, A., Illeris, K., Sederberg, M.-L., & Simonsen, B. (1998). *Voksenuddannelse og deltagermotivation. (Adult education and participant motivation).* Roskilde, Denmark: Roskilde Universitetsforlag.

Assarsson, L., & Sipos-Zackrisson, K. (2006). Att delta i vuxenstudier. In Larsson, S., & Olsson, L. E. (Eds.), *Om vuxnas studier. (On adult studies).* Lund, Sweden: Studentlitteratur.

Bozionelos, N. (2001). Computer anxiety: relationship with computer experience and prevalence. *Computers in Human Behavior, 17*(2), 213–224. doi:10.1016/S0747-5632(00)00039-X

Broos, A., & Roe, K. (2006). The digital divide in the playstation generation: Self-efficacy, locus of control and ICT adoption among adolescents. *Poetics, 34*(4/5), 306–317. doi:10.1016/j.poetic.2006.05.002

Brosnan, M., & Lee, W. (1998). A cross-cultural comparison of gender differences in computer attitudes and anxieties. The United Kingdom and Hong Kong. *Computers in Human Behavior, 14*(4), 559–577. doi:10.1016/S0747-5632(98)00024-7

Clift, R. T., Mullen, L., Levin, J., & Larson, A. (2001). Technologies in contexts: implications for teacher education. *Teaching and Teacher Education*, *17*, 33–50. doi:10.1016/S0742-051X(00)00037-8

Colley, A., & Comber, C. (2003). Age and gender differences in computer use and attitudes among secondary school students, what has changed? *Educational Research, 45*(2), 155–165. doi:10.1080/0013188032000103235

Compeau, D. R., & Higgins, C. A. (1995). Computer self-efficacy: Development of a measure and initial test. *Management Information Systems Quarterly, 19*(2), 189–211. doi:10.2307/249688

Cooper, J. (2006). The digital divide: the special case of gender. *Journal of Computer Assisted Learning, 22*(5), 320–334. doi:10.1111/j.1365-2729.2006.00185.x

Cooper, J., & Weaver, K. D. (2003). *Gender and Computers: Understanding the digital divide.* Mahwah, NJ: Erlbaum.

Corneliussen, H. (2003). Male positioning strategies in relation to computing. In Lie, M. (Ed.), *He, she and IT revisited. New perspectives on Gender in the Information society* (pp. 103–134). Olso, Norway: Gyldendal.

Crossan, B., Field, J., Gallagher, J., & Merrill, B. (2003). Understanding participation in learning for non-traditional adult learners: learning careers and the construction of learning identities. *British Journal of Sociology of Education, 24*(1), 55–67. doi:10.1080/01425690301907

Edwards, P. N. (1990). The army and the microworld. Computers and the politics of gender identity. *Signs: Journal of Women in Culture and Society, 16*(1), 102–127. doi:10.1086/494647

Faulkner, W., & Kleif, T. (2003). Edinburgh women's training course: An old idea still working. In Lie, M., & Sörensen, K. H. (Eds.), *Strategies of Inclusion: Gender in the Information Society (Vol. I,* pp. 201–236). Trondheim, Norway: NTNU, Centre for Technology and Society.

Fidishun, D. (2001). Listening to our side. Computer training issues of middle age and older women. *Women's Studies Quarterly, 29*(3), 103–127.

Fuller, L., & Meiners, E. (2005). Reflections. Empowering women, technology and (feminist) institutional changes. *Frontiers, 26*(1), 168–180. doi:10.1353/fro.2005.0009

Fürst, G. (2004). *Slutrapport från GIT-projektet. Genus, integration och teknologi – pedagogiskt nytänkande när 22 kvinnor utbildar sig till nätverksutvecklare. (Final report from the GIT project. Gender, integration and technology – educational innovation when 22 women study to become network developers).* Halmstad, Sweden: Högskolan i Halmstad.

Gansmo, H. J., Lagesen, V. A., & Sörensen, K. H. (2003). Forget the hacker? A critical re-appraisal of Norwegian studies of gender and ICT. In Lie, M. (Ed.), *He, She and IT Revisited. New Perspectives on Gender in the Information Society* (pp. 34–68). Oslo, Norway: Gyldendal.

Green, E., & Keeble, L. (2001). The technological story of a women's centre. A feminist model of user-centred design. In Keeble, L. (Ed.), *Community Informatics* (pp. 53–70). Florence, KY: Routledge.

Hägerström, J. (2004). Vi och dom och alla dom andra på Komvux. Etnicitet, genus och klass i samspel.(We and them and all the others at Komvux: The interplay of ethnicity, gender and class.) Lund, Sweden: Lunds universitet, Sociologiska institutionen.

Hargittai, E., & Shafer, S. (2006). Differences in actual and perceived online skills: the role of gender. *Social Science Quarterly*, *87*(2), 432–448. doi:10.1111/j.1540-6237.2006.00389.x

Hartzel, K. (2003). How self-efficacy and gender issues affect software adoption and use. *Communications of the ACM*, *46*(9), 167–171. doi:10.1145/903893.903933

Hayes, E. (2000). Social Contexts. In Hayes, E., & Flannery, D. D. (Eds.), *Women as Learners. The Significance of Gender in Adult Learning* (pp. 23–52). San Francisco: Jossey-Bass.

Hayes, E., & Flannery, D. D. (Eds.). (2000). *Women as Learners. The Significance of Gender in Adult Learning*. San Francisco: Jossey-Bass.

Illeris, K. (2003). Adult education as experienced by the learners. *International Journal of Lifelong Education*, *22*(1), 13–23. doi:10.1080/02601370304827

Jenson, J., & Rose, C. B. (2003). Women@ work: listening to gendered relations of power in teachers' talk about new technologies. *Gender and Education*, *15*(2), 169–181. doi:10.1080/09540250303854

Jubas, K., Butterwick, S., Zhu, H., & Liptrot, J. (2006). Learning a living: practices and recognition of women's on-the-job and informal learning in the information technology field. *Journal of Vocational Education and Training*, *58*(4), 483–496. doi:10.1080/13636820601005867

Kleif, T., & Faulkner, W. (2003). 'I'm no athlete but I can make this thing dance!' Men's pleasures in technology. *Science, Technology & Human Values*, *28*(2), 296–325. doi:10.1177/0162243902250908

Lagesen, V. A. (2003). Advertising computer science to women (or was it the other way around?). In Lie, M. (Ed.), *He, she and IT revisited. New perspectives on Gender in the Information society* (pp. 69–102). Olso, Norway: Gyldendal.

Lie, M. (1998). *Computer dialogues: Technology, Gender and Change*. Trondheim, Norway: NTNU.

(2003). InLie, M., & Sörensen, K. H. (Eds.). Strategies of Inclusion: Gender in the Information Society.: *Vol. 1. Experiences from public sector initiatives*. Trondheim, Norway: NTNU.

Lior, K., D'Aarcy, M., & Morais, A. (2001). *Tacit skills, informal knowledge and reflective practice*. (NALL Working Paper, 24). Toronto, Canada: University of Toronto, Ontario Institute for Studies in Education.

MacKeogh, C. (2003). The Cork institute of Technology and Fasttrack to IT. Initiatives for the lone parents and the longterm unemployed. In Lie, M., & Sörensen, K. H. (Eds.), *Strategies of Inclusion: Gender in the Information Society* (*Vol. I*, pp. 419–438). Trondheim, Norway: NTNU, Centre for Technology and Society.

Marcoulides, G. A. (1989). Measuring computer anxiety. The computer anxiety scale. *Educational and Psychological Measurement*, *49*(3), 733–739. doi:10.1177/001316448904900328

Marcoulides, G. A., Stocker, Y.-O., & Marcoulides, L. D. (2004). Examining the psychological impact of computer technology. An updated cross-cultural study. *Educational and Psychological Measurement*, *64*(2), 311–318. doi:10.1177/0013164403258451

Margolis, J., & Fisher, A. (2002). *Unlocking the clubhouse. Women in computing*. Cambridge, MA: MIT Press.

Rogers, A. (2005). Lifelong learning and the absence of gender. *International Journal of Educational Development, 26*(2), 189–208. doi:10.1016/j.ijedudev.2005.07.025

Rommes, E. (2003). 'I don't know how to fit it into my life'. Courses, computers and the internet for 'everybody' in Amsterdam. In Lie, M., & Sörensen, K. H. (Eds.), *Strategies of Inclusion: Gender in the Information Society* (*Vol. I*, pp. 151–166). Trondheim, Norway: NTNU, Centre for Technology and Society.

Rommes, E., Faulkner, W., & van Slooten, I. (2005). Changing Lives. The case for women-only vocational technology training revisited. *Journal of Vocational Education and Training, 57*(3), 293–218. doi:10.1080/13636820500200288

Selwyn, N. (1997). Teaching information technology for the 'computer shy': a theoretical perspective on a practical problem. *Journal of Vocational Education and Training, 49*(3), 395–408. doi:10.1080/13636829700200023

Skolverket (2006). *Beskrivande data. Förskoleverksamhet, skolbarnomsorg, skola och vuxenutbildning.* Rapport 283 (Descriptive data: Pre-school, out of school care, school and adult education. Report 283). Stockholm, Sweden: Skolverket.

Statistics Sweden. (2002). *Dator och Internet i hemmet. (Computers and internet in the home)* Retrieved July 8, 2007, from http://www.scb.se/statistik/LE/LE0101/1976I02/LE0101_1976I02_BR_10_LE103SA0401.pdf

Statistics Sweden. (2003). *Tid för vardagsliv. Kvinnors och mäns tidsanvändning 1990/91 och 2000/01.* (Time for everyday life. Women's and men's use of time 1990/91 and 2000/01) Stockholm: Statistiska centralbyrån (SCB) Retrieved May, 29, 2009, from http://www.scb.se/statistik/LE/LE0103/2003M00/LE99SA0301.pdf.

Statistics Sweden. (2006). *Levnadsförhållanden. Undersökningarna av levnadsförhållanden. Tillgång till samt användning av dator på fritiden 1994-2006.* (Living conditions: Studies of living conditions. Access to and use of computers in leisure time) Retrieved July 7, 2007, from http://www.scb.se/templates/tableOrChart____207316.asp.

Statistics Sweden. (2007). *Utbildningsstatistisk årsbok 2007* Stockholm: Statistics Sweden. Retrieved July 7, 2007, from http://www.scb.se/statistik/_publikationer/UF0524_2007A01_BR_11_UF0106TAB.pdf

Statistics Sweden. (2009a) *Statistikdatabasen.* Datoranvändning bland privatpersoner 16-74 år efter kön, ålder och hur ofta man använt persondator (urvalsundersökning). År 2003-2008. (Statistical database. Computer usage among private individuals 16-74 years of age, according to gender, age and frequency of use of personal computers (A selective study) 2003-2008). Retrieved June 1, 2009, from www.scb.se.

Statistics Sweden. (2009b) *Statistikdatabasen.* Internetanvändning bland privatpersoner 16-74 år (andel) efter kön, ålder, hur ofta man använt Internet och tid. År 2003-2008. (Statistical database. Internet use among private individuals 16-74 years of age, according to gender, age and frequency and length of internet usage) Retrieved June 1, from www.scb.se

Upitis, R. (1998). From hackers to luddites, game players to game creators: profiles of adolescent students using technology. *Journal of Curriculum Studies, 30*(3), 293–318. doi:10.1080/002202798183620

Volman, M., van Eck, E., Heemskerk, I., & Kuiper, E. (2005). New technologies, new differences. Gender and ethnic differences in pupils' use of ICT in primary and secondary education. *Computers & Education, 45*(1), 35–55. doi:10.1016/S0360-1315(04)00072-7

Ware, M. C., & Stuck, M. F. (1985). Sex-role messages vis-à-vis microcomputer use: a look at the pictures. *Sex Roles, 13*(3-4), 215–228. doi:10.1007/BF00287911

Weil, M. M., & Rosen, L. D. (1995). The psychological impact of technology from a global perspective – A study of technological sophistication and technophobia in university students from 23 countries. *Computers in Human Behavior, 11*(1), 95–133. doi:10.1016/0747-5632(94)00026-E

Wilson, K. R., Wallin, J. S., & Reiser, C. (2003). Social stratification and the digital divide. *Social Science Computer Review, 21*(2), 133–143. doi:10.1177/0894439303021002001

Wistedt, I. (Ed.). (2000). Datateknisk ingång för kvinnor. En utvärdering. (The computer engineering entrance for women: An evaluation) Teknisk rapport/ Luleå tekniska universitet; 2000:15. Luleå, Sweden: Luleå tekniska universitet.

Zohar, A. (2006). Connected knowledge in science and mathematics education. *International Journal of Science Education, 28*(13), 1579–159. doi:10.1080/09500690500439199

KEY TERMS AND DEFINITIONS

Adult Education: Non-compulsory education for individuals older than the ordinary secondary school age, normally compensating for missed primary or secondary school or providing more general and practical skills and knowledge than higher education (which in this article is not regarded as part of adult education).

Adult Education Centre: In this article, a public organizer of a number adult education courses on a municipal level. Commonly, but not always, even a building where the courses are taught.

Computer Student: In this paper, a person participating in a basic computer course, arranged by an adult education centre.

Computer Attitudes: In this article, a range of positive and negative emotions towards computers and computing. Positive computer attitudes correlate to some extent with computer interest.

Computer Interest: The propensity to use and learn to use computers for different purposes. Correlates to some extent with computer use – the difference arising for example from the practical possibilities for computer use.

Computer Use: The actual use of computers for different tasks. A crude measure is the amount of time spent at a computer.

Gender: Here, basically biological sex. This article does not pay regard to the fact that biological women and biological men can adopt a range of different positions in relation to what is regarded as masculine and feminine.

Gendered: Here, refers to a difference between men and women

Self-Esteem: Favourable appreciation or opinion of oneself (Oxford English dictionary) In this paper primarily the appreciation of one's ability to learn about and use computers and, thus, to large degree synonymous with computer self-efficacy = "individuals' beliefs about their abilities to competently use computers" (Compeau & Higgins, 1995).

ENDNOTES

1   Following the usage which is gaining ground in English in the research literature, even in this paper, when referring to the sample of the study, gender equals biological sex. I am critical of this usage, as I think there are several useful points that can be made by separating the way people do masculinity and femininity (gender) from their biological sex. However, such points are not made in this analysis of the material, and so I adopt the present convention.

2   I have no official figures on what kind of computer courses students in adult education

attend, but in my discussions with teachers in computer courses in adult education I have been told that men more often than women go to higher level courses. If that is true, the female dominance in the basic level courses that this study deals with is even higher than 70%.

Section 5
Digital Learning

Chapter 13
Gendered Knowledge Production in Universities in a Web 2.0 World

Gill Kirkup
Open University, UK

ABSTRACT

This chapter examines the access women have had historically to engage in knowledge production as university scholars or students. It discusses the changing nature of knowledge production in universities, and the impact of some Web 2.0 tools on this activity. It asks, through a detailed discussion of wikis and blogging if Web 2.0 tools can challenge the traditional gendering of university knowledge production,.

INTRODUCTION

Universities, traditionally, have been concerned principally with two main functions: research or the production of knowledge, and teaching or its dissemination and acquisition. Universities are, and have been historically, the central knowledge institutions of the modern state, although significantly, they pre-date the development of the nation- state. (Peters, 2007, p 21)

This chapter is concerned with gender and the knowledge production function of universities. Phrases

like the 'knowledge economy' the 'knowledge society' and 'knowledge workers' are familiar twenty first century concepts in discussions about the role of education, and higher education in particular. Digital technologies have been important drivers of the knowledge society (Castells, 2000), where the production and exchange of knowledge is a major economic activity and they have been a force for change in universities. Political forces challenge universities to provide wider access to a larger proportion of the population; this is sometimes called 'massification'. Ideological forces, in particular the commodification of knowledge, put an emphasis on efficiency and quantifiable measures of quality in the production and distribution of knowledge (Lyotard, 1984; Delanty, 1998; Peters, 2007), and

DOI: 10.4018/978-1-61520-813-5.ch013

have had a dramatic impact on the work of scholars and researchers. Technological forces in the form of digital tools and systems to support learning, scholarship, research and assessment, are drivers for change and support political and ideological forces. Digital technologies have been seen as the tools to enable economies of scale in research and teaching and to measure outputs of various kinds (Kirkup, 2009). There is little gender analysis of these changes and in particular of the impact of what are known as Web 2.0 technologies on the social role of universities as creators, defenders and disseminators of knowledge. This is surprising given the radical critiques of higher education by feminist academics in the later years of the twentieth century.

Feminist scholars have criticized universities as being historically gendered places of knowledge production, and for producing gendered knowledge (May, 2008). In the last fifty years universities have changed the gendered composition of their students and workforce. Academia is now a more welcoming profession for women. The increasing numbers of women working in universities (see HESA, 2008 for UK universities), as well as the fact that in the USA and Europe women make up over 50% of university students, has contributed to the notion of the 'feminization of education'; a criticism that higher education is now an activity that appeals to women and girls rather than to men and boys[1]. Is it possible that the increase in numbers of women, plus the opportunities provided by new digital forms of knowledge production, are creating a feminization of knowledge production, or at least a challenge to the hegemonic male activity of university knowledge production?

This chapter looks particularly at Web 2.0 applications that might offer ways to create and share knowledge; ways which support the ideals of critical and feminist pedagogy (see Kirkup et al, 2010), and challenge gendered knowledge production (Harding, 1991, Haraway, 1997) It looks in particular at 'wikis' and 'blogs', asking: Who is engaged in using these tools and how are they used?

THE STRUGGLE FOR THE POWER TO KNOW

Universities are places where knowledge is created through research and scholarship, and also through the interaction that students have with subject content, with each other and with subject experts. Knowledge production is not simply the job of salaried scholars and researchers, although it is their role to lead and direct this activity. Students are active creators of knowledge when they interact with, and come to be expert in, a discipline area. Proponents of the social construction of knowledge argue that knowledge production is a group process:

'*Together, members construct and negotiate a shared meaning, bringing the process of the group along collectively rather than individually. In the process, they become what the literary critic Stanley Fish [1980] calls a "community of interpretation" working towards a shared understanding of the matter under discussion.*'(Brown and Duguid, 2000, p 222)

Theorists such as Brown et al (1989) who argue that it is from our own embodied experience that we use 'situated reasoning' to make meaning for ourselves and for others echo feminist writing about knowledge creation (Haraway, 1997, Harding, 1991). Haraway (1997) argues that historically not only bodily attributes of gender, but of race, class and language has defined who can validly 'know' about the world. She studied early modern scientific practices and noted that the authority to be a 'witness' of a scientific process, to record it and discuss it in professional circles was restricted to a peer group of upper class men. Feminist theory of the body – as a material object (Haraway's cyborg, 1985), as a social actor (Harding's situated knower, 1991), as a set of discursive practices (Butler's performative actor, 1999) and as a material system (Barad, 2003) has always seen embodiment as centrally involved in the production of gendered knowledge. Bodies produce knowledge and the meaning we make is inescapably located in them. Gender is inscribed on our bodies, it is produced in the interactions our bodies with human and non-human others, and our bodies are, for others, always gendered signs. We are all gendered knowledge makers.

Professional researchers and scholars have the authority through their work to change the content of knowledge for the rest of the world. They are officially accredited to speak as experts, and they have membership of influential professional organizations that determine the content of a field or discipline and its theories and its practices. It is because of this, as well as the more commonly acknowledged benefits such as accrediting entry level knowledge for professions, that it is so important that no group in society is excluded from university. The excluded are not only excluded from learning, they are denied the power to make knowledge. By the second half of the twentieth century, women and other groups new to university education challenged the knowledge that universities produced, and it was in this context that a space opened for women's studies and gender studies to challenge the content and the methodology of disciplines

In 2007 (the latest available data at the time of writing) women averaged 55.2% of the total population of university students across 27 European Union countries (Eurostat, 2009), this is still lower than the figure for the USA where women were 57.3% of students for the same year. But historically universities have been elite male organisations. The elite men who went there both produced and consumed knowledge. In eighteenth and nineteenth century England, Oxford and Cambridge aimed to produce gentlemen and clerics; and new institutions were established at the end of the nineteenth century to teach applied arts and sciences. In France the Grande Ecoles were basically research institutions, where elite men were educated in order to take up roles as senior civil servants. In Germany (Prussia), elite students learned to be 'spiritual' leaders of a newly emerging nation; they embodied Humboldt's idea of 'Bildung', the cultivation of the whole (male) person – combining liberal arts as well as science. In all these countries nineteenth century universities provided important ideological and technocratic bases for the growing European Nation States. American universities, in the same period, were concerned to build a new national identity: one based on a relationship with civil society rather than with an elite (Delanty, 2001). These universities were not homes for radical thinking. Radicals, including all the women intellectuals of the their times (such as Mary Wollstonecraft, 1792), worked outside universities as authors and self-financed intellectuals, often excluded from professional accreditation, practice and remuneration.

In the second half of the twentieth century, universities became tools for social integration. They acquired a social mission to make knowledge available to all – or all who merited it – rather than for an already existing elite. 'Credentialising' this meritocracy became more important than ever, and for the first time large numbers of women obtained qualifications that gave them access to careers and professions. Governments also saw universities as core state institutions for the production of commercial knowledge, and funding for this activity increased both from the state and from commercial organizations. In a globalised network society (Castells, 2000, 2001) the nature of the internet, i.e. to allow anyone with access to the technology to create and disseminate content, is seen by many as providing the biggest challenge to the role of universities as creators, defenders, disseminators and accreditors of knowledge since their inception. Knowledge making has always been a restricted privilege, even within universities. Much of the worry about the future of universities is about the possible removal of this activity elsewhere, and the loss of the traditional academic values of 'truth' and 'disinterested' research (Delanty, 2001, Webster, 2001 Robins and Webster, 1999). It seems that networked digital communications, in particular the content generation possibilities of Web 2.0 could allow students and others outside accredited universities and professional bodies to publish their ideas in ways previously restricted to accredited experts: to make new knowledge. With the increased numbers of women scholars and students working in universities is there any need to for continued concern that the knowledge universities are making might be gendered?

The influx of women into universities in the 1970s brought with it a challenge to established disciplines through the development of gender studies as a critical discipline and of feminist pedagogy elaborated as a new way of teaching. Feminist pedagogy blended ideas from the radical liberatory pedagogy of Paulo Freire, with ideas coming out of a gender critique of psychology. Freirian pedagogy included the student as an expert in their own lives, and involved a critical engagement with subject experts who are potentially contributing to systems of oppression. Education in this model is primarily about empowerment, but not of an individual in a neoliberal sense - as someone free to make choices and optimize their personal potential - but as an individual indissolubly a member of a group or class whose empowerment depends on the empowerment of the group. For Freire the terms teachers and students are interchangeable with 'leaders' and 'people':

'Teachers and students (leadership and people), co-intent on reality, are both Subjects, not only in the task of unveiling that reality and thereby coming to know it critically, but in the task of re-creating that knowledge.' (Freire, 1970online)

This use of personal reflection, and group discussion was combined with a critique of 'male ways of knowing' in books by Belenkey et al (1986) and Gilligan (1982). These authors argued that the systems of moral and intellectual development of psychologists such as Piaget and Kohlberg were gendered. These systems had been developed through observing and then generalizing from the behaviour of young men. Belenky and Gilligan argued that women incorporate other values into their moral and intellectual world that are focused on supporting human relationships and entail an ethic of care, and if these are incorporated into knowledge production they create new and different knowledge.

Although the principles that underpin feminist pedagogy are ideological and political and those underpinning social constructivism and the theory of situated cognition (Brown et al, 1989) are psychological, the model of knowledge as a product of social interaction is very similar. The possibilities provided by digital communication and the explosion of user-generated content (for example the popular web sites such as YouTube, Wikipedia and blogging sites) have challenged universities to incorporate these tools into teaching and learning (Weller, 2007). There is as yet no consistent strategy for their use in (*or for their exclusion from*) knowledge production by scholars and researchers (Borgman, 2007).

KNOWLEDGE MAKING WITH WEB 2.0

Computers have been used for research and scholarship for over half a century. They have developed from computational devices used mainly in the numerical sciences into tools to record and recall, analyze, synthesize and model, data and events. They have become increasingly sophisticated tools to 'think with' (Turkle, 1984), and are now tools which enable us to do our thinking collectively. The newest applications which support this collective activity are labeled 'Web 2.0' to distinguish them from the first generation of internet applications. By the mid 1980s academic computing was no longer a specialist occupation. Researchers and scholars had personal computers on their desks that they used for everyday academic activities such as data analysis and writing. By the 1990s the early internet was offering communication though email and conferencing systems to all academic staff in rich nations.

Soon the 'World Wide Web' was offering content as well as communication. At first this content came from people and organizations who could afford web designers and relatively expensive server systems to make their content available, this was the first generation of web applications. However, technical improvements in hardware and the development of easy to use programming languages in particular XML (extensible markup language) have rapidly expanded the number of different user functions. It is these functions that constitute Web 2.0: in particular the development of social computing and user-generated content. Wesch (2007) asserts that, in the internet, message form and message content have become separated. All web content has become infinitely portable. It can be categorized and organized through the use of tagging: a form of user-generated indexing. Content can be exchanged, or combined ('mashed up') automatically. Wesch argues that the web is effectively a learning machine, learning from what users upload and download, and how they describe (tag and link) this. As well as enabling us to create user generated content the web is about social computing. It presumes individuals want to make contact with others and share digital 'stuff' (for example text, audio or images) and which could be something they have created for themselves, or something created by someone else that they think is worth sharing. Content is in a constant process of development, change and expansion. The web, it is asserted is now our collective intelligence.

Borgman (2007) has explored some of the differences between the traditional systems of scholarly research like book publishing and peer reviewing and those that are needed to make use of newer digital tools. She tended to focus on those digital systems that looked similar to those used in traditional research – archives, databases, and professional online publication media. She discounts a great deal of Web 2.0 content as not useful for scholarship because it is unverifiable. However, it is these newer kinds of social net-

working applications that are the most interesting when thinking about new forms of knowledge production and they offer the greatest challenge to traditional scholarly forms.

Examples of Web 2.0 applications that are in common use for knowledge production inside and outside the university include sites like YouTube which allow sharing of video content. Photographs, music - in fact any kind of content - can be shared through a web site somewhere on the internet. Blogs or weblogs are a Web 2.0 phenomenon, where people or groups can create content in a chronological journal that is made available for others to read and comment on. Blogs potentially offer scholars a new medium through which to discuss their ideas. A Wiki is a different kind of collaborative website that allows a number of people to engage individually in creating, adding and editing content. The collaboratively produced content may remain in a process of constant change and development. Wikipedia is the most well known example of this. Wikis are a clear example of socially constructed knowledge. Blogging and wikis are two applications that will be explored in more detail later, for their challenge to gendered knowledge production

Web 2.0 applications are tools for twenty-first century knowledge creation and knowledge management which challenge previous systems of knowledge creation and control. They challenge conceptions of authorship and authority. Texts are often multi-authored. They are linked to other texts by different authors, which have been published elsewhere, and the links are crucial to the meaning of the text. Authors may choose to be anonymous. There are no gatekeepers to web publishing, no peer review systems; and consequently evaluating the authority of web texts is complex. Web 2.0 content challenges copyright and ownership. The ability to disseminate and reproduce web content has been the cause of a number of law suits, and spurred the development of technologies to both track copied material and delete it. It has also fuelled the growth of the 'open content' movement that is trying to change copyright laws so that ownership of ideas is protected but content is freely available for use. There has been concern in education about plagiarism, and the ease with which people, and students in particular, can copy the work of others and represent it as their own.

Web 2.0 applications challenge privacy. Once a person's name appears somewhere on the web, whether through self-authored content or in the content of others, they lose control over information linked to it. There is a need for everyone to monitor web content that refers to them, and to actively manage it. The nature of web content is to be in a state of constant flux, while at the same time retaining copies of older materials. When this is the case for information about individuals, it challenges the concept of stable and authentic identity. Web content also challenges the concept of authorship, as web authors create personal, anonymous and group content. Managing an online identity (or identities) and the reputation that goes with them is important.

There has been little research on the gendering of Web 2.0 applications, who uses them and how and whether the content they support is gendered. However, the capacity to create knowledge is an exercise of power, and the right to be a knowledge creator must be asserted afresh with every new knowledge creation tool. The next two sections of this chapter examine two of the most significant Web 2.0 activities: blogging and wikis, to see what they might offer for knowledge production that makes visible the operations of gender and power.

Knowledge Making Through Wikis

The form of the wiki came from programs which allow multiple authors to work online with a single text held in one location. The final version of a wiki web page is therefore the product of group knowledge production, but this fact is invisible to the reader who sees only the most recent version. Even those who are co-authoring may not know who the other authors are. Unlike blogs, which are discussed later, most readers of wikis cannot see how the final entry is created; the multiple authors and their different contributions are made invisible.

Scholars and researchers have always produced collective writing; on large projects rather than small, and in some fields more than others. This was done in the past in an iterative fashion, and the possibility of working faster synchronously on the same text is very appealing. Academics have certainly incorporated wikis into student activity as a way to encourage students to produce group products. They have so far been less interested in using them for academic publishing, although many academics do contribute anonymously to large open wikis like Wikipedia. In scholarly publications it remains important to identify individual contributions, both for accountability as well as for professional recognition. Academic debate goes forward by challenging both the ideas and the authors of ideas; and these are located and named by well-recognized referencing systems. There is a concern that without the ability to provenance ideas, and challenge them through dialectic reasoning; what is at work is 'hive mind' (Lanier, 2006), and the result is mediocrity and 'group think'.

'I've participated in a number of elite, well-paid wikis and Meta-surveys lately and have had a chance to observe the results. I have even been part of a wiki about wikis. What I've seen is a loss of insight and subtlety, a disregard for the nuances of considered opinions, and an increased tendency to enshrine the official or normative beliefs of an organization'. (Lanier, 2006, online)

Scott (2004) agrees with Lanier that an apparent burgeoning of web content through wikis is actually disguising the fact that very little new is being created:

'Content creators are relatively rare in this world. Content commentators less so. Content critics are a dime a hundred and content vandals lurk in every doorway.' (Scott, 2004, online)

For most people a wiki is not only about collective knowledge making it is also about free (to the user) knowledge. Wikipedia has spearheaded the 'open content' movement in which anyone can participate in content production; the final (or most recent) product is then made freely available. The theory is that content stabilizes when people stop wanting to correct it. The knowledge in public wikis like Wikipedia is consensus knowledge 'good enough' knowledge (Schiff, 2006), rather than expert knowledge. There were concerns that consensus was not the equivalent of accuracy, and attempts to present balance and neutrality could lead to lack of representation for novel and critical perspectives, and too much recognition of dubious material on the grounds of achieving 'balance' of opinion. This does not seem to have happened to any significant measure. Recent tests of the accuracy of Wikipedia content have shown that this process is at least as accurate in its factual data as an encyclopedia written by experts (Rector, 2008). It does appear that as long as there are active Wikipedia 'citizens' who are willing to spend time checking the content of entries that they have expertise in then Wikipedia will be both up to date and reliable. However in 2009 (Coleman, 2009) it became known that Wikipedia employees were actively editing and censoring the content of the pages about the US President, and questions were again raised about how far Wikipedia was a self governing community. Traditional publication methods, through expert peer systems attempt to make transparent issues of censorship and conflict over content. The operation of wikis makes this much less transparent for the reader.

What are the Affordances of Wikis for Challenging the Gendering of Knowledge Production?

Wikis have a number of problems for anyone wanting to use them to make visible the ways in which knowledge becomes biased towards some sets of ideas and some kinds of knowledge makers. Although wikis facilitate the collaborative construction of knowledge they make the processes of content production and authorship invisible to those who only access the product. Their capacity to connect ideas across websites through internal links enriches content, but does not necessarily challenge the previous problem in traditional publishing of individuals citing the work of friends and allies, to the exclusion of others. Wikis raise questions about the relationship between content and authorship. No author can own a wiki's content, and no author can therefore guarantee its content. Wikis will always be in the process of development and change by others. A wiki is not the place to create new knowledge expressly situated in an individual context or an embodied in individual experience. It is quite the opposite of situated, and embodied knowledge – it is distributed or apparently disembodied (or multiple) bodied knowledge. It is therefore not an obvious tool to challenge gendered knowledge production.

Knowledge Making Through Blogging

The activity of blogging is now widespread. It began with the creation of a simple program that allowed anyone, without programming skills, to write in a chronological journal style and have their content uploaded to a public website, where it could be read by others. The program allowed readers to add comments, so that a blog became an interactive journal or record. Since blogging was recognized as an identifiable activity in the 1990s, many forms of blogging have developed;

the most recent, micro-blogging, involves the posting, and broadcasting of small amounts of text (as in Twitter) or images to a group of 'subscribers'. However, it is the activity of creating and publishing longer pieces of content in blogs that is discussed here because it is in this kind of blogging that the nature of academic knowledge production is the most clear.

Blogs fall into two main kinds: personal journals and 'expert filters'. The personal journal is closest to traditional diary writing. It is a genre of reflective writing and usually contains a strong textual identity of the author. Personal journal blogs such as that of Salam Pax the Baghdad Blogger (Pax, 2003) become popular because they give readers privileged access to events, or privileged access to insightful reflections on aspects of life. An expert filter is a blog which aggregates information from other websites, often using the technology of an RSS (really simple syndication) feed to automatically collect new postings from other blogs and websites. It serves its readers by bringing together a selection of sources about a particular topic that the blog author is interested/expert in. Both kinds of blog are clearly very personalized knowledge creation. Readers understand and trust them, and many have become highly influential, so much so that commercial organizations now use blogging for marketing 'conversations' with customers (Scoble and Israel, 2006). As well as students and scholars writing blogs, some universities have heeded Scoble's advice and started institutional blogs. In the university where I work an institutional blog called 'Platform'[2] has been set up on the university's public website. It aggregates selected student blogs and also recruits subject specialist scholars to write about newsworthy items of the day. It functions as an expert aggregator, a social platform and a web magazine.

Saper (2006) was the first to categorise academic blogging as being a particular genre of blogging which he labeled 'Blogademia'. Academic bloggers, he argued, did not see blogging as part of the production of knowledge in their disciplines because blogs did not go through any peer review or editorial process. Academic blogs he asserted '*often air dirty laundry, gripes, complaints, rants, and raves, what those blogs add to research seems outside scholarship*' (Saper, 2006, online). This kind of writing makes visible the social processes of knowledge production. Blogs he asserted were one of the future tools of academia. Walker (2006) in her research identified three genres of academic blog: public intellectuals, research logs, and pseudonymous blogs about academic life. She speculated about whether blogs were a good medium to popularise research. Gregg (2009) has more recently examined the public blogs of a number of post-graduate students and young academics using Walker's categories. She sees these particular academic blogs as an expression of a subculture, of people who are struggling to make a life in their chosen careers as scholars and researchers. This kind of blogging contains the potential for a radical critique of academic knowledge production because it is engaged in examining and critiquing the role and function of the academy and the employment practices within it.

Blogging has also been described as a Foucauldian 'technology of the self' (Lovink, 2008), and since academics (and students) are engaged in the continuous development of a professional 'self', blogging could play a significant role in such professional identity creation. In many institutions students are required as part of their course activities to keep blogs as a form of reflective journal. This activity is much less popular as an activity for academic staff, and it is not yet accepted fully as valid scholarly knowledge production. There is still a stress on traditional forms of publication as the main product of academic activity (or academic performativity) which also ignores the fact that academics produce a variety of other, interrelated products using various media. Borgman (2007) in her book on scholarship in the digital age, discounts blogging on the first page where she lists it with other ' "*stuff*" – *the unverified and unverifiable statements of individuals, discussions on listservs ... questionable advertisements for questionable products and services, and political and religious screeds in all languages.*' (Borgman, 2007, p 1). She contrasts this "stuff" with 'the *substantial portion of online content [that] is extremely valuable for scholarship*'. However, as productivity measures increasingly look for 'impact', more academics are likely to see blogging as offering the potential for their ideas to have more impact than through traditional academic publication routes.

Blogging is particularly interesting because it is one of the few areas of Web 2.0 content creation that have been argued to be particularly accessible to women's working and writing styles. Journal writing has been described as a women's genre (Heilbrun, 1988), contrasted with scientific writing, which along with other aspects of scientific practice (Haraway, 1997) has been classified as a masculine genre, traditionally produced by men, and associated with rationality and objectivity rather than reflection (Tillery, 2005). Can blogging provide the tool for producing what Helene Cixous (Sellers, 1994) called 'écriture feminine': the act of writing which creates not only new knowledge about gender but a new 'feminine'; a new way of using language to create different knowledge about the world?

Argomon and Koppel (2007) carried out a textual analysis of some thousands of blogs using an automated tool called 'Gender Genie' which classified texts as 'masculine' or 'feminine' depending on features of the style. Blog text which was classified in the research as being in a female style was seen as being more interactive and those in a masculine style as more informative. Female bloggers demonstrated styles which suggested that they were more interpersonally involved with their content and their readers, and male bloggers used a more informative style. However Argomon and Koppel suggest that interactivity and informativity are properties of genres of blogs those

which were journals had a more female style, and blogs which were expert filters had a more masculine style. When groups interact online the composition of the group can influence the style of writing produced. Herring and Paolillo (2006) found that an analysis otexts produced by contributors to online forums indicated that participants on female-majority lists tend to employ female stylistic features, and participants on male-majority lists tend to employ male stylistic features, regardless of their sex. So it appears that men and women can adopt different styles to fit in with the group norm. However, in order to have a group norm in which female styles of writing are preferred or even acceptable there needs to be a significant mass of women writing.

Despite these possibilities for women to create knowledge though blogs that use a genre that they may find more comfortable than others, it is still the case that most 'A' list blogs in the Technorati top 100 blogs[3] are male.

What are the Affordances of Blogging for Challenging the Gendering of Knowledge Production?

Blogs are technically simple tools and many web sites offer free hosting for blogs. Like wikis blogs can include of many features of Web 2.0 allowing for the easy uploading of images, RSS feeds, and links to social sharing sites, and to other content. Students and scholars can find themselves space to publish, outside the structures (and strictures) of an institution if they wish. This offers a freedom for critical and controversial knowledge production, including knowledge production about gender. Blogs are usually individually owned and authored, but even when they are group authored they are accountable spaces. It has been impossible for most bloggers to remain anonymous even when they wished. It is therefore possible to identify the gender of authors and to address this. The possibility of reader comments being published alongside blog postings enables readers to engage with and challenge the content of a blog, while keeping a clear separation between the content creator and commentators,

Blogs provide space for critical reflection, even those that operate mainly as expert filters allow blog owners to comment on the sources they filter. Blogs are generally understood as being part of the genre of diaries and journals, and there is an expectation of subjective writing that is not possible in other kinds of academic publication. It is possible to have a 'private' semi-private blog – that is one that only a select list of subscribers has access to. This allows restricted access and protects the author from harassment or from the premature publication of ideas to the world. A blog also offers the possibility of keeping a long term life-journal or eportfolio, which can provide a scholar with a searchable record the development of projects and ideas, for their own benefit and for sharing with others

Unlike wikis blogs are embodied, designed to be created and owned by individuals, or recognized groups having their roots in the lives and embodied experiences of those who create them. The appear to offer a form of writing sympathetic to traditional female forms of writing and knowledge production, being more subjective and personal. However the statistics about blogs suggest that women have not been as active as men in using them to demonstrate their expertise and engage as public intellectuals.

CONCLUSION

This chapter has discussed the changing nature of knowledge production in universities, and the fact that historically women have not been equally involved in this activity with men. It has looked the impact of some Web 2.0 tools with a particular focus on how they might be used in a way that challenges the traditional gendering of university knowledge production. Blogs, it has been argued have the potential to support a

tradition of 'écriture feminine', grounding it as a reputable form of academic practice. Wikis on the other hand have the danger of making gender invisible in the way they collaboratively construct knowledge so that authorship is disguised - even impossible to ascertain - and in their stress on objectivity and consensus as measures of quality. However, there is no evidence that either of these Web 2.0 activities is having a significant impact on the gendered inequality of university knowledge production. It would seem that women scholars have become successful in the more traditional knowledge production medium of print, but they have yet to compete equally with men in the newer Web 2.0 media.

We are in a rapidly changing environment with respect to knowledge production. Universities struggle to get access the funding necessary to allow them to employ staff with the time to the do research and scholarship necessary for knowledge production. They find themselves competing as authoritative knowledge producers with commercial organizations and with 'amateur' experts who use the web to share and distribute their knowledge beyond any system of quality assurance such as those in place in academic and professional work. So this would be an opportune moment for those of us working on gender issues to identify the opportunities as well as threats that have been created by Web 2.0 tools, for us to continue, with our students, to create knowledge about gender and make visible the role of gender in knowledge creation.

ACKNOWLEDGMENT

Thank you to the GLIT Research Network for providing me with the opportunity of presenting an earlier version of this paper at the *Symposium on Gender, Learning and IT*, organized in Helsingborg, August 2007 as part of the activities of the *GLIT Research Network.* This network and symposium received support from *the KK-Foundation*

(The Knowledge Foundation of Sweden) and its research programme *LearnIT*.

REFERENCES

Argamon, S., Koppel, M., Pennebaker, J. W., & Schler, J. (2007). Mining the Blogosphere. Age, gender and the variety of self expression [Electronic Version]. *First Monday, 12*, 2007. Retrieved from http://firstmonday.org/01.09.2009.

Barad, K. (2003). Posthumanist Performativity: Toward an Understanding of How Matter Comes to Matter. *Signs, 28*(3), 801–831. doi:10.1086/345321

Belenky, M. F., Goldberger, N. R., & Tarule, J. M. (Eds.). (1986). *Women's ways of knowing: the development of self, voice, and mind*. New York: Basic Books.

Borgman, C. L. (2007). *Scholarship in the Digital Age. Information, Infrastructure and the Internet*. Cambridge, MA: MIT Press.

Brown, J. S., Collins, A., & Duguid, P. (1989). Situated cognition and the culture of learning. *Educational Researcher, 18*(1), 32–42.

Brown, J. S., & Duguid, P. (2000). *The social life of information*. Boston, MA: Harvard Business School Press.

Butler, J. (1999). *Gender Trouble. Feminism and the Subversion of Identity* (2nd ed.). London: Routledge.

Castells, M. (2000). *The rise of the network society* (2nd ed.). Oxford, UK: Blackwell.

Castells, M. (2001). *The Internet galaxy: reflections on the Internet, business, and society*. New York: Oxford University Press.

Coleman, M. (2009, March 10). Barack Obama 'receives preferential treatment on Wikipedia', report claims. *Telegraph newspaper,* London

Delanty, G. (2001). *Challenging knowledge: the university in the knowledge society. Milton Keynes*. UK: Open University Press.

Eurostat. (2009). Share of women among tertiary students. Retrieved August 20, 2009, 2009, from http://epp.eurostat.ec.europa.eu/

Freire, P. (1970). *Pedagogy of the Oppressed*. London: Penguin. Online version retrieved August 20, 2009, from http://www.marxists.org/subject/education/freire/pedagogy

Gilligan, C. (1982). *In a different voice: psychological theory and women's development*. Cambridge, MA: Harvard University Press.

Gregg, M. (2009). Banal Bohemia: Blogging from the Ivory Tower Hot-desk. *Convergence, 15*, 4.

Haraway, D. (1985). A manifesto for cyborgs: Science, technology, and social feminism in the 1980s. *Socialist Review, 15*(80), 65–107.

Haraway, D. J. (1997). *Modest_Wintess@Second Millenium.FemaleMan_Meets_Onco-Mouse*. London: Routledge.

Harding, S. (1991). *Whose science? Whose knowledge? Thinking from women's lives*. Buckingham, UK: Open University Press.

Heilbrun, C. G. (1988). *Writing a Woman's Life*. New York: Ballantine Books.

Herring, S. C., & Paolillo, J. C. (2006). Gender and genre variation in weblogs. *Journal of Sociolinguistics, 10*(4), 439–459. doi:10.1111/j.1467-9841.2006.00287.x

HESA. (2008). *Resources of Higher Education Institutions 2006/07*. Retrieved August 20, 2009, from http://www.hesa.ac.uk/

Kevin Robins, F. W. (1999). *Times of the technoculture: from the information society to the virtual life*. London: Routledge.

Kirkup, G. (2009). Flying under the radar: The importance of small scale e-learning innovation within large-scale institutional e-learning implementation. In Stansfield, M., & Connolly, T. (Eds.), *Institutional Transformation through Best Practices in Virtual Campus Development: Advancing e-learning policies* (pp. 81–95). Hershey, PA: IGI Global.

Kirkup, G., Schmitz, S., Kotkamp, E., Rommes, E., & Aino-Maija Hiltunen. (2010). Towards a feminist manifesto for e-learning. In S. Booth, S. Goodman & G. Kirkup (Eds.), *Gender Issues in Learning and Working with Information Technology: Social Constructs and Cultural Contexts*. Hershey, PA: IGI Global.

Lanier, J. (2006). Digital Maoism: the Hazards of the new Online Collectivism [Electronic Version]. *Edge. The Third Culture*. Retrieved August 20, 2007 from http://www.edge.org/3rd_culture/lanier06/lanier06_index.html

Lovink, G. (2008). *Zero Comments. Blogging and Critical internet culture*. London: Routledge.

Lyotard, J. F. (1984). *The postmodern condition: a report on knowledge*. Manchester, UK: Manchester UP.

May, A. M. (2008). Gender and the political economy of knowledge. In Bettio, F., & Verashchagina, A. (Eds.), *Frontiers in the Economics of Gender* (pp. 267–285). London: Routledge.

Pax, S. (2003). *The Baghdad Blog*. London: Guardian Books.

Peters, M. A. (2007). Higher Education, Globalisation and the Knowledge Economy: Reclaiming the Cultural Mission [Electronic Version]. *Ubiquity, 8*.

Phillips, M. (2002, August 19). *The feminisation of education*. London: Daily Mail, Rector, L. H. (2008). Comparison of Wikipedia and other encyclopaedias for accuracy, breadth, and depth in historical articles [Electronic Version] [from http://www.emeraldinsight.com/]. *RSR. Reference Services Review, 36*, 7–22. Retrieved June 6, 2009.

Robins, K., & Webster, F. (1999). *Times of the Technoculture: Information, Communication and the Technological Ord*. London: Routledge.

Saper, C. (2006). Blogademia. *Reconstruction, 6*(4), 1–15.

Schiff, S. (2006). *Know it all. Can Wikipedia conquer expertise?* New Yorker, 31.07.2006

Scoble, R., & Israel, S. (2006). *Naked Conversations. How blogs are changing the way businesses talk with customers*. Hoboken, NJ: John Wiley and Sons.

Scott, J. (2004, November 19). The Great Failure of Wikipedia. *ASCII*. Retrieved August 20, 2007, from http://ascii.textfiles.com/archives/000060.html

Sellers, S. (Ed.). (1994). *The Helene Cixous Reader*. London: Routledge.

Tillery, D. (2005). The plain style in the seventeenth century: gender and the history of scientific discourse. *Journal of Technical Writing and Communication, 35*(3), 273–289. doi:10.2190/MRQQ-K2U6-LTQU-0X56

Turkle, S. (1984). The second self: computers and the human spirit. London: Granada.

Walker, J. (2006). Blogging from Inside the Ivory Tower. In Bruns, A., & Jacobs, J. (Eds.), *Uses of Blogs* (pp. 127–138). New York: Peter Lang.

Webster, F. (2001). The postmodern university? the Loss of Purpose in British Universities. In Lax, S. (Ed.), *Access Denied in the Information Age* (pp. 69–92). Hampshire, UK: Palgrave.

Weller, M. (2007). *Virtual Learning Environments. Using, choosing and developing your VLE*. London: Routledge.

Wesch, M. (2007). The Machine is Us/ing Us. Retrieved Augst 20, 2009, from http://www.youtube.com/watch?v=NLlGopyXT_g

Wollstonecraft, M. (1792). *A Vindication of the Rights of Woman. With Strictures on Political and Moral Subjects*. Retrieved June 19, 2009, from http://www.bartleby.com/144/Key

KEY TERMS AND DEFINITIONS

Blog/Blogging: The word is a contraction of 'web log' - a website which has regular entries, usually in reverse chronological order. Blogs often take the form of personal journals.

Feminization of Education: Education as a process carried out mainly by women and with practices that appeal mainly to female students.

Gendered Knowledge: The assertion that knowledge is never 'objective' but always reflects aspects of the identities of those who made it, therefore knowledge will reflect the gender of those who made it.

Knowledge Economy: An economy which uses knowledge products and tools for economic gain.

Knowledge Society: A society where knowledge making is a primary form of production and the exchange of knowledge (buying and selling) is the primary form of economic exchange.

Massification of Education: A phrase describing the that change from education as an activity for an elite minority to education designed for the masses, i.e. the majority of a population

Wiki: Any website that uses software that allows for the collaborative creation and editing of linked web pages by users working online in different locations.

ENDNOTES

[1] This criticism has been applied mainly to teaching (Phillips 2002) and is also given as an explanation for the under-achievement of boys.

[2] http://www.open.ac.uk/platform/blogs retrieved 20.08.2009

[3] See http://technorati.com/pop/blogs/ retrieved 20.08.2009 The Technorati list contains a large number of blogs that discuss web sites and computer applications, but it also contains sites that discuss politics, and culture.

Chapter 14

Queen Bees, Workers and Drones:
Gender Performance in Virtual Learning Groups

Gwyneth Hughes
Institute of Education, London

ABSTRACT

Collaborative learning online is increasingly popular and the interaction between learners is documented and discussed, but gender is largely absent from this work. This chapter attempts to remedy this gap by offering a review of a study of undergraduate online collaboration. Using a metaphor of bees in the hive, the chapter explores gendered 'performance' in online groups through comparing learners' behaviours with that of queen bees, workers and drones. The frustrated queens, sub-groups of workers and excluded drones identified in the study do not lead to harmonious and productive working. The study concluded that a shift from face-to-face to online does not necessarily promote shifts in gender performances and that finding new ways of performing gender online might help resolve some of the conflicts arising from learning collaboratively.

INTRODUCTION: THE GROWTH OF COLLABORATIVE E-LEARNING AND THE INVISIBILITY OF GENDER ISSUES

Take up of online learning has snowballed over the past decade. This growth mirrors the expansion in Internet use and widening broadband connectivity. While much e-learning consists of a repository for documents to be printed off for more conventional uses, there has been growing interest in using online spaces for collaboration between learners. Even more recently, new read/write web tools, sometimes know as Web 2.0, have been heralded as offering a diverse range of online spaces to supplement the more established virtual learning environments (Mason & Rennie, 2008). Alongside these developments, a shift in thinking about learning and teaching away from the idea of the solo learner to understanding that learning takes place in learning groups and communities is occurring, with wide recognition that learners

DOI: 10.4018/978-1-61520-813-5.ch014

benefit from social contact with peers (Wenger, 1998; McConnell, 2006).

In universities and colleges there is plenty of evidence for interaction between peers. In a social 'backstage', students discuss matters outside of the academic context of their studies, share information about teachers, practical details for assignments and occasionally also discuss the course content. Much of this activity now occurs online using email and social networking tools such as 'MySpace' and 'Facebook' (Selwyn, 2007; Salmon, 2000; Palloff & Pratt, 2001). A recent study of first year undergraduates in the UK suggested that learners value such social support and friendships highly (Yorke & Longden, 2007).

As well as this co-operative social activity, peer supported learning can be built into a programme of study more formally. Collaborative learning occurs where a group of learners undertakes a joint enterprise of producing a product which requires a deeper level of engagement. An example of this could be where learners are required to produce pieces of work for assessment collectively, or give group presentations or solve a problem as a group. Again such activity is taking place online as well as offline.

With the increasing importance of virtual learning comes recognition that not everyone has access to the technologies commonly in use for online co-operation and collaboration. Women and men from poorer economic backgrounds experience particular difficulties with the latest technologies which require computers with broadband (high bandwidth) to access the latest Web 2.0 technologies with multimedia content (Johnson *et al.*, 2008). Researchers have also noted some particular disadvantages women might face with virtual learning such as access to computers at home and fitting virtual learning into a 'third shift' after time spent on work and family (Kramarae, 2001; Kirkwood & Kirkup, 1991), and these issues have not gone away.

But gaining access to the technology is only a first step, and although gender and other issues do not disappear when learners succeed in getting online, much research leaves gender invisible. Research on virtual learning has highlighted some of the problems of group and community working using the permanent traces of virtual interactions. Virtual groups do not attract full participation from all members: some may be passive observers or 'lurkers' or others may opt out altogether (Palloff & Pratt, 2005), while some groups have unresolved problems with 'dynamics' (McConnell, 2006). However, despite the relative ease of recording data, studies of learner behaviours online do not usually appreciate that gender and other social factors have a significant influence on how the group interacts.

In this chapter I attempt to remedy the invisibility of gender in virtual learning by presenting findings from a study which produced some data on gender and participation in virtual collaborative learning (Hughes, 2009). The study included undergraduate and postgraduates who worked collaboratively online as part of what might be termed blended learning courses - that is the courses were partly online and partly based in traditional classroom settings. The groups were mixed in terms of gender with other identity issues such as age and ethnicity also of significance. To interpret learner participation in the collaborative group and learners' sense of 'belonging' to the group, I view gender as a performance rather than a fixed characteristic and the first section of this chapter explores what this might mean.

In the next section, I present some of the learners' accounts of their online group participation. To illustrate the gendered learner performances which emerged in the study, I use a metaphor of bees in the hive. The bees represent the learners and the hive the online or blended learning environment in which they interact and the wax and honey are the products of learning. A hive contains a queen bee who is the means of reproduction and who is the focus of all activity in the hive. She is fed by the worker bees, who do the work for the hive: collecting food and making wax. Drones are male bees, who are also fed by workers, but they do not collect food and their only purpose is to fertilise the queen. If conditions in the hive are not suitable they must leave and soon die on their own. This analogy of course already gendered from a biological perspective, but it has resonance with the behaviour of the learners in their online groups and hence it has illustrative value. Like any metaphor there are limitations and I will allude to these as the chapter progresses.

It has been suggested that being online offers much potential for challenging and reconfiguring gendered performances in virtual leisure activities (Turkle, 1995) and there is no reason why this would not be possible in educational situations too. Therefore, in the final section of the chapter I will consider how far these examples of gendered behaviours online are different from commonly perceived offline gendered behaviours and consider how the use of technology might make a difference for successful collaboration.

GENDER: FROM REPRESENTATION TO PERFORMANCE

Participation in education has long been associated with social identities of gender, class, profession and ethnicity. Statistics from advanced industrial countries, such as the UK, show that higher education favours success by females and those from high socio-economic groups and, in the UK and US, those from working class and ethnicity minority groups attend lower status institutions (Universities UK, 2005) and are more likely to withdraw (Barefoot, 2004). The figures can be explained by exclusive structural factors such as quality of schooling, or college or university entrance requirements, but this is an oversimplification which views identity in terms of deficit and does not capture the complexity of individual experiences of learning.

Much of the research on gender concerns representation at this institutional level and there

is much less research on gender at the level of learning and teaching in classrooms or online (Harrop *et al.* 2007). As I explained earlier, my work therefore focussed on this micro-level and in particular examines collaborative learning, the benefits of which are increasingly being recognised. But, to understand gender and participation in collaborative learning it is useful to move beyond gender as a category and view gender as a performed rather than a given identity.

Goffman (1978) argued as far back as the late 1950s that identity is a performance which depends on the performer's intentions, the setting and the audience. Consider the performance of a waiter while politely serving the tables and how this changes as s/he moves into the kitchen area and urgently requests the next order. The performance is very convincing as Goffman says: "We all act better than we know how" (Goffman, 1978, p. 80), although occasionally the audience will recognise that they are being misled. The feminist Judith Butler (1990) also argued that gender is a continuous act in an ever changing context and this means that there is no authentic self. If gender is not a fixed product of social context then the question arises about how we know how to 'do' gender.

What counts as a feminine (female) or masculine (male) performance depends upon widely established discourses of gender. For example, collaborative learning is itself often a feminised whereas independent working is usually constructed as masculine (Leathwood, 2006). A gender identity is constructed from the appropriate performance so females might collaborate as part of a feminine performance and not doing so might be regarded as unfeminine and inappropriate.

We all belong to many communities and this can give rise to tensions between identity performances of class, gender, ethnicity etc. Learners in formal education will be members of family and friendship groups as well as learning communities. Because of this multiplicity of identity performances, contradictions can surface which cause emotional and other challenges to identity positions which will not always be available or possible to maintain. Belonging to a formal learning community or learning group requires reconciliation of conflicting identities of class, gender and ethnicity with educational communities and practices (Read, *et al.*, 2003; Ball, Reay & David, 2002). For example, in their study of mature learners, Baxter & Britton (2001) explored learner experiences of contradictions between academic language used in universities and language used by their working class communities. Managing such identity contradictions requires a good understanding and skilled negotiation of identity performances. If the tensions remain unresolved, then working class students may feel alienated or may even withdraw from study.

Online Gender Performance-A Greater Opportunity for Re-Invention of Self?

I have already alluded to the possibility that being online might offer new possibilities for performing gender. Internet aficionados are familiar with reinventing themselves online and challenging the idea that identity is stable. The Internet has made it easy to invent a whole gamut of identities in online personae, avatars etc. for online communities and games (Turkle, 1995; Kirkup, 2001). Turkle claims that through the Internet "our views of the self, new images of multiplicity, heterogeneity, flexibility, and fragmentation dominate current thinking about human identity" (Turkle, 1995, p.178). She cites examples where deliberate exploration of new identities in online chat rooms, for example, gender swapping, is a liberating experience as males were able to experience what it was like to be female and vice versa.

The new read/write web - the so called Web 2.0 technologies such as social networking sites and virtual worlds - have brought both opportunities for networking online and recreating oneself for wider audiences. Using previous web technolo-

gies only those with access to computer language and coding could produce content online. Now increasing numbers of people are uploading video, photos and networking online without the need for advanced technical skills. In a virtual world such as Second Life, three dimensional representations of self can move about, gesture as well as talk through text (Guest, 2007). All these innovations potentially provide an even richer opportunity for exploring new forms of gender (Van Doorn *et al.* 2007).

But although promoting a new visual image of oneself through a photograph or avatar online is straightforward for many, transforming or even slightly adjusting gender performance and textual communication behaviours is not so easy. Herring (1994) has also demonstrated that there are gendered styles of communication online, such as dominant styles or co-operative styles, which mirror offline conversational discourse. Unequal power relationships can reproduce online as, for example, in virtual sexual harassment (Adam, 2001; Spender, 1995). While creating a new virtual self might be easy with the right software, experiencing it in any depth might not as straightforward as it might initially seem.

This brings me back to the question about gender performance in formalised virtual learning groups in higher education. How is gender manifested online in groups which might meet in person as well as virtually in what is often called blended learning? To explore this I next present some findings from my research.

A STUDY OF BLENDED LEARNING GROUPS

A study of identity and belonging in learning groups (Hughes, 2009) was initially conducted in two UK 'teaching' universities both based in a large city and with a very diverse student intake. I selected three modules because they were taught through blended learning and included collaborative online group work. These were from different disciplines: IT, Sports Science and Education, each with different gender, ethnicity and age profiles to provide richness of data.

The undergraduate IT and sports science modules both required groups to work collaboratively online for an assessment, while the postgraduate education module enabled groups to co-operate in a discussion board to give each other feedback on specific tasks and to discuss new concepts and ideas. Participants were either interviewed or asked to reflect on their experiences of working collaboratively online.

Although both the IT and Sports Science students were mixed in terms of age, ethnicity and gender, white females were over-represented, perhaps because the students were invited to volunteer for interviews (the interviewer was a white female and males may be less keen to volunteer). For the IT module 13 (11 female, 2 male) students were interviewed. For the Sports Science module 12 (10 female, 2 male) volunteered. The education students were professionals with a majority of mature, white women (19 female, 6 male) and this further skewed the sample. Ethnic minorities were also under-represented in the study (11 in total from ethnic minorities out of a total of 50) again perhaps because of voluntary interviews. However, since the results were not used statistically, I considered that there was sufficient diversity to provide insight into group online behaviours for the purposes of the study.

BEES IN THE HIVE: GENDER PERFORMANCE IN COLLABORATIVE WORK

Using this analogy of a beehive, three types of leaner identities that were often performed in the study were co-operative workers, queen bees and drones. The hive in this metaphor might represent the learning environment in which these learners are situated. Like the worker bees who gather pol-

len, make honey and build the hive, the workers in collaborative groups bring material (pollen) to share for the joint activity, form sweet social bonds (honey) and build a joint product usually for assessment (the wax). Queen bees lead or co-ordinate the group and have responsibility for submitting the joint product for assessment which is analogous to the reproductive function of the queen. Queens may express superiority or a strong need to control. Drones are inactive, alienated or independent students who can easily be excluded from the group or leave the course; drones cannot survive outside the hive, although occasionally one of these can unexpectedly provide material for the queen just as drones occasionally have a function of fertilising the queen. I shall next explore through some examples below how these group performances were gendered.

Workers, Drones And Collaboration

Workers exhibit feminine collaborative and conscientious attributes and it is not therefore surprising that the workers in the learning groups were often female. For example, a white younger female on the IT module drew on an accessible feminine language of explicit emotions in constructing her performance of collective working for a group online assessment:

I think it was quite nice to see what people in other groups had put up for everybody to see. That was quite a nice sort of feeling thinking that people were sharing their information and things like that, that was quite nice.

The education course in particular promoted social rather than independent learning both in the classroom and online and not surprisingly most students valued peer knowledge. However, there was some tension between peer knowledge and the authority of teacher knowledge. Several students negotiated a position of being a collective learner provided that the tutor was present to authenticate the collective knowledge, as in this example from a white female:

I also feel it was a strength having comments posted on (the VLE) by the tutor. There was a visible presence which I valued. I guess I found this useful as it gave me sense of security knowing that we were on the right track.

Drones were those who rejected collaborative working and these were not surprisingly mostly males performing masculinity through rejecting this feminine activity, although both female and male students were alienated. A mixed-race male education student was dismissive of collective knowledge in favour of the supposed authentic knowledge ascribed to the tutor. He gave his views on a 'legitimate academic source of information':

They (students) may not value the opinions of other students on the discussion forum as much as they value the tutors (sic) opinion and if this is not forthcoming they may lose motivation.

He uses 'they' to refer to other students rather than the first person, which is normally used in written reflective statements, although it is likely that he is portraying a personal experience of being de-motivated by peer learning. This detached objective style of writing is consistent with a masculine style of discourse and in particular with scientific discourse (his first degree was in psychology). Such an identity performance which devalues peer knowledge was inconsistent with the views of the majority in the education cohort and in showing this drone-like behaviour it is not surprising that he later disengaged from the course.

In another testimony from a white mature male from the IT cohort a difference in commitment arose from different levels of interest between him and a female peer.

I read everything up there but to be honest, a lot of them (messages) were of no interest. (Female name) was more into it and I let her get on with it really. I saw them (the group) several times in the week anyway so there was no point in me using it really.

He does not appear to identify with the collective discussion: the messages were of 'no interest'. His dissociation from the conscientious female who is 'into it' provides a comfortable masculine identity and thus in the online environment he appears to be a drone. However, to disassociate himself from a masculinity that is disinterested in learning as described by Connell (1995), he shifts to using a preference for meeting the group physically rather than virtually to justify his lack of interest in the online text and, consistent with his maturity, manages to present himself as an engaged student.

The concept of learning from peers is more of a challenge for science and technology students because in science and technology education factual knowledge is privileged over any social and contextual knowledge about science (Hughes, 2000). By contrast, a social science, arts or history student who is familiar with multiple perspectives and knowledge as socially contingent would find the notion of learning from peers as well as authoritative 'experts' much more palatable.

A black male from a visual arts background taking the education module was a collective worker. He stated:

From the different messages posted, one could almost pinpoint members' understanding viewpoints about a given subject. Also by reading the messages, it was possible to fill in the gaps or add to one's own knowledge/understanding of the topic being discussed.

Interestingly, he also does not use the first person commonly used by the females in their reflective writing and although he identifies with collective knowledge, he gives his statement a flavour of masculine objectivity by using 'one's own' instead of 'my'. Thus, this male student is able to present a comfortable 'worker' identity in relation to collective knowledge building

Worker Bees Excluding Others

Sometimes learners formed sub-groups, based on identity congruence within the sub-group, to differentiate themselves from the rest of the student group. In the IT module, a sub-group identity of visibly active commitment to the collaborative task was performed by three white females who also presented themselves as friends. The youngest sub-group member stated:

There weren't enough members of our group logging on; there wasn't much communication apart from the beginning where they would say 'hi my name is and I am in your group' and that's it, that's all it would be geared for. But there were three members who used to log on and we used to try and communicate with each other but we felt that we did most of it. We did nearly everything.

These three conscientious mature female students could be described as the workers in the hive: they logged on and wrote the joint assignment and submitted it on behalf of the group.

The inactive students mentioned above might have been excluded because they could not access the technology or they might be alienated students or lone workers. But, forming sub-groups is not an inclusive way of working and no attempt was made to explore why other members were passive or perhaps waiting to be drawn in after introducing themselves. It was assumed that the others were complicit with being drones as one of the trio put it: "the sort of people that were quite happy to let someone else do it."

Asynchronous discussion boards are often claimed to give campus-based learners who work, mature learners and part-time learners flexibility

of study (Littlejohn & Pegler, 2007). Another example from the use of asynchronous discussion boards illustrates how workers must navigate both the technologies and methods employed by the group and that groups do not necessarily take responsibility for exclusive actions. In the education module there was an online activity in which collective discussion from the whole cohort was expected. Several students whose first posting for the discussion was much later than the group majority were not able to collaborate with the others.

An Asian mature female was an example of a latecomer. She reflected on her experience:

There was a "sell by date" to the contributions... As much as I appreciated I could go to the discussion board at any time, it appeared late entrants rarely got any feedback.... This technical aspect was particularly retarding for me when I had to send my work online.

This learner, although a conscientious worker, was unable to collaborate with her group. Her consistently gendered performance of self as having limited IT skills, exercising caution over using IT and delaying her message posting was not congruent with the way the group functioned to give feedback only to early entrants to the discussion. Her experience goes against popular assumptions that the flexibility of asynchronous communication - of which this student was clearly aware - guarantees access for all. Had this student taken part in the negotiation of group process, she might have been able to interact with others who joined later or persuaded others to give her feedback, but her position as an ethnic minority 'outsider' in a predominantly white group might mean that such negotiation is not easy. This hive is not a very friendly one, and the group apparently did nothing to help with including latecomers. Thus, this learner could easily shift performance from worker to drone.

The Frustrated Queen Bee

All the groups interviewed in the undergraduate modules had elected, or voluntary, female group co-ordinators who were responsible for collating each group member's work and submitting it as a joint product for assessment purposes. These I term the queen bees because of their high responsibility and reproductive role (but not biologically) in producing the assignment. Some of the queens found the role very frustrating either because of a sense of superiority or over-conscientiousness.

The sports science students worked in groups on an assessed task, both face-to-face and online, so they were perhaps more aware of each other's physical identities than students in the IT module. A mature, female sports science student described herself as senior to her group:

Most of them were young people anyway so I wouldn't have much in common with them, they were all rather shy .... and to be honest I helped loads of people, that's the irony of it all, and some people realised that at the end of the course .... I gave them quite a lot of my time and helped them with computer skills and essay writing skills and research skills .... So, the younger ones kind of look to you for guidance even though you got a lot more on than they do, you know it's amazing.

Mature students are widely assumed to be conscientious despite external commitments, and here this student presents a consistent identity which also includes an acceptable gendered role of nurturer of others. But, she constructs herself here as superior to the group on the basis of age, confidence (not shy) and her perceived role as teacher or mentor to the other students. In doing so she appears resentful at having to spend time helping others rather than proud of her unique role in the group.

In the IT module there was another example of the frustrated queen. A mature white female took over leadership of a group and responsibil-ity for submitting the group assignment online. But group members who left their input until the eleventh hour gave her anxiety:

I always check my emails in the morning, some-times in the evening anyway and some of it was checking to see if anybody in our group had put anymore work on because I was getting a bit panicked. And some of it was just like at the end to see if the other groups had got theirs done ... I kept thinking 'oh god, oh god' and it was 10.50 when I got it on and it had to be on by 11 and I kept thinking 'oh oh they have got theirs on'... There were members of the group that didn't re-ally put an awful lot of input in until right at the end and I was thinking 'oh my god' this is going to be a nightmare.

In this example the group co-coordinator performs the gendered role of a frustrated, over-conscientious queen in the hive. Being a conscientious female means submitting the final product in good time and depended on all other members producing material well in advance of the deadline. She continued:

Then at the end they just went 'there you go, loads of work, really good work' and one seemed like a real space cadet and the stuff that he come up with was phenomenal. You know saw him the first week and saw him the last week and he was like 'don't worry, don't worry' and I was thinking 'oh I am worried'.

By contrast, the 'space cadet', a younger white male, performed a laissez-faire approach with trust in the ability of the group to produce a successful product close to the deadline. He, like many others, perceived the group's function to be supporting individuals preparing their contribu-tions to combine just before the cut-off time for the group submission without the need for group interaction, in his words to "put in our statements at the very last day".

This is a risky approach, but in this case it paid off and the group produced a successful product. We might extend the hive analogy to assert that this male drone who appeared not to be contributing did succeed in getting the queen's attention in the end. Such a risk-taking gender performance is consistent for confident males, working or busy students or those who are less committed to academic study. There might of course be female drones as well as males as we are not taking the biology of bees literally, although not apparently in this study.

CONCLUSION: REPRODUCING OR TRANSFORMING GENDER PERFORMANCE IN COLLABORATIVE E-LEARNING

This online study has made visible some of the gendered performances which learners negotiate when taking part in e-learning groups and cohorts. I have explored some of these gender performances through an analogy of a beehive containing workers, queens and drones.

The performance of a worker bee who does much of the activity of gathering and exchanging information to bring to the collective, just as the worker bee gathers pollen for the hive, is associated with feminine attributes of conscientiousness and giving to others or servicing others and so it is not surprising that this role was performed by many females in the study although there are possibilities for male workers to perform this identity too.

The voluntary leaders of these groups were perhaps more surprisingly female as we might have expected male 'queens' in a human context. As queen bees, these learners had responsibility for reproducing knowledge and ensuring that the material reached its destination on time, and this is quite consistent with the feminine attributes of conscientiousness and giving time to others as well. These queen bees sometimes took on far more nurturing work and group management than they could cope with and became frustrated and anxious when the workers and drones needed help or appeared not to be delivering to target.

Finally, in most groups there were the drones who were barely visible and who did not contribute to the work except perhaps to satisfy the queen by submitting something at the very last minute. They did not see themselves as part of the group learning environment (hive), were not interested in collective work and were easily excluded. These performances are consistent with males rejecting collaborative working and other disaffected students who find themselves on the margins of learning situations where other identities of class, disability and ethnicity could be as significant as gender, if not more so.

It is interesting to consider whether or not there is any evidence that virtual gender interactions are different from gendered performances in the classroom. From this study it would seem not: all the performances of the mainly female workers and queens and mainly male drones reproduce gender performances which occur offline in groups where females also perform co-operative and nurturing activities (Cohen & Mullender, 2003). Nevertheless, this is only one relatively small study and groups may behave differently in other learning situations (Hartley, 2005).

The gendered performances described in this study are not ideal for inclusive learning and go some way to explain the lack of persistence of some learners and the frustrations of others. Educators thus have a role in creating learning environments - or different kinds of hives to continue the metaphor - that enable learners to explore new and different performances of gender so that they can make a shift from under-active drones to workers, or from over-controlling and frustrated queens to assertive facilitators or leaders. Use of the beehive metaphor for helping learners to understand and challenge group roles might be a possible way forward. With the expansion of the read/write web and increasing informal social networking, it would be useful to have more studies of online collaboration which might confirm whether or not learners who recreate themselves through inventing names and avatars also undergo a deeper gender transformation of their gendered performance and gain more insight into their practice.

REFERENCES

Adam, A. (2001). Cyberstalking: gender and computer ethics. In Green, E., & Adam, A. (Eds.), *Virtual Gender: Technology, consumption and identity*. London: Routledge.

Ball, S., Reay, D., & David, M. (2002). 'Ethnic Choosing': minority ethnic students, social class and higher education choice. *Race, Ethnicity and Education*, 5(4), 333–357. doi:10.1080/1361332022000030879

Barefoot, B. (2004). Higher education's revolving door: confronting the problem of student drop out in US colleges and universities. *Open Learning, 19*(1), 9–18. doi:10.1080/0268051042000177818

Baxter, A., & Britton, C. (2001). Risk, Identity and Change: becoming a mature student. *International Studies in Sociology of Education, 11*, 87–102. doi:10.1080/09620210100200066

Butler, J. (1990). *Gender Trouble: Feminism and Subversion of Identity*. London: Routledge.

Cohen, M. B., & Mullender, A. (2003). Introduction. In Cohen, M. B., & Mullender, A. (Eds.), *Gender and Groupwork*. London: Routledge. doi:10.4324/9780203163795

Connell, R. (1995). Masculinities. Cambridge, UK: Polity in association with Blackwell.

Goffman, I. (1978). The presentation of Self in Everyday Life. London: The Penguin Press (first pub UK 1969 USA by Anchor Books in 1959).

Guest, T. (2007). *Second Lives. A Journey Through Virtual World*. London: Hutchinson.

Harrop, A., Tattersall, A., & Goody, A. (2007). Gender matters in higher education. *Educational Studies, 33*(4), 385–396. doi:10.1080/03055690701423531

Hartley, P. (1997). *Group Communication*. London: Routledge.

Herring, S. (1994). *Gender differences in computer-mediated communications: bringing familiar baggage to the new frontier*. Retrieved February 2005, from http://www.mith2.umd.edu/WomensStudies/Computing/Articles+ResearchPapers/gender-differences-communication

Hughes, G. (2000). Marginalization of Socio-scientific Material in Science-Technology-Society Science Curricula: Some implications for Gender Inclusivity and Curriculum Reform. *Journal of Research in Science Teaching, 37*(5), 426–440. doi:10.1002/(SICI)1098-2736(200005)37:5<426::AID-TEA3>3.0.CO;2-U

Hughes, G. (2009). Identity and belonging in social learning groups: the value of distinguishing the social, operational and knowledge-related dimensions. *British Educational Research Journal*, iFirst Article, 1–17. Retrieved from http://www.informaworld.com/smpp/content~db=all~content=a910357382

Johnson, N. F., Macdonald, D., & Brabazon, T. (2008). Rage against the Machine? Symbolic Violence in E-learning Supported Tertiary Education. *E-learning, 5*(2), 275–283. doi:10.2304/elea.2008.5.3.275

Kirkup, G. (2001). Cyborg teaching. *ACM SIGCAS Computers and Society, 31*(4), 23–32. doi:10.1145/572306.572311

Kirkwood, A., & Kirkup, G. (1991). Access to computing for home-based students. *Studies in Higher Education, 16*(2), 199–208. doi:10.1080/03075079112331382984

Kramarae, C. (2001). The third shift: women learning online. Washington, DC: American association of University Women Educational Foundation.

Leathwood, C. (2006). Gender, equity and the discourse of the independent learner in higher education. *Higher Education, 33*(4), 385–396.

Littlejohn, A., & Pegler, C. (2007). *Preparing for Blended e-Learning.* Abingdon, UK: Routledge.

Mason, R., & Rennie, F. (2008). *E-Learning and Social Networking Handbook Resources for Higher Education.* London: Routledge.

McConnell, D. (2006). *E-learning Groups and Communities.* Buckingham, UK: Open University Press.

Palloff, R., & Pratt, K. (2001). *Lessons from the Cyberspace Classroom: The Realities of Online Teaching.* San Francisco: Jossey-Bass.

Palloff, R., & Pratt, K. (2005). *Collaborating Online: Learning Together in Community.* San Francisco: Jossey-Bass.

Read, B., Archer, L., & Leathwood, C. (2003). Challenging Cultures? Student Conceptions of 'Belonging' and 'Isolation' at a Post-1992 University. *Studies in Higher Education, 28*(3), 261–277. doi:10.1080/03075070309290

Salmon, G. (2000). *E-moderating: The Key to Teaching and Learning Online.* London: Kogan Page.

Selwyn, N. (2007, November 15) 'Screw Blackboard... do it on Facebook!': an investigation of students' educational use of Facebook. Paper presented *'Poke 1.0 - Facebook social research symposium'*, University of London.

Spender, D. (1995). *Nattering on the Net: Women, Power and Cyberspace.* Melbourne, Australia: Spinifex Press.

Turkle, S. (1995). *Life on the Screen: Identity in the Age of the Internet.* New York: Simon & Schuster.

Universities UK and Standing Conference of Principals SCOP (2005). *From Margins to Mainstream: embedding widening participation in Higher Education* Retrieved November 29, 2006 from http://bookshop.universitiesuk.ac.uk/downloads/margins_fullreport.pdf

Van Doorn, N., van Zoonen, L., & Wyatt, S. (2007). Writing from experience: Presentations of gender identity on weblogs. *European Journal of Women's Studies, 14*(2), 143–158. doi:10.1177/1350506807075819

Wenger, E. (1998). *Communities of Practice: Learning, Meaning and Identity.* Cambridge, UK: Cambridge University Press.

Yorke, M., & Longden, B. (2007). The first year experience in higher education in the UK. York, UK: Higher Education Academy Report. Key Terms Gender performance: an understanding that gender continually arises through actions rather than through permanent biological or social constructions.

KEY TERMS AND DEFINITIONS

E-Learning: Any form of learning that takes place using information and communication technologies and especially used to refer to learning online.

Virtual: Occurring online rather than in the real world.

Collaborative Learning: Learning that occurs when groups or pairs work to together on a joint enterprise or activity.

Group: More than two persons interacting together.

Chapter 15
Towards a Feminist Manifesto for E–Learning:
Principles to Inform Practices*

Gill Kirkup
Open University, UK

Sigrid Schmitz
University of Freiburg, Germany

Erna Kotkamp
Utrecht University, Netherlands

Els Rommes
Radboud University, Netherlands

Aino-Maija Hiltunen
University of Helsinki, Finland

ABSTRACT

This chapter argues that the future development of European e-learning needs to be informed by gender theory, and feminist and other critical pedagogies. The authors explore four themes that have been important in gender theory: embodiment, knowledge, power and ethics, and illustrate how these would give a new and more critical perspective for future e-learning developments, and for social progress if they were incorporated into educational policy and practice. The chapter ends with a framework for using this analysis to inform future action, expressed as the first draft of a manifesto.

INTRODUCTION: WHY DO WE NEED A MANIFESTO?

Why do we need a feminist manifesto for e-learning? A manifesto is a call for action. A feminist manifesto for e-learning is a call for action for the development

and use of e-learning driven by a feminist agenda which places 'gender' as a central explanatory concept for understanding inequality and difference in educational systems, pedagogy and learning. In this chapter we review what we consider to be the main arguments and justifications for e-learning in higher education in particular – which is the field

DOI: 10.4018/978-1-61520-813-5.ch015

in which we, the authors, all work. We illustrate these arguments through some of the most recent e-learning activities and applications. The list of our affiliations at the top of this chapter indicates that we work in a number of different countries. What it does not show is that we come from different disciplines: computer science, educational technology, psychology, and gender studies. In working together on a framework for a feminist manifesto for e-learning what we clearly had in common was our underlying explanatory gender theories. However, we found that our disciplines and the four different languages we work in meant that we often used different words to describe the same thing, or that the words we were using had different connotations for us. This has involved us in long discussions about our writing, and we have decided in the end to leave alternative words and expressions in the paper, in the hope that this will increase accessibility without causing confusion.

One set of values that we hold in common are those of feminist pedagogy. These are a set of values and practices which were developed by gender studies teachers and feminist educators in the last two decades of the twentieth century. The five main practices that we consider to be central to feminist pedagogy are:

- Reformation of the relationship between professor and student
- Empowerment of all participants
- Building communities through education
- Respect for the diversity of personal experience
- Challenging traditional views (of knowledge, curricula and values)

However, although we use e-learning technologies in our own pedagogy and we are involved in other aspects of theorizing the impact of digital technologies on gender and lived experience, we felt that the principles and practices of feminist pedagogy and the practices of e-learning had never been integrated. This is the task we have set ourselves, a task for which this chapter forms the first stage. The creation of a manifesto, we felt, would provide a focus to bring together our developing ideas, and the conclusions of this chapter comprise a draft of theses for our feminist manifesto for e-learning.

In this chapter we argue that neither the justifications made for state investment in e-learning in Europe nor most e-learning activities themselves are informed by critical thinking about feminist pedagogy or feminist theory; if these were applied, they would produce an evaluative perspective which would make e-learning a better tool for knowledge production and for social change. This is especially important in a twenty first century Europe, where the permeability of previously rigid national borders inside Europe and the influx of workers from outside have created a diverse and mobile population. The success of this new European depends on its ability to capitalize on the dynamic potential of this diverse population, rather than excluding or marginalizing them. Understanding gender diversity and implementing gender equality action initiatives can provide a model of inclusion that can be applied to other aspects of diversity.

We focus our discussion on four issues that have received significant attention from feminist scholars outside the field of education: embodiment, knowledge, power, and ethics, and explore what a serious consideration of these issues might mean if applied to e-learning pedagogy. We selected these issues in particular because they directly influence the way we look at teaching, learning and technology. They are not an exhaustive list of all possible issues but they provide what we consider to be key planks for a platform to debate what should be the key principles for critical inclusive e-learning,.

The idea of a manifesto is a familiar one, but for many of us manifestos belong to history, like the 'Communist Manifesto' of Marx and Engels (1848), or to party politics. Political parties produce manifestos which describe the principles that are core to their values, and a statement about the party's intended policies and actions – once in power. However, manifestos come in all shapes and sizes; for instance, they have been a popular form for artists to publish their aims. Feminism has a long history of producing its own manifestos; the earliest, Wollstonecraft's Vindication of the Rights of Women (1792), although not called a manifesto, clearly contains the kind of analysis of a problem, and a call for action which make it one. Donna Haraway's 'Manifesto for Cyborgs' (1985), has remained the most significant influence on feminist theorizing of gender and technology in the last twenty years, and is a core influence in our thinking about a feminist manifesto for e-learning.

There are a number of manifestos attempting to address the future of the internet. The Cluetrain Manifesto (Levine et al., 2000) with its 95 theses – a combination of assertions about the internet and about the future of business – is probably the most famous. However, in our view the most recent manifestos for the digital world do not contain the kinds of critical analysis of power and gender that we would like to see in an emancipatory educational manifesto. They seem to accept neo-liberal, technicist, and economic arguments for digital technologies uncritically. These kinds of arguments are also implicit in the literature on e-learning. The inaugural issue of the International Journal on E-Learning contained one of the first e-learning manifestos (Landis et al., 2002), written by a group of educationalists who were worried about the commercialization of the internet and about learner safety and equity as well as the quality of the knowledge accessible to internet as learning resource. The four tenets of this manifesto were:

- Maximize the Internet as a tool for learning and growth.
- Promote learner safety.
- Commit to equity.
- Respect property rights. (Landis et al. 2002, pp 6-7)

The first three tenets would find support amongst most educators, while the fourth is more controversial, challenged now by the 'Open (free) Content' movement. However, Landis et al.'s manifesto is not alone in educational writing about e-learning in its omission of any analysis of power, gender or difference in the production and dissemination of knowledge, or of the 'cyborg' nature of all e-learners. All these are significant issues in feminist thought.

Uncritical Arguments for e-Learning.

The authors of this chapter are all e-learning practitioners and scholars; we are NOT making an argument against e-learning or encouraging a retrogressive resistance to tools and techniques which will empower both scholars and learners. Like others in the field we believe e-learning can provide powerful tools and techniques of benefit to education at all levels. The difference between ourselves and others is that we believe that e-learning tools and techniques operate in a world in which there is a constant ongoing power struggle over the creation of, and access to, ideas, knowledge, and resources; and gender plays a significant part in this. First we will consider some of the arguments that are put forward for the promotion of e-learning, and discuss why we see these as flawed.

Current educational theories and discourses about the purposes of e-learning rarely touch on the power struggle that concerns us except to argue at the most fundamental level for equity of access to resources. Briefly, we see the two strongest arguments used by governments and educational policy makers to justify the allocation of resources to educational spending on e-learning – as expounded, for example, by Schank (2002) – as technically and economically determinist[1]. Summarized briefly, these arguments are based on the one hand on the belief that technology automatically enhances learning for everyone by adding increased functionality to the system, and by enabling more forms of media to be incorporated into the educational experience. This technological determinist argument usually goes in parallel with an economic argument that e-learning is cost effective because it produces economies of scale which make higher education and training more accessible to more learners. Thus, not only does the key measure of student participation rise, but national productivity, wealth, and the international competitiveness in a global market of a country's goods and services improve as a correlate of education and training. However, these arguments rarely address the unequal distribution of productivity and wealth within and between nations, and there is rarely any acknowledgement that e-learning might be contributing to inequalities. There is also rarely any discussion of the conflicts around defining the content of education, who specifies what is taught and what are the values underlying the choice of the content and skills that comprise a curriculum.

Another kind of what we consider to be uncritical argument for e-learning is one often employed by educational researchers and practitioners who – though interested in gains at the classroom rather than institutional or national level – use discourses about education which sit comfortably with economic rationality and technical determinist arguments. These include the idea of students as 'customers', and education as a form of student empowerment. The needs of students – or customers – then become the driving value of the system so that individualized learning is prioritized and subject content and the tasks of learning and assessment are tailored to an individual student's needs and capacity. These needs are often implicitly economic ones, and the student is seen repository of human capital and education as investment in this capital, and investment that is valued most when it give an economic return. Despite the emphasis on added value to the individual, there is also a very popular discourse about the value of collaborative learning through group activities as the basis for learning or knowledge creation.

Peer- and self-assessment are valued because students are deemed to be good judges of what they and their peers have learned; workplace and practice-based learning are valued, as helping to break down what is seen as a detrimental barrier between formal institutions of learning and 'the real world' of the workplace. E-learning is seen as instrumental in removing this barrier. this. In many e-learning models the teacher's role is understood as primarily that of facilitator and support rather than subject expert – because digital resources are seen as embodying expertise. E-learning, while being apparently only a 'tool' or 'method' for the delivery of content and skills plays, we argue, a significant role in helping determine what these skills and content are. For example a major skill set that students gain through education is that of information and communication technology skills, learned in the process of engaging in e-learning and rarely critically examined.

As educators we find ourselves aligned with many of the positions discussed above, including the importance of collaborative and practice based learning, however we are aware of the tensions and contradictions inherent in many of these positions, as well at the issues that are disguised by them. There are internal contradictions such as the tension between individualized and collaborative learning. There are developments, such as the changed role of the teacher in e-learning, which need a more sophisticated elaboration then they have had until now. Most arguments promoting e-learning have no overt 'political' analysis and therefore are inadequate as a basis for providing us with a feminist or any critical, foundation for an e-learning manifesto. The arguments that have outline above will provide a contrast to the issues that a gender perspective brings, when we start our grounding for a feminist manifesto for e-learning through a feminist analysis of embodiment, knowledge, power, and ethics. But before doing that we also wish to discuss some examples of popular e-learning applications and activities, in order to give a concrete foundation to our later discussion, especially for readers who are not familiar with the range of elearning now being practices across Europe.

INTRODUCING SOME OF THE PRESENT DEVELOPMENTS IN E-LEARNING

Five of the most important developments in e-learning in 2010 are: the easy creation of content, free access to educational content, personalisation (Green et al., 2005), mobile learning and virtual environments. This list is loosely based on those identified by Rubens, a Dutch e-learning advisor who presented them in reaction to those identified by Vlasveld (Rubens, 2009). The attempt to distinguish between the different forms and developments of e-learning are examples of the way that arguments about, and descriptions of, e-learning are taking place.[2] These different separate developments are also often referred to as a group constituting 'e-learning 2.0', in which the pedagogical model of learning with technology is seen as social constructivism (O'Hear, 2006).

The first important development – that of facilitating simple creation of content – is the outcome of the technological affordance offered for learning when content, freely accessible to learners, can be created by teachers and other content providers (Wiley, 2000; Rubens, 2009). An example of this is the development of so called 'reusable learning objects' and the debate about the ease with which these can be integrated into different learning frameworks. This development has encouraged another, that of 'open content', to which we will return later. Another form of easy content creation is the ability to create and incorporate video and other audio visual materials into learning materials. Many universities have adapted their technical infrastructure to accommodate simple video recording of lectures and easy access to these recordings through digital downloads. Websites like TeacherTube or LearnerTV.com further accommodate this and expand on it by allowing the easy uploading of other files (e.g. PDF and PowerPoint) associated with a video lecture.

The interest in easy content creation has also been fuelled by commercial organizations. Vlasveld (2008) argues that (commercial) publishing companies and other content providers are making material easily exchangeable in order to make it possible for teachers to combine different learning objects from different publishers, and content providers, into courses. The business model for this and its ability to create commercial income has yet to be tested.

This approach to developing teaching material is still focused on the notion of the teacher (or other content provider) as the source of 'true information'. Within educational discussions on e-learning attention is drawn to the notion that students can be content creators themselves and that they have a greater expectation of interactivity with content material. Furthermore in some instances there is a more critical attitude towards the value of lectures, even technology enhanced ones.

Related to the ease with which content is created and accessed online, is another development: a shift in thinking about the ownership of teaching materials, from belonging to the teacher or even the institution, to belonging to the world. Some higher education institutions offer some teaching content at no cost; others go as far as offering whole courses online for free. The business model for this is that income is generated from examinations and accreditation rather than from the teaching material itself. 'Teaching' as a process of human engagement of teacher with students, has in some cases become deleted from the process completely. A well known example of this is the Massachusetts Institute of Technology (MIT) who offer Open Courseware: *"Free lecture notes, exams, and videos from MIT. No registration required"* (MIT, 2009; also see Open University, 2009) A wide range of the materials from MIT courses are made available, including Women's and Gender

Studies. The above mentioned LearnerTV.com also offers most of its material under a 'Creative Commons' license which enables free re-use by others (teachers and students) in any non-profit making context.

A third development is the increasing focus on how e-learning environments can be personalized for learners. Rubens describes this as being about enabling the learner to take control of their own learning trajectory (Rubens, 2009). This can be done through the introduction of a virtual tutor, a program which helps the student design a personal route through learning. Personalization can also involve the notion that a student becomes a participant designer of the e-learning environment itself, not just the route through it. The drive for personalization stems from the importance given to the learner as an individual with individual learning needs and a particularized context.

A fourth important development is that of mobile learning or location-based learning. This term is usually reserved for e-learning that does not rely on a computer (either desk-top or lap-top) to mediate content. The most well-known examples are the use of mobile phones, personal digital assistants (PDAs) and iPhones in the learning processes. Often, the use of a Global Positioning System (GPS) is crucial so that students have mobile access to information about buildings or other objects of interest in their physical surroundings. Location-based learning is seen as creating the possibility for a more meaningful experience through enrichment of the student's experience when it is embodied in a location outside a formal educational context like a class-room or lecture theatre, by connecting the learner to resources and to other learners, while allowing them to remain in their location.

Probably the best known and most discussed development in e-learning is that of social software. The term itself can be seen as a portmanteau concept that is used for different types of software that puts the user at the center of a network of other users. This type of software en- ables extensive communication so that learners, as users of the software, can work together and create content collaboratively. Although, like the other developments in e-learning, the availability and development of the technology is crucial, the focus here lies more on what users do with the technology than on access to it. It is this use of technology in particular that fueled the move towards collaborative learning, peer assessment, workplace and practice-based learning. Here the liberal educational discourse becomes most apparent. For example McLoughlin and Lee state '*social software offers the possibility to move away from the last century's highly centralized, industrial model of learning and toward individual learner empowerment through designs that focus on collaborative, networked interaction*' (McLoughlin and Lee, 2008, online).

Or as much quoted Peter Duffy suggests, a pedagogical paradigm shift might be taking place:

The implication here is a possible shift from the basic archetypical vehicles used for e-learning today (lecture notes, printed material, PPTs, websites, animation) towards a ubiquitous user-centric, user-content generated and user guided experience. (Duffy, 2008, 119)

He goes on to say: 'It is not sufficient to use online learning and teaching technologies simply for the delivery of content to students. A new "Learning Ecology" is present where these Web 2.0 technologies can be explored for collaborative and (co)creative purposes as well as for the critical assessment, evaluation and personalization of information.' (Duffy, 2008, 119)

Some social software tools popular at the time of writing include wikis, blogs and online discussion forums that are used in both formal and informal learning situations (see also Kirkup in this book). Serious gaming and the use of virtual worlds can also be included under the umbrella concept of 'social software'. Virtual worlds like Second Life have been used for simulation in work-related learning and there are serious immersive games that are also designed for this purpose (Boulos et al., 2007). Second Life has inspired wide discussion on how to accommodate different pedagogical styles and activities in virtual worlds (Baker et al., 2009). The importance of the rules of play as introduced by Salen and Zimmerman (2004) and the game experience itself have become a focus of attention for educational practitioners (see for example the Games and Education Research Network, GERN at http://www.bris.ac.uk/education/research/networks/gern)

Other new developments like microblogging (Twitter), cloud computing, digital mind mapping as well as the further development of intelligent agents and customized tutors, can be seen as an extension of the developments in social software. These new applications are often adopted first by students for their own purposes some time before they are adopted – if they ever are - into formal education. In the near future Tim Berners-Lee's vision of a 'semantic web' (Berners-Lee et al., 2001) to replace the present relatively anarchic web we are used to, might be the beginning of another significant shift in e-learning as we move towards the next stage: what is being called e-learning 3.0 by some writers.

These applications are the ones we identify as the most influential developments in e-learning. It has been important to sketch these out before discussing how feminist debates on embodiment, knowledge, power and ethics can offer a critical perspective to our understanding of the affordance and challenges that the kinds of technologies discussed here offer to e-learning. We will now move from discussing practical examples of e-learning to addressing aspects of feminist theory that we can build on to start creating a framework for a feminist manifesto for e-learning.

We begin with a discussion of embodiment, one of the most crucial issues to engage with when evaluating technologies which appear to disembody the learner, and the teacher.

THE FEMINIST QUESTION OF EMBODIMENT

Learning is a deeply embodied process and this embodiment is relevant for several reasons. In this section, we discuss ontological aspects of embodiment and learning, asking: In what ways are gendered bodies relevant in learning and in having access to the learning process? In the next section, we follow with a discussion of the relevance of embodiment for the epistemological issues of learning, asking, how are knowledge and meaning mutually connected with body and matter? Perhaps embodiment is most obviously relevant in the learning of embodied practices, such as how to use a computer 'mouse', how to envision 3D images or how to fly an airplane. Physicality is also relevant in educational settings, where questions can be asked about how the body is accommodated, how repetitive strain injury (RSI) is prevented and what is the importance of emotions such as pleasure or resistance in the learning context. Some of these embodied practices have been identified as creating or increasing inequalities between men and women, for instance, by facilitating some kinds of bodies more than others (Weber, 1999; Webster, 1995). However, in this chapter, we focus our discussion of gendered embodiment in education primarily on four aspects: access, motivation, capabilities and support for learning technologies. Clearly, people differ in their 'inclusion needs' (Sorensen, Faulkner, & Rommes, forthcoming) and learning situations differ in the extent to which these needs are relevant.

In order to learn, people need to have access to the learning situation. Feminist researchers have shown that this access can be more or less restricted for some groups in society, depending on the subject taught, the context in which it is taught and the role of teacher and other learners. Classroom practices (both on- and off-line) may be outright sexist, racist or facilitate (sexual) harassment of some students. Practices may be more subtly gendered or exclusionary where for example women, sexual minorities, or members of lower social class groups get the message that an educational context is not 'their' place (Clegg, 2001; Stepulevage, 2001). Access may also be restricted as some people may be incapable of being physically present in the classroom, as e.g. parents with children or people with disabilities (Rommes, Faulkner, & Slooten, 2005).

A second factor affecting inclusion is motivation (or lack of it) for learning. This can result from the feeling that certain knowledge, or skills, are particularly relevant or interesting to one's life, experiences and circumstances, or that some kinds of knowledge or learning method is fun or exciting. The questions of 'whose knowledge?' is being taught and 'which knowledge?' is being taught are highly relevant from a feminist perspective, as is the question of how teaching is being carried out. Such questions also relate to issues of identity and of symbolic connections between fields of knowledge and femininities and masculinities. If learners get the message, whether from society or from teachers and teaching material, that some knowledge is 'for them' and that this knowledge speaks to their particular life experiences, motivation to learn or to join into the learning experience will rise (Sorensen, Faulkner, & Rommes, forthcoming).

Motivation, or even the message 'this is for me', also improves the third inclusion factor, which is capability for learning. As the well-known self-fulfilling prophecy thesis shows, the expectation[3] that a person will be successful will increase the chance of that person indeed being successful (Geis, 1993; Koch, 2008). Self confidence is an important factor in a person's capabilities to learn. Most fields of knowledge and work are highly gendered in the sense that there are different numbers of men and women

working in, for example healthcare occupations or engineering and they consequently have different gender connotations. Hence, self confidence, motivation and thus capabilities are for these occupations also unequally distributed in society. In addition, as people's experiences prior to any learning situation differ, some will have a head-start, both in their capabilities and in their expectation of these capabilities, whereas others will have to catch up on knowledge, skills or practices, and this will influence their capabilities to learn in a new situation.

Last but not least, the fourth inclusion issue is that of access to networks of support. The support and social networks a person has access to can influence their educational access (e.g. in the form of people willing to take care of the children so that a parent can attend class), their motivation (e.g. by giving personalized recognizable examples of relevance or by being a role model) and their capabilities (e.g. by informal learning or by giving encouragement) to learning in a particular subject area.

What happens if we see learning no longer as simply humanly embodied, but as embodied as cyborg? As Haraway asserted, we are all cyborg; that is we are all a hybrid of machine and organism, a reality with which teachers who incorporate ICTs in their teaching most consciously deal with in their teaching practices (Goodman, Kirkup, & Michielsens, 2003). Barad (2007) has elaborated this further with the concept of 'intra-action': that matter and meaning, or in this case the organic and the technical, can not exist separately, they mutually constitute each other. Learning has become integrated with technologies, and the learner incorporates organic and machine elements, is part of a network in which students, teachers, hardware, software, knowledge and skills are 'intra-acting'. But as Haraway argued: cyborgs are not 'innocent' or without bias in this system, they are partial and constructed and can be constructed differently (Haraway, 1985). One network, or rather one cyborg is not equal to another.

Different networks open up different spaces for new forms of agency and new forms of exclusion and inclusion. The parent with children who was once excluded from learning, may now become included as a result of the use of new technologies, whereas a person who had a lot of experience and capabilities in hierarchically organized classes may now feel insecure and incompetent working with the same learning material on-line or interactively constructing knowledge via social software. Becoming cyborg offers different challenges to each learner.

Differences between cyborgs may take the form of aspects of the human actor (for example age, level of education, level of experience and self-confidence, ethnicity, gender), but they may also be aspects of the technological actor (for example which hardware and software is used, what kind of network connection is available) and they may also take the shape of aspects of the human-technology intra-action: a particular human actor with a particular technology may be supported or disempowered by a particular kind of teaching. For each of these three dimensions of difference there are diversities between students (and teachers), as Haas states: we should '*better understand and respect the differing cultural and material conditions that influence individual access to and attitudes about technology rather than to assume that all students and teachers approach technology in the same way at the same time*' (Chegwidden, 2000; Haas, Tulley & Blair, 2002).

The digital and verbal capabilities of learners as well as experiences and attitudes and preferred ways of learning (e.g. contextual, problem-based or reflective) combined with different e-learning applications create considerable variety between cyborg students (and teachers). A Turkish-Dutch woman with experience and confidence in using Windows-based computers and with a preference for mastering, individual and impersonal learning, who uses an Apple to access a Finnish Wiki e-learning environment is in a different intra-action than she is when using a Turkish Wiki. Taking these differences into account is crucial but complicated, as they may influence the learning process and the assessed performance of the student. Therefore, in designing e-learning environments, questions need to be asked about how inequalities between cyborgs in access, motivation, capabilities and support networks can be taken into account in developing e-learning tools, and providing supportive learning contexts. In the next section we move from the learner to the 'what' of learning, in particular knowledge.

THE FEMINIST QUESTION OF KNOWLEDGE

Some of the central goals of feminist teaching have been to develop an awareness of the origins of different concepts and viewpoints in knowledge domains and make visible the development of personal reflective standpoints by teachers and learners. In this context, knowledge production and presentation (through literature or by teachers), and critical reflection on this presented knowledge, and even on the construction of new knowledge by students is a highly embodied process. Therefore, knowledge constitution is a crucial part of the embodied aspects of e-learning and it should be grounded in a feminist perspective. For a long time, cognitive engagement with knowledge acquisition and reflection was assumed to be a more or less purely rational process, being connected to mind and meaning, but not involving the body. New approaches provided by feminist materialism, however, emphasize the inseparability of body and mind in understanding mind and meaning as embodied processes. Feminist materialism criticizes the long held separation of biology and sociality (e.g. Ahmed, 2008) and tries to offer an understanding of how knowledge and meaning are mutually connected with body and matter. The inclusion of these concepts in feminist e-learning leads to a differentiated understanding of the processes, the agencies, and power relations that sometimes influence and are sometimes erased in the intra-actions that take place in the networks of human and technological encounters.

With her concept of 'agential realism' Barad (2003, 2007) has provided a new theoretical framework to analyse the productive relations between matter, causality, and agency. Barad aims to overcome what she sees as the inherent separation of these things produced by traditional scientific representationalism. In this traditional mode, an object (of matter or nature) was held as having a given essence (ontology) the existence and form of which could be explained by science in linguistic terms (epistemology). Representation, in this dichotomised system, is stated as the knowledge a subject has over an object. Barad argues against this separation, she sees phenomena in the world as not preformed and not existing outside of meaning. Matter and meaning are thoroughly interwoven. At the same time, Barad denies those constructivist approaches that consider the meaning of matter as fully linguistically constructed; which is the position usually credited to Butler (1990). Thus, knowledge cannot be conceptualized outside of the processes and actors all of whom are engaged in knowledge construction. Referring to Haraway's concept of situated knowledges (Haraway, 1988) Barad also sees the issue of embodied knowledge as a material-semiotic matrix at the core of her arguments. Like Haraway, Barad gives matter an active role in these networks; she sees it as an agency in the development of worldly phenomena. In order to combine both, matter and discourse, Barad sets out a framework she calls Epistem-onto-logy.

By developing the term *'post-humanist performativity'* Barad (like Haraway, 1985) also widens Butler's concept of performativity (Butler, 1990) to the consideration of intra-active practices between human and non-human actors in the process of knowledge constitution. With reference to Nils Bohr, she points out that the technological components of research apparatuses as well as the experimenter's background assumptions, his/her interpretations and viewpoints, and the process of experimentation itself intra-act with the research object, that is they "are productive of (and part of) phenomena produced; they enact a local cut that produces 'objects' of particular knowledge practices within the particular phenomena produced." (Barad 2003, 819).

This framework locates phenomena as ongoing practices; they are not 'things' but 'doings'. Thus, phenomena come to exist through iterative intra-actions, with bodily and cultural agencies; objects, subjects and technologies; matter and discourse being not separable and not traceable back to isolated causes. The analysis of phenomena then calls for a reformulation of traditional notions of causality. An understanding of phenomena can only be attained when we disengage ourselves from the classic linear logic of cause and effect and follow the intra-actors in their 'doing' from different vantage points or different optics. Barad uses the term 'agential situated cut' to describe the foci of a particular perspective that is set by particular components. It is important to note that, in this framework, no description of a phenomenon can be fixed. Phenomena are always in a process of change and even the viewpoint of the observer changes the phenomenal intra-actions.

Using this concept to consider embodied intra-action in the course of knowledge acquisition, reflection, and construction for feminist e-learning means that we must look for a more detailed analysis of the intra-active practices in which engagement with technology as well as with other learners and teachers through technological hard- and software constitute the phenomena of knowledge. Students are not only embodied learners; they are agents who are part of the intra-actions which produce knowledge. The following part of this section gives a brief outline of some components that crucially mediate (a) knowledge distribution, discussion and reflection, (b) the development of standpoints and opinions, (c) the practices of communication and collaboration, and (d) the awareness of self and others in e-learning networks. All these components are engaged in the production of gender and gender inequalities.

Knowledge Distribution, Discussion, and Reflection

What knowledge becomes available to students via intra-actions in the human-technological apparatuses of e-learning? The general availability of online resources through open access and open content produces both inclusions and exclusions of content, and thus contributes to forming knowledge in any discipline. In addition, the technological equipment and the digital literacy of students or teachers also mediate their access to knowledge. Some digital content may be available for only some parts of a subject. The format in which content can be downloaded, e.g. as written text, slides or video lectures, intra-acts with the student and with the quantity and quality of knowledge production and acquisition.

Compacting content and producing hypertextual material in technologically mediated formats (e.g. Wikipedia) intra-acts with the comprehension of a topic. We do not know the impact of including annotations in digital texts, or how the ability to visualize relations between topics in the format of hypertext and web links influences the development of a learner's view of a particular topic. All these aspects also beg the question of the location of power. Who decides on the arguments, knowledge perspectives and discourses that are presented, while others are dropped? Who sets the annotations or links and, thereby structures the knowledge?

Development of Standpoints and Opinions

The technologically mediated exchange of information, perspectives and opinions between subjects may produce other kinds of knowledge than those we are used to, those which have come from the study of linear texts and face-to-face

discussion. For example, when writing a text in a collaborative wiki, and annotating the arguments of others, the digital 'fixing' of all of these intra-actions may impact on the author's as well as the audience's opinions differently from what would have occurred in discussing the same topic in personal intra-action with others. This impact is not only on the production of the phenomena of individual knowledge or personal standpoint, but, in an attempt to strengthen collaborative e-learning it also impacts on the intra-active formation of group opinions and perspectives.

To take another example: concept mapping is an upcoming e-learning tool for visualizing the relationships among different terms or information sources in order to improve overviews of knowledge domains from different perspectives. However, the creation of terms and knowledge concepts, and the visualization of their interrelations in concept maps also constitute a particular intra-active dynamic between the user and the software. The 'doing' of these arrangements, the handling of software features, the process of negotiation about concept terms and relations differs from a verbal discussion or from concept mapping using paper cards. Research on student engagement with this form of knowledge management and acquisition shows gendered differentiations (see Schmitz & Grunau, 2009).

Communication and Collaboration

As discussed earlier one important aspect of e-learning has been the strengthening of digital communicative and collaborative intra-actions between students, and between students and teachers, respectively, over time and space. However, different communication practices, e.g. synchronously in chat or asynchronously in forums or blogs, intra-act in the development of a discourse. In synchronous communication in particular, the speed of technology as well as the subject's power over language, can provide crucial agency to some, allowing them to gain argumentative power for their opinion over others. Commonly used text-based computer-mediated communication and collaboration arrangements opened up a whole set of questions concerning gender issues (see Herring, 2001), and although these issues are a focus of interest for a small number of researchers, gender has not been accepted widely as having a significant impact on what is considered valid and authoritative knowledge.

Awareness of Self and Others in e-Learning Networks

Finally in this discussion about the intra-active development of knowledge in e-learning comes the question: Does the presentation and 'fixing' of biographical texts, and the kinds of portrait photographs that are widely distributed in social networks, modulate our self presentation and our self-awareness? And how is this gendered? Different forms of inclusions and exclusions, and reification of stereotypes occurs not just in the practices of e-learning but in the knowledge that is created through it. The concept of intersectionality has developed to describe the mutual intra-actions of a range of different factors (technological or social) or aspects of any individual so gender is now observed as a process in interaction with, for example, age, race, and culture. Different aspects of a person's identity are more important than others at any one time, and lead to different inclusions and exclusions. Engagement in collaborative e-learning should modulate the relation between the individual and other learners, and gender will be involved in this.

Barad's theory of agential realism argues that material bodies and discourses produce knowledge that is always in flux, and always relative to the agency of the actors and the power they can mobilise. In the next section we revisit earlier feminist theories of power, to add to those of embodiment and knowledge, to continue developing the foundation for our e-learning manifesto.

THE FEMINIST QUESTION OF POWER

Feminism, and subsequently feminist pedagogy, can be seen in a historical context of waves of feminism. The first wave, having campaigned for access to education and female suffrage, was followed by the second wave which included campaigning for changes to the nature of educational practices, in particular changes to pedagogy (Thompson 1983). The question of gender and power, access to power through education and the operation of power in education became core issues in twentieth century feminist pedagogy, distinct from, but linked to questions of gender embodiment and knowledge, Feminist pedagogy is aligned with critical pedagogy, which aims to engage otherwise disempowered students in critical consciousness, so that by using the authority of their own experience they are able see through dominant (false) discourses which have disempowered them. The ultimate aim is that learners, through developing critical consciousness can ultimately formulate 'praxis', which is the ability to act in a socially engaged, and empowered way. Critical and feminist pedagogy focuses on making power-relations visible and challenging them to achieve social and political change through personal development in informal and formal education (Freire, 1970; Habermas, 1968; Foucault, 1988; Giroux, 1991). Critical pedagogy focuses on personal empowerment for disempowered groups, through the use of problem-based and solution-centered pedagogic practices. Becoming aware of the politics of a situation, engaging in dialogue between groups, and working at a grass-roots level, usually at the adult education level, are some of the practices of critical pedagogy. Questions about power are acknowledged and addressed, and emancipation is seen as changing power relations. It is obvious why feminist educators who were concerned about the potential of education to either support the gender status quo or challenge it, aligned themselves to this tradition of critical education.

Access to education as learners and access to teaching as a profession has been a major route to empowerment for women globally, but second wave feminism was reflexive about these activities. The personal was seen as not only political but also pedagogical. A major premise of feminist pedagogy was the commitment to taking personal experience seriously, and seeing it as a valid source of knowledge which could lead to epistemological questions. This commitment to the importance of personal experience has meant that feminist pedagogy has included an analysis of race (hooks, 1994) and of other issues of inequality producing new critical perspectives such as queer-pedagogy (Britzman, 1995; de Castell & Bryson, 1997) all of which address issues of power.

E-learning is and has been a strong part of current policies and strategies in European higher education, which is part of global education market and it is rarely promoted by those involved in critical pedagogy because of this. For governments e-learning is seen as one of the key factors promoting European higher education to the rest of the world and an added attraction when competing globally for students. At this global economic level power through online education is involved in political and economical power, seen by critics as a new form of imperialism. However, the proponents of e-learning argue that its power is a democratizing or equalizing one. When e-learning is promoted by feminist scholars and critical pedagogues, it can seem that we are sympathetic to these global educational marketers, when in fact we are critical of many aspects of this activity. We need to keep asking who has the power to decide about resources, who shapes learning outcomes and curricula development? Teachers, students and policy makers will always have unequal resources, possibilities, choices and options. As feminist educators how do we bring our critical feminist pedagogy to this analysis?

At the e-classroom level, teaching is always linked with questions of power, about the ownership of knowledge, authority and expertise. Academic leadership is gained not only through research and scholarship, but also through teaching. A teacher's pedagogical presence can promote shared expertise and encourage the growth of diversity. A teacher's power in a learning context lies in their responsibility for the quality of the learning process – and defining that quality is also a question of power. E-learning courses designed and taught with an explicit acknowledgement of power can support students learning together and from each other, to develop not only cognitive, writing or technical competencies, but also those social skills and competencies that are part of critical consciousness.

Critical e-learning skills, alongside feminist critical pedagogy, are becoming core academic competencies whether we wish it or not – in the same way that 'reading' once was in book based learning. Their development though the whole of academia will mean new orientations for scholars toward their academic work, as they model new academic practices for students. This can mean new orientations towards their "scholarly products". This might also lead to an alignment with the previously mentioned 'Open (free) Content' movement and the notion of making academic work available under a Creative Commons license. This possibility and a better and critical use of constructive collaborative learning and an increased use of social platforms in teaching, gives students more of the rights and responsibilities of power and empowerment. E-learning skills do not themselves give access to power, but their creative and critical application opens up more possibilities. An absence of e-learning skills is likely to be a barrier to access to power.

Questions of power are also questions of agency, and if we adopt Barad's understanding of agency we have a very complicated picture for e-learning. We need to identify the key actors in virtual classrooms, and the key actors in developing policies for e-learning inside institutions. Who or what are the key actors developing national and international e-learning policies? We need to understand the technologies we use as actors themselves. Bourdieu (1980) as well as Barad are most useful in identifying who (or what) is responsible for creating, wielding or maintaining agency. Bourdieu's concept of 'habitus': those ways of thinking and being which empower and dis-empower us, and which are solidly embodied in us, and in the technologies we use, brings this argument back to the earlier discussion of embodiment and knowledge. Our attitudes towards e-learning and our skills in using it is part of our habitus, and the habitus of the technologies we use: both of these are gendered.

Finally our discussion of power leads to a discussion of the question of ethics. With the notion that e-learning yields power, we accept Winner's (1986) proposition that technologies, including e-learning technologies, have politics. We also support the notion that they have gender. Do they have ethics? They are certainly agents in ethical systems and feminist scholarship has asked questions about whether there are alternatives to the ethical systems we are used to.

THE FEMINIST QUESTION OF ETHICS

Feminism and gender theory have always had an ethical component. The question has been asked, How should men and women behave towards each other, for example as equals, as partners, as protectors and protected? What should the nature of gendered relations be, for example how should brothers and sisters, husbands and wives, relate to each other? What kind of gendered behaviour is of value and how is it to be valued, for example mothering? These questions have been asked about teaching, learning and the relationships between teachers, learners and knowledge. In

the 1980s there was a flowering of writing about feminist teaching (Culley and Portuges, 1985) and a research strand developed which claimed that ways of knowing were gendered, in women were identified as 'connected knowers' (Belenky et al., 1986). This was a way of interacting with the world which was seen to have ethical value.

This work grew out of psychological research on gendered differences in moral and intellectual development (Gilligan, 1982), reinforced by feminist theories of knowledge (Harding, 1991). Gilligan took issue with Kohlberg (1981) over his model of stages of ethical development in human beings, which put 'justice' as the pinnacle of moral development. She used object relations theory to argue that women and men have different stages of development and these reflected the different ways they learned to value relationships with people and things. Women, she argued, prioritise building and maintaining connection with others over abstract justice – they are 'connected knowers' rather than individual knowers. She did not locate this as a biological determined way of thinking but as a cultural product of the way in which we all become gendered adults with particular roles and habitus.

Harding (1991) argued that groups were placed in different relationships to the world and to each other which produced different knowledge about the same material world. This is simplistic description of 'Standpoint Theory', a more political version of the theory of 'connected knowing'; because it argued that the view from 'below' was a more accurate view of the material and social world than that from 'above'. It was the view from below that provided the engine for change – both epistemological and social. This is the kind of position that proponents of critical pedagogy take with respect to the importance of the knowledge held by the powerless and dispossessed (Freire, 1970).

This concern with ethics was picked up again in feminist thinking nearly twenty years later by Noddings (2003) and Held (2005) who developed what has come to be called an 'Ethic of Care'. This ethic, which values trust, mutual consideration and solidarity with others, it is argued, is more appropriate to our present world and its problems and should have at least equal priority with the ethics of justice, equality and individual rights. Clearly if this is the case then it needs to be embedded in the structures, and technologies of teaching and learning.

In the 1980s, feminist ethics of care and connection were embedded in feminist pedagogy. This body of theory about gender and teaching (Thompson, 1983) places particular responsibilities on the teacher, to embed an ethics of caring into their practices and encourage it in student behaviour. Although a few writers on feminist pedagogy (e.g. McWilliam and Taylor, 1998; Morley 2002) have worked through some aspects of this in e-learning contexts; the move generally to a central concern with e-learning technologies has left many feminist educators continuing to try to apply these ethics in the face-to-face classroom, while being alienated from a critical involvement with e-learning. As we discussed in the introduction, the values underpinning many developments in e-learning appear to be very individualist – which contradicts the values of the connected knower. They are also embedded in an economic model which places high value on return on investment – a very different focus from that of critical pedagogy, A feminist ethic of care could provide a challenge to the predominant ideology which understands education as the optimisation of an individual's talents and opportunities related to employment and the nation's economic development (Gouthro, 2005), by offering alternative values that are to do with social capital and the valuing of skills and knowledge that are of no direct economic value. We need alternative ethical models integrated into our educational systems to develop values other than those of the market, which at the time of writing this chapter (2009) have proved devastating globally for the poorest and weakest. The challenge is to incorporate the understanding of

the connected learner with feminist insights on embodiment, knowledge and power into a statement of the values on which to build a manifesto for e-learning and also show what it would mean to implement them in practice.

Reconsidering e-Learning in the Light of These Feminist Questions

The sections so far have outlined what we, the authors, consider to be the four main pillars of feminist theory, namely the concepts of embodiment, approaches to human-machine intra-actions to create knowledge, the operation of power and the re-integration of feminist ethics. We argue that these could provide the foundation for a systematic feminist conception and use of e-learning. As we have argued throughout this chapter, current theories about and even manifestos for e-learning lack any feminist analysis of these issues. Feminist perspectives on e-learning acknowledge and attempt to address a range of inequalities in access to technology, in computer literacy, user strategies, the skills levels of learning communities and of individuals. Gender critical pedagogy is sensitive to intersectionality, and to the mutual intra-actions of a range of different actors in any one learning event. Age, disability, race, culture, language, sexuality, amongst others, have to be addressed in an e-learning event, as does technology, and as does knowledge/content.

In the introduction to this chapter we described five principles of traditional (pre e-learning, and pre-cyborg and materialist feminist theory) feminist pedagogy. We can now elaborate these as a basis for a manifesto for e-learning which includes a critical engagement with e-learning technologies and humans intra-acting as agents in the learning process.

All e-learning should:

1. Reform the power relationships between teachers, student, knowledge and learning

technologies. There is a need for sensitization of students and teachers to pedagogical power relations in the classroom, to epistemological power relations in knowledge production, and to the creation of power in the intra-actions of people and technology.

2. Empower all human computer intra-actions in the learning encounter, but prioritise the empowerment of human actors.

3. Build global networked communities of learners and their technologies, to include solidarity and loyalty in an ethic of care for all community members.

4. Respect diversity in human-computer intra-actions, whether in the design of e-learning environments, or in the teaching and participation of the learning process. Respect for diversity also includes respect for knowledge, scholarship and technology as agents. Encourage and enable all participants to develop an understanding of their own standpoints, or their own partial perspectives while developing as scholars and researchers.

5. Engage in positive challenges to knowledge and to technology with the aim of building new socially engaged knowledge in intra-action with others (human and non-human).

The next step will be to take these five principles and apply them to the current developments in e-learning to develop a feminist praxis for e-learning. For example, we can ask what it means for easy electronic content creation if we take into account the feminist idea of knowledge and partial perspectives. In what ways can easy content creation support situated and connected learning and how does this relate to ownership of teaching materials? How do power differences take shape in this context and how do we deal with issues of embodiment, knowledge and ethics in this context? How do we manage global networks of learners and balance an ethic of care with the requirement to challenge knowledge.

Clearly these questions are not easily answered. In this chapter we have attempted to lay a theoretical and political ground by showing how feminist work on embodiment, knowledge, power and ethics could re-energise our thinking about what principles should underpin our praxis. The next step will be to formulate answers which will turn these principles into a practical manifesto of action.

ACKNOWLEDGMENT

We would like to acknowledge that this article has been written as a cooperation within ATHENA3 - the Advanced Thematic Network in Women's Studies in Europe - with the support of the Socrates/Erasmus programme for Thematic Network Projects of the European Commission through grant 227623-CP-I-2006-INL-ERASMUS-TNPP.

REFERENCES

Ahmed, S. (2008). Open Forum. Imaginary Prohibitions: Some Preliminary Remarks on the Founding Gestures of the "New Materialism". *European Journal of Women's Studies*, *15*(1), 23–39. doi:10.1177/1350506807084854

Baker, S. C., Wentz, R. K., & Woods, M. M. (2009). Using Virtual Worlds in Education: SecondLife® as an Educational Tool . *Teaching of Psychology*, *36*(1), 59–64. doi:10.1080/00986280802529079

Barad, K. (2003). Posthumanist Perfomativity: Toward an Understanding of How Matter Comes to Matter. *Signs: Journal of Women in Culture and Society*, *28*(3), 801–831. doi:10.1086/345321

Barad, K. (2007). *Meeting the Universe Halfway*. Durham, NC: Duke University Press.

Belenky, M. F., Clinchy, B. M., Goldberger, N. R., & Tarule, J. M. (Eds.). (1986). *Women's ways of knowing: the development of self, voice, and mind*. New York: Basic Books.

Berners-Lee, T., Hendler, J. J., & Lassila. O. (2001, May 17). The Semantic Web, *Scientific American*.

Boulos, M. N. K., Hetherington, L., & Wheeler, S. S. (2007). Second Life: an overview of the potential of 3-D virtual worlds in medical and health education. *Health Information and Libraries Journal*, 2007, 233–245. doi:10.1111/j.1471-1842.2007.00733.x

Bourdieu, P. (1980). *Questions de sociologie* [Sociology in Question]. Paris: Minuit.

Britzman, D. (1995). Is there a queer pedagogy – Or, stop reading straight. *Educational Theory*, *45*(2), 151–165. doi:10.1111/j.1741-5446.1995.00151.x

Butler, J. (1990). *Gender Trouble: Feminism and the Subversion of Identity*. New York: Routledge.

Chegwidden, P. (2000). Feminist Pedagogy and the Lap Top Computer. In E. Balka & R. Smith (Eds.), Women, Work and Computerization, Charting a Course to the Future (pp. 292-299). Boston: Dordrecht.

Clegg, S. (2001). Theorising the Machine: gender, education and computing. *Gender and Education*, *13*(3), 307–324. doi:10.1080/09540250120063580

Culley, M., & Portuges, C. (Eds.). (1985). *Gendered Subjects. The dynamics of feminist teaching*. London: Routledge.

de Castell, S., & Bryson, M. (1997). *Radical in<ter>ventions: Identity, politics and difference in educational praxis*. New York: SUNY Press.

Duffy, P. (2008). Engaging the YouTube Google-eyed generation: Strategies for using web 2.0 in teaching and learning. *Electronic Journal of e-Learning, 6*(2), 119-129.

Foucault, M. (1988). Technologies of the Self. In Martin, Gutman, Huck & Hutton (eds.), Technologies of the Self. A Seminar with Michel Foucault.: The University of Massachusetts Press, 16-49.

Freire, P. (1970). *Pedagogy of the Oppressed*. New York: Continuum Publishing Company.

Geis, F. L. (1993). Self-fulfilling prophecies; a social psychological view of gender . In Beall, A. E., & Sternberg, R. J. (Eds.), *The Psychology of Gender* (pp. 9–54). London: Guilford Press.

Gilligan, C. (1982). *In a different voice: psychological theory and women's development*. Cambridge, MA: Harvard University Press.

Giroux, H. A. (1991). *Postmodernism, Feminism and Cultural Politics: Rethinking Educational Boundaries*. Albany, NY: State University of New York Press.

Goodman, S., Kirkup, G., & Michielsens, M. (2003). *ICTs in Teaching and Learning Women's Studies - Perspectives and Practices in Europe. The use of new information and communication technologies in women's studies teaching*. Lund: Athena, Universiteit Utrecht & Lund University.

Gouthro, P. A. (2005). A critical feminist analysis of the homeplace as learning site: expanding the discourse of lifelong learning to consider adult women learners. *International Journal of Lifelong Education, 24*(1), 5–19. doi:10.1080/026037042000317310

Green, H., Facer, K., Ruddwith, T., Dillon, P., & Humphreys, P. (2005) Personalisation and Digital Technologies Future Lab, Bristol. Retrieved September 1, 2009, from http://www.futurelab.org.uk/resources/documents/opening_education/Personalisation_report.pdf

Haas, A. T., Tulley, C., & Blair, K. (2002). Mentors versus masters: Women's and girls' narratives of (re)negotiation in web-based writing spaces. *Computers and Composition, 19*, 231–249. doi:10.1016/S8755-4615(02)00128-7

Habermas, J. (1968). *Erkenntnis und Interesse* [Knowledge and human interests]. Frankfurt, Germany: Suhrkamp.

Haraway, D. (1985). A manifesto for cyborgs: Science, technology, and social feminism in the 1980s. *Socialist Review, 15*(80), 65–107.

Haraway, D. (1988). Situated Knowledges: The Science Question in Feminism and the Privilege of Partial Perspective. *Feminist Studies, 14*(3), 575–599. doi:10.2307/3178066

Harding, S. (1991). *Whose science? Whose knowledge?: Thinking from women's lives*. Buckingham, UK: Open University Press.

Held, V. (2005). *The Ethics of Care: Personal, Political, and Global*. New York: Oxford University Press.

Herring, S. C. (2001). Gender and power in online communication. *Center for Social Informatics Working Papers*. Retrieved August 10, 2009, from http://rkcsi.indiana.edu/archive/CSI/WP/WP01-05B.html.

hooks, b. (1994). *Teaching to Transgress. Education as the Practice of Freedom*. London: Routledge.

Koch, A. C., Muller, S. M., & Sieverding, M. (2008). Women and computers. Effects of stereotype threat on attribution of failure. *Computers & Education, 51*, 1795–1803. doi:10.1016/j.compedu.2008.05.007

Kohlberg, L. (1981). *The philosophy of moral development: moral stages and the idea of justice*. London: Harper & Row.

Landis, M., Boire, J., Hanson, K., Niguidula, D., Tsikalas, K., & VanderVeen, A. (2002). An e-Learning manifesto. *International Journal on E-Learning, 1*(1), 6–8.

Locke, C., Levine, R., Searles, D., & Weinberger, D. (2000). *The Cluetrain Manifesto. The end of Business as Usual*. London: Pearson Education.

Marx, K., & Engels, F. (1848). *The Communist Manifesto*. London: Penguin.

McLoughlin, C., & Lee, M. (2008). Future learning landscapes: Transforming pedagogy through social software. *Innovate, 4*(5). Retrieved June 26, 2009, from http://www.distance-educator.com/dnews/Article15911.phtml

McWilliam, E., & Taylor, P. G. (1998). Teacher Im/Material: Challenging the new Pedagogies of Instructional Design. *Educational Researcher, 27*(8), 29–35.

(MIT)Massachusetts Institute of Technology. (2009) *MITOpenCourseWare*. Retrieved September 1, 2009, from http://ocw.mit.edu/

Morley, L. (2002). Lifelong Yearning. Feminist Pedagogy in the Learning Society . In Howie, G., & Tauchert, A. (Eds.), *Gender, Teaching and Research in Higher Education*. London: Ashgate Press.

Noddings, N. (2003). *Caring: a feminine approach to ethics and moral education*. Berkeley, CA: University of California Press.

O'Hear, S. (2006, August 8). e-Learning 2.0 - how Web technologies are shaping education, *ReadWriteWeb*. Retrieved September 9, 2009, from http://www.readwriteweb.com/archives/e-learning_20.php

Open University. (2009). *OpenLearn*. Retrieved September 1, 2009, from http://www.open.ac.uk/openlearn/home.php

Rommes, E., Faulkner, W., & Slooten, I. V. (2005). Changing Lives: the case for women-only vocational technology training revisited. *Journal of Vocational Education and Training*, *57*(3), 293–317. doi:10.1080/13636820500200288

Rubens, W. (2009) *Trends in e-learning*. Retrieved June 26, 2009, from http://www.frankwatching. com/archive/2009/01/07/trends-in-e-learning/

Salen, K., & Zimmerman, E. (2004). *Rules of Play. Game design fundamentals*. Cambridge, MA: MIT Press.

Schank, R. C. (2002). *Designing world class e-learning: How IBM, GE, Harvard Business School, and Columbia University are succeeding at e-learning*. New York: McGraw-Hill.

Schmitz, S., & Grunau, E. (2009, March). *Concept Mapping from a Perspective of Gendered Diversity*. Paper presented at the 5th European Symposium on Gender & ICT, Bremen. Retrieved June 26, 2009, from http://www.informatik. uni-bremen.de/soteg/gict2009/proceedings/ GICT2009_Schmitz.pdf

Sorensen, K., Faulkner, W., & Rommes, E. (in press). *Technologies of Inclusion; Bridging the Gender Gap in the Information Society*. Cambridge, MA: MIT Press.

Spender, D. (2003). *Nattering on the Net. Women, Power and Cyberspace*. Melbourne, Australia: Spinifix Press.

Stepulevage, L. (2001). Gender/Technology Relations: complicating the gender binary. *Gender and Education*, *13*(3), 325–338. doi:10.1080/09540250120082525

Thompson, J. L. (1983). *Learning Liberation. Women's Response to Men's Education*. London: Croom Helm.

Vlasveld, F. (2008). *Zes trends in e-learning*. Retrieved June 26, 2009, from http://www. frankwatching.com/archive/2009/01/07/trends-in-e-learning/

Weber, R. C. (1999). Manufacturing gender in military cockpit design . In MacKenzie, D., & Wajcman, J. (Eds.), *The social shaping of technology* (2nd ed., pp. 372–381). Philadelphia: Open University Press.

Webster, J. (1995). What Do We Know About Gender and Information Technology at Work? A Discussion of Selected Feminist Research. *European Journal of Women's Studies*, *2*, 315–334. doi:10.1177/135050689500200303

Wiley, D. A. (2000). *Learning object design and sequencing theory*. Unpublished doctoral dissertation, Brigham Young University. Retrieved June 26, 2009, from http://davidwiley.com/papers/ dissertation/dissertation.pdf

Winner, L. (1986). *The Whale and the Reactor: A Search for Limits in an Age of High Technology*. Chicago: University of Chicago Press.

Wollstonecraft, M. (1792). *A Vindication of the Rights of Woman. With Strictures on Political and Moral Subjects*. Retrieved June 19, 2009, from http://www.bartleby.com/144/

Wright, M. M. (2005). Finding a Place in Cyberspace. *Frontiers: A Journal of Women Studies, 26*(1), 48-59.

KEY TERMS AND DEFINITIONS

Embodiment: The integration of biological and socio-cultural aspects in a concept of mutual intra-actions that constitute the subject as a whole.

Collaborative Learning: Collaborative learning denotes learning in group work. In e-learning mediated collaboration, the focus is on the collective effort to complete all tasks that are intended for the learning process. Effective communication is a central prerequisite for effective collaboration.

Critical Pedagogy: Educational theory and teaching and learning practices intended to raise learners' critical consciousness about oppressive social conditions as part of a larger collective political struggle.

Ethics: A system for determining conduct based on a moral a framework of moral values. Also debates about the nature and validity of these values

Inclusion Needs: Aspects which need to be in place for the embodied inclusion of people in the information society, or in e-learning situations. These needs are access, motivation, capabilities and support.

Manifesto: A declaration of principles, intentions and sometimes a programme of action.

Personalisation: In digital technologies this refers to systems which store information about individual users and respond to the user on the basis of this information. In e-learning it refers to digital systems which use the information about the interests and performance of an individual student to offer individualized support and pathways through content.

Power: "Power" is a term with philosophical, political, social, cultural and many other uses and connotations. In philosophy power is a measure of an entity's ability to control the environment around itself, including the behavior of other entities. It can be seen as authority of influence, as a goal or a capability. Power functions in relations and social structures, and as such it has been a classic subject for women's and gender studies.

ENDNOTES

[1] European government policy documents such as the UK Higher Education Funding Council's 2005 policy document: ' HEFCE Strategy for e-learning' is an example of this kind or rationale. See http://www.hefce.ac.uk/pubs/hefce/2005/05_12/, last accessed 18.06.09

[2] This discussion took place on the Dutch website Frankwatching zes trends in e-learning at the end of 2008/beginning of 2009. http://www.frankwatching.com/archive/2008/12/29/zes-trends-in-e-learning/

[3] This expectation may either be by others, which is called the Pygmalion thesis, or by the person themselves. In the latter case, the opposite may also happen, if someone is informed that generally a group of people (to which the person belongs) performs badly on a test, the 'stereotype threat' will cause the person to perform less good than without that information.

Compilation of References

Adam, A. (2001). Cyberstalking: gender and computer ethics. In Green, E., & Adam, A. (Eds.), *Virtual Gender: Technology, consumption and identity*. London: Routledge.

Adams, V. (2002). Randomized Controlled Crime: Postcolonial Sciences in Alternative Medicine Research. *Social Studies of Science*, *32*(5-6), 659–690. doi:10.1177/030631270203200503

Adya, M., & Kaiser, K. (2005). Early determinants of women in the IT workforce: a model of girls' career choices. *Information Technology & People*, *18*(3), 230–259. doi:10.1108/09593840510615860

Ahmed, S. (2008). Open Forum. Imaginary Prohibitions: Some Preliminary Remarks on the Founding Gestures of the "New Materialism". *European Journal of Women's Studies*, *15*(1), 23–39. doi:10.1177/1350506807084854

Ahrenkiel, A., Illeris, K., Sederberg, M.-L., & Simonsen, B. (1998). *Voksenuddannelse og deltagermotivation. (Adult education and participant motivation)*. Roskilde, Denmark: Roskilde Universitetsforlag.

Akerlind, G. (2005). Variation and commonality in phenomenographic research methods. *Higher Education Research & Development*, *24*, 321–334. doi:10.1080/07294360500284672

Akrich, M. (1992). The De-Scription of Technical Objects. Shaping Technology/Building Society: Studies in Sociotechnical Change. In Bijker, W. E., & Law, J. (Eds.), *Shaping Technology Bulding Society Studies in Sociotechnical Change* (pp. 205–224). Cambridge, MA: MIT Press.

Altmejd, A., & Vallinder, A. (2007). *Betydelsen av en virtuell agents sociala förmåga [The Significance of the Social Skills of Virtual Agents]*. Student research paper, Lund University, Lund, Sweden. Retrieved May 31, 2009, from http://www.lucs.lu.se/Agneta.Gulz/selected_student_works/AA-AV_StudReport_2007.pdf

Anderson, B. (1991). *Imagined communities: reflections on the origin and spread of nationalism*. London: Verso.

Argamon, S., Koppel, M., Pennebaker, J. W., & Schler, J. (2007). Mining the Blogosphere. Age, gender and the variety of self expression [Electronic Version]. *First Monday*, *12*, 2007. Retrieved from http://firstmonday.org/01.09.2009.

Ariffin, O. (1993). *Bangsa Melayu: Malay Concepts of Democracy and Community 1945-1950*. Oxford, UK: Oxford University Press.

Ariffin, R. (1999). Feminism in Malaysia: A Historical and Present Perspective of Women's Struggles in Malaysia. *Women's Studies International Forum*, *22*(4), 417–423. doi:10.1016/S0277-5395(99)00039-4

Assarsson, L., & Sipos-Zackrisson, K. (2006). Att delta i vuxenstudier. In Larsson, S., & Olsson, L. E. (Eds.), *Om vuxnas studier. (On adult studies)*. Lund, Sweden: Studentlitteratur.

Aull Davies, C. (1999). *Reflexive Ethnography – A Guide to Researching Selves and Others*. London, New York: Routledge.

Bakardjieva, M. (2005). *Internet Society. The internet in everyday life*. London: Sage Publications.

Baker, S. C., Wentz, R. K., & Woods, M. M. (2009). Using Virtual Worlds in Education: SecondLife® as an Educational Tool. *Teaching of Psychology, 36*(1), 59–64. doi:10.1080/00986280802529079

Ball, S., Reay, D., & David, M. (2002). 'Ethnic Choosing': minority ethnic students, social class and higher education choice. *Race, Ethnicity and Education, 5*(4), 333–357. doi:10.1080/1361332022000030879

Bandura, A. (1977). *Social Learning Theory.* Englewood Cliffs, NJ: Prentice Hall.

Bandura, A. (2000). *Self-efficacy: The Foundation of Agency.* Mahwah, NJ: Lawrence Erlbaum.

Barad, K. (1998). Getting Real: Technoscientific Practices and the Materialization of Reality. *A Journal of Feminist Cultural Studies, 10*(2), 87-128.

Barad, K. (1999). Agential Realism – Feminist Interventions in Understanding Scientific Practices. In Biagioli, M. (Ed.), *The Science Studies Reader* (pp. 1–11). New York: Routledge.

Barad, K. (2003). Post-humanist performativity: Toward an understanding of how matter comes to matter. Signs. *Journal of Women in Culture and Society, 28*(3), 801–831. doi:10.1086/345321

Barad, K. (2007). *Meeting the universe halfway – quantum physics and the entanglement of matter and meaning.* Durham, NC: Duke University Press.

Barad, K. (2007). *Meeting the Universe Halfway.* Durham, NC: Duke University Press.

Barefoot, B. (2004). Higher education's revolving door: confronting the problem of student drop out in US colleges and universities. *Open Learning, 19*(1), 9–18. doi:10.1080/0268051042000177818

Barry, A. (2001). *Political machines: Governing a technological society.* London: Athlone.

Baxter Magolda, M. B. (1992). *Knowing and reasoning in college: Gender related patterns in students' intellectual development.* San Francisco: Jossey-Bass.

Baxter, A., & Britton, C. (2001). Risk, Identity and Change: becoming a mature student. *International Studies in Sociology of Education, 11*, 87–102. doi:10.1080/09620210100200066

Baylor, A., & Plant, A. (2005). Pedagogical agents as social models for engineering: The influence of appearance on female choice. In Looi, C. K., McCalla, G., Bredeweg, B., & Breuker, J. (Eds.), *Artificial intelligence in education: Supporting learning through intelligent and socially informed technology* (Vol. 125, pp. 65–72). Amsterdam, The Netherlands: IOS Press.

Baylor, A., Rosenberg-Kima, R., & Plant, A. (2006). Interface agents as social models: The impact of appearance on females' attitude toward engineering. In CHI'06 Extended Abstracts on Human Factors in Computing Systems (pp. 526-531). New York: ACM.

Beck, E. (2002). P for Political – Participation is Not Enough. *Scandinavian Journal of Information Systems, 14*, 77–92.

Belenky, M. F., Clinchy, B. M., Goldberger, N. R., & Tarule, J. M. (1986/1987). *Women's ways of knowing: The development of self, voice and mind.* New York: BasicBooks.

Bengtsson, J. (2004). *Med livsvärld som grund (Grounded in the life-world).* Lund, Sweden: Studentlitteratur.

Berner, B. (1996). *Sakernas tillstånd: Kön, klass och expertis* [The state of things: Gender, class and technical expertise]. Lund, Sweden: Carlsson.

Berner, B., & Mellström, U. (1997). Looking for Mister Engineer. Understanding Masculinity and Technology at two Fin-de-Siecles. In Berner, B. (Ed.), *Gendered Practices. Feminist Studies of Technology and Society.* Stockholm: Almqvist & Wiksell.

Berners-Lee, T., Hendler, J. J., & Lassila. O. (2001, May 17). The Semantic Web, *Scientific American.*

Birkett, W. P., & Evans, E. (2005). Theorising professionalisation: a model for organising and understanding histories of the professionalising activities of occupational associations of accountants. *Accounting History, 10*(1), 99–127. .doi:10.1177/103237320501000105

Bjerknes, G., & Bratteteig, T. (1995). User Participation and Democracy: A Discussion of Scandinavian Research on Systems Development. *Scandinavian Journal of Information Systems*, *7*(1), 73–98.

Björkman, C. (2005). *Feminist Technoscience Strategies in Computer Science.* Doctoral Dissertation, Blekinge Institute of Technology, Sweden.

Blagojevic, M., Bundule, M., Burkhardt, A., Calloni, M., Ergma, E., & Glover, J. (2004). *Waste of talents: turning private struggles into a public issue. Women and science in the Enwise countries.* Luxembourg: European Commission.

Blomqvist, M. (2007, June 27-29). Working conditions in the ICT sector mediated by newspapers *Gender, Work and Organisation 5th biennial international interdisciplinary conference*, Keele University, UK

Bødker, K., Kensing, F., & Simonsen, J. (2004). *Participatory IT Design, Designing for Business and Workplace Realities*. Cambridge, MA: The MIT Press.

Boivie, I. (2005). *A Fine Balance, Addressing Usability and Users' Needs in the Development of IT Systems for the Workplace*. Published doctoral dissertation, Uppsala University, Sweden.

Bolsø, A. (2002). *Power in the Erotic; feminism and lesbian practice*. Trondheim, Norway: NTNU.

Borgman, C. L. (2007). *Scholarship in the Digital Age. Information, Infrastructure and the Internet*. Cambridge, MA: MIT Press.

Bossen, C. (2008). How to analyze IT. Strategies, Methodologies and Challenges. Presentation at PhD workshop 2nd-4th June 2008, Aarhus, Denmark.

Boulos, M. N. K., Hetherington, L., & Wheeler, S. S. (2007). Second Life: an overview of the potential of 3-D virtual worlds in medical and health education. *Health Information and Libraries Journal*, 2007, 233–245. doi:10.1111/j.1471-1842.2007.00733.x

Bourdieu, P. (1980). *Questions de sociologie* [Sociology in Question]. Paris: Minuit.

Bowden, J. A., & Walsh, E. (2000). *Phenomenography*. Melbourne, Australia: RMIT University Press.

Bozionelos, N. (2001). Computer anxiety: relationship with computer experience and prevalence. *Computers in Human Behavior*, *17*(2), 213–224. doi:10.1016/S0747-5632(00)00039-X

Brandell, G., & Staberg, E. (2008). Mathematics: a female, male or gender-neutral domain? A study of attitudes among students at secondary level. *Gender and Education*, *20*(5), 495–509. doi:10.1080/09540250701805771

Bras-Klapwijk, R. M., & Rommes, E. (2005). Voorbij de twee seksen: inspelen op uiteenlopende loopbaan-oriëntaties van middelbare scholieren. In M. v. S. Z. e. Werkgelegenheid (Ed.), De Glazen Muur. Essaybundel over beroepensegregatie. (pp. 53-68). Den Haag: Ministerie van Sociale Zaken en Werkgelegenheid, Directie Coördinatie Emancipatiebeleid.

Bratteteig, T. (1997). Mutual learning. Enabling cooperation on systems design. In Kristin Braa & Eric Monteiro (Eds.), *IRIS Conference '20: Proceedings* (pp. 1-20). Oslo, Norway: Dept. of Informatics, University of Oslo.

Bratteteig, T. (2004). *Making Change, Dealing with relations between design and use*. Published doctoral dissertation, University of Oslo, Norway.

Brave, S., & Nass, C. (2005). *Wired for Speech*. Cambridge, MA: MIT Press.

Bray, F. (2007). Gender and Technology. *Annual Review of Anthropology*, *36*, 1–21. doi:10.1146/annurev.anthro.36.081406.094328

Britzman, D. (1995). Is there a queer pedagogy – Or, stop reading straight. *Educational Theory*, *45*(2), 151–165. doi:10.1111/j.1741-5446.1995.00151.x

Broos, A., & Roe, K. (2006). The digital divide in the playstation generation: Self-efficacy, locus of control and ICT adoption among adolescents. *Poetics*, *34*(4/5), 306–317. doi:10.1016/j.poetic.2006.05.002

Brosnan, M., & Lee, W. (1998). A cross-cultural comparison of gender differences in computer attitudes and anxieties. The United Kingdom and Hong Kong. *Computers in Human Behavior, 14*(4), 559–577. doi:10.1016/S0747-5632(98)00024-7

Brown, J. S., & Duguid, P. (2000). *The social life of information*. Boston, MA: Harvard Business School Press.

Brown, J. S., Collins, A., & Duguid, P. (1989). Situated cognition and the culture of learning. *Educational Researcher, 18*(1), 32–42.

Bruun Jensen, C. (2004). *Researching Partially Existing Objects: What is an Electronic Patient Record? Where do you find it? How do you study it?* Working Papers from Centre for STS Studies, Department of Information & Media Studies, University of Aarhus, Denmark.

Bryant, S. (2000). At home on the electronic frontier: Work, gender and the information highway. *New Technology, Work and Employment, 15*(1), 19–34. doi:10.1111/1468-005X.00062

Buder, C. (2003). Frauen und Informations- und Kommunikationstechnologien im globalen Süden. In Frauen und IKT im globalen Süden – Research Report (pp. 37–50). Wien: Frauensolidarität.

Buis, T. (2003). *Technomonitor 2003. Een kwantitatieve analyse van het technisch onderwijs en de technische arbeidsmarkt*. Nijmegen: Kenniscentrum Beroepsonderwijs Arbeidsmarkt.

Burke, K. (1969). *A Grammar of Motives*. Berkley, CA: University of California Press.

Butler, J. (1990). *Gender Trouble: Feminism and Subversion of Identity*. London: Routledge.

Butler, J. (1993). *Bodies that Matter. On the Discursive Limits of "Sex"*. London, UK: Routledge.

Butler, J. (1993). *Bodies that Matter: on the discursive limits of 'sex*. New York: Routledge.

Butler, J. (1999). *Gender Trouble, Feminism and the Subversion of Identity*. London: Routledge.

Butler, J. (1999). *Gender Trouble. Feminism and the Subversion of Identity* (2nd ed.). London: Routledge.

Butler, J. (2004). *Undoing Gender*. New York: Routledge.

Butler, J. (2006). *Undoing Gender*. New York: Routledge.

Camp, T. (1997). The incredible shrinking pipeline. *Communications of the ACM, 40*(10), 103–110. .doi:10.1145/262793.262813

Carr-Chellman, A. A. (Ed.). (2005). *Global perspectives on e-learning*. London: Sage.

Carstensen, G. (2004). *Sexuella trakasserier finns nog i en annan värld: Konstruktioner av ett (o)giltigt problem.* (Sexual harassment probably happens in another world: Constructions of an (in)valid problem in academia). Doctoral Dissertation, Uppsala University, Sweden. (In Swedish).

Castell, S. D., & Bryson, M. (1998). From the Ridiculous to the Sublime: On Finding Oneself in Educational Research. In Pinar, W. F. (Ed.), *Queer Theory in Education* (pp. 245–250). Mahwah, NJ: Lawrence Erlbaum Associates.

Castells, M. (2000). *The rise of the network society* (2nd ed.). Oxford, UK: Blackwell.

Castells, M. (2001). *The Internet galaxy: reflections on the Internet, business, and society*. New York: Oxford University Press.

Chegwidden, P. (2000). Feminist Pedagogy and the Lap Top Computer. In E. Balka & R. Smith (Eds.), Women, Work and Computerization, Charting a Course to the Future (pp. 292-299). Boston: Dordrecht.

Chess, S. (2006). *Working with Sex, Playing with Gender: Locating Androgyny in Video Games*. Retrieved December 12, 2007, from http://www.shiraland.com/Work/gender_media.pdf

CIA-The World Factbook. *Afghanistan*. Retrieved April, 2009, from https://www.cia.gov/library/publications/the-world-factbook/geos/af.html

Clark, H. H. (1996). Using language. Cambridge, UK: Cambridge University Press. doi:10.1017/CBO9780511620539

Clarke, J., Harrison, R., Reeve, F., & Edwards, R. (2002). Assembling spaces: The question of "place" in further education. *Discourse: Studies in the cultural politics of education, 23*(3), 285-297.

Clegg, S. (2001). Theorising the Machine: gender, education and computing. *Gender and Education, 13*(3), 307–324. .doi:10.1080/09540250120063580

Clift, R. T., Mullen, L., Levin, J., & Larson, A. (2001). Technologies in contexts: implications for teacher education. *Teaching and Teacher Education, 17,* 33–50. doi:10.1016/S0742-051X(00)00037-8

Cockburn, C. (1983). *Male Dominance and Technological Change*. London: Pluto Press.

Cockburn, C. (1985). *Machinery of dominance: Women, men and technical know-how*. London: Pluto Press.

Cockburn, C., & Ormod, S. (1993). *Gender and Technology in the Making*. Thousand Oaks, CA: Sage Publications.

Cohen, M. B., & Mullender, A. (2003). Introduction. In Cohen, M. B., & Mullender, A. (Eds.), *Gender and Groupwork*. London: Routledge. doi:10.4324/9780203163795

Coleman, M. (2009, March 10). Barack Obama 'receives preferential treatment on Wikipedia', report claims. *Telegraph newspaper,* London

Colley, A., & Comber, C. (2003). Age and gender differences in computer use and attitudes among secondary school students, what has changed? *Educational Research, 45*(2), 155–165. doi:10.1080/0013188032000103235

Collins, P. H. (1998). It's All in the Family: Intersections of Gender, Race and Nation. *Hypatia, 13*(3), 62–82. doi:10.2979/HYP.1998.13.3.62

Coltrane, S., & Adams, M. (1997). Work-family imagery and gender stereotypes: Television and the reproduction of difference. *Journal of Vocational Behavior, 50,* 323–347. doi:10.1006/jvbe.1996.1575

Compeau, D. R., & Higgins, C. A. (1995). Computer self-efficacy: Development of a measure and initial test. *Management Information Systems Quarterly, 19*(2), 189–211. doi:10.2307/249688

Connell, R. (1995). Masculinities. Cambridge, UK: Polity in association with Blackwell.

Connell, R. W. (1987). *Gender and Power, Society, the Person and Sexual Politics*. Oxford, UK: Polity Press.

Connell, R. W. (1997). The big picture: Masculinity in recent world history. In Halsey, A. H., Lauder, H., Brown, P., & Stuart Wells, A. (Eds.), *Education. Culture Economy Society*. Oxford, UK: Oxford University Press.

Connell, R. W. (2000). *The Men and the Boys*. Berkeley, CA: University of California Press.

Connell, R. W., & Messerschmidt, J. W. (2005). Hegemonic masculinity. Rethinking the concept. *Gender & Society, 19*(6), 829–859. doi:10.1177/0891243205278639

Cooper, J. (2006). The digital divide: the special case of gender. *Journal of Computer Assisted Learning, 22*(5), 320–334. doi:10.1111/j.1365-2729.2006.00185.x

Cooper, J., & Weaver, K. D. (2003). *Gender and Computers: Understanding the digital divide*. Mahwah, NJ: Erlbaum.

Corneliussen, H. (2003). Konstruksjoner av kjönn ved hoyre IKT-utdanning i Norge. (Constructions of gender in higher ICT education in Norway) *Kvinneforskning 4.*

Corneliussen, H. (2003). Male positioning strategies in relation to computing. In Lie, M. (Ed.), *He, she and IT revisited. New perspectives on Gender in the Information society* (pp. 103–134). Olso, Norway: Gyldendal.

Corneliussen, H. (2003, November 14-16). *Negotiating gendered positions in the discourse of computing*. Presented at Information Technology, Transnational Democracy and Gender. Luleå.

Crenshaw, K. W. (1991). Mapping the Margins: Intersectionality, identity politics, and violence against women of colour. *Stanford Law Review, 43*(6), 1241–1299. doi:10.2307/1229039

Crossan, B., Field, J., Gallagher, J., & Merrill, B. (2003). Understanding participation in learning for non-traditional adult learners: learning careers and the construction of learning identities. *British Journal of Sociology of Education*, *24*(1), 55–67. doi:10.1080/01425690301907

Cukier, W. (2003, April 10-12). Constructing the IT Skills Shortage in Canada: The Implications of Institutional Discourse and Practices for the Participation of Women. In *Proceedings of the 2003 SIGMIS conference on Computer personnel research.* Philadelphia.

Cukier, W., Shortt, D., & Devine, I. (2002). Gender and Information Technology: Implications of Definitions. *SIGCSE Bulletin*, *34*(4), 142–148. .doi:10.1145/820127.820188

Culley, M., & Portuges, C. (Eds.). (1985). *Gendered Subjects. The dynamics of feminist teaching.* London: Routledge.

Curtis, P. (2009). Girls do better without boys, study finds, *The Guardian*. Retrieved March 18, 2009, from http://www.guardian.co.uk/education/2009/mar/18/secondary-schools-girls-gcse-results

Davies, N. (2008). *Flat Earth News.* London: Chatto & Windus.

de Castell, S., & Bryson, M. (1997). *Radical in<ter>ventions: Identity, politics and difference in educational praxis.* New York: SUNY Press.

Delanty, G. (2001). *Challenging knowledge: the university in the knowledge society. Milton Keynes.* UK: Open University Press.

DfES. (2007). *Gender and Education: the evidence on pupils in England.* Department of Education and Skills.

Duffy, P. (2008). Engaging the YouTube Google-eyed generation: Strategies for using web 2.0 in teaching and learning. *Electronic Journal of e-Learning, 6*(2), 119-129.

Dunn, S., & Ridgeway, J. (1991). Naked into the World: IT experiences on a final primary school teaching practice: a second survey. *Journal of Computer Assisted Learning, 7*(4), 229–240. doi:10.1111/j.1365-2729.1991.tb00254.x

Dutton, W., Helsper, E. J., & Gerber, M. M. (2009). *The Internet in Britain 2009 Oxford Internet Surveys.* UK: University of Oxford.

Dyer, R. (1997). *White: Essays on race and culture.* London: Routledge.

Eck, E. V., & Volman, M. (1999). *Techniek. Leuke hobby, saaie baan?* Amsterdam: SCO-Kohnstamm Instituut.

Edwards, P. N. (1990). The army and the microworld. Computers and the politics of gender identity. *Signs: Journal of Women in Culture and Society, 16*(1), 102–127. doi:10.1086/494647

Edwards, P. N. (1990). The Army and the Microworld: Computers and the Politics of Gender Identity. SIGNS. *Journal of Women in Culture and Society, 16*(1), 102–107. doi:10.1086/494647

Edwards, R., & Clarke, J. (2002). Flexible learning, spatiality and identity. *Studies in Continuing Education, 24*(2), 153–165. doi:10.1080/0158037022000020965

Edwards, R., & Usher, R. (2007). *Lifelong learning: Signs, discourses, practices.* Dordrecht, The Netherlands: Springer.

Elovaara, P. (2004). *Angels in Unstable Sociomaterial Relations: Stories of Information Technology.* Published doctoral dissertation, Blekinge Institute of Technology.

Elovaara, P., Igira, F. T., & Mörtberg, C. (2006, July 5-August). Whose participation? Whose knowledge? – Exploring PD in Tanzania-Zanzibar and Sweden. In Proceedings of *Participatory Design Conference: Vol. 1, 31,* Trento, Italy.

Engels, R. C. M. E., Braak, D. T., Eyndhoven, S., Overbeek, G., Scholte, R. H. J., & Kemp, R. A. T. d. (forthcoming). The Impact of Alcohol Portrayal in Soaps on Adolescent Drinking. *Psychology & Health.*

Engels, R. C. M. E., Hermans, R., Van Baaren, R. B., Hollenstein, T., & Bot, S. M. (2009). Alcohol portrayal on television affects actual drinking behaviour. *Alcohol and Alcoholism (Oxford, Oxfordshire), 44*(3), 244–249. doi:10.1093/alcalc/agp003

EOC. (2004). *Occupational Segregation, gender gaps and skills gaps*, Occupational Segregation Working Paper Series No.15. EOC e-Skills(2008). *Technology Counts IT and Telecoms Insights 2008*. Retrieved February 10, 2009, from http://www.e-Skills.com/Research-and-policy/Insights-2008/2205

Epstein, D., & Johnson, R. (1998). *Schooling Sexualities*. Buckingham, UK: Open University Press.

Eriksson, K. (2003). *Manligt läkarskap, kvinnliga läkare och normala kvinnor: Köns- och läkarskapande symbolik, metaforik och praktik.* (Physicianship, Female Physicians and Normal Women: The Symbolical, Metaphorical and Practical Doing(s) of Gender and Physicians). Doctoral Dissertation, Uppsala Universitet, Sweden. (In Swedish).

Errington, S. (1990). Recasting Sex, Gender, and Power: A Theoretical and Regional Overview. In Atkinson, J., & Errington, S. (Eds.), *Power and Difference: Gender in Island Southeast Asia* (pp. 1–158). Stanford, CA: Stanford University Press.

Esterberg, K. G. (1996). "A Certain Swagger When I Walk": Performing Lesbian Identity. In Seidman, S. (Ed.), *Queer Theory/Sociology* (pp. 259–279). Cambridge, UK: Blackwell Publishers.

European Commission (1999, June 19). *The European Higher Education area: Joint declaration of the European Ministers of Education.*

Eurostat. (2009). Share of women among tertiary students. Retrieved August 20, 2009, 2009, from http://epp.eurostat.ec.europa.eu/

Evans, T. (1994). *Understanding learners in open and distance education.* London: Kogan Page.

Faulkner, W. (2000a). Dualisms, Hierarchies and Gender in Engineering. *Social Studies of Science, 30*(5), 759–792. .doi:10.1177/030631200030005005

Faulkner, W. (2000b). The Power and the Pleasure? A Research Agenda for "Making Gender Stick" to Engineers. *Science, Technology & Human Values, 25*(1), 87–119. .doi:10.1177/016224390002500104

Faulkner, W. (2001). The technology question in feminism: A view from feminist technology studies. *Women's Studies International Forum, 24*(1), 79–95. doi:10.1016/S0277-5395(00)00166-7

Faulkner, W. (2003). Teknikfrågan i feminismen [The technology issue in feminism]. In B. Berner (Ed.), Vem tillhör tekniken? [Who Owns Technology]. Lund, Sweden: Arkiv förlag.

Faulkner, W. (2005). Becoming and Belonging: Gendered processes in engineering. In Archibald, J., Emms, J., Grundy, F., Payne, J., and Turner, E. (Eds.) *Women into Computing (WIC) Conference Proceedings: The Gender Politics of ICT* 15-25. Middlesex, UK: Middlesex University Press.

Faulkner, W., & Kleif, T. (2003). Edinburgh women's training course: An old idea still working. In Lie, M., & Sörensen, K. H. (Eds.), *Strategies of Inclusion: Gender in the Information Society* (Vol. I, pp. 201–236). Trondheim, Norway: NTNU, Centre for Technology and Society.

Faulkner, W., & Kleif, T. (2004). Included women, excluded men: users and nonusers of rural community resource centres. In N. Oudshoorn, E. Rommes & I. v. Slooten (Eds.), Strategies of Inclusion: Gender in the Information Society, Vol. III: Surveys of Women's User Experience (pp. 137-166). Trondheim, Norway: NTNU.

Fidishun, D. (2001). Listening to our side. Computer training issues of middle age and older women. *Women's Studies Quarterly, 29*(3), 103–127.

Fisher, A., & Margolis, J. (2002). Unlocking the Clubhouse: The Carnegie Mellon Experience. *SIGCSE Bulletin, 34*(2), 79–83. .doi:10.1145/543812.543836

Foucault, M. (1980). *Power/Knowledge: Selected interviews and other writings 1972-1977* (Gordon, C., Ed.). Brighton, UK: Harvester.

Foucault, M. (1988). Technologies of the Self. In Martin, Gutman, Huck & Hutton (eds.), Technologies of the Self. A Seminar with Michel Foucault.: The University of Massachusetts Press, 16-49.

Foucault, M. (1991). *Discipline and Punish: the Birth of the Prison.* London: Penguin.

Foucault, M. (1991). *Discipline and punish: the birth of the prison*. Harmondsworth, UK: Penguin.

Foucault, M. (2007). Spaces of security: The example on the town Lecture of 11ᵗʰ January 1978. *Political Geography, 26*(1), 48–56. doi:10.1016/j.polgeo.2006.08.004

Fox, K. E. (1985). *Reflections on Gender and Science*. New Haven, CT: Yale University Press.

Fralick, B., Kearn, J. Thompson, S., & Lyons, J. (2008). How middle schoolers draw engineers and scientists. *Science education technology, 18*, 60-73.

Fraser, N. (1992). Introduction. In Fraser, N., & Lee Bartky, S. (Eds.), *Revaluing French Feminism: Critical Essays on Difference, Agency and Culture* (pp. 1–24). Bloomington, IN: Indiana University Press.

Freire, P. (1970). *Pedagogy of the Oppressed*. London: Penguin. Online version retrieved August 20, 2009, from http://www.marxists.org/subject/education/freire/pedagogy

Freire, P. (1970). *Pedagogy of the Oppressed*. New York: Continuum Publishing Company.

Frosh, S., Phoenix, A., & Pattman, R. (2002). Policing young masculinities. In Young masculinities. Palgrave: Handmills.

Fuller, L., & Meiners, E. (2005). Reflections. Empowering women, technology and (feminist) institutional changes. *Frontiers, 26*(1), 168–180. doi:10.1353/fro.2005.0009

Fürst, G. (2004). *Slutrapport från GIT-projektet. Genus, integration och teknologi – pedagogiskt nytänkande när 22 kvinnor utbildar sig till nätverksutvecklare. (Final report from the GIT project. Gender, integration and technology – educational innovation when 22 women study to become network developers)*. Halmstad, Sweden: Högskolan i Halmstad.

GameGirlAdvance. (2003). *It's Time for Androgyny, It's just Vaan!* Game+Girl=Advance Weblog. Retrieved May 31, 2009, from http://www.gamegirladvance.com/archives/2003/12/02/its_time_for_androgyny_its_just_vaan.html

Gansmo, H. J., Lagesen, V. A., & Sorensen, K. (2003). Forget the hacker? A critical re-appraisal of Norwegian studies of gender and ICT. In Lie, M. (Ed.), *He, She and IT Revisited. New Perspectives on Gender in the Information Society* (pp. 34–68). Trondheim, Norway: Gyldendal Norsk Verlag.

Gedenryd, H. (1998). *How Designers Work – making sense of authentic cognitive activities*. Doctoral Dissertation, Lund University, Sweden.

Geis, F. L. (1993). Self-fulfilling prophecies; a social psychological view of gender. In Beall, A. E., & Sternberg, R. J. (Eds.), *The Psychology of Gender* (pp. 9–54). London: Guilford Press.

Ghosh, R. A. (2004). *The opportunities of Free/Libre/Open-Source-Software for developing countries*. Retrieved December, 2006, from: http://www.iprsonline.org/unctadictsd/bellagio/docs/Gosh_Bellagio4.pdf

Gill, R., & Grint, K. (1995). *The Gender and Technology Relation: Contemporary Theory and Research*. London: Taylor and Francis.

Gilligan, C. (1982). *In a different voice. Psychological theory and women's development*. Cambridge, MA: Harvard University Press.

Gilmour, H. (1999). What Girls Want: The intersections of leisure and power in female computer game play. In Kinder, M. (Ed.), *Kids' Media Culture* (pp. 263–292). Durham, NC: Duke University Press.

Giroux, H. A. (1991). *Postmodernism, Feminism and Cultural Politics: Rethinking Educational Boundaries*. Albany, NY: State University of New York Press.

Goffman, I. (1978). The presentation of Self in Everyday Life. London: The Penguin Press (first pub UK 1969 USA by Anchor Books in 1959).

Goh, B. L. (2002). *Modern Dreams: An Enquiry into Power, Cultural Production and the Cityscape in Contemporary Urban Penang, Malaysia*. New York: Cornell University Press.

Gomes, A. (1994). *Modernity and Identity: Asian Illustrations*. Bundoora, Victoria: La Trobe University Press.

Goodman, S., Kirkup, G., & Michielsens, M. (2003). *ICTs in Teaching and Learning Women's Studies - Perspectives and Practices in Europe. The use of new information and communication technologies in women's studies teaching.* Lund: Athena, Universiteit Utrecht & Lund University.

Gouthro, P. A. (2005). A critical feminist analysis of the homeplace as learning site: expanding the discourse of lifelong learning to consider adult women learners. *International Journal of Lifelong Education, 24*(1), 5–19. doi:10.1080/026037042000317310

Gras-Velazquez, A., Joyce, A., & Derby, M. (2009). *Women and ICT, why are girls are still not attracted to ICT studies and careers?* European Schoolnet Brussels, Retrieved August 20, 2009 from www.eun.org

Green, E., & Adam, A. (1998). On-line leisure. Gender and ICT's in the Home. *Information Communication and Society, 1*(3), 291–312.

Green, E., & Keeble, L. (2001). The technological story of a women's centre. A feminist model of user-centred design. In Keeble, L. (Ed.), *Community Informatics* (pp. 53–70). Florence, KY: Routledge.

Green, H., Facer, K., Ruddwith, T., Dillon, P., & Humphreys, P. (2005) Personalisation and Digital Technologies Future Lab, Bristol. Retrieved September 1, 2009, from http://www.futurelab.org.uk/resources/documents/opening_education/Personalisation_report.pdf

Greenbaum, J., & Kyng, M. (1991). *Design at Work: Cooperative Design of Computer Systems.* Hillsdale, NJ: Lawrence Earlbaum Associates.

Gregg, M. (2009). Banal Bohemia: Blogging from the Ivory Tower Hot-desk. *Convergence, 15*, 4.

Griffiths, M., Moore, K., Burns, B., & Richardson, H. (2007). *The Disappearing Women: North West ICT Project Final Report.* University of Salford.

Grundy, F. (1996). *Women and Computers.* Exeter, UK: Intellect Books.

Guest, T. (2007). *Second Lives. A Journey Through Virtual World.* London: Hutchinson.

Gulliksen, J., & Göransson, B. (2002). *Användarcentrerad systemdesign.* Lund, Sweden: Studentlitteratur. [*User centred systems design*]

Gulz, A., & Haake, M. (2006a). Pedagogical agents – design guide lines regarding visual appearance and pedagogical roles. In Méndez-Vilas, A., Solano Martin, A., Mesa Gonzalez, J., & Mesa Gonzalez, J. A. (Eds.), *Current Developments in Technology-Assisted Education (2006)* (Vol. III, pp. 1848–1852). Badajoz, Spain: FORMATEX.

Gulz, A., & Haake, M. (2006b). Visual design of virtual pedagogical agents: Naturalism versus stylization in static appearance. In *Proceedings of the 3rd International Design and Engagability Conference @ NordiChi 2006.*

Haake, M., & Gulz, A. (2007). Virtual pedagogical agents: Stylization for engagement. *Interfaces, 70*, 12–13.

Haas, A. T., Tulley, C., & Blair, K. (2002). Mentors versus masters: Women's and girls' narratives of (re)negotiation in web-based writing spaces. *Computers and Composition, 19*, 231–249. doi:10.1016/S8755-4615(02)00128-7

Habermas, J. (1968). *Erkenntnis und Interesse* [Knowledge and human interests]. Frankfurt, Germany: Suhrkamp.

Habib, L., & Cornford, T. (2001). Domestication and Gender: Computers in the Home. Global Co-operation in the New Millenium. *ECIS 2001 9th European Conference on Information Systems,* Bled, Slovenia.

Hacker, S. (1989). *Pleasure, Power and Technology.* Boston: Unwin Hyman.

Hacker, S. (1990). *Doing it the hard way: Investigations of gender and technology.* Boston: Unwin Hyman.

Hafkin, N., & Taggart, N. (2001). Gender, Information Technology, and Developing Countries: An Analytic Study. New York: Academy for Educational Development (AED)

Hägerström, J. (2004). Vi och dom och alla dom andra på Komvux. Etnicitet, genus och klass i samspel. (We and them and all the others at Komvux: The interplay of ethnicity, gender and class.) Lund, Sweden: Lunds universitet, Sociologiska institutionen.

Hammersley, M. (2006). *Media bias in reporting social research*. London: Routledge.

Handlingsplan för eFörvaltning (2008) [The Action Plan for eGovernment]. Stockholm: Näringsdepartementet. Retrieved February, 2008, from http://www.sweden.gov. se/content/1/c6/09 /65/12/4ffd1319.pdf

Hannover, B., & Kessels, U. (2004). Self-to-prototype matching as a strategy for making academic choices. Why high school students do not like math and science. *Learning and Instruction, 14*, 51–67. doi:10.1016/j.learninstruc.2003.10.002

Haraway, D. (1985). A manifesto for cyborgs: Science, technology, and social feminism in the 1980s. *Socialist Review, 15*(80), 65–107.

Haraway, D. (1985). A manifesto for cyborgs: Science, technology, and social feminism in the 1980s. *Socialist Review, 15*(80), 65–107.

Haraway, D. (1988). Situated Knowledges: The Science Question in Feminism and the Privilege of Partial Perspective. *Feminist Studies, 14*(3), 575–599. doi:10.2307/3178066

Haraway, D. (1991). A cyborg manifesto: Science, technology, and socialist-feminism in the late twentieth century. In Haraway, D. (Ed.), *Simians, Cyborgs and Women: The Reinvention of Nature* (pp. 149–181). New York: Routledge.

Haraway, D. (1991a). A Cyborg Manifesto: Science, Technology, and Socialist-Feminism in the Late Twentieth Century. In Haraway, D. (Ed.), *Simians, Cyborgs and Women – The Reinvention of Nature* (pp. 149–181). New York: Routledge.

Haraway, D. (1991b). Situated Knowledges: The Science Question in Feminism and the Privilege of Partial Perspective. In Haraway, D. (Ed.), *Simians, Cyborgs and Women – The Reinvention of Nature* (pp. 183–201). New York: Routledge.

Haraway, D. (1997). *Modest_Witness@Second_Millennium. FemaleMan©_Meets_OncoMouse™. Feminism and Technoscience*. London: Routledge.

Haraway, D. (2000). *How Like a Leaf – Interview with Thyrza Nichols Goodeve*. London: Routledge.

Haraway, D. (2004). Cyborgs, Coyotes, and Dogs: A Kinship of Feminist Figurations and There Are Always More Things Going on Than You Thought! Methodologies as Thinking Technologies. An interview with Donna Haraway in two parts by Nina Lykke, Randi Markussen, & Finn Olesen. In Haraway, D. (Ed.), *The Haraway Reader* (pp. 321–342). London: Routledge.

Haraway, D. J. (1991). *Simians, cyborgs, and women: The reinvention of nature*. London: Routledge.

Haraway, D. J. (1994). A Game of Cat's Cradle: Science studies, feminist theory, cultural studies. *Configurations, 2*(1), 59–71. doi:10.1353/con.1994.0009

Haraway, D. J. (1997). *Modest_Wintess@Second Millenium. FemaleMan_Meets_Onco-Mouse*. London: Routledge.

Haraway, D. J. (1997). *Modest_witness@second_millenium. Female man©_meets_oncomouse™: Feminism and technoscience*. London: Routledge.

Haraway, D. J. (1999). The promesis of monsters: A regenerative politics for inappropriate/d others. In J. Wolmark (Ed) Cybersexualities: a reader on feminist theory, cyborgs and cyberspace (pp. 314-366). Edinburgh, UK: Edinburgh Univ. Press. hooks, B. (2000). Feminism is for Everybody: passionate politics. Cambridge MA: South End Press.

Harding, S. (1991). *Whose science? Whose knowledge? Thinking from women's lives*. Buckingham, UK: Open University Press.

Harding, S. (1991). *Whose science? Whose knowledge?: Thinking from women's lives*. Buckingham, UK: Open University Press.

Harding, S. (2006). *Science and social inequality: feminist and postcolonial issues*. Urbana, IL: University of Illinois Press.

Hargittai, E., & Shafer, S. (2006). Differences in actual and perceived online skills: the role of gender. *Social Science Quarterly*, 87(2), 432–448. doi:10.1111/j.1540-6237.2006.00389.x

Harrop, A., Tattersall, A., & Goody, A. (2007). Gender matters in higher education. *Educational Studies*, 33(4), 385–396. doi:10.1080/03055690701423531

Hartley, P. (1997). *Group Communication*. London: Routledge.

Hartzel, K. (2003). How self-efficacy and gender issues affect software adoption and use. *Communications of the ACM*, 46(9), 167–171. doi:10.1145/903893.903933

Hayes, E. (2000). Social Contexts. In Hayes, E., & Flannery, D. D. (Eds.), *Women as Learners. The Significance of Gender in Adult Learning* (pp. 23–52). San Francisco: Jossey-Bass.

Hayes, E., & Flannery, D. D. (Eds.). (2000). *Women as Learners. The Significance of Gender in Adult Learning*. San Francisco: Jossey-Bass.

Heilbrun, C. G. (1988). *Writing a Woman's Life*. New York: Ballantine Books.

Held, V. (2005). *The Ethics of Care: Personal, Political, and Global*. New York: Oxford University Press.

Henning-Loeb, I. (2006). *Utveckling och förändring i kommunal vuxenutbildning: En yrkeslivshistorisk ingång med berättelser om lärarbanor* [Development and Change in Municipal Adult Education. Life History Studies and Narrative Analysis of Teacher Trajectories]. Göteborg, Sweden: Acta Universitatis Gothoburgensis.

Henriksen, D. L. (2002). Locating virtual field sites and a dispersed object of research. *Scandinavian Journal of Information Systems*, 14(2), 31–45.

Henwood, F. (1998). Engineering Difference: discourses on gender, sexuality and work in a college of technology. *Gender and Education*, 10(1), 35–49. doi:10.1080/09540259821087

Henwood, F. (2000). Engineering Difference: Discourses on Gender, Sexuality and Work in a College of Technology. *Gender and Education*, 10(1), 35–49. doi:10.1080/09540259821087

Herman, C. (forthcoming). *Re-engineering gender? Public discourses and private lives of women SET professionals in East and West Europe*.

Herring, S. (1994). *Gender differences in computer-mediated communications: bringing familiar* baggage to the new frontier. Retrieved February 2005, from http://www.mith2.umd.edu/WomensStudies/Computing/Articles+ResearchPapers/gender-differences-communication

Herring, S. C. (2001). Gender and power in online communication. *Center for Social Informatics Working Papers*. Retrieved August 10, 2009, from http://rkcsi.indiana.edu/archive/CSI/WP/WP01-05B.html.

Herring, S. C., & Paolillo, J. C. (2006). Gender and genre variation in weblogs. *Journal of Sociolinguistics*, 10(4), 439–459. doi:10.1111/j.1467-9841.2006.00287.x

HESA. (2008). *Resources of Higher Education Institutions 2006/07*. Retrieved August 20, 2009, from http://www.hesa.ac.uk/

Hill, J. P., & Lynch, M. (1983). The Intensification of Gender-Related Role Expectations during Early Adolescence. In Brooks-Gunn, J., & Petersen, A. C. (Eds.), *Girls at Puberty; Biological and Psychosocial Perspectives* (pp. 201–228). New York, London: Plenum Press.

Hirdman, Y. (2003). *Genus* [Gender]. Stockholm: Liber AB.

Holloway, S. L., Valentine, G., & Bingham, N. (2000). Institutionalising technologies: masculinities, feminities, and the heterosexual economy of the IT classroom. *Environment & Planning A*, 32(4), 617–633. doi:10.1068/a3238

hooks, b. (1994). *Teaching to Transgress. Education as the Practice of Freedom*. London: Routledge.

Hoplight Tapia, A. (2003, April 10-12). Hostile_work_environment.com. *Proceedings of the 2003 SIGMIS conference on Computer personnel research*. Philadelphia.

Hoyles, C. (1985). *The learning machine: The gender gap.* BBC1 on 9 May 1985.

Hughes, G. (2000). Marginalization of Socioscientific Material in Science-Technology-Society Science Curricula: Some implications for Gender Inclusivity and Curriculum Reform. *Journal of Research in Science Teaching, 37*(5), 426–440. doi:10.1002/(SICI)1098-2736(200005)37:5<426::AID-TEA3>3.0.CO;2-U

Hughes, G. (2009). Identity and belonging in social learning groups: the value of distinguishing the social, operational and knowledge-related dimensions. *British Educational Research Journal*, iFirst Article, 1–17. Retrieved from http://www.informaworld.com/smpp/content~db=all~content=a910357382

Hylland-Eriksen, T. (1998). *Common denominators: ethnicity, nation-building and compromise in Mauritius.* Oxford, UK: Berg Publishers.

ICM. (2001). *IT Technology Tracker.*

Illeris, K. (2003). Adult education as experienced by the learners. *International Journal of Lifelong Education, 22*(1), 13–23. doi:10.1080/02601370304827

Ingraham, C. (1997). The Heterosexual Imaginary: Feminist Sociology and Theories of Gender. In Seidman, S. (Ed.), *Queer Theory/Sociology* (pp. 168–193). Malden, Oxford, UK: Blackwell Publishers.

International Telecommunication Union. (2007). *ITU ICT Eye.* Retrieved July 2008 from ITU. Website: http://www.itu.int/ITU-D/icteye/

Jackson, S. (2003). Lifelong Earning: Working-class women and lifelong learning. *Gender and Education, 15*(4), 365–376. doi:10.1080/09540250310001610571

Jackson, S. (2005). Gender, Sexuality and Heterosexuality. The Complexity (and limits) of Heteronormativity.

Jakupec, V., & Garrick, J. (Eds.). (2000). *Flexible learning, human resource and organisational development: Putting theory to work.* London: Routledge.

JämO (2000). Rapport från en granskning av 22 IT-företags jämställdhetsplaner. (Report on survey of 22 IT companies' plans for gender equality)

Jenson, J., & Rose, C. B. (2003). Women@work: listening to gendered relations of power in teachers' talk about new technologies. *Gender and Education, 15*(2), 169–181. doi:10.1080/09540250303854

Jenson, J., De Castell, S., & Bryson, M. (2003). "Girl talk": gender, equity, and identity discourses in a school-based computer culture. *Women's Studies International Forum, 26*(6), 561–573.

Johansson, P., & Martinsson, S. (2000). Det nationella IT-programmet – en slutrapport om SwIT. (The national IT programme – final report on SwIT) [Uppsala, Sweden: IFAU.]. *Forskningsrapport, 2000*, 8.

Johnson, N. F., Macdonald, D., & Brabazon, T. (2008). Rage against the Machine? Symbolic Violence in E-learning Supported Tertiary Education. *E-learning, 5*(2), 275–283. doi:10.2304/elea.2008.5.3.275

Jones, R. B. A. (2006). The CSI effect. *Science scope.*

Jubas, K., Butterwick, S., Zhu, H., & Liptrot, J. (2006). Learning a living: practices and recognition of women's on-the-job and informal learning in the information technology field. *Journal of Vocational Education and Training, 58*(4), 483–496. doi:10.1080/13636820601005867

Kahn, J., & Loh, F. (1992). *Fragmented Vision. Culture and Politics in Contemporary Malaysia.* Sydney, Australia: Allen & Unwin.

Kamjou, A. (1998) "Han, hon, den, det" ("He, she, it") in Westerberg, Bengt (ed).

Karasti, H. (2001). *Increasing sensitivity towards everyday work practice in system design.* Doctoral Dissertation. Oulu: Oulun Yliopisto.

Karim, W. J. (1995). *'Male' and 'Female' in Developing Southeast Asia.* Oxford, UK: Berg Publishers.

Kelkar, G., Shrestha, G., & Veena, N. (2005). Women's Agency and the IT industry in India. In Ng, C., & Mitter, S. (Eds.), *Gender and the Digital Economy: Perspective from the Developing World* (pp. 110–131). London: Routledge.

Kessels, U. (2005). Fitting into the stereotype: How gender-stereotyped perceptions of prototypic peers relate to liking for school subjects. *European Journal of Psychology of Education, 20*(3), 309–323. doi:10.1007/BF03173559

Kevin Robins, F. W. (1999). *Times of the technoculture: from the information society to the virtual life*. London: Routledge.

Kihl, M. (2003). *Välkommen i LTH? – en studie av D02:s och C02:s första år på Teknis [Welcome to LTH? A study of the first year at the Lund Institute of Technology for computer and information & communication engineering students]*. Sweden: Report. Lund Institute of Technology, Lund University.

Kimmel, M. (1994). Masculinity as Homophobia: Fear, Shame, and Silence in the Construction of Gender Identity. In Masculinities, T. (Ed.), *H. Brod & M* (pp. 119–141). London: Sage.

Kirkup, G. (2001). Cyborg teaching. *ACM SIG-CAS Computers and Society, 31*(4), 23–32. doi:10.1145/572306.572311

Kirkup, G. (2009). Flying under the radar: The importance of small scale e-learning innovation within large-scale institutional e-learning implementation. In Stansfield, M., & Connolly, T. (Eds.), *Institutional Transformation through Best Practices in Virtual Campus Development: Advancing e-learning policies* (pp. 81–95). Hershey, PA: IGI Global.

Kirkup, G. E. (2001). "Getting our hands on it": Gendered inequality in access to information and communications technologies. In Lax, S. (Ed.), *Access Denied in the Information Age* (pp. 45–66). Basingstoke, UK: Palgrave.

Kirkup, G. E. (2002*). ICT as a tool for enhancing women's education opportunities; and new educational and professional opportunities for women in new technologies*. Expert paper produced for a UN expert meeting, United Nations Division for the Advancement of Women (UN-DAW), Seoul, Korea. Retrieved August, 2009, from http://www.un.org/womenwatch/daw/egm/ict2002/reports/Kirkup%20paperwith%20refs.PDF

Kirkup, G., & Abbott, J. (1997). *The gender gap. A gender analysis of the 1996 computing access survey. Milton Keynes, PLUM Paper number 80*. Programme on Learner Use of Media, Open University.

Kirkup, G., Schmitz, S., Kotkamp, E., Rommes, E., & Aino-Maija Hiltunen. (2010). Towards a feminist manifesto for e-learning. In S. Booth, S. Goodman & G. Kirkup (Eds.), *Gender Issues in Learning and Working with Information Technology: Social Constructs and Cultural Contexts*. Hershey, PA: IGI Global.

Kirkwood, A., & Kirkup, G. (1991). Access to computing for home-based students. *Studies in Higher Education, 16*(2), 199–208. doi:10.1080/03075079112331382984

Kitzinger, J., & Barbour, R. S. (1999). The challenge and promise of focus groups. In Barbour, R. S., & Kitzinger, J. (Eds.), *Developing focus group research: politics, theory and practice*. London: Sage.

Kleif, T., & Faulkner, W. (2003). 'I'm no athlete but I can make this thing dance!' Men's pleasures in technology. *Science, Technology & Human Values, 28*(2), 296–325. doi:10.1177/0162243902250908

Koch, A. C., Muller, S. M., & Sieverding, M. (2008). Women and computers. Effects of stereotype threat on attribution of failure. *Computers & Education, 51*, 1795–1803. doi:10.1016/j.compedu.2008.05.007

Kohlberg, L. (1981). *The philosophy of moral development: moral stages and the idea of justice*. London: Harper & Row.

Kramarae, C. (2001). The third shift: women learning online. Washington, DC: American association of University Women Educational Foundation.

Kramer, P. E., & Lehman, S. (1990). Mismeasuring women: A critique of research on computer ability and avoidance. SIGNS: Journal of women in culture and society, 16(1), 158-171.

Kyng, M. (1991). Designing for Cooperation: Cooperating in Design. *Communications of the ACM, 34*(12), 65–73. doi:10.1145/125319.125323

Laclau, E., & Mouffe, C. (1985). *Hegemony and Socialist Strategy: Towards a Radical Democratic Politics.* London: Verso.

Lagesen, V. A. (2003). Advertising computer science to women (or was it the other way around?). In Lie, M. (Ed.), *He, she and IT revisited. New perspectives on Gender in the Information society* (pp. 69–102). Olso, Norway: Gyldendal.

Lagesen, V. A. (2005). *Extreme Make-Over? The Making of Gender and Computer Science. PhD-Dissertation, STS-Report 71*. Trondheim, Norway: NTNU.

Lagesen, V. A. (2007a). The Strength of Numbers: Strategies to Include Women into Computer Science. *Social Studies of Science, 37*(1), 67–92. doi:10.1177/0306312706063788

Lagesen, V. A. (2007b). A Cyberfeminist Utopia? Perceptions of Gender and Computer Science among Malaysian Women Computer Science Students and Faculty. *Science, Technology & Human Values, 33*, 5–27. doi:10.1177/0162243907306192

Landis, M., Boire, J., Hanson, K., Niguidula, D., Tsikalas, K., & VanderVeen, A. (2002). An e-Learning manifesto. *International Journal on E-Learning, 1*(1), 6–8.

Landström, C. (2007). Queering feminist technology studies. *Feminist Theory, 8*(1), 7–26. doi:10.1177/1464700107074193

Langen, A. V., & Vierke, H. (2009). *Wat bepaalt de keuze voor een natuurprofiel? De invloed van de leerling, de school, de ouders en de peergroup.* Den Haag: Platform Bèta Techniek.

Lanier, J. (2006). Digital Maoism: the Hazards of the new Online Collectivism [Electronic Version]. *Edge. The Third Culture*. Retrieved August 20, 2007 from http://www.edge.org/3rd_culture/lanier06/lanier06_index.html

Law, J. (2004). *After method: Mess in social science research.* London: Routledge.

Law, J. (2006). Pinboards and Books: Juxtaposing, Learning and Materiality. Retrieved February, 2008, from http://www.heterogeneities.net/publications/pinboardsandbooks.pdf

Leathwood, C. (2006). Gender, equity and the discourse of the independent learner in higher education. *Higher Education, 33*(4), 385–396.

Lee, F. (2008). Technopedagogies of mass-individualization: Correspondence education in the mid twentieth century. *History and Technology, 24*(3), 239–253. doi:10.1080/07341510801900318

Lee, M. N. N. (1999). The Impact of the Economic Crisis on Higher Education in Malaysia. *Industry and Higher Education, 15*, 26–27.

Lefebvre, H. (1991). *The production of space.* Oxford, UK: Basil Blackwell.

Levidow, L. (1996). In Ghorayshi, P., & Bélanger, C. (Eds.), *Women, Work, and Gender Relations in Developing Countries* (pp. 43–56). Santa Barbara, CA: Greenwood.

Lie, M. (1998). *Computer dialogues: Technology, Gender and Change.* Trondheim, Norway: NTNU.

Lie, M. (2003). *He, She and IT revisited. New Perspectives on gender in the Information Society.* Oslo, Norway: Gyldendal Akademisk.

Lie, M., & Lund, R. (1994). *Renegotiating Local Values: Working Women and Foreign Industry in Malaysia.* Richmond, UK: Curzon Press.

Lior, K., D'Aarcy, M., & Morais, A. (2001). *Tacit skills, informal knowledge and reflective practice.* (NALL Working Paper, 24). Toronto, Canada: University of Toronto, Ontario Institute for Studies in Education.

Lippa, R. (2001). On deconstructing and reconstructing masculinity-femininity. *Journal of Research in Personality, 35*, 168–207. doi:10.1006/jrpe.2000.2307

Littlejohn, A., & Pegler, C. (2007). *Preparing for Blended e-Learning.* Abingdon, UK: Routledge.

Locke, C., Levine, R., Searles, D., & Weinberger, D. (2000). *The Cluetrain Manifesto. The end of Business as Usual.* London: Pearson Education.

Lovink, G. (2008). *Zero Comments. Blogging and Critical internet culture*. London: Routledge.

Löwgren, J., & Stolterman, E. (2004). *Thoughtful interaction design. A Design Perspective on Information Technology*. Cambridge, MA: The MIT Press.

Luke, C. (2002). Globalisation and Women in Southeast Asian Higher Education Management. *Teachers College Record, 104*(3), 625–662. doi:10.1111/1467-9620.00174

Lyotard, J. F. (1984). *The postmodern condition: a report on knowledge*. Manchester, UK: Manchester UP.

MacKenzie, D., & Wacjman, J. (1999). Introductory essay: the social shaping of technology. In MacKenzie, D., & Wacjman, J. (Eds.), *The social shaping of technology*. Philadelphia: Open University Press.

MacKeogh, C. (2003). The Cork institute of Technology and Fasttrack to IT. Initiatives for the lone parents and the longterm unemployed. In Lie, M., & Sörensen, K. H. (Eds.), *Strategies of Inclusion: Gender in the Information Society* (Vol. I, pp. 419–438). Trondheim, Norway: NTNU, Centre for Technology and Society.

MacKeogh, C. (2003). Women in Technology and Science Role Model Project. In M. Lie & K. Sorensen (Eds.), Strategies of Inclusion: Gender in the Information Society. Vol. 1: Experiences from public sector initiatives (pp. 401-418). Trondheim, Norway: NTNU.

Mahatmir, M. (1991). *Malaysia: The Way Forward*. Kuala Lumpur: Centre for Economic Research and Services, Malaysian Business Council.

Mahr, B., & Peroz, N. (Eds.). (2006). Establishing Academic Structures in Computer Science at Herat University. Frankfurt, Germany: IKO Verlag.

Marcoulides, G. A. (1989). Measuring computer anxiety. The computer anxiety scale. *Educational and Psychological Measurement, 49*(3), 733–739. doi:10.1177/001316448904900328

Marcoulides, G. A., Stocker, Y.-O., & Marcoulides, L. D. (2004). Examining the psychological impact of computer technology. An updated cross-cultural study. *Educational and Psychological Measurement, 64*(2), 311–318. doi:10.1177/0013164403258451

Marcus, G. E. (1995). Ethnography in/of the World System: The Emergence of Multi-Sited Ethnography. *Annual Review of Anthropology, 24*, 95–117. doi:10.1146/annurev.an.24.100195.000523

Margolis, J., & Fischer, A. (2002). *Unlocking the Clubhouse: Women in Computing*. Cambridge, MA: MIT Press.

Margolis, J., & Fisher, A. (2002). *Unlocking the clubhouse. Women in computing*. Cambridge, MA: MIT Press.

Martinsson, S. (1999). *Det nationella IT-programmet – en delrapport om SwIT. (The national IT programme – interim report on SwIT)*. Uppsala, Sweden: IFAU.

Marton, F. (1981). Describing conceptions of the world around us. *Instructional Science, 10*, 177–200. doi:10.1007/BF00132516

Marton, F., & Booth, S. (1997). *Learning and awareness*. Mahwah, NJ: Lawrence Erlbaum.

Marton, F., & Pang, M. F. (2006). On some necessary conditions of learning. *Journal of the Learning Sciences, 15*(2), 193–220. doi:10.1207/s15327809jls1502_2

Marx, K., & Engels, F. (1848). *The Communist Manifesto*. London: Penguin.

Mason, R., & Rennie, F. (2008). *E-Learning and Social Networking Handbook Resources for Higher Education*. London: Routledge.

Massey, D. (1994). *Space, place and gender*. Cambridge, UK: Polity Press.

Massey, D. (1999a). Space-time, 'science' and the relationship between physical geography and human geography. *Transactions of the Institute of British Geographers, 24*(3), 261–276. doi:10.1111/j.0020-2754.1999.00261.x

Massey, D. (1999b). *Power-geometries and the politics of space. Hettner lecture, 1998*. Heidelberg, Germany: University of Heidelberg.

Massey, D. (2004). Geographies of responsibility. *Geografiska Annaler, 86B*(1), 5–18.

May, A. M. (2008). Gender and the political economy of knowledge. In Bettio, F., & Verashchagina, A. (Eds.), *Frontiers in the Economics of Gender* (pp. 267–285). London: Routledge.

McCloud, S. (1993). *Understanding Comics*. New York: Harper Perennial.

McConnell, D. (2006). *E-learning Groups and Communities*. Buckingham, UK: Open University Press.

McGivney, V. (1999). Men earn, women learn: Bridging the gender divide in education and training. Leicester, UK: The National Organisation for Adult Learning, NIACE.

McLoughlin, C., & Lee, M. (2008). Future learning landscapes: Transforming pedagogy through social software. *Innovate, 4*(5). Retrieved June 26, 2009, from http://www.distance-educator.com/dnews/Article15911.phtml

McNay, L. (2003). Agency, Anticipation and Indeterminacy in Feminist Theory. *Feminist Theory, 4*(2), 139–148. doi:10.1177/14647001030042003

McWilliam, E., & Taylor, P. G. (1998). Teacher Im/Material: Challenging the new Pedagogies of Instructional Design. *Educational Researcher, 27*(8), 29–35.

Mellström, U. (1995). *Engineering Lives, Technology, Time and Space in a Male-Centred World*. Linköping, Sweden: Linköping Studies in Art and Science.

Mellström, U. (2002). Patriarchal machines and masculine embodiment. *Science, Technology & Human Values, 27*(4), 460–478. doi:10.1177/016224302236177

Mellström, U. (2003). *Masculinity, Power and Technology: A Malaysian Ethnography*. Aldershot, UK: Ashgate.

Mellström, U. (2004, April). Machines and masculine subjectivity, technology as an integral part of men's life experiences. Men and Masculinities, Special Issue: Masculinities and Technology, (Eds) Faulkner, W. & Lohan, M., 6(4), 368-383.

Mendick, H. (2005). A beautiful myth? The gendering of being/doing 'good at maths'. *Gender and Education, 17*(2), 203–219. .doi:10.1080/0954025042000301465

Mendick, H. (2005). A beautiful myth? The gendering of being/doing 'good at maths'. *Gender and Education, 17*(2), 203–219. doi:10.1080/0954025042000301465

Mercer, P. (2008). *Cattle farms lure Australia women*. BBC News.

Messer-Davidow, E. (1995). Acting Otherwise. In Kegan Gardiner, J. (Ed.), *Provoking agents: gender and agency in theory and practice* (pp. 23–51). Urbana, IL: University of Illinois Press.

Michel, L. P., & Pelka, B. (2004). *Die Darstellung von Berufen im Fernsehen und ihre Auswirkungen auf die Berufswahl - Ergebnisse einer Pilotstudie": Dream jobs for all? Representation of jobs on TV and consequences for job choices - results of a pilot study*. MMB Institut für Medien- und Kompetenzforschung.

Ministry of Communication. (2003). *Information and Communication Technologies (ICT) Policy*. Retrieved July, 2008, from Ministry of Communication/Afghanistan. Web site: http://www.mcit.gov.af/Documents/PoliciesandLaws/Afghanistan%20ICT%20Policy-english.pdf

Ministry of Education/Afghanistan. (2006). *National Education Strategic Plan for Afghanistan 1385-1389*, Retrieved July, 2008, from Ministry of Education/Afghanistan. Web site: http://moe.gov.af/National%20Education%20Strategic%20Plan.pdf

Ministry of Education/Afghanistan. (2007). *School Survey 1386 Report*, Retrieved January, 2009, from Ministry of Education/Afghanistan. Web site: http://www.moe.gov.af/EMIS/School%20Survey%201386%20Report%20v2.3_2.zip

Mohamad, M. (2002). At the Centre and the Periphery: The Contribution of Women's Movements to Democratization. In F. Loh Kok Wah and Khoo Boo Teik (Eds.), Democracy in Malaysia: Discourses and Practices, Richmond, UK: Curzon Press.

Moore, M. G. (1993). Theory of transactional distance. In Keegan, D. (Ed.), *Theoretical principles of distance education* (pp. 22–38). London: Routledge.

Morley, L. (2002). Lifelong Yearning. Feminist Pedagogy in the Learning Society. In Howie, G., & Tauchert, A. (Eds.), *Gender, Teaching and Research in Higher Education*. London: Ashgate Press.

Morley, L. (2005). Opportunity or exploitation? Women and quality insurance in higher education. *Gender and Education, 17*(4), 411–429. doi:10.1080/09540250500145106

Mörtberg, C. (1987). *Varför har programmeraryrket blivit manligt? (Why have programming become a male occupation?). Research report, 1987:42*. Luleå, Sweden: Luleå University of Technology.

Mörtberg, C. (1997). *'Det beror på att man är kvinna-': gränsvandrerskor formas och formar informationsteknologi*. ['It's because one is a woman...' Transgressors are shaped and shape information technology]. Doctoral Dissertation. Luleå: Luleå tekniska universitet.

Mörtberg, C. (2003). In Dreams Begin Responsibility – Feminist Alternatives to Technoscience. In C. Mörtberg, P. Elovaara & A. Lundgren (eds.) How do we make a difference? Information Technology, Transnational Democracy and Gender (pp. 57-69). Division Gender and Technology, Luleå University of Technology, Sweden.

Mörtberg, C., & Due, B. (2004) "Med IT och kön som prisma i studier av nordiska IT-policies" in Mörtberg, C. & Due, B. (ed) (2004) Informationsteknologi och kön som prisma i analyser av nordiska IT-policies. (Information technology and gender as prisms in analyses of Nordic IT policies) NIKK Småskrifter nr. 9.

Mörtberg, C., Stuedahl, D., & Elovaara, P. (forthcoming). Designing for Sustainable Ways of Living with Technologies. In Wagner, I., Bratteteig, T., & Stuedahl, D. (Eds.), *Exploring digital design multi-disciplinary design practices*. London: Springer.

Moss, D. (2004). Creating space for learning: Conceptualising women and higher education through space and time. *Gender and Education, 16*(3), 283–302. doi:10.1080/09540250042000251452

Mouffe, C. (2005). *On the political*. New York: Routledge.

Mumtaz, S. (2001). Children's enjoyment and perception of computer use in the home and the school. *Computers & Education, 36*(4), 347–362. doi:10.1016/S0360-1315(01)00023-9

Na, M. (2001). The Home Computer in Korea: Gender, Technology, and the Family. *Feminist Media Studies, 1*(3). doi:10.1080/14680770120088909

Nass, C., Isbister, K., & Lee, E.-J. (2000). Truth is beauty: Researching embodied conversational agents. In Cassell, J., Sullivan, J., Prevost, S., & Churchill, E. (Eds.), *Embodied Conversational Agents* (pp. 374–402). Cambridge, MA: MIT Press.

Newman, S. E. (1998). Here, There, and Nowhere at all: Distribution, Negotiation, and Virtuality in Postmodern Ethnography and Engineering. *Knowledge and Society, 11*, 235–267.

Newmarch, E., Taylor-Steele, S., & Cumpston, A. (2000). *Women in IT – what are the barriers*. New South Wales: Department of Education, Training and Youth Affairs.

Ng, C. (1999). *Positioning women in Malaysia. Houndsmill, Basingstoke*. Hampshire, UK: Macmillan Distribution Ltd.

Ng, C., & Mitter, S. (2005). Valuing Women's Voices: Call Centers Workers in Malaysia and India. In Ng, C., & Mitter, S. (Eds.), *Gender and the Digital Economy: Perspective from the Developing World*. London: Routledge.

Ng, C., & Mohamad, M. (1997). The Management of Technology and Women in Two Electronic Firms in Malaysia. *Gender, Technology and Development, 1*(2), 177–203. doi:10.1177/097185249700100201

Ng, C., & Munro-Kua, A. (Eds.). (1994). *Keying into the Future. The Impact of Computerization on Office Workers*. Kuala Lumpur, Malaysia: Vinlin Press.

Ng, C., & Thambiah, S. (1997 March 5-6). Women and Work in the Information Era: Levelling the Playing Field? Paper presented at the Regional Conference on Women and Work: Challenges in Industrializing Nations, Putrajaya, Sepang.

Ng, C., & Yong, C. (1995). Information technology, gender and employment. A case study of the telecommunications industry in Malaysia. In Mitter, S., & Rowbotham, S. (Eds.), *Women Encounter Technology: Changing Patterns of Employment in the Third World*. London: Routledge.

Nielsen, S. H., von Hellens, L. A., Beekhuyzen, J., & Trauth, E. M. (2003, April 10-12). Women Talking About IT Work: Duality or Dualism? *Proceedings of the 2003 SIGMIS conference on Computer personnel research*. Philadelphia(68-74).

Nitsche, S. (2006, July). Null Bock auf Technik – warum sich in Deutschland nicht mehr sondern weniger Frauen für ein Ingenieurstudium entscheiden. *TU Intern - University Press*, p. 12.

Noble, D. (1998). Digital diploma mills: The automation of higher education. First Monday, *3*(1), Retrieved August 2009, from http://www.firstmonday.org

Noddings, N. (2003). *Caring: a feminine approach to ethics and moral education*. Berkeley, CA: University of California Press.

Nonini, D. M. (1997). Shifting Identities, Positioned Imagineries: Transnational Traversal and Reversals by Malaysian Chinese. In Ong, A., & Nonini, D. M. (Eds.), *Ungrounded Empires: The Cultural Politics of Modern Chinese Transnationalism*. New York: Routledge.

Nonini, D. M. (1998). 'Chinese Society', Coffeshop Talk, Possessing Gods: The Politics of Public Space among Diasporic Chinese in Malaysia. positions: east asia cultures critique, *6*(2), 339-369.

Nonini, D. M. (1999). The dialectics of 'disputatiousness' and 'rece-eating money': class confrontation and gendered imagineries among Chinese men in West Malaysia. *American Ethnologist, 26*(1), 47–68. doi:10.1525/ae.1999.26.1.47

Nordicom–Sveriges Mediebarometer. (1998-2006). (Nordicom – Sweden's Media Barometer) Retrieved February, 2008, from http://www.nordicom.gu.se

O'Hear, S. (2006, August 8). e-Learning 2.0 - how Web technologies are shaping education, *ReadWriteWeb*. Retrieved September 9, 2009, from http://www.readwriteweb.com/archives/e-learning_20.php

Öhman, P. J. (2004). *The Obvious and the Essential: Interpreting Software Development & Organizational Change*. Doctoral Dissertation. Uppsala University, Sweden.

Oldenziel, R. (1999). *Making Technology Masculine; Men, women and modern machines in America 1870-1945*. Amsterdam: Amsterdam University Press.

Ong, A. (1987). *Spirits of Resistance and Capitalist Discipline. Factory women in Malaysia*. Albany, NY: State University of New York Press.

Oost, E. V. (2000). Making the computer masculine. In Balka, E., & Smith, R. (Eds.), *Women, Work and Computerization, Charting a Course to the Future* (pp. 9–16). Dordrecht, The Netherlands: Kluwer Academic Publishers.

Open University. (2009). *OpenLearn*. Retrieved September 1, 2009, from http://www.open.ac.uk/openlearn/home.php

Othman, M., & Latih, R. (2006). Women in Computer Science: No Shortage Here! Communications of the ACM, *49*(3), 111–114. doi:10.1145/1118178.1118185doi:10.1145/1118178.1118185

Oudshoorn, N., Rommes, E., & Stienstra, M. (2004). Configuring the User as Everybody: Gender and Design Cultures in Information and Communication Technologies. *Science, Technology & Human Values, 29*(1), 30–63. doi:10.1177/0162243903259190

Pacey, A. (1999). *Meaning in Technology*. Cambridge, MA: MIT Press.

Palloff, R., & Pratt, K. (2001). *Lessons from the Cyberspace Classroom: The Realities of Online Teaching*. San Francisco: Jossey-Bass.

Palloff, R., & Pratt, K. (2005). *Collaborating Online: Learning Together in Community*. San Francisco: Jossey-Bass.

Parkins, W. (2000). Protesting like a Girl: Embodiment, Dissent and Feminist Agency. *Feminist Theory, 1*(1), 59–78. doi:10.1177/14647000022229065

Pax, S. (2003). *The Baghdad Blog*. London: Guardian Books.

Peletz, M. G. (1996). *Reason and Passion: Representations of Gender in a Malay Society*. Berkeley, CA: University of California Press.

Perry, W. G., Jr. (1968/1970/1999). Forms of ethical and intellectual development in the college years: A scheme. San Francisco: Jossey-Bass.

Peters, M. A. (2007). Higher Education, Globalisation and the Knowledge Economy: Reclaiming the Cultural Mission [Electronic Version]. *Ubiquity, 8*.

Peters, O. (1994). Distance education and industrial production: a comparative interpretation in outline (1967). In Keegan, D. (Ed.), *Otto Peters on distance education: The industrialization of teaching and learning* (pp. 107–127). London: Routledge.

Peters, O. (1998). *Learning and teaching in distance education*. London: Kogan Page.

Peterson, H. (2005). *Gender, Power and Post-Bureaucracy: Work Ideals in IT Consulting*. Doctoral Dissertation, Uppsala University, Sweden.

Phillips, M. (2002, August 19). *The feminisation of education*. London: Daily Mail, Rector, L. H. (2008). Comparison of Wikipedia and other encyclopaedias for accuracy, breadth, and depth in historical articles [Electronic Version] [from http://www.emeraldinsight.com/]. *RSR. Reference Services Review, 36*, 7–22. Retrieved June 6, 2009.

Pinckard, J. (2003). *Genderplay: Successes and Failures in Character Designs for Videogames*. Game+Girl=Advance. Retrieved December 3, 2007, from http://www.gamegirladvance.com/archives/2003/04/16/genderplay_successes_and_failures_in_character_designs_for_videogames.html

Platman, K., & Taylor, P. (2004). *Workforce Ageing in the New Economy: A Comparative Study of Information Technology Employment*, Cambridge, UK: University of Cambridge. Retrieved from http://www.wane.ca/PDF/Platman&TaylorSummaryReport2004.pdf

Pollit, C., & Bouchaert, G. (2004). *Public management reform. A comparative analysis* (2nd ed.). Oxford, UK: University Press.

Quinn, J. (2003). *Powerful Subjects. Are women really taking over the university? Stoke on Trent*. UK: Trentham Books.

Rasmussen, B., & Hapnes, T. (2003). Gendering technology; Young girls negotiating ICT and gender. In Lie, M. (Ed.), *He, She and IT Revisited; New Perspectives on Gender in the Information Society* (pp. 173–197). Oslo, Norway: Gyldendal Akademisk.

Read, B., Archer, L., & Leathwood, C. (2003). Challenging Cultures? Student Conceptions of 'Belonging' and 'Isolation' at a Post-1992 University. *Studies in Higher Education, 28*(3), 261–277. doi:10.1080/03075070309290

Reeves, B., & Nass, C. (1996). *The Media Equation: How People Treat Computers, Televisions and New Media like Real People and Places*. New York: Cambridge University Press.

Regeringens proposition (1999-2000):86, *Informationssamhälle för alla* [Government Bill 1999/2000:86, Information Society for All]. Stockholm, Regeringen. Retrieved February, 2008, from http//:www.regeringen.se

Reilly, C. A. (2004). Sexualities and technologies: how vibrators help to explain computers. *Computers and Composition, 2004*, 363–385.

Rich, A. (1993). Compulsory Heterosexuality and Lesbian Existence. In Abelove, H., Barale, M. A., & Halperin, D. M. (Eds.), *The Lesbian and Gay Studies Reader* (pp. 227–254). New York: Routledge.

Richardson, H., & French, S (2002, November). *Exercising different choices – the gender divide and government policy making in the 'global knowledge economy*. 6th International ETHICOMP conference. Lisbon, Portugal.

Rittel, H. W. J., & Webber, M. M. (1973). Dilemmas in a General Theory of Planning. *Policy Sciences, 4*, 155–169. .doi:10.1007/BF01405730

Robins, K., & Webster, F. (1999). *Times of the Technoculture: Information, Communication and the Technological Ord*. London: Routledge.

Rogers, A. (2005). Lifelong learning and the absence of gender. *International Journal of Educational Development, 26*(2), 189–208. doi:10.1016/j.ijedudev.2005.07.025

Rommes, E. (2003). 'I don't know how to fit it into my life'. Courses, computers and the internet for 'everybody' in Amsterdam. In Lie, M., & Sörensen, K. H. (Eds.), *Strategies of Inclusion: Gender in the Information Society* (*Vol. I*, pp. 151–166). Trondheim, Norway: NTNU, Centre for Technology and Society.

Rommes, E. (2007 August 23-25). Heteronormativity Revisited; Teenagers and their Occupational Choices for IT. Paper presented at the Symposium on Gender, Learning and IT, Helsingborg Sweden.

Rommes, E. (2007). *Images and Identities; Sex, Sexuality and Soaps*. Invited speaker manuscript at The 3rd Christina Conference in conjunction with The 4th European Gender & ICT Symposium, Helsinki, Finland. Retrieved May 25, 2007, from www.helsinki.fi/kristiina-instituutti/conference/pdf/rommes.pdf

Rommes, E., & Schönberger, M. (in press). *Report WP 4 Motivation*. Wuppertal, Germany. *EU Coordinated Action Motivation*.

Rommes, E., Faulkner, W., & Slooten, I. V. (2005). Changing Lives: the case for women-only vocational technology training revisited. *Journal of Vocational Education and Training, 57*(3), 293–317. doi:10.1080/13636820500200288

Rommes, E., Overbeek, G., Scholte, R., Engels, R., & de Kemp, R. (2007). 'I'm not interested in computers': Gender-based Occupational Choices of Adolescents. *Information Communication and Society, 10*(3), 299–319. doi:10.1080/13691180701409838

Rommes, E., Overbeek, G., Scholte, R., Engels, R., & Kemp, R. D. (2007). 'I'm not interested in computers', Gender-based occupational choices of teenagers. *Information Communication and Society, 10*(3), 299–319. doi:10.1080/13691180701409838

Roos, G. (2001). "Nya" studerande eller "gamla"? Rekrytering till studiecentra i Hälsingland ["New students" or "old"? The recruitment to study centres in Hälsingland]. *Pedagogisk forskning i Sverige, 6*(1), 1-18.

Rose, N. (1999). *Powers of Freedom: Reframing political thought*. Cambridge, UK: Cambridge University Press. doi:10.1017/CBO9780511488856

Rubens, W. (2009) *Trends in e-learning*. Retrieved June 26, 2009, from http://www.frankwatching.com/archive/2009/01/07/trends-in-e-learning/

Runesson, U. (2006). What is it Possible to Learn? On Variation as a Necessary Condition for Learning. *Scandinavian Journal of Educational Research, 50*, 397–410. doi:10.1080/00313830600823753

Salen, K., & Zimmerman, E. (2004). *Rules of Play. Game design fundamentals*. Cambridge, MA: MIT Press.

Salminen-Karlsson, M. (1999). Bringing women into computer engineering. Curriculum reform processes at two institutes of technology. Linköping, Sweden: Linköping Studies in education and psychology, no 60.

Salminen-Karlsson, M. (1999). *Bringing women into computer engineering. Curriculum reform processes at two institutes of technology. Linköping studies in education and psychology*. Linköping, Sweden: Linköping University.

Salmon, G. (2000). *E-moderating: The Key to Teaching and Learning Online*. London: Kogan Page.

Saloma-Akpdeonu, C. (2005). *Female Spaces in the Philippines' ICT Industry'. Gender and the Digital Economy: Perspective from the Developing World*. New Delhi: Sage Publications.

Sanders, J (2005). *Gender and technology in education: a research review*. Retrieved March 10, 2009, from www.josanders.com

Saper, C. (2006). Blogademia. *Reconstruction, 6*(4), 1–15.

Schank, R. C. (2002). *Designing world class e-learning: How IBM, GE, Harvard Business School, and Columbia*

University are succeeding at e-learning. New York: McGraw-Hill.

Schein, E. H. (1987). Individuals and careers. In Lorsch, J. W. (Ed.), *Handbook of Organizational Behavior* (pp. 155–171). Englewood Cliffs, NJ: Prentice-Hall.

Schiff, S. (2006). *Know it all. Can Wikipedia conquer expertise?* New Yorker, 31.07.2006

Schinzel, B. (2004). *Kulturunterschiede beim Frauenanteil im Informatik-Studium.* Retrieved July, 2008, from University of Freiburg, Department of Modelling and Social Impacts. Web site: http://mod.iig.uni-freiburg.de/cms/fileadmin/publikationen/online-publikationen/Frauenanteil.Informatik.International.pdf

Schmitz, S., & Grunau, E. (2009, March). *Concept Mapping from a Perspective of Gendered Diversity.* Paper presented at the 5th European Symposium on Gender & ICT, Bremen. Retrieved June 26, 2009, from http://www.informatik.uni-bremen.de/soteg/gict2009/proceedings/GICT2009_Schmitz.pdf

Schneider, D. (2003). *The Psychology of Stereotyping.* New York: Guilford Press.

Schutz, A., & Luckman, T. (1974). *The Structures of the life-world.* London: Heinemann Educational Books Ltd.

Scoble, R., & Israel, S. (2006). *Naked Conversations. How blogs are changing the way businesses talk with customers.* Hoboken, NJ: John Wiley and Sons.

Scott, J. (2004, November 19). The Great Failure of Wikipedia. *ASCII.* Retrieved August 20, 2007, from http://ascii.textfiles.com/archives/000060.html

Selby, L., Ryba, K., & Young, A. (1998). Women in computing: what does the data show? *SIGCSE Bulletin, 30*(4), 62a–67a. .doi:10.1145/306286.306318

Selby, L., Young, A., & Fisher, D. (1997). *Increasing the participation of women in tertiary level computing courses: what works and why.* ASCILITE'97.

Sellers, S. (Ed.). (1994). *The Helene Cixous Reader.* London: Routledge.

Selwyn, N. (1997). Teaching information technology for the 'computer shy': a theoretical perspective on a practical problem. *Journal of Vocational Education and Training, 49*(3), 395–408. doi:10.1080/13636829700200023

Selwyn, N. (2007, November 15) 'Screw Blackboard... do it on Facebook!': an investigation of students' educational use of Facebook. Paper presented '*Poke 1.0 - Facebook social research symposium*', University of London.

Senger, P. (1998). *Anti-Boxology: Agent Design in Cultural Context. CMU-CS-98-151.* Pittsburgh, PA: Carnegie Mellon University.

Siann, G. (1997). We Can, We Don't Want to: Factors Influencing Women's Participation in Computing. In Lander, R., & Adam, A. (Eds.), *Women in Computing.* Exeter, UK: Intellect.

Siann, G. (1997). We Can, We Just Don't Want To. In Lander, R., & Adam, A. (Eds.), *Women and Computing.* Devon, UK: Intellect.

Siann, G., Durndell, A., Macleod, H., & Glissov, P. (1988). Stereotyping in relation to the gender gap in computing. *Education Research, 30*, 8–103.

Sjöberg, C. (1998). *Utbildning och arbetsmarknad för IT-specialister. (Education and the labor market for IT specialists).* Stockholm: Nutek.

Skolverket (2006). *Beskrivande data. Förskoleverksamhet, skolbarnomsorg, skola och vuxenutbildning.* Rapport 283 (Descriptive data: Pre-school, out of school care, school and adult education. Report 283). Stockholm, Sweden: Skolverket.

Sondergaard, D. M. (2002). Poststructuralist Approaches to Empirical Analysis. *Qualitative Studies in Education, 15*(2), 187–204. doi:10.1080/09518390110111910

Sørensen, K. H. (2002). Love, Duty and the S-curve: An Overview of Some Current Literature on Gender and ICT. In Sørensen, K. H., & Stewart, J. (Eds.), *Digital Divides and Inclusion Measures. A Review of Literature and Statistical Trends on Gender and ICTs. STS Report 59.* Trondheim, Norway: NTNU, Centre for Technology and Society.

Sorensen, K., Faulkner, W., & Rommes, E. (in press). *Technologies of Inclusion; Bridging the Gender Gap in the Information Society*. Cambridge, MA: MIT Press.

SOU 2003:55, *Digitala tjänster – hur då?* [Digital Services- How?]. Retrieved February, 2008, from http//:www.regeringen.se

Speilhofer, T., O'Donnell, L., Benton, T., Schagen, S., & Shagen, I. (2002). *The impact of school size and single-sex education on performance*. Local Government Association. National Foundation for Educational Research (NfER).

Spender, D. (1995). *Nattering on the Net: Women, Power and Cyberspace*. Melbourne, Australia: Spinifex Press.

Spender, D. (2003). *Nattering on the Net. Women, Power and Cyberspace*. Melbourne, Australia: Spinifix Press.

Spijkerman, R. (2005). *An Image to Die For; Prototypes of Smoking and Drinking Peers and Adolescents' Substance Use*. Nijmegen, The Netherlands: Radboud University Nijmegen, Stepulevage, L. (2001). Gender/Technology Relations: complicating the gender binary. *Gender and Education, 13*(3), 325–338.

Star, S. L., & Strauss, A. (1999). Layers of silence, arenas of voice: The ecology of visible and invisible work. *Computer Supported Cooperative Work, 8*(1/2), 9–30. doi:10.1023/A:1008651105359

Statistics Sweden & the Swedish National Agency of Higher Education (2007, April 20). Higher education: Students and graduated students in undergraduate education 2005/06. Serie utbildning och forskning.

Statistics Sweden. (2002). *Dator och Internet i hemmet. (Computers and internet in the home)* Retrieved July 8, 2007, from http://www.scb.se/statistik/LE/LE0101/1976I02/LE0101_1976I02_BR_10_LE-103SA0401.pdf

Statistics Sweden. (2003). *Tid för vardagsliv. Kvinnors och mäns tidsanvändning 1990/91 och 2000/01.* (Time for everyday life. Women's and men's use of time 1990/91 and 2000/01) Stockholm: Statistiska centralbyrån (SCB)

Retrieved May, 29, 2009, from http://www.scb.se/statistik/LE/LE0103/2003M00/LE99SA0301.pdf.

Statistics Sweden. (2006). *Levnadsförhållanden. Undersökningarna av levnadsförhållanden. Tillgång till samt användning av dator på fritiden 1994-2006.* (Living conditions: Studies of living conditions. Access to and use of computers in leisure time) Retrieved July 7, 2007, from http://www.scb.se/templates/tableOrChart_____207316.asp.

Statistics Sweden. (2007). *Utbildningsstatistisk årsbok 2007* Stockholm: Statistics Sweden. Retrieved July 7, 2007, from http://www.scb.se/statistik/_publikationer/UF0524_2007A01_BR_11_UF0106TAB.pdf

Statistics Sweden. (2009a) *Statistikdatabasen*. Datoranvändning bland privatpersoner 16-74 år efter kön, ålder och hur ofta man använt persondator (urvalsundersökning). År 2003-2008. (Statistical database. Computer usage among private individuals 16-74 years of age, according to gender, age and frequency of use of personal computers (A selective study) 2003-2008). Retrieved June 1, 2009, from www.scb.se.

Statistics Sweden. (2009b) *Statistikdatabasen*. Internetanvändning bland privatpersoner 16-74 år (andel) efter kön, ålder, hur ofta man använt Internet och tid. År 2003-2008. (Statistical database. Internet use among private individuals 16-74 years of age, according to gender, age and frequency and length of internet usage) Retrieved June 1, from www.scb.se

Steenberg, A. (1997) *Flickor och pojkar i samma skola. (Girls and boys in the same school.)* Solna: Ekelunds Förlag.

Stepulevage, L. (2001). Gender/Technology Relations: complicating the gender binary. *Gender and Education, 13*(3), 325–338. doi:10.1080/09540250120082525

Suchman, L. (2002). Located Accountabilities in Technology Production. *Scandinavian Journal of Information Systems, 14*(2), 91–105.

Suchman, L. (2005). *Agencies in technology design: Feminist reconfigurations*. Retrieved February, 2008, from http://www.lancs.ac.uk/fass/sociology/papers/suchman-agenciestechnodesign.pdf

Suchman, L. (2007). *Human-Machine Reconfigurations – Plans and Situated Actions* (2nd ed.). New York: Cambridge University Press.

Sullivan, A. (2008). (forthcoming). Academic self-concept, gender and single-sex schooling. [Routledge]. *British Educational Research Journal*.

Swedish Government Bill. (2002). *Den öppna högskolan.* [Reforms in Higher education – A more open system]. Regeringens proposition. *Prop, 2001*(02), 15.

Swedish Government Bill. (2005). *Ny värld – ny högskola.* [New world – a new higher education]. Regeringens proposition. *Prop, 2005,* 162.

Swedish Ministry of education and Ecclesiastic Affairs. (1962). Korrespondensundervisning inom skolväsendet [Correspondence study in the school system]. *Brevskoleutredningen, SOU, 1962,* 16.

Swedish Ministry of Education and Science. (1998a). Utvärdering av distansutbildningsprojekt med IT-stöd [Evaluation of IT-supported distance education projects]. *Commission of Distance Education, SOU, 1998,* 57.

Swedish Ministry of Education and Science. (1998b). *På distans: Utbildning, undervisning och lärande* [At a distance: Education, teaching and learning]. *Kostnadseffektiv distansutbildning.* [Cost-effective distance education]. *Commission of Distance Education, SOU, 1998,* 83.

Swedish Ministry of Education and Science. (1998c). Flexibel utbildning på distans [Flexible education at a distance]. *Commission of Distance Education, SOU, 1998,* 84.

Thompson, J. L. (1983). *Learning Liberation. Women's Response to Men's Education*. London: Croom Helm.

Tillery, D. (2005). The plain style in the seventeenth century: gender and the history of scientific discourse. *Journal of Technical Writing and Communication, 35*(3), 273–289. doi:10.2190/MRQQ-K2U6-LTQU-0X56

Toresson, G. W. (2002). Kvinnor skapar kunskap på nätet. Datorbaserad fortbildning för lärare. (Women create knowledge on the Net. Data-based further education for teachers.) Umeå: Umeå universitet.

Trauth, E. M., Quesenberry, J. L., & Morgan, A. J. (2004, April 22-24). *Understanding the Under Representation of Women in IT: Toward a Theory of Individual Differences*. Presented at SIGMIS'04, Tucson, AZ.

Traweek, S. (1988). *Beamtimes and Lifetimes: The World of High Energy Physicists*. Cambridge, MA: Harvard University Press.

Traweek, S., & Reid, R. (2000). *Cultural Studies of Science, Technology, and Medicine*. New York: Routledge.

Turkle, S. (1984). The second self: computers and the human spirit. London: Granada.

Turkle, S. (1995). *Life on the Screen: Identity in the Age of the Internet*. New York: Simon & Schuster.

Turkle, S., & Papert, S. (1990). Epistemological Pluralism: Styles and Voices within the Computer Culture. *Signs, 16*(1), 128–157. .doi:10.1086/494648

Tuuva-Hongisto, S. (2007). *Tilattuja tarinoita: etnografinen tutkimus pohjoiskarjalaisesta tietoyhteiskunnasta*. [Negotiated stories of the information technology: en ethnographic study of the Northcarelian information society]. Doctoral Dissertation. Joensuu: Joensuun yliopisto.

Udén, M. (2000). *Tekniskt sett av kvinnor. (Women technically speaking.)* Luleå: Tekniska högskolan. Institutionen för Arbetsvetenskap.

Universities UK and Standing Conference of Principals SCOP (2005). *From Margins to Mainstream: embedding widening participation in Higher Education* Retrieved November 29, 2006 from http://bookshop.universitiesuk. ac.uk/downloads/margins_fullreport.pdf

Upitis, R. (1998). From hackers to luddites, game players to game creators: profiles of adolescent students using technology. *Journal of Curriculum Studies, 30*(3), 293–318. doi:10.1080/002202798183620

Usher, R. (2002). Putting space back on the map: Globalisation, place and identity. *Educational Philosophy and Theory, 34*(1), 41–55. doi:10.1111/j.1469-5812.2002. tb00285.x

Valenduc, G. (2004). *Widening Women's Work in Information and Communication Technology*. Namur, Belgium: European Commission.

Valian, V. (1998). *Why So Slow? The Advancement of Women*. Cambridge, MA: The MIT Press.

Van den Bulck, J., & Beullens, K. (2007). The Relationship between Docu Soap Exposure and Adolescents' Career Aspirations. *European Journal of Communication, 22*(3), 355–366. doi:10.1177/0267323107079686

Van Doorn, N., van Zoonen, L., & Wyatt, S. (2007). Writing from experience: Presentations of gender identity on weblogs. *European Journal of Women's Studies, 14*(2), 143–158. doi:10.1177/1350506807075819

Verran, H. (1998). Re-imagining Land Ownership in Australia. *Postcolonial Studies, 1*, 237–254. doi:10.1080/13688799890165

Verran, H. (1999). Staying True to Laughter in Nigerian Classrooms. In Law, J., & Hassard, J. (Eds.), *Actor Network Theory and After*. London: Routledge.

Visser, I. (2002). Prototypes of gender: Conceptions of feminine and masculine. *Women's Studies International Forum, 25*(5), 529–539. doi:10.1016/S0277-5395(02)00312-6

Vlasveld, F. (2008). *Zes trends in e-learning*. Retrieved June 26, 2009, from http://www.frankwatching.com/archive/2009/01/07/trends-in-e-learning/

Volman, M., van Eck, E., Heemskerk, I., & Kuiper, E. (2005). New technologies, new differences. Gender and ethnic differences in pupils' use of ICT in primary and secondary education. *Computers & Education, 45*(1), 35–55. doi:10.1016/S0360-1315(04)00072-7

von Prümmer, C. (2000). *Women and distance education: Challenges and opportunities*. New York: Routledge.

von Prümmer, C. (2004). Gender issues and learning online: from exclusion to empowerment. In U. Bernath & A. Szücs (Eds.) Supporting the learner in distance education and e-learning. (pp. 474-480). Oldenburg, Denmark: BIS-verlag.

Wajcman, J. (1991). *Feminism confronts technology*. London: Polity Press.

Wajcman, J. (2000). Reflections on gender and technology studies: in what state is the art? *Social Studies of Science, 30*(3), 447–464. doi:10.1177/030631200030003005

Wajcman, J. (2004). *Technofeminism*. Cambridge, UK: Polity Press.

Wajcman, J. (2004). *Technofeminism*. London: Polity Press.

Wajcman, J. (2007). From Women and Technology to Gendered Technoscience. *Information Communication and Society, 10*(3), 287–298. doi:10.1080/13691180701409770

Wajcman, J. (2009). Feminist theories of technology. *Cambridge Journal of Economics Advance Access*. First published in January 8, 2009, doi:10.1093/cje/ben057.

Wajcman, J., & Anh Pham Lobb, L. (2007). The Gender Relations of Software Work in Vietnam. *Gender, Technology and Development, 11*(1), 1–25. doi:10.1177/097185240601100101

Walker, J. (2006). Blogging from Inside the Ivory Tower. In Bruns, A., & Jacobs, J. (Eds.), *Uses of Blogs* (pp. 127–138). New York: Peter Lang.

Walkerdine, V. (2003). Reclassifying upward mobility: Femininity and the neoliberal subject. *Gender and Education, 15*(3), 237–248. doi:10.1080/09540250303864

Walsh, E. (2000). Phenomenographic analysis of interview transcripts. In Bowden, J., & Walsh, E. (Eds.), *Phenomenography*. Melbourne, Australia: RMIT Publishing.

Waltz, S. B. (2003). Everything New is Old Again: Technology and the Mistaken Future. *Bulletin of Science, Technology & Society, 23*(5), 376–381. doi:10.1177/0270467603259792

Wännman-Toresson, G. (2002). *Kvinnor skapar kunskap på nätet: Datorbaserad fortbildning för lärare* [Women creating knowledge on the Net. Computer-based further education for teachers]. Umeå, Sweden: Dissertation of the faculty of social science.

Ware, M. C., & Stuck, M. F. (1985). Sex-role messages vis-à-vis microcomputer use: a look at the pictures. *Sex Roles, 13*(3-4), 215–228. doi:10.1007/BF00287911

Warner, M. (1991). Introduction: Fear of a Queer Planet. *Social Text, 9*(4), 3–17.

Weber, R. C. (1999). Manufacturing gender in military cockpit design. In MacKenzie, D., & Wajcman, J. (Eds.), *The social shaping of technology* (2nd ed., pp. 372–381). Philadelphia: Open University Press.

Webster, F. (2001). The postmodern university? the Loss of Purpose in British Universities. In Lax, S. (Ed.), *Access Denied in the Information Age* (pp. 69–92). Hampshire, UK: Palgrave.

Webster, J. (1995). What Do We Know About Gender and Information Technology at Work? A Discussion of Selected Feminist Research. *European Journal of Women's Studies, 2*, 315–334. doi:10.1177/135050689500200303

Webster, J. (2005a). Why Are Women Still So Few in ICT? Understanding the persistent under-representation of women in IT professions. In Archibald, J., Emms, J., Grundy, F., Payne, J., and Turner, E. (Eds.) *Women into Computing (WIC) Conference Proceedings: The Gender Politics of ICT*, 3-14. Middlesex, UK: Middlesex University Press.

Weil, M. M., & Rosen, L. D. (1995). The psychological impact of technology from a global perspective – A study of technological sophistication and technophobia in university students from 23 countries. *Computers in Human Behavior, 11*(1), 95–133. doi:10.1016/0747-5632(94)00026-E

Weller, M. (2007). *Virtual Learning Environments. Using, choosing and developing your VLE*. London: Routledge.

Wenger, E. (1998). *Communities of Practice: Learning, Meaning and Identity*. Cambridge, UK: Cambridge University Press.

Wentzel Winther, I. (2006a). Kid's rooms as plus territory. *Interacções, 2*(2), 9-26. Retrieved August 2009, from http://nonio.eses.pt/interaccoes/artigos/B1%281%29.pdf

Wentzel Winther, I. (2006b). *Hjemlighed: Kulturfænomenologiske studier* [Homeness: Anthropological studies]. København: Danmarks Pædagogiske Universitets Forlag.

Wesch, M. (2007). The Machine is Us/ing Us. Retrieved Augst 20, 2009, from http://www.youtube.com/watch?v=NLlGopyXT_g

West, C., & Zimmerman, D. H. (1987). Doing Gender. *Gender & Society, 1*(2), 125–151. .doi:10.1177/0891243287001002002

Westerberg, B. (1998). *Han, hon, den, det. Om genus och kön. (He, she, it. About gender and sex.)*. Stockholm: Ekerlids Förlag.

Whitelegg, E. (2006). *Invisible witnesses? How scientists, technologists, engineers and mathematicians are represented on UK television*. Paper presented at the British Educational Research Association Annual Conference.

Widerberg, K. (1992). Om kjønnets logikk. (About the logic of gender). In Brantsaeter, M. C., & Widerberg, K. (Eds.), *Sex i arbeid(et)*. Norway: Tiden Norsk Førlag. (In Norwegian)

Wigforss, E., & Booth, S. (2006, April 10-12). Experiencing the University Context. In *Proceedings for the Symposium Research into Learning in Networked Outreach Initiatives at Networked learning 2006 – Fifth International Conference*, Lancaster, University, UK.

Wigforss, E., Nordin, L., Hylander, J., Badersten, L., & Johansson, K. (2004). *Rekrytering till universitet och högskolor via fria studier*. (Recruitment to higher education through free studies) Slutrapport till Rekryteringsdelegationen, Utbildningsdepementet (Final report to the Recruitment Committee, Ministry of Education).

Wiley, D. A. (2000). *Learning object design and sequencing theory*. Unpublished doctoral dissertation, Brigham Young University. Retrieved June 26, 2009, from http://davidwiley.com/papers/dissertation/dissertation.pdf

Willamson, T. (2002). Incorporating a Malaysian Nation. *Cultural Anthropology, 17*(3), 401–430. doi:10.1525/can.2002.17.3.401

Wilson, K. R., Wallin, J. S., & Reiser, C. (2003). Social stratification and the digital divide. *Social Science Computer Review, 21*(2), 133–143. doi:10.1177/0894439303021002001

Winner, L. (1986). *The Whale and the Reactor: A Search for Limits in an Age of High Technology.* Chicago: University of Chicago Press.

Wistedt, I. (2001). *Five Gender-Inclusive Projects Revisited. A Follow-up Study of the Swedish Government's Initiative to Recruit More Women to Higher Education in Mathematics, Science, and Technology. National Agency for Higher Education.* Stockholm: Högskoleverket.

Wistedt, I. (Ed.). (2000). Datateknisk ingång för kvinnor. En utvärdering. (The computer engineering entrance for women: An evaluation) Teknisk rapport/ Luleå tekniska universitet; 2000:15. Luleå, Sweden: Luleå tekniska universitet.

Wittig, M. (1993). One Is Not Born a Woman. In Abelove, H., Barale, M. A., & Halperin, D. M. (Eds.), *The Lesbian and Gay Studies Reader* (pp. 103–109). New York: Routledge.

Wollstonecraft, M. (1792). *A Vindication of the Rights of Woman. With Strictures on Political and Moral Subjects.*

Retrieved June 19, 2009, from http://www.bartleby.com/144/Key

Wright, M. M. (2005). Finding a Place in Cyberspace. *Frontiers: A Journal of Women Studies, 26*(1), 48-59.

WWW-ICT. (2004). *Widening Women's Participation in ICT: Synthesis Report of the European Project.* Brussels, Belgium: European Commission.

Yorke, M., & Longden, B. (2007). The first year experience in higher education in the UK. York, UK: Higher Education Academy Report. Key Terms Gender performance: an understanding that gender continually arises through actions rather than through permanent biological or social constructions.

Young, I. M. (1997). *Intersecting voices: dilemmas of gender, political philosophy, and policy.* Princeton, NJ: Princeton University Press.

Yuval-Davis, N. (1997). *Gender and Nation.* London: Sage Publications.

Zohar, A. (2006). Connected knowledge in science and mathematics education. *International Journal of Science Education, 28*(13), 1579–159. doi:10.1080/09500690500439199

About the Contributors

Shirley Booth is, at the time of writing, Professor at the Wits School of Education at the University of the Witwatersrand in South Africa, and at the same time visiting professor in the Department of Education at University of Gothenburg in Sweden. She initiated the network of researchers with interests in gender, learning and IT under the auspices of the LearnIT research programme of the Knowledge Foundation of Sweden, which ultimately led to this book. Her own research interest is primarily learning and teaching in higher education, in particular in the areas of the mathematical, natural and engineering sciences, and also in teacher education. Her doctoral thesis concerned students learning to programme, and the methodological approach she used there, phenomenography, has remained an abiding research interest. She co-authored the book Learning and Awareness with Professor Ference Marton, where phenomenography was developed further into a theory of variation and learning.

Sara Goodman, FL, MS is a lecturer at the Centre for Gender Studies, Lund University, Sweden and coordinates the international masters program *Master of Science in Social Studies of Gender at the Faculty of Social Science.* Between 1998 and 2004, she lead the development of the gender studies education at Lund University and has received two awards for contributions in teaching: in 2005, the Lund University Prize for Teaching and in 2002, the Social Science Faculty Award for the Course of the Year. Her research interests are interdisciplinary and have focused on work, knowledge, gender, science and technology studies, information technology as well as the Third World studies in different constellations. More recently her research interests have also focused upon the teaching and development of gender studies as well as critical feminist pedagogy. Sara Goodman has represented Lund University in ATHENA(Advanced Thematic Network on Higher Education in Women's Studies 1998 – 2009) since its inception and she has served as a member of the ATHENA taskforce for the last nine years. She currently is a member of a research project, *Physics and Learning in Groups* based at Chalmers School of Engineering and Gothenburg University.

Gill Kirkup, Dr., B.A., B.Ed., M. Phil, Ph.D, is a Senior Lecturer in the Institute of Educational Technology, Open University, UK. She is also, at the time of writing the Head of Research, Data and Policy at the UK Resources Centre for Women in Science Engineering and Technology 2008-2010, part-time secondment. Gill Kirkup has researched and written about gender and technology for more than twenty years. Her publications record is very long it includes three co-authored books and three co-edited books: over forty chapters in books and over 30 journal articles. The book she co-authored with Ruth Carter "Women in Engineering: A Good Place to Be?" Macmillan (1990) remains a foundational text on the work and lives of women engineers. Her work is also involved with understanding the operation of gender in distance education and the gendering of ICTs for learning. Since the 1980s this work has been done in collaboration with colleagues from a number of European countries, in particular Germany, Netherlands and Sweden. Gill Kirkup is also a Fellow of the UK Higher Education Academy, member of the Association of Learning Technologies, member of the Fawcett Society. Represented the Open University (UK) in Athena (Advanced Thematic Network on Higher Education in Women's Studies) 1999- 2009.

* * *

Annika Bergviken Rensfeldt, PhD student in Educational Science at the University of Gothenburg, focuses on the latest decades' official documents on distance higher education in Sweden in her doctoral project. Her knowledge interest concerns discursive aspects of higher education change and expansion, how policy ideas around openness, flexibility and mobility are produced through new spatial imaginaries and subjectivities and the possible democratic implications for higher education participation. Annika has worked with IT and flexible learning since 1996 as a university lecturer, consultant and at executive level, and lately also in the Linnaeus centre of excellence on Learning and interaction in contemporary society (LinCS).

Martha Blomqvist is Associate Professor in Sociology and senior lecturer at the Centre for Gender Research, Uppsala University. Her main research interest is gender in working life, with a focus on information technology and organizational change. She is the editor of Crossroads of Knowledge, an interdisciplinary research publication. A current interactions research project aims at studying and initiating change in gendered and gendering processes within and together with a technological research centre in central Sweden.

Inger Boivie has a Ph.D. in human-computer interaction and her research focused on user-centred systems design (UCSD) and usability and the relations between the systems development process and health issues in computer-supported work. Her dissertation is titled *A Fine Balance: Addressing Usability and Users' Needs in the Development of IT Systems for the Workplace*(Uppsala 2005). Inger Boivie has also been interested in gender issues in systems development and discusses such issues briefly in her thesis. Boivie has extensive practical experience from more than ten years as a practitioner and consultant in UCSD and usability in bespoke systems development. After her Ph.D., Inger returned to the IT industry, and now works as a usability designer in an IT consulting company.

Pirjo Elovaara, PhD, is senior lecturer in Technoscience Studies at the School of Planning and Medie Design, Blekinge Institute of Technology, Sweden. Her research field is based on feminist technoscience and focuses on design and use of information and communication technology. She is especially interested in the concepts and practices of participation and agency. She has also been involved in a number of local and regional ICT development projects in the region of Blekinge, in the southeast of Sweden. Her latest research project, together with Christina Mörtberg, was about gender, skills, technology and e-government with the title 'From government to e-government: gender, skills, learning and technology' (2005–2007).

Marie Griffiths is an ESPRC Academic Fellow at the University of Salford, previously she has been involved in a number research project focusing on the under-representation of women in IT/ICT sector. Currently, Marie is a member of ISOS Research Centre (Information Systems, Society and Organisation) and her research interest also include young people and technologies/new media, the domestication and consequences of technologies in the home and the use of new media in education.

Agneta Gulz is an associate professor in Cognitive Science at Lund University in Sweden. Her main research area is digital learning technologies, in particular learning technologies that are based on virtual pedagogical characters. Some focus issues are: educational benefits and drawbacks with the use of virtual environments and virtual pedagogical characters, human cognitive differences (e.g. learning style differences) and the adaptation to such differences by means of digital learning environments, gender issues and digital learning environments. During 2009-2011 she leads an internationally oriented research project "Digital Dialogues" on chat-based interaction between teenagers and virtual characters in learning contexts. Agneta is the author of more than 30 papers published in international journals, books and conference proceedings.

Magnus Haake, PhD, MSc in Engineering Physics, Lund University. His PhD dissertation (2009) is on virtual embodied pedagogical characters and was carried out at the Department of Design Sciences at Lund University in Sweden. Magnus has a background in Human-Computer Interaction and information visualization in interactive digital media. He has been enrolled as an expert in different projects, both within business and research. Magnus is also trained in visual arts and graphic design. Since 2003 he has focussed on virtual characters in social and educational contexts. The specific topic of his PhD studies regards the basic, underlying visual design of virtual characters in relation to social psychology and to pedagogical intentions and outcomes. Magnus has published around 30 papers in journals, books and proceedings.

Aino-Maija Hiltunen works as a co-ordinator at the University of Helsinki, in the national network of gender studies. Organizing e-learning for gender studies students, university pedagogy for teachers, network knowhow in general and quality assurance has been among her activities, as well as co-ordinating the Gender and ICT's in Women's Studies –working group of European network Athena.

Eva Maria Hoffmann studied Computer Science at the University of Erlangen and Technische Universitaet Berlin (TU Berlin), Germany. Since 2005 she has been working at the Center for international and Intercultural Communication (ZiiK) at the TU Berlin. The ZiiK is building up academic structures in the higher education in Afghanistan in the area of IT. Eva Hoffmann is responsible for the establishment of the Computer Science Faculty in Heart University. She was 2005 and 2009 lecturing at Herat University for one semester. As women's representative at the School of Electrical Engineering and Computer Science at TU Berlin, the advancement of women is in focus of her work, and she is working on several projects to attract women to study electrical engineering and computer science at TU Berlin. Due to this, the situation of women in Afghanistan is an interesting field to explore, since the studies in Computer Science in Afghanistan has a high proportion of female students compared to German universities.

Gwyneth Hughes, Dr., is Senior Lecturer in Higher Education at the Institute of Education, London. She is also Faculty Director of Learning and Teaching and is responsible for enhancing teaching at both faculty and institute levels and she chairs an E-Learning Implementation Group as part of this role. Her research has followed the growth of use of e-learning over the past decade and she is particularly interested in addressing issues of equality, diversity and inclusion as they apply to virtual learning and teaching, and she has published extensively in this area.

Erna Kotkamp is a teacher researcher at Utrecht University at the Department of Media and Culture Studies where she is also an e-learning consultant. She combines technical ICT skills with academic research on where and how pedagogical choices are made in the desiging process of educational software.

Ulf Mellström is professor of Gender and Technology Studies at Luleå University of Technology, Sweden. He has published widely on technology and masculinity, engineering studies, and crosscultural comparisons of gender and technology relations. Currently he is also a guest professor at the Department of Gender Studies at Linköping University, Sweden. His research intersects anthropology, gender theory, and Science and Technology Studies. He has conducted fieldwork in Sweden and Malaysia. Mellström also holds several positions of trust in the Scandinavian gender studies community. He is member of Swedish Government's delegation on Gender Equality in Higher Education, chair of board the Swedish Secretariat for Gender Research 2006-2009, member of the program committe for gender studies in the Norwegian Research Council and has also served on the gender committe at Swedish Research Council between 2001 to 2007.

Christina Mörtberg, PhD, docent/reader, is an associate professor at the Department of Informatics, University of Oslo/University of Umeå, Norway/Sweden. Mörtberg's current research interests can be described in two interrelated areas that link to each other. In the first, systems design, she bases her research on situated perspectives and participatory design approaches and in the second, a theoretical/methodological perspective is in focus where systems design is studied in combination with theory/methodology based on feminist technoscience and science and technology studies. Mörtberg has been involved in numerous national, Nordic, and international research projects throughout the years and has also been one of the founders of several transnational research networks. Together with Pirjo Elovaara she conducted the project 'From government to e-government: gender, skills, learning and technology'. Mörtberg has published and continues to publish her research on her own as well as in collaboration with doctoral students and colleagues.

Helen Richardson is a Senior Lecturer in Information Systems (IS) and joined the University of Salford in 1998 after a varied career including working in the field of Social Care and running a Research and Training Unit promoting Positive Action for Women at Work. She works in the Research Centre for People, Work and Organization and is engaged in Critical Research in IS including issues of gender in the ICT labour market and the global location of service work.

Sandra Riomar is a PhD student in Educational Science at the University of Gothenburg. Her doctoral project focuses on the spatial dimensions of open, flexible and distributed forms of learning, the political dimensions of institutional change and the gendered spatial orderings of these developments. Drawing on field-data from adult educational settings and students homes, the analytical focus is the diminishing spatial boundaries of private/public spheres and new forms of creating 'enclosure' and a sense of place for learning. Sandra also works as a university lecturer in the program for Human Resource Development and Labour Relations and in the field of Distance Education.

Els Rommes, Dr., is assistant Professor 'Gender, ICT and Pedagogy' at the Institute for Gender Studies, Radboud University Nijmegen. Her research interests and main publication areas include strategies of inclusion of gender in the information society, design and use of ICTs, gendered images of gender and SET (science, engineering and technology) and teenagers' gendered professional choices. She has been coordinator of the advanced PhD-training of Netherlands Graduate School of Science, Technology and Modern Culture (50 junior and senior PhD students), guest Professor at Bremen university and postdoctoral researcher in the European research project SIGIS (Social Inclusion of Gender in the Information Society). Presently, Els is researcher and Dutch team leader of the EU project 'Motivation; Promoting positive images of Science, Engineering and Technology in young people' and of the Dutch historical media research project 'Changing Images of science-technology in society'.

Minna Salminen-Karlsson has a PhD in education from Linköping University, with a thesis entitled "Bringing Women into Computer Engineering. Curriculum Reform Processes at Two Universities of Technology". She has worked for a number of years in the cross-disciplinary area of social studies of technology and is currently associate professor in sociology at Uppsala University. Her research interests are the various intersections of gender, education, organization and technology. The underlying question in her research is how technology as a knowledge domain is constructed as masculine and how this influences women's possibilities to become technologically competent. She has studied engineering education in a gender perspective, workplace learning and gender in high-tech workplaces and technology courses for school-age children. She has lectured widely on gender and teaching methods in engineering education.

Sigrid Schmitz (Dr. habil.) is university lecturer at the University of Freiburg/Germany (until June 2009) and at the University of Oldenburg/Gemany (from October 2009). With a study in biology her main research and teaching is on gender aspects at the intersection between computer and brain sciences, on gender and e-learning, and on the development of didactic concepts for gender studies in SET-disciplines. She is also engaged in the feminist discourse on embodiment approaches, feminist epistemology, and transdisciplinary teaching and research. Since 2002 she leads the Forum of Competence "Gender Studies in Computer and Natural Sciences" [gin] together with Prof. Britta Schinzel. She was visiting professor for "Gender Research in Natural Sciences" at the Unviersität of Graz/Austria (2003) and for "Transdiscipinary Gender and Science Studies" an the Humboldt University of Berlin/ Germany (2008).

Johanna Sefyrin is a Ph D Student in informatics at Mid Sweden University in Sundsvall. Her Ph D project concerns user participation and gender in systems design projects. Her primary focus is on explorations of how to further increase the analytical and methodological sensibility in order to tune in to the lower frequencies of participation and gender in systems design. The central issues are aspects of marginalisation, and how these relate to systems design approaches, practices, methods and techniques. An important context for her research is the development of public eAdministration and public eServices.

Her theoretical points of departure are Participatory Design and feminist technoscience. Her publications include: Sefyrin, Johanna (2005). Understandings of gender and competence in ICT. In Jacqueline Archibald, Judy Emms, Frances Grundy, Janet Payne, Eva Turner (Eds.), *The Politics of ICT.* Middlesex, UK: Middlesex University Press; and Sefyrin, Johanna (2009, forthcoming), "We do not talk about this" – Problematical silences in eGovernment. Accepted for *Electronic Journal of e-Government.*

Eva Wigforss, PhD is senior lecturer at the Department of Logopedics, Phoniatrics and Audiology, School of Medicine at Lund University in Sweden. Her main research areas concern various aspects of lifelong learning, learning difficulties (dyslexia and other language related deficits) and distance learning. Recent works have been related to the project Learning in the extended ICT-mediated university and the Grundtvig project Dys-Learn looking at lifelong learning conditions for adults and more specifically adults with dyslexia.

Index

E

e-administration 83, 98
earlier studies 223
early modern scientific practices 232
e-classroom 267
economic activity 231
economic fluctuations 135
economic model 269
economic value 269
economically advantageous 213
economies of scale 232
écriture feminine 239, 240
editing content 235
editorial column 140, 142, 144
education colleges 193
education gendered 192, 194
education policy documents 193, 195
educational attainment 104
educational communication 195
educational communities 247
educational content 259
educational context 260, 262
educational expansion 195
educational experience 201, 258
educational field 48
educational forms 195
educational guidance 176
educational manifesto 257
educational marketplace 213
educational modes 198, 203
educational opportunities 192, 206
educational policy 255, 257
educational practitioners 261
educational programme 115, 118, 125
educational researchers 258
educational software 128
educational systems 151, 255, 269
educational technology 256
educational theories 257
educational trajectories 197
educators 133
efficiency 231
efficient solutions 15
e-government 83, 84, 92, 95, 98
e-learners 257

e-learning 244, 252, 253, 254, 255, 256,
257, 258, 259, 260, 261, 263, 264,
265, 266, 267, 268, 269, 270, 272,
273, 274
e-learning 2.0 259
e-learning environments 260, 263, 270
electrical engineer 106
electronics industry 34, 35
elite male organisations 233
elite students 233
emancipatory 257
embodied knowledge 7, 237
embodiment 255, 256, 258, 261, 266, 268,
269, 270
emerging Islamic modernity 34
emerging new middle-class 36
emigration 50
emotional strain 212
empirical material
65, 66, 71, 75, 83, 85, 86,
192, 194, 197, 201, 207
employability 107
employer 213
employment practices 238
empowerment 95, 234
encouraging co-operation 223
engagement 219
engineering 107, 110
engineering program 1, 4, 139
engineering students 127, 132
engineering-oriented 6
engineering-oriented problem solving 6
England 233
English language skills 49, 53
entanglement 87, 93, 94, 96, 97, 98
entry level knowledge 233
environment 260, 263, 274
environmental problems 143
episodic interviews 105
epistemological base 20, 21
epistemological questions 267
Epistem-onto-logy 264
eportfolio 240
equal opportunities 137, 198, 203
equal opportunity discourse 143
equal opportunity issues 135